The period between 1500 and 1700 was the most decisive one in the formation of standard modern English, yet there is remarkably little teaching material. Manfred Görlach's *Introduction to Early Modern English* fills a very real need. It provides a thorough and linguistically informed synchronic description of Early Modern English, dealing with its varieties, with writing and orthography, phonetics and phonology, syntax and the lexicon, including sections on problems of language contact and the lexicographical tradition. In addition, it provides a valuable anthology of texts from a wide range of sources: the texts exemplify features from Early Modern English discussed in the main body of the text, and have also been effectively chosen so as to provide something of the cultural background to the processes of linguistic change of the period.

This textbook is admirably suited to undergraduate courses on English in the early modern period. It will be welcomed by all students of English language and literature studying this period.

INTRODUCTION TO
EARLY MODERN ENGLISH

INTRODUCTION TO

Early Modern English

MANFRED GÖRLACH
Professor of English Language and
Medieval Studies, University of Cologne

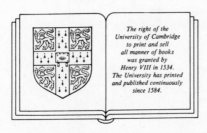

The right of the
University of Cambridge
to print and sell
all manner of books
was granted by
Henry VIII in 1534.
The University has printed
and published continuously
since 1584.

CAMBRIDGE UNIVERSITY PRESS

Cambridge
New York   Port Chester   Melbourne   Sydney

Published by the Press Syndicate of the University of Cambridge
The Pitt Building, Trumpington Street, Cambridge CB2 1RP
40 West 20th Street, New York, NY 10011, 4211 USA
10 Stamford Road, Oakleigh, Melbourne 3166, Australia

Originally published in German as Einführung ins Frühneuenglische
by Quelle & Meyer, Heidelberg 1978
and © Quelle & Meyer, Heidelberg 1978
First published in English by Cambridge University Press 1991 as
Introduction to Early Modern English
English translation © Cambridge University Press 1991

Printed in Great Britain at the University Press, Cambridge

British Library cataloguing in publication data

Görlach, Manfred
Introduction to Early Modern English.
1. English language; history
I. Title II. Einführung ins Frühneuenglische. English.
420.9

Library of Congress cataloguing in publication data

Görlach, Manfred.
[Einführung ins Frühneuenglische. English]
Introduction to Early Modern English / Manfred Görlach.
    p. ca.
Translation of: Einführung ins Frühneuenglische.
Includes bibliographical references.
ISBN 0–521-32529–3. – ISBN 0–521-31046–6 (paperback)
1. English language – Early modern. 1500–1700 – Grammar.
2. English language – Early modern, 1500–1700 – Texts. I. Title.
PE821.G613 1990
420'.9'031 – dc20 89–77389 CIP

ISBN 0 521 32529 3 hardback
ISBN 0 521 31046 6 paperback

Contents

Contents

Contents

Texts

x

List of texts

List of texts

Figures

List of figures

Preface

The Early Modern English (EModE) period has been greatly neglected by historical linguists. Although there are very useful studies relating to pronunciation and phonological systems (Dobson 1968, Horn and Lehnert 1954), to inflexion (Graband 1965), to individual problems of syntax (Ellegård 1953, Jacobsson 1951, Rydén 1966), to the theoretical linguistic background (Michael 1970, Padley 1976 and 1985), to educational history (Michael 1987, Howatt 1984), or to the position of EModE vis-à-vis Latin (Jones 1953), other important areas, especially of syntax, lexis and semantics, have so far not been satisfactorily treated.

Linguistic data and interpretations, moreover, have frequently been adduced only for philological textual discussions, in particular in the case of Shakespeare's works. And this has been done mainly in a contrastive manner: only features likely to cause misunderstanding to a modern English reader have been commented upon. Franz's work (1939) is an exception, since he offers much more than the title of his book *Shakespeare's Language* indicates. His work in fact proves to be a fairly comprehensive treatment of EModE grammar.

The neglect of the EModE period is especially hard to understand if one considers how important this stage was for the history of the English language: it was the period when many of the characteristic structures of the modern written language developed. The same neglect is found in academic teaching. Introductions to EModE are far less frequent than classes in Old English or Middle English.

All this easily explains why manuals on EModE are almost nonexistent. Barber's *Early Modern English* of 1976 was the first exhaustive attempt. His book was published when the planning of the German version of my book (1978) was nearing completion. I gratefully acknowledge the help that his book gave me for some ideas in the final stages of writing my German manual. Since Barber's book is so different in style, scope, method and purpose, I still feel there is room for another introduction to EModE published in English. This new, adapted translation takes into account some of the findings of the research done in the last ten years. It is intended to be a manual for undergraduate teaching. The idea is that a student should be introduced to EModE and learn to analyse it from the original texts. Therefore the first section, the grammar, is closely correlated with the texts presented in an appendix, almost all specimens used for illustration being taken from them. These texts have, naturally, been selected from a linguistic point of view, but a considerable number illustrating the literature and the cultural history of the time has also been included. My selection reflects a process of many years' reading. Although it is not claimed to be representative, I still hope that it will serve to illustrate all the grammatical developments that took place in the EModE period.

Most of the texts are excerpts only, but the Bibliography is intended as a guide to students who wish to read the texts in full, if at all possible. The German version of this book has been tested in undergraduate teaching over the last ten years. The results of my own experience, as well as critical comments by colleagues, have been incorporated in this English version, but it has proved impossible to take into account all the recent publications on EModE with their various theoretical stances, in particular, the largely neglected light that historical reconstructions of present-day dialects in England (Anderson 1987), Scotland (Romaine 1982), Ireland (Harris 1985, Bliss 1979, Braidwood 1964), America (Kytö and Rissanen 1983) and the Caribbean (Harris 1986) have thrown on varieties of EModE: this would have meant writing a completely new book. (I have included the most important publications in English of the past few years in the Bibliography.) I have recently dealt with variation and some of the sociolinguistic problems of EModE in detail elsewhere (Görlach 1985a, 1988 and a forthcoming article), articles that can serve to supplement chapter 2. I hope that this book will contribute towards rectifying the neglect of one of the most important periods in the development of the English language.

For the English version, it has been possible to add a few more texts (T51–T66): the great number of references to the texts included in the grammar made it necessary to retain T1–T50 without change of numbering, and therefore to add the new texts as a separate group of "Additional Texts", arranged in purely chronological order. Note that the new texts (unlike T1–T50 of the original collection) are not normally referred to in chapters 1–7. It has also been possible to add to this version a chronological table (found on pages xx–xxix) detailing the important events, inventions and artistic landmarks which came about between the years 1485 and 1700 (this table is taken from W. Frerichs *et al.*, *Dates and Documents, Facts and Figures*. Frankfurt: Hirschgraben-Verlag (1970).

This book has greatly profited from the kind help of Dr Charles Barber and Vivian Salmon, who have prevented me from making various blunders; and it would have been impossible without the patient and meticulous help of Helen Weiss, who has gone through my draft translation with exemplary care and improved the book throughout.

Symbols and abbreviations

>	becomes
<	comes from
*	reconstructed form
**	ungrammatical
≠	opposition, contrast
~	in complementary distribution, equivalent
≅	in free variation
→	derivation; borrowing
Ø	zero; loss (of a sound, word)
‖	replaced by
¯	etymologically long (vowel)
+	morpheme boundary
#	word boundary
⟨ ⟩	grapheme
[ ]	sound; semantic feature
/ /	phoneme
{ }	morpheme
' '	meaning
" "	quoted text, article or chapter title

AmE	American English
AN	Anglo-Norman
AV	Authorized Version
BL	British Library, London
BrE	British English
c	century
c.	circa
C	consonant
CC	continuative clause
CED	*A Chronological English Dictionary* (Finkenstaedt *et al.* 1970)

List of symbols and abbreviations

DEMEP	*English Pronunciation 1500–1800*
DNB	*Dictionary of National Biography*
EE	English Experience (reprint series)
EETS	Early English Text Society
EF	expanded form
EL	English Linguistics (reprint series)
EModE	Early Modern English (1500–1700)
Engl	English
Fr	French
G	German
GVS	Great Vowel Shift
Ital	Italian
Lat	Latin
ME	Middle English (1100–1500)
MS	manuscript
NP	noun phrase
OE	Old English (–1100)
OED	*The Oxford English Dictionary*
PC	participial clause
PrE	Present-day English
Q	(study) question
STC	*Short Title Catalogue* (Pollard and Redgrave)
SVO	subject verb object
T	major text of appendix (referred to by the nos. 1–66 and by line, e.g. T1/39, 41–5; T50/2)
t	minor text of Introduction
V	vowel
VP	verb phrase
Wing	*Short-Title Catalogue 1641–1700*

Chronological table

General and Social History		Britain Overseas	
1485–1509	Henry VII (House of Tudor) – married with Elizabeth of York	1496–8	Voyages of the Cabots, Eng. claims to Canada and the east coast based on their discoveries
1509–47	Henry VIII – policy of balance of power (Charles V, Francis I)		
1513	The English defeat the Scots at Flodden		
1521	The title of "Fidei Defensor" conferred on Henry VIII by the pope (appreciation of Henry's pamphlet defending the papacy against Luther's attack on it)		
1532–4	The Breach with Rome		
1534	Act of Supremacy; Henry VIII "only Supreme Head in earth of the Church of England called Anglicana Ecclesia" Beginning of the Reformation		
1535	Thomas More (b. 1478) and John Fisher (b. 1459) beheaded for not accepting Henry VIII as head of the church		
1536	Wales definitely annexed		
1536–8	Dissolution of the monasteries		
1542	Henry VIII King of Ireland		
1542–	New colleges fd. in Oxford and Cambridge (Camb.: Magdalen C. 1542; Trinity C. 1547. Oxf.: Christ C. 1546; Trinity C. 1555)		
1547–53	Edward VI – Catholic service abolished; churches stripped of images		
1553–8	Mary I ("Bloody Mary") – married with Philip of Spain; Catholic reaction, papal power restored, penal laws against heresy revived		
1556	T. Cranmer (b. 1489), Archbishop of Canterbury, tried for heresy and burned on the stake		
1558–1603	Elizabeth I	1558	Calais lost (Eng. since 1347)
1559	Act of Supremacy: the sovereign supreme head of the realm in spiritual matters; Reformation restored, papal power abolished Act of Uniformity: Prayer Book the only legal form of worship; rise of Dissent		

Science, Invention, Economics		Literature, Philosophy, Fine Arts, Music
	1503	Dunbar (1460–1520), Scottish satirical poet, *The Thistle and the Rose*
	1509	*Everyman*, greatest Eng. morality play;
	1515	Douglas' trans. of *Aeneid* (T18A, T21)
	1516	Thomas More (1478–1553), *Utopia*, describes an ideal state
	1525	Tyndale's (1492–1536) New Testament in Eng. (T19)
	1526–8	Hans Holbein the Younger (1497–1543) in England
	1532–1533	John Heywood (*c.* 1497–1580), poet and playwright
	1535	Eng. lyrical poetry, Surrey (T21), (?1517–47), Wyatt (?1503–42); Eng. humanism, Elyot (?1490–1547), Ascham (1515–68), T. Wilson (1525–81) (T4)
	1549	Lily and Colet, *Grammar* (T3)
	1549	Archbishop Cranmer's *Common Prayer Book* (revised and wholly in Eng. 1552)
c. 1550– Transition from farm to pasture land in Eng., enclosure of open fields; sheep farming Development of weaving industry	*c.* 1550–	The madrigal cultivated in Eng. (orig. Italian verse form); some great madrigal writers of that period: Byrd (1543–1623), Gibbons (1583–1625), Morley (1557–1602), Weelkes (1557–1623), Wilbye (1574–1638)
1552– New Poor Laws, relief of the impotent poor, setting vagabonds and beggars to continual labour (valid down to 1832)		Nicholas Udall (d. 1556), *Ralph Roister Doister*, the first Eng. comedy
	1553	T. Wilson, *Arte of Rhetorique* (T4)
	1559	*Translation of Seneca* into Eng. (by Jasper Heywood)
	1562	*Gorboduc or Ferrex and Porrex*, the first regular Eng. tragedy in blank verse (by Sackville and Norton)
	1564	William Shakespeare born at Stratford on Avon (d. 1616) (T31)

Chronological table (*cont.*)

	General and Social History		Britain Overseas
1560	The (Presbyterian) Church of Scotland fd. by John Knox	1562	Beginning of Eng. slave trade (John Hawkins)
c. 1565	Beginning of Puritanism		
1570	The Independents fd. (the religion of the Pilgrim Fathers and of Cromwell's army) Sir W. Raleigh (?1552–1618), poet, courtier and discoverer	1570–	Voyages of Francis Drake to the West Indies
		1570–90	English "sea-dogs" plunder the Spanish Main
		1577–80	Francis Drake circumnavigates the globe
		1583–5	First Eng. plantation in North America (unsuccessful)
1587	Execution of Mary Queen of Scots		
1588	Battle of the Armada; end of Spanish naval supremacy	1588	Gambia (West Africa), settled for trading purposes (patent granted by Queen Elizabeth)
1589–1600	Hakluyt's *Principal Navigations*		
		1600	The East India Company chartered
1601	First important Poor Law	1601	Conquest of Ireland

xxii

Science, Invention, Economics		Literature, Philosophy, Fine Arts, Music	
1566	Royal Exchange fd. in London	1569	J. Hart, *An Orthographie* (T6)
1572	Introduction of the Gregorian Calendar into Eng.	1570	R. Ascham, *Scholemaster*
		1575–	Edmund Spenser (*c.* 1552–99), *Shepherd's Calender*; *Faerie Queene* (T23 and T24)
		1577	Holinshed (*c.* 1520–*c.* 1580), Eng. chronicler, *Chronicles of England, Scotland, and Ireland*, the source of nearly all of Shakespeare's historical plays (T36A)
		1579	Norton's *Plutarch*
		1580–2	Bullokar and Mulcaster (T7 and T8)
		1582	Rheims New Testament (T19)
		1586	John Knox, *History of the Reformation in Scotland* (see 1560, col. 1)
		1587–	Christopher Marlowe (1564–93), *Tamburlaine, Doctor Faustus, The Jew of Malta*
		1554–86	P. Sidney, *Arcadia* 1590 (T26), *Apologia* 1595 (T27)
		1591–	Shakespeare's plays; beginning of the golden age of the English stage John Lyly (1554–1606), dramatist and novelist, *Endymion; Euphues, the Anatomy of Wit* (hence "euphuism") (T25) T. Kyd (1558–94), *The Spanish Tragedy* Ben Jonson (1573–1637), *Everyman in his Humour* (T14) Beaumont (1584–1616) and Fletcher (1579–1625)
1600	William Gilbert (*c.* 1544 to 1603), *Treatise on Magnetism* (in Latin); G. is "the father of the science of magnetism"	1594	Richard Hooker (1554–1600), theologian, *Laws of Ecclesiastical Polity*, 8 vols. T. Nashe (1567–1601), pamphleteer and satirist; first Eng. novel of adventure, *The Life of Jack Wilson*
		1596–	Shakespeare's great comedies: *The Merchant of Venice, As you like it, Twelfth Night* (T31)
		1601–	Shakespeare's great tragedies: *Julius Caesar, Hamlet, Othello, King Lear, Macbeth*

Chronological table *(cont.)*

	General and Social History		Britain Overseas
1603–25	James I King of England (= James VI of Scotland) – House of Stuart		
1603	Personal Union of England and Scotland		
1605	Gunpowder Plot (Guy Fawkes) fails		
		1607	First permanent Eng. settlement in the New World
		1609	Under James I 12,000 Eng. and Scottish Protestants settle in Northern Ireland (Ulster)
		1607–11	Henry Hudson (*c.* 1550 to 1611) discovers Hudson River and Hudson Bay
		1612	The Bermudas settled
		1616	William Baffin discovers "Baffin Bay" (between Greenland and Canada)
1622	Nathaniel Butter the first to print all the news of the day upon a single sheet; he brought out the *Weekly News*	1620	Landing of the Pilgrim Fathers at Plymouth (Massachusetts) (T54)
1625–49	Charles I – rule by "Divine Right"	*c.* 1620	First negro-slaves sent to North America
1628	Petition of Rights forced upon the king	1627	Barbados British
1629–40	Arbitrary rule of Charles I, no Parliament summoned	1629	The Bahamas settled
1633	The Baptist Church fd.		
1640	Long Parliament		
1642–9	Civil War – Roundheads (= Puritans) against Cavaliers (= Royalists)	1643	Tasman (a Dutch navigator) discovers the south of New Zealand and the Fiji Islands

Science, Invention, Economics		Literature, Philosophy, Fine Arts, Music
	1605	Bacon, *Advancement* (T13) Douai Old Testament: Roman Catholic Bible complete (T19)
	1608–	Shakespeare's romantic dramas: *A Winter's Tale, Cymbeline, The Tempest*
	1611	The Authorized Version of the Bible ("King James' Bible") (T19) John Donne (1572–1631), metaphysical poetry Francis Bacon (1561–1626), *Novum Organum* (B. demands facts, not opinions), *Essays*
1614 John Napier (1550 to 1617) publishes his invention of logarithms	*c.* 1615–	Inigo Jones (1573–1652), the first to introduce pure Renaissance architecture to England
	1616	Death of William Shakespeare
	1620	Collection of Eng. tragedies and comedies translated into German
	1623	Complete edition of Shakespeare's Works (First Folio) (T31)
	1625	Virginal Book ("Fitzwilliam Virginal Book") written; the collection contains 416 pieces by John Bull (1562–1628), T. Morley (1557–1602), P. Philipps (1560–1633), T. Tallis (1505–85), J. Dowland (1563–1612) and other composers
1628 William Harvey publishes an essay on the circulation of the blood		
1637 *Analytical Geometry* (Fermat, Descartes)		
	1642	Decree against stage plays, secular music, public sports, etc.
	1644	John Milton (1608–74), poet and prose writer, *Areopagitica* (a vindication of the freedom of the press); *Paradise Lost* (1667) (T33 and T34) Milton "Latin Secretary" to Cromwell

Chronological table *(cont.)*

	General and Social History		Britain Overseas
1645	Cromwell's victory at Naseby		
1649	Charles I executed on Jan. 30		
1649–60	England a Commonwealth (= Republic); the House of Lords abolished; beginning of England's naval greatness, popular foreign policy	1649–50	Cromwell's Irish campaign, massacres of Drogheda and Waterford
1651	Navigation Act (importation of goods into England on Eng. ships only); in force until 1849		
1652	Society of Friends (Quakers) fd. by George Fox (T50)		
1652–4	First War with Holland; end of Dutch naval supremacy (see 1588)		
1654	Cromwell, Protector of the British Commonwealth; strict Puritan régime and military despotism	1655	Conquest of Ireland Capture of Jamaica
1656	Resettlement of Jews in England by Oliver Cromwell		
1658	Death of Oliver Cromwell; his son Richard his successor		
1660–85	Charles II – restoration of the Stuarts hailed with enthusiasm by the majority of the nation; restoration of the Church of England – rise of Nonconformity		
1662	Act of Uniformity (against Nonconformists)	1663 1664	Carolina an Eng. Colony Capture of New Amsterdam (New York)
1665	Great Plague in London		
1666	Great Fire in London (see Wren, 1660–, col. 3) The Dutch fleet sails up the Thames		
		1667	Acquisition of the Dutch Gold Coast
1670	Treaty of Dover: Charles a pensioner of the French king; his pledge to overthrow protestantism in England		
1673	Test Act (against Roman Catholics and Dissenters)		

Science, Invention, Economics		Literature, Philosophy, Fine Arts, Music
	1649–1651	Thomas Hobbes (1588–1679), *Leviathan* (defence of absolute monarchy)
1660	The Royal Society fd.	1660–	Theatres reopened John Dryden (1631–1700), poems and plays; first Poet Laureate (T15, 18H) Restoration Comedy: William Wycherley (1640–1715) and William Congreve (1670–1729)
1660–	Christopher Wren (1632–1723), surveyor general of buildings, rebuilds the City of London (St Paul's, etc.)		
1661	Robert Boyle (1627–91), *The Sceptical Chemist* ("the foundation stone of modern chemistry")	1663–	Samuel Butler (1612–80), *Hudibras* (satire on the Puritans)
1666–	Sir Isaac Newton (1642–1727), natural philosopher, pioneer of new mathematics, physics, and astronomy; invented differential and integral calculus; discovers laws of gravity (1682)	1665–1667 1668	*The London Gazette* published T. Sprat, *History of the Royal Society* (T17) T. Wilkins, *Essay*
1667	Robert Hooke (1635–1703), horologist and physicist, *Micrographia*, first description of plant cells – "Hooke's Law"		
1675	Greenwich Observatory fd.		

Chronological table (*cont.*)

	General and Social History		Britain Overseas
1679	Habeas Corpus Act. The names of Whigs and Tories appear instead of Roundheads and Cavaliers		
1685–8	James II, the Catholic king	1682	Foundation of Pennsylvania by William Penn, the Quaker
1687	Declaration of Indulgence (in favour of Roman Catholics)		
1688	The "Glorious Revolution", James flees the land		
1689–94	Mary II, daughter of James II, but a Protestant, joint sovereign with William III		
1689–1702	William III of Orange, Queen Mary's husband		
1689	William and Mary sign Bill of Rights which guarantees the supremacy of Parliament		
1689	Grand Alliance against Louis XIV; the balance of power the guiding principle of William's foreign policy – Toleration Act (not for Roman Catholics)	1690	Battle of the Boyne; William III of Orange (a Protestant) defeats James II (the Catholic king)
1692	Last case of Royal Veto		
1693	Ministers chosen from the majority of the Commons; beginning of party government		
1695	Licensing Act not renewed: Freedom of the Press		

Science, Invention, Economics		Literature, Philosophy, Fine Arts, Music	
1676	Edmund Halley (1656–1742), astronomer and mathematician	1678	John Bunyan (1628–88), *The Pilgrim's Progress*, part I (T60)
1682	Halley's Comet		
		1688–	Henry Purcell (1659–95), *Dido and Aeneas*
c. 1690	Beginning of capitalism and free enterprise	1690–	John Locke (1632–1704), empiricism: *Essay concerning Humane Understanding, Two Treatises of Government, Letter on Toleration* (intellectual revolt against absolutism) (T63)
1694	Bank of England fd.		
1696	Lloyd's, marine insurance organization fd.		

1 Introduction

1.1 Synchronic and diachronic methods

The English language, like every living language, is continually changing. All texts dating from an earlier period illustrate this fact. These changes mean that every period needs its own particular description or grammar. It also means that this grammar must clearly define its object of description, e.g. the beginning and the end of the period, geographical and social components, uses of the language described, etc.

Shakespeare's, Ben Jonson's, Milton's and Dryden's works as well as the Authorized Version (AV) of the Bible of 1611 were originally written in EModE, but they are also part of PrE. They belong to the PrE system in that they form part of the passive competence of present-day speakers. Such 'diachrony in synchrony', however, is never complete and brings with it problems of description.

The orthography and punctuation of EModE texts are normally adapted to suit present-day needs; pronunciation of the original texts, whether delivered on the stage or from the pulpit, is modern. However, the syntax remains more or less as in the original and except in some highly Latinized texts, it does not cause serious problems of comprehension. Such texts can, of course, sound artificial and odd, or even seem to the modern ear to contain mistakes.

Problems are most evident as regards the lexis. For simple contexts which are intelligible without the aid of a dictionary, a translation from the archaic register is still necessary: the AV's "with a girdle of a skin about his loines" (Mark 1.6), for example, is translated in the New English Bible (NEB) as "with a leather belt round his waist". Other passages remain unintelligible or cause predictable misunderstandings. Thus Hamlet's "Thus Conscience does make Cowards of vs all" (*Hamlet* II.1.83) is problematic: *does make* is likely to be misunderstood as an emphatic use and the sense of *conscience* that Shakespeare intended cannot be understood from its PrE meaning.

These few examples will be sufficient to show that EModE cannot be satisfactorily described as a subsystem of PrE, but needs a separate description that is based on the structures of EModE itself. Moreover, the archaic function that some EModE texts have in PrE makes us aware of the possibility that there were similarly archaic registers in EModE.

1.2 Model of grammar

A synchronic description of EModE can be attempted in various ways. It would be ideal if we could describe the linguistic competence of a speaker of EModE and the change in English as a change in linguistic competence. But such a grammar would necessarily be defective as it would lack one central prerequisite: there is no speaker of EModE who could decide on the grammaticality and acceptability of new, not yet attested utterances generated by such a grammar. Also there is the problem of the very conspicuous variation apparent in EModE and in view of the unsolved problems of description of PrE varieties in transformational grammars, I do not see much sense in attempting a variety grammar of this type for EModE.

It would seem much better to describe EModE in a way that combines functional structuralism, as developed by such scholars as Martinet and the Prague linguists, with methods and insights of modern sociolinguistics. Even then we are, of course, restricted by the limitations of the sources, although EModE is comparatively well documented.

1.3 Sources

1 There is a wealth of texts available on which a grammar of EModE can be based. But any grammar deriving from these texts will not be more than a grammar of the texts described, and not a

complete grammar of EModE. It is uncertain whether, and how far, a modern linguist is entitled to claim to have found mistakes in historical texts and then to correct them, or whether every single document of the period ought to have more authority than the insight of a modern linguist. Statistical data are a dubious basis on which to judge grammaticality – but even statistics are not normally available for EModE.

(a) This rather shaky basis is reduced even further by gaps among the texts that have come down to us. Although printed texts of the period were more likely to survive than, for instance, medieval manuscripts, we do know of lost literature of the time. No copy of the first seven editions of Deloney's *Jack of Newbury* is extant, and many plays are only known as titles in Henslowe's *Diary*. Texts which survive in manuscript form and were first printed as late as the nineteenth or twentieth century include texts of both linguistic and literary importance, such as Nisbet's 'translation' of the Wyclif Bible into Scots (t7), Cheke's partial translation of the Gospels, Hart's *The Opening of the Unreasonable Writing of our Inglish Toung...*, or Sidney's original version of *Arcadia*. Even more likely to have been lost, of course, are personal documents such as letters or diaries, which were often discarded after they had served their function. Since these types of texts were least susceptible to standardizing influences, they bear important witness to variation in EModE.

(b) The homogeneity of the written language, or rather of the printed texts of the period, has left little trace of the variation that is certain to have existed in the spoken language. Where dialectal utterances are found in print, in plays or pastoral lyrics, they are stylized and idealized as part of a literary convention, and the same is true of the portrayal of colloquial speech or the language of the lower classes in contemporary plays.

(c) The doubtful originality of texts adds further problems. Printed texts only occasionally reflect the uncontaminated idiolect of their authors. Even written texts such as letters or diaries were often copied by secretaries or exist only in later copies. Shakespeare's plays may serve as a very impressive example of what could happen in the course of a play's textual history. Manuscripts owned by the players or texts copied during performances often served as the basis for early editions. The folio edition (1623, T31A–F) is based on manuscripts which were carefully checked by players. This text was later printed by at least five compositors, of whom A "albeit he sometimes misread his copy, was on the whole very faithful to it", B "took all manner of liberties", and E "though he tried hard, (...) succeeded badly" (Hinman 1968: xviii), and finally the text was corrected with varying degrees of care. The author's original text is therefore doubtful in many places and even very careful textual criticism cannot guarantee to reconstruct it in many cases.

2 Dictionaries provide information about the vocabulary and meanings of words; before 1604 the only dictionaries were bilingual, most of them Latin–English.

3 Statements by grammarians are valuable sources for linguistic structures *and* attitudes. Intensive study of the English language started in the Renaissance period. This study was partly prompted by comparison with Latin and the resulting impression was that English lacked order, a full vocabulary and stylistic elegance (2.9). In the sixteenth century grammarians concentrated on problems of orthography and its reform (3.5) and on the lexicon (7.3). The value of such statements varies. The following factors must be taken into account if one wishes to arrive at an objective evaluation:

(a) provenance, life, social class and age of the individual grammarian, whose status may vary from that of a naive describer to that of a scholar basing his work on a particular linguistic theory;

(b) aim of the grammar (descriptive or – more likely – normative?);

(c) dependence upon a particular tradition: how strong is the influence of Latin grammar?

(d) the commonly conservative attitude of sixteenth-century grammarians.

All this means that we must expect gaps or doubtful judgements in the description, such as in the case of the pronunciation of homophones whose sounds are perceived as different only because the spelling differs; or the description, following the Latin pattern, of case and tense forms which may be non-existent in English (5.2.1). On the other hand, grammarians tended to overlook English categories which had no counterpart in Latin, such as the emerging category of aspect and the function of auxiliary *do* (6.5.6, 6.6).

4 The opinions of poets, critics and antiquaries reflect how the norms of correctness were interpreted. As shown in texts T1–T34, the wealth and variety of statements on the EModE language is considerable. However, we must not forget that most views are in some sense biased and must be carefully interpreted in their individual contexts. Moreover, the levels of grammar are very unevenly represented – there is much on the lexicon, a certain amount on pronunciation, but very little on syntax; also, almost all comments are concerned with the emerging standard form of EModE.

1.4 Cultural background

The gaps mentioned above are also found in other disciplines dealing with the period between 1500 and 1700. Historical geography, sociology, the history of religion, economic history and other areas can only provide some of the information that a sociolinguist working on present-day issues can easily obtain and use as a basis for empirical research. But even where documents from Early Modern times have been interpreted as required for the purposes of various disciplines, it is hardly possible for the individual scholar to have all this information at hand to apply to the linguistic data and thus interpret language use and change. Although we know from Labov's and other sociolinguists' research how linguistic variation can be described as patterned heterogeneity, there are considerable restrictions on the application of this procedure to language history before 1900.

One point, which is of special importance to the interpretation of linguistic data, can be regarded as representative of the problem as a whole.

1.5 Book production and literacy (Bennett 1952, 1965, 1970)

Cheap paper, the decreasing use of Latin and French, and growing interest in religious and encyclopaedic literature and also in light entertainment caused the production of books to rise dramatically in the early fifteenth century; yet the fact that every single copy had to be written out by hand limited the number of books. These works were chiefly religious or devotional manuals for monasteries or a private readership, such as catechisms, Latin grammars or dictionaries, encyclopaedic writings on housekeeping, agriculture, hunting, medicine or English history and literature in the narrower sense, such as the works of Chaucer and Lydgate. Private reading increasingly replaced reading aloud and public lecturing.

The bulk of everyday literature remained the same in the sixteenth century. (This is even true of medical texts, which by and large did not take into account new discoveries but reflected the knowledge and the medical system of the late Middle Ages.) The continuing increase in English books on the popular sciences, on history and geography is quite remarkable. Besides this, there was also a very extensive literature available in translation, mostly from the French, and predominantly concerned with practical and devotional topics. Classical authors, especially complete works, were not normally translated in England (unlike France) before 1560–90 (cf. 7.4.2). The invention of printing by Caxton and its subsequent spread throughout England after 1476 meant a speedy increase in book production, which was accelerated by a rapidly growing literate public. In the *Short Title Catalogue* as printed between 1476 and 1640, 25,000 titles are listed, which is certainly more than all the titles produced in the preceding periods of the English language put together.

Little is known about the number of copies printed. In many cases it will have been limited to 100 copies. But a school-book like Lily's grammar sold up to 10,000 copies each year.

The number of literary works published depends on a great number of factors. In the late sixteenth century in particular, several favourable circumstances coincided:

(a)   The expansion of grammar-school education meant that literacy was more widespread than ever before – a situation that was unparalleled until the nineteenth century.

(b)   Numerous theatres and their audiences drawn from all social classes gave rise to a great number of new plays.

(c)   The new sciences and the increasing interest in language, literature and rhetoric encouraged people to read books on these subjects.

(d)   Numerous university graduates tried to earn a living from writing if they were excluded from a government or ecclesiastical position.

It is impossible to determine exactly how many people were literate. There are only a few vague contemporary statements on this. The increasing number of printers and book titles serves as indirect evidence of the expanding market (1500: 54 titles, 1550: 214, 1640: 577), as does the foundation of a great number of grammar schools in the sixteenth century. Literacy appears to have reached a peak around 1600; it spread among members of the upper classes, including women, and even extended to the lower classes. Grammars and dictionaries from the early seventeenth century onwards were explicitly aimed at compensatory linguistic education, in particular of the young and of women (cf. t43).

In judging the impact that education had on the language of the time, it is important to stress how widely education was understood as a linguistic discipline. This explains the great influence of rhetoric and the delight in linguistic puns that is evident in contemporary drama. Linguistic education, which included education in English, was a very important precondition for social upward mobility.

2 Varieties of Early Modern English

2.1 Introduction

A language as spoken over a period of 200 years (that is to say, of seven generations) during which a standard was emerging can be described as homogeneous only if we exclude linguistic change and geographical and social variation, that is, if the language is described on a highly abstract level. To speak of *the* Early Modern English language is therefore unjustified. EModE could indeed be taken as a typical example to illustrate the fact that language systems are neither homogeneous nor stable: the existence of a great number of individual lects was a precondition for linguistic change in EModE, a change which is largely the result of the selection and later codification of one of the existing variants.

If we wish to explain within a Labovian framework the functioning of the co-existing varieties in an EModE social setting, we find that in most cases the relevant information is lacking. This means that we must again limit ourselves to describing subsystems extracted from the analysis of texts. Comparative description in the form of diasystems is possible and would be interesting on the basis of texts such as T36 vs T36A, but in other cases would not repay the effort.

In the sixteenth century, the emerging standard and the increasing importance of linguistic and literary theory took the first step in the history of the English language towards creating some kind of recognizable and mandatory order out of the chaos of co-existing regional, social, diachronic and stylistic variants. Increasing centralization, the disproportionate growth of London and the growing mobility of the population in general, combined to spread London prestige forms in waves out to the regional

8

dialects (T11, t3), the language of written documents being affected first. The social varieties affected one another increasingly: the speech of the educated determined the norms of the middle class. Nevertheless lower-middle-class pronunciation largely prevailed (especially after the political upheavals of the seventeenth century), though exhibiting the corrective influence of the grammar-school tradition. The causes, formulated quite generally in terms of the spread of the standard around 1600, have been described by Reyce (t3) and Puttenham (T11).

In consequence, the basis for diachronic change in one subsystem can often be discerned in the synchronic occurrence of variants in co-existing social or regional subsystems (4.3.4). On the other hand, reflexes of the wavelike spread of innovations brought about by the new standard language can still be recognized today on the geographical dimension (Horn and Lehnert 1954: 69–70: "A linguistic journey from Scotland via Northern England and the Midlands allows one to experience a substantial slice of language history.").

2.2 Dating Early Modern English

Linguistic development is a continuous process; boundaries separating postulated periods must therefore always be subjective or even appear to be arbitrary. It is opportune to draw such lines where the largest possible number of changes in the internal (structural) and external (cultural) history of a language 'bundle', to adapt a model developed for areal linguistics. The following delimiting dates have been proposed for the EModE period:

1500–1700 (Dobson 1968, Graband 1965, without detailed arguments; Görlach 1982)
1500–1660 (Baugh and Cable 1978, Schlauch 1959 "The Renaissance")
1540–1750 (Partridge 1969: 13 "New English")
1500–1800 (DEMEP 1976)
1476–1776 (the forthcoming *Cambridge History of the English Language*).

The following factors can be adduced in favour of dating the beginning of the EModE period from c. 1500:

Introduction to Early Modern English

1   The expansion of a written standard form and its increas-
     ing homogeneity (after 1450, English texts can no longer
     be localized); book printing began in England in 1476.
2   Inflexion is restricted to /s, əθ, əst, ər, ɪŋg, əd, ən/.
3   The end of the medieval feudal system and the rise of
     Renaissance dukes and courtiers (the Wars of the Roses
     ended in 1471, and the Tudors came to the throne in
     1485).
4   The beginning of humanism in England (Oxford Reform-
     ers 1485–1510).
5   The breakaway of the English church from Rome in 1534.
6   The discovery of America in 1492 (for the historical dates,
     see the conspectus on pages xx–xxix).

The fifteenth century is, however, a transitional period, both
linguistically and culturally. It must be realized that many sixteenth-century features have their beginnings or precursors in the
preceding century: the reduction of inflexions, the rise of
chancery English as the standard after 1430, the increase in the
middle-class readership (1.5). The *aureate terms* of fifteenth-century poetic diction are similar to the *inkhorn terms* of the sixteenth
(in form, though not in function) (7.3.5), purism in Pecock in the
fifteenth century matches Cheke's in the sixteenth, and the
influence of Latin syntax was more pronounced in the fifteenth
century than in the sixteenth.

It is even more difficult to settle on a date for the end of the
EModE period. Political history justifies the selection of 1660,
the end of the Civil War. There are also linguistic considerations
in favour of this date:

Dobson's (1968) detailed investigations have shown that,
regardless of variability, the pronunciation of the educated, and of
schoolmasters in particular, remained surprisingly stable until the
mid-seventeenth century (4.2). Phonemic mergers were largely
avoided, and the upper classes did not adopt the 'progressive'
pronunciation system. This homogeneity and relative stability is
explained by the strong school tradition, in which attempts were
made to stabilize pronunciation by reference to spelling (based on
late ME distinctions). Thus the upheavals of the Civil War appear
to have opened the floodgates to developments (especially in pro-

nunciation) long common among the lower classes, before a new phase of stabilization set in in the eighteenth century.

The following points, therefore, would support the choice of 1660.

1   Phonemic merger in words like *tale:tail* and *sole:soul*, coalescence of the initial sounds in *knot:not*, *gnat:not* and *wring:ring*, the phonemic split into /ʊ/ and /ʌ/ in *put:but*, and the re-allocation of the vowels in *cat:what* have all become effective.

2   Spelling has, more or less, become fixed in its modern form.

3   Reduction in the pronominal system and the introduction of *its* (cf. 5.4) have become effective.

Moreover, Dryden's verdicts on Ben Jonson and Shakespeare in 1672 (T15) reveal the self-confidence of a new era, particularly in attitudes to language. This sense of distance between the two periods is even more pointedly expressed in Pope's lines:

> As Augustus Rome, so Dryden found
> English brick, and left it marble.

In spite of these reflections, 1700 seems a reasonable date to select, since by this time the language has reached the state of considerable homogeneity characteristic of the eighteenth century. 'EModE' should, then, be defined as the period during which the London-based language spread outwards until relative homogeneity was achieved, the period of co-existing variants, so typical of all levels of EModE, being over by 1700. Two major indications may be given special mention:

1   Remaining syntactic redundancies had virtually disappeared and existing grammatical categories were rapidly being re-defined (6.1.6).

2   The use of Latin for expository prose had been discontinued (see 2.9.2).

2.3 Written and spoken language

The reconstruction of any language before 1900 must, in the first phase at least, be that of the written language, which may vary to a greater or lesser extent from the spoken. Direct evidence of the spoken English of the time is very scarce, as is pointed out by Barber (1976: 48–56). Whether in allegedly literal protocols of court proceedings, popular dramatic scenes (King 1941) or texts representing EModE dialects – the standardizing effect of editing must always be reckoned with. Sermons and speeches, which are still extant in great numbers and which were written down for oral delivery diverge from spoken English on the rhetorical level, although sermons such as Latimer's (T39) may well preserve many features typical of extempore preaching.

The spoken and written forms of a language also differ in modern times as a consequence of the requirements of different types of communicative situations, despite the fact that most native speakers are also writers (and listeners/readers) of the language and that users frequently have occasion both to speak and to write on the same topic. Since in EModE times competence in written English was not as common as it is today, and the need to switch from the spoken to the written language and back again was less frequent, it may be assumed that the two subsystems were further apart then than they are in modern speech communities.

Then as now, written language was more supraregional and homogeneous but also more dependent on style and literary traditions. Two counterdirectional developments occurred within EModE, affecting the interrelationship of the two subsystems.

1   The increasing influence of the schools brought spelling and pronunciation closer together, the spelling most often affecting the pronunciation of a particular word (spelling pronunciation, 4.8).
2   Increasing use of the written form as a consequence of changing communicative needs and conventions and its 'improvement' in accordance with Latin models meant that the written language diverged from spoken English, in particular at the level of text syntax.

The stabilizing influences of an existing written tradition were recognized quite early, but possibly exaggerated, as in the observation that Swift ascribes to the Earl of Oxford (1712):

t1   if it were not for the *Bible* and *Common Prayer Book* in the
      vulgar Tongue, we should hardly be able to understand any
      Thing that was written among us an hundred Years ago:
      Which is certainly true: For those Books being perpetually
5   read in Churches, have proved a kind of Standard for
      Language, especially to the common People.   1712

2.4 Dialects of Early Modern English

2.4.1 Standard and dialect

As late as around 1400, a poet wrote in his native dialect or in that
of his expected audience; if texts moved beyond their sphere of
origin they were translated into the dialect of the new readers.
That Chaucer used London English is due to his provenance, to
the language of the court, and to the London readers for whom
the poems were written. The *Gawain* poet, however, used the
West Midland dialect, which was difficult for Londoners to
understand, and the language of the *York Plays* is, of course, that
of York. The rise of the standard language in the fifteenth century
meant that it quickly became equated with correct speech,
whereas dialect came to be associated with uneducated and incorrect usage. The printing presses soon ironed out the remaining
local differences in written English, as was only to be expected in
view of the fact that 98 per cent of all English books were printed
in London (for Scots, see 2.5).

The more firmly the standard came to be established, the
greater was the pressure to conform. There are quite early statements on "What the best English is", such as Hart's of 1569:

t2   there is no doubt, but that the English speach, which
      the learned sort in the ruled Latin, togither with
      those which are acquainted with the vulgars Italian,
      French, and Spanish doe vse, is that speach which
5   euery reasonable English man, will the nearest he can,
      frame his tongue therevnto: but such as haue no con-
      ference by the liuely voice, nor experience of reading,
      nor in reading no certaintie how euery letter shoulde
      be sounded, can neuer come to the knowledge and vse,
10   of that best and moste perfite English.   1569

'Good' English also came to be limited geographically (according to Puttenham (T11/50–1) to sixty miles around London). In consequence, tolerance towards dialect speakers diminished; the much-quoted example of Sir Walter Raleigh, of whom Aubrey said that he did not disown his Devonshire dialect (accent?), is telling because it points to the conformity of others. Conformity is also found in Shakespeare's works, in which few traces of his native Stratford dialect can be detected. James I, at least in his written usage, also took pains to avoid Scotticisms after he had moved to London in 1603.

EModE dialect material should be interpreted in the light of the above indications of contemporary sociolinguistic evaluation; the available material is of three types:

1 Dialect texts: because of the early standardization of 'public' texts, these are most likely to be private letters and diaries, which may exhibit deviances caused by dialect interference. (Also, see statements in court such as in T64 which were expected to be taken down verbatim.)

As regards literary texts, dialect was used in sixteenth-century plays mainly for country bumpkins; it was not until later that Ben Jonson, for instance, used (urban) dialect to individualize characters in his comedies. The representation of dialect in literature is, however, limited to certain conspicuous phonetic or lexical features which are enough to signal to the audience that a speaker is of either southern or northern origin. The much-quoted Cotswold dialect, too, is an Elizabethan stage convention: standard speech with a few typical and stereotyped deviances. Even if dramatists had been able to render dialect speech realistically and with phonetic precision (and most of them certainly were not), they would not have dared to, for fear of rendering their plays unintelligible (see T31C). A new age was ushered in by the 'gentleman dialectologist' Meriton, whose fictional dialogue (T61) was intended as a realistic portrayal of rural Yorkshire speech, a device much imitated in the eighteenth and nineteenth centuries.

2 Diachronic reconstructions on the basis of recorded ME or EModE dialects.

3 Contemporary comments on dialects: in view of the prescriptive and evaluative attitudes of the period, any interpretation

ought to be treated with caution (see T11). In general, statements are comparatively few in number and often anecdotal and impressionistic. However, Reyce's observations (t3) may be compared with Puttenham's (T11), which precede those of the former by fourteen years; and Verstegan (t4) provides some apparently accurate specimens:

t3　To come now vnto the persons them selues, & the Inhabitantes of this contry, when I remember there names & language I doe fynde no dialecte or Ideome in the same differente from others of the beste speeche or pronun-
5　ciation; For as we border not vpon any forreigne lymitts of differinge tongue or pronunciation, by whose vycinitie in our comon traffacke wee haue cawse by encrochenge vpon others to dyversefye our owne naturall language, so havinge no naturall defecte proper to this soyle, do wee
10　disgrace that with any broade or rude accente, which wee do receyve at the handes of Schollers, & other of the better sorte for education, where of wee haue many trayned vp in the beste & purest language. Howbeit I muste confesse our honest toylinge contry villager, to
15　expresse his meaninge to his lyke neighbour, wyll many tymes lett slyppe some strange vnvsuall differente tearmes, not so well intelligible, to anye of cyvyll education, vntyll by the rude Commente of some skyllfull in that homely Iargon, which by dayly vse amonge
20　them is familiar, thay be after there manner explaned. But this beinge only amonge the rudest contrymen the artificer of the good towne, scorneth to followe them, when he naturally prydeth in the cownterfaittinge imitation of the beste sorte of Language, & therefore no
25　cawse to observe any thinge therein.　　1603

t4　and of this different pronountiation one example in steed of many shall suffice, as this: for pronouncing according as one would say at London *I would eat more cheese if I had it*, the Northern man saith, *Ay sud eat mare cheese*
5　*gin ay hadet*, and the Westerne man saith *Chud eat more cheese an chad it*. Lo heere three different pronountiations in our owne Country in one thing, and hereof many the like examples might be alleaged.　　1605

A positive attitude towards dialect in the sixteenth century can be detected in Spenser's use of it in his pastoral poetry (T23B), where it serves to meet the demands of *decorum* (2.6) and, at the same time, to satisfy the ideal of linguistic purism (7.3.7). Compare his solution with that chosen by Ramsay, who, in the early eighteenth century, was in the much easier position of having Scots to contrast with Standard English for the 'rural' speech of his shepherds. It was not until the second half of the seventeenth century that an antiquarian-scholarly interest in dialects arose. This is shown by Evelyn's attitude as expressed in T16/87–92, and the *Collections* of John Ray, who, in 1674, started the tradition of dialect dictionaries in England (also, see T59/42–6):

t5   In my travels through several parts of *England*, besides
      other things, which I principally minded and pursued,
      I could not but take notice of the difference of Dialect
      and variety of local words (for so I will take leave to
5   call such as are not of general use) in divers Counties,
      by Reason whereof in many places, especially in the
      North, the Language of the common people is to a stran-
      ger very difficult to be understood. Where upon I
      thought it might be worth the while to make a Collection
10   of such words for my own use, and began first to set
      down those that occurred to me in common discourse. But
      making short stayes in particular places, and conversing
      but with few persons, I found that what I could take
      notice of my self would be but an inconsiderable part
15   of what were in use among the vulgar. Therefore I desired
      my friends and acquaintance living in several Countreys
      to communicate to me what they had observed each of their
      own Countrey words, or should afterwards gather up out
      of the mouths of the people; which divers of them accord-
20   ingly did. To whose contributions I must acknowledge my
      self to owe the greatest part of the words, I now present
      the *Reader* with, in these Catalogues. The considerations
      which induced me to make them publick were. *First*, be-
      cause I knew not of any thing that hath been already done
25   in this kind. 2. Because I conceive, they may be of some
      use to them who shall have occasion to travel the North-
      ern Counties, in helping them to understand the common
      language there. 3. Because they may also afford some di-
      version to the curious, and give them occasion of making
30   many considerable remarks.   1674

2.4.2 The geographical spread of English (Leith 1983: 151–212; Bailey 1985)

> t6 And who in time knowes whither we may vent
> The treasure of our tongue, to what strange shores
> This gaine of our best glorie shal be sent,
> T'enrich vnknowing Nations with our stores?
> 5 What worlds in th'yet vnformed Occident
> May come refin'd with th'accents that are ours?   1599

At the beginning of the EModE period, the use of English was restricted to England and some parts of Scotland, Wales and Ireland (T10). In the west and the north, Celtic languages (Cornish, Manx, Irish and Scottish Gaelic) covered a much larger area than they do today, and the use of English, even as a second language, was very rare. Scotland's official language was Scots (2.5); the Celtic Border dividing the Gaelic-speaking Highlands from the Scots-speaking Lowlands was a comparatively stable linguistic boundary, despite official attempts to promote the use of Scots (or English) in the Highlands, as laid down in the Statutes of Iona (T53).

Parts of Sutherland, Orkney and Shetland gradually shifted from Scandinavian Norn to Scots in the course of the sixteenth to eighteenth centuries. Ireland was almost completely Celtic-speaking in the early sixteenth century, with pockets of English speakers in the east remaining from the medieval settlements (T52). In the second half of the sixteenth century the colonization of Ireland became official policy, a process that made substantial progress in the seventeenth century with the Plantation of Ulster (1606, Scottish settlers predominating, see Braidwood 1964) and with Cromwell's conquests in central Ireland (Ó Muirithe 1978). This expansion resulted in new contact varieties of English: these were based on southern English and Welsh/Cornish in the south and west of England, on English and Irish in Ireland, and on Scots and English and Irish in Ulster (cf. T52, T62).

From 1607 onwards, there were permanent settlements of English speakers in America ("New England"), but there is little evidence that a distinctive AmE variety ("Colonial AmE") separated off at this time (cf. T54, T64 and texts printed in Fisher and Bornstein 1974: 259–89); such early texts, however, do illustrate what kinds of texts and dialectal and sociolectal features the settlers brought with them and used as patterns, forms of speech that later developed into the AmE of the Atlantic states. From 1600, the year of the foundation of the *East India Company*, English was also present in India – but the development of Indian English dates only from the nineteenth century. The origins of various forms of English-related pidgins in West Africa and the Caribbean also date back to the sixteenth/seventeenth centuries, but no coherent and realistic textual representations survive from that period.

2.5 Scots (Templeton 1973, Romaine 1982, Görlach 1985b)

Although Scots can (and possibly should) be described as an independent language in the Renaissance period, it also functions in some ways as a subsystem of English as early as the sixteenth century, and increasingly so after 1603. If it is regarded as belonging to the history of EModE, then its linguistic distinctiveness, its political status as the language of the Scottish court and of books printed in Edinburgh, and its gradual merging with written *Sudron* ('southern English'), all give it a unique importance in the linguistic history of the period.

A national literature emerged from the late fourteenth century onwards, and especially in the fifteenth century (see Jack 1988), when court poets, emulating Chaucer and Lydgate, used the vernacular in their poems. Prose followed in the sixteenth century, comprising translations, an adaptation of the Wyclif Bible, historiography, writings on law and popular medicine, and works of devotion or religious instruction. There was little drama worthy of note, with the notable exception of Lyndsay's *Satire of the Thrie Estaitis*.

The fact that Scots did not develop into a modern national language (as did other vernaculars, such as English, French or German, during the Renaissance) is a result of a mixture of political, economic and cultural factors. Although printing presses existed in Edinburgh, the number of titles printed in Scots (and the number of copies) was minimal in comparison with book production in London. Bald (1926) has calculated the ratio of Scots to English/anglicized books printed in Edinburgh in each decade. Her figures show that, while Scots texts predominated before 1580, there was a rapid decline after 1603, when Scots ceased to be used as a book language except for certain antiquarian purposes:

	Scots	Eng
1560	18	0
1570	43	12
1580	35	5
1590	10	13
1600	18	38
1610	7	25
1620	3	47
1625	2	21
Total	136	161

It was also of great importance that the language of the Scottish reformers, and of religion in general, was largely English. Knox had lived in England for a long period before spending many years in Frankfurt and Geneva (where he married an English-woman). Even after his return to Scotland, he wrote almost exclusively in English (with some Scots admixtures), a fact which provoked Ninian Winzet's criticism:

> Gif ye, throw curiositie of novationis hes foryet our auld plane Scottish quhilk your mother lerit you, I sall wryte to you my mynd in Latin, for I am nocht acquyntit with your Southeron.   (Quoted from Lewis 1954: 203)

The only attempt to translate the Bible into Scots remained unprinted: in the years 1513–22 M. Nisbet adapted the text of the Late Version of the Wyclif Bible by making the most necessary changes in orthography/phonology. Just how close he kept to the lexis of his source, however, is shown by a comparison of T19B/1–6 with Nisbet's rendering:

> t7 And quhen ye tyme of promissioun com nere quhilk god hadde knawlechit to abraham ye pepile waxit and multi-plijt in egipt. Til ane vthir king raase in egipt quhilk knew nocht ioseph. y^{is} begilet oure kin and tormentit
> 5   oure fadris y^t y^{ai} suld put away y^{ar} 3onng childir for y^{ai} suld nocht leeue.   *c.* 1520

Finally, imitation of Chaucer by the Scottish court poets (the "Makars") led, in the language of the poets, to a considerable mixing of Scots and southern words and word-forms (besides the adoption of numerous loans from French and Latin). In 1512, Gavin Douglas explained in the prologue to his translation of Virgil's *Aeneid* that he intended to write in conservative Scots ("kepand na sudron bot our awyn langage"), but that he was forced to accept loans from Latin, French and *English* "quhar scant was Scottis" (T18A/7, 12–14). It is difficult to imagine a contemporary English poet borrowing from Dunbar or Douglas. (Surrey's use of Douglas' *Aeneid* in his own translation (T21) did *not* involve the borrowing of Scots words.)

Such tendencies towards convergence increased in the sixteenth century with the growing prestige of English. Although James I attempted a literary handbook for Scots (T28) and stressed the exemplary function of the monarch's speech (T29/55–9), he made increasing use of English elements in his own writings – and not only in his letters to Queen Elizabeth (T42). He did not conceal his admiration for the English in other respects either, as can be seen in a letter to Cecil:

> Alace it is a farre more barbarouse and stiffe nekkit
> people that I rule ouer. Saint george surelie rydes
> vpon a touardlie rydding horse, quhaire I ame burstin
> in daunting a wylde vnreulie coalte.

Of his books, T28 and T29 are largely Scots in the manuscripts, but T28 was anglicized by the printer Vautrouiller, and T29 twice underwent anglicization by Waldegrave (1599, 1603); James' *Counterblaste to Tobacco*, however, published in London after his accession to the throne, is in pure English.

In view of such tendencies, and of the flow of English books on to the Scottish market, it is not surprising that neither writers nor printers used pure Scots between 1575 and 1603, and that their texts are marked by deliberate or unconscious interference from English (see Devitt 1989). The Union of the Crowns in 1603, therefore, only consolidates a development that had been in full swing throughout the second half of the sixteenth century. Englishmen normally came into contact with Scots in the sixteenth century only in written or printed form. The kind of breakdown in oral communication that could occur is illustrated by the fictional tale from *The Merie Tales of the Mad men of Gotam* printed below. (The text is also remarkable because the English author, A.B., tried to render some stereotyped features of Scots – compare Shakespeare's text for *Jamie* in *Henry IV*):

t8   And he wente to London to haue a Bores head made. He dyd
     come to a Caruer (or a Joyner) saying in his mother tonge,
     I saye spek, kens thou meke me a Bare heade? Ye said the
     Caruer. Than sayd the skotyshman, mek me a bare head
  5 anenst Yowle, an thowse bus haue xx pence for thy hyre.
     I wyll doe it sayde the Caruer. On S. Andrewes daye be-
     fore Chrystmas (the which is named Yowle in Scotland, and
     in England in the north) the skottish man did com to Lon-
     don for his Bores heade to set at a dore for a signe.
 10 I say speke said the skotish man, haste thou made me a
     Bare head? Yea said the Caruer. Then thowse a gewd fellow.
     The Caruer went and did bryng a mans head of wod that was
     bare and sayd, syr here is youre bare head. I say sayde
     the skotyshman, the mokyl deuill, is this a bare head?
 15 Ye said the caruer. I say sayd the Skotishman, I will
     haue a bare head, syk an head as doth follow a Sew that
     hath Gryces. Syr said the caruer, I can not tel what is
     a Sew, nor what is a Gryce. Whet horson, kenst thou not a
     sew that wil greet and grone, and her gryces wil run after
 20 her and cry a weke a weke. O said the Caruer, it is a
     pigge. Yea said the skotish man, let me haue his fathers
     head made in timber, and mek me a bird and set it on his
     skalps, and cause her to singe whip whir, whip whir. The
     caruer sayde, I can not cause her to singe whip whir.
 25 Whe horson sayde the skotish man gar her as she woulde
     singe whip whir. Here a man maye see that euerye man
     doth delight in his owne sences, or doth reioice in his
     fantasie.   1540

This tale shows why the authorities employed translators for Scots in the port of London until 1617.

Some authors who translated Scots texts into English also made it clear that their task was not easy; cf. Harrison, who based his History of Scotland (for Holinshed's *Chronicles*, T36 and T36A) on Bellenden's Scots version:

t9   I haue chosen rather, onely with the losse of three or
     foure dayes to translate Hector out of the Scottish
     (a tongue verie like vnto ours) than with more expense

of time to diuise a newe, or follow the Latin copie...

5   Hetherto I haue translated Hectors description of Scotland out of the Scottish into the English toung, being
not a little ayded therein by the Latine.   1577

English authors differed in their evaluation of Scots. Some claimed that Scots (and northern English) retained the original character, the purity and the correct pronunciation of the language much better than English (t36/1–2, T11/46; see Zachrisson 1914). On the other hand, appreciation of Scottish culture as something independent came only by degrees. For example, T10/95–101 and similar passages were inserted by Hooker only in the second edition of the *Chronicles*.

To sum up: to decide whether Scots in the sixteenth and seventeenth centuries should be described as a separate language or as a dialect of English is not easy. On the one hand, Scots fulfilled the criteria usually assumed to be constitutive for a language.

1   It was a national language whose use coincided with the political boundaries of the Scottish kingdom.

2   It had developed a literary/written standard.

3   The court at Edinburgh and the University of St Andrew's provided a norm of written (and presumably also of spoken) Scots.

4   There are several statements extant indicating that some users considered Scots an independent language (T18A/7–10, etc. and cf. Bald 1928).

On the other hand, the weight of these criteria is diminished by the increasing convergence of Scots with English in the course of the period; and there are other factors which argue against independent language status.

1   The reciprocal intelligibility of Scots and English was not seriously endangered even when the two were furthest apart (in spite of the remarks made above).

2   Structural differences were most marked in phonology/orthography and – in some texts – in lexis, but much less so in inflexion and syntax.

3   Educated speakers remained conscious of the common descent of Scots and northern English, and of the close

historical relationship between Scots and English in general.

It can therefore be argued that Scots is and has always been a subsystem of English, whose incipient separation from EModE was slowed down as a consequence of political, economic and cultural factors in the sixteenth century and finally blocked by the adoption of English as the written (and, later, the spoken) language of higher prestige.

In the following chapters no full description of Scots as a linguistic system is attempted; the few chapters (3.7; 5.5.3; 7.1.6) and occasional remarks on Scots serve only to point to some characteristic divergences from EModE.

2.6 Sociolectal variation

t10   *Clo.* ⁹ He fir, that muft marrie this woman: Therefore
you Clowne, abandon: which is in the vulgar, leaue the
focietie: which in the boorifh, is companie, of this female: which in the common, is woman: which toge-
5   ther, is, abandon the fociety of this Female, or Clqwne
thou perifheft: or to thy better vnderftanding, dyeft; or
(to wit) I kill thee, make thee away, tranflate thy life into death, thy libertie into bondage: I will deale in poy-
fon with thee, or in baftinado, or in fteele: I will bandy
10   with thee in faction, I will ore-run thee with police: I
will kill thee a hundred and fifty wayes, therefore tremble and depart.   1623

Social differences in speech are reflected in historical texts especially where:

1   members of different social classes are represented as speaking, e.g. in plays or in other forms of dialogue;

2   individual features characteristic of a specific class are either described as worthy of imitation (most frequently the speech of the educated) or stigmatized as barbarisms and corrupt forms;

3   literary texts are written for readers of one specific social class, such as prose romances for the lowest class of literates, or scholarly texts for the educated.

The most conspicuous class markers appear to have been – then as now – on the level of pronunciation (T11/37 *strange accents or ill shapen soundes*). Since divergent pronunciation was normally not reflected in the orthography, social stratification in the surviving texts is most clearly discernible in vocabulary – most obviously in the Latinate diction (often technical terms) which was considered appropriate for the educated, but which often came out as malapropism (7.3.6) in the speech of the lower classes.

The existence of features characteristic of female speech is also first mentioned in EModE, for instance when Gil (1621: 17–18) criticizes the advanced pronunciation of London middle-class women, or in John Harington's anecdote about Iaques Wingfield, whose name caused embarrassment: "she brought her Ladie word, not without blushing, that it was M. *Priuie* Wingfield…" (1596, full text in Barber 1976: 156). Note Stanyhurst's reference to Cicero on the topic of female consciousness of linguistic standards – and the Irish counterexample (T52/38–50).

Thieves' cant occupied a unique position as the language of a group outside mainstream society; it was first recorded in the sixteenth century (T9; also cf. T59/47–9). Its distinctiveness lies exclusively on the level of the vocabulary, which abounds in cryptic expressions intelligible only to the initiated; once accepted into slang, they can of course become part of the more general vocabulary.

From the Middle Ages onwards (John of Garland, *c.* 1230), the social stratification of (written) language was correlated with the three stylistic levels of classical rhetoric: *altus, grande* is appropriate for *curiales/courtiers; medius* for *civiles/citizens, burghers; humilis* for *rurales/simple countrymen.* This tripartite division is found, for example, in Chaucer (*Clerk's Prologue* 15–20, Benson 1987: 137). The ubiquitous influence of rhetoric on Renaissance linguistic thought would lead one to expect what is indeed confirmed by detailed analysis: the attitudes of grammarians and the practice of poets were largely determined by this correlation and the principle of decorum. As with representations of 'dialect' in EModE writings, renderings of sociolect are therefore bound to be somewhat stylized.

As early as the sixteenth century the rapid spread of the standard meant that dialect came to function as a sociolect (t4,

T11). This view is not vitiated by, for instance, the deliberate use of certain dialect words in Spenser's poetry.

2.7 Diachrony

2.7.1 The co-existence of diachronically different forms of speech

It is true of all linguistic communities with literary, especially written, traditions that earlier forms of speech can co-exist with more modern varieties in certain registers. As regards EModE, the retention of earlier English is found in poets who, following the principle of *imitatio*, appealed to Chaucer as the *fyrst fynder* of English poetry and took over certain parts of his language in a deliberately archaizing fashion (7.1.4). Stressing the continuity of the Church of England, the 'translators' of the AV did not attempt a completely new translation, but chose to retain as much as possible of Tyndale's versions (1526/35), whose morphology and syntax, vocabulary and rhythm they largely preserved, with some substitutions from later sixteenth-century translations (cf. T19A and T19B). In consequence, an archaizing style started to be associated with poetic or biblical registers as early as the sixteenth/seventeenth centuries, and has remained so down to the present day.

Not so conspicuous, but nevertheless influential, was the practice of some printers from Caxton (T1: 1380/1480) to Batman (t12: 1390/1592), who reprinted medieval texts, changing their language only where necessary to enable modern readers to understand them (the complete rewriting of the preface t12 is an exception).

2.7.2 Awareness of linguistic change

At least since the time of Chaucer (*Troilus* II.22–5 in Benson 1987: 489, ultimately based on Horace) writers have been aware of, and have commented on, the sequence of chronolects in historical succession and the problems arising from linguistic change. However, it was only from the seventeenth century onwards that comments became frequent; these were predominantly negative, claiming that:

1   the adoption of loanwords affected the purity of the Germanic language;

2   'sloppy' articulation made pronunciation deviate from correctness;

3   the changing English language was not the equal of Latin. This was advanced as an argument against translating the Bible, since only in Latin would it remain unaffected by linguistic change. The instability of the language also made some English poets fear for the survival of their literary works as Waller did in 1693 (T65).

This perpetual change, and the fact that only the use of Latin secured international fame, even made Bacon publish the second, enlarged edition of *The Advancement of Learning* (1605) as *De augmentis scientiarum* (1623). Etymology (7.1.5) and historical grammar had not yet developed into scholarly disciplines. Therefore writers who were aware of the principle of linguistic change still often erred in details, as Dryden did, in T15, when he criticized Ben Jonson's use of English even though some of the 'errors' were correct in Jonson's time. Dryden, too, confessed that he was often puzzled about what constituted proper English usage, a state of affairs he contrasts with the stability of Latin:

t10a   I am often put to a stand, in considering
       whether what I write be the idiom of the
       tongue, or false grammar, and nonsense
       couched beneath that specious name of
       Anglicism; and have no other way to clear
       my doubts, but by translating my English
       into Latin, and thereby trying what sense
       the words will bear in a more stable
       language.   (Dedication to *Troilus and Cressida*, 1679)

The history of the classical languages suggested an analogy between language development and an organism which matures towards a perfect state, but which then ages and deteriorates. A variant concept saw the development as a cycle of heights and depths (T8/1–5). What solution could seem more obvious than to try to perfect a language by enriching its vocabulary and regulating its grammar, and then to attempt to fix it in the resultant state of perfection?

Renaissance writers saw the English language as being close to this ideal state or even as having achieved it, but from the Restoration onwards the idea of decay (implying that the acme was past) became dominant. Stabilization could not be achieved by custom alone (be it of the court, be it of the educated), it would have taken an academy. The history of the proposals for an academy is one of failure and defeat (Flasdieck 1928). The English came closest to establishing one in the period 1660–1724: prompted by the foundation of the Académie Française (1634) and the English translation of its history, the Royal Society set up a committee on language (T16, T17), Defoe submitted a detailed project in 1698, and Swift published his *Proposal* in 1712 (cf. the texts in Bolton 1966: 91–101, 107–23). However, it was the largely prescriptive dictionaries of the eighteenth century and the great number of prescriptive school grammars that brought about what stability could be expected from a living language and the norms of usage that writers had hoped for from an academy.

2.8 Registers

2.8.1 Rhetoric

Register can be seen as language variation according to subject matter, style and medium. According to Renaissance views, discussion of it consequently came under the heading of rhetoric, a discipline which, with its concept of decorum ('appropriateness of speech'), provided a stylistic yardstick. Rhetoric was developed in classical times as a forensic art: it was concerned with legal discourse. In the Middle Ages one of its five parts, *elocutio*, had been given special emphasis so that rhetoric had largely become the discipline of literary expression and was often equated with poetics. In the *trivium*, rhetoric was one of the basic disciplines, together with grammar and logic (6.1.3), and by refining a scholar's sensitivity to Latin style it also schooled his powers of expression in the vernacular.

The impact of *elocutio*, which may be roughly divided into figures of speech and figures of thought, and which were classified into over 200 categories in Renaissance manuals (cf. Sonnino 1968), was felt at all levels of expression, ranging from lexical meaning and correct inflexion to word-order rules, the structure of texts (speeches, letters as in T43, essays) and appropriateness of style. Rhetoric thus served to structure arguments properly and to provide them with linguistic brilliance.

Since education in the grammar schools, which was available to large sections of the male population, was dominated by rhetoric, it is easy to explain the readiness to undertake linguistic experiments, the rhetorical exuberance and witty punning which was enjoyed by readers and theatre audiences alike. On the other hand, these facts are probably the greatest obstacle to a modern reader's appreciation of Renaissance poetry (see Lewis 1954: 161). Rhetorical cultivation of the mother tongue was one of the most important aspects of the attempt to overcome the inadequacy of English vis-à-vis Latin. It is therefore no surprise that the influences of rhetoric are to be found everywhere, ranging from the greatest works of literature to the letter-writing manual of Angel Day (T43). They are conspicuous in the 'artful' prose of Sidney (T26) and Lyly (T25) and in Shakespeare's plays, especially his early ones, such as *Love's Labours Lost* I.2.1–129.

From its beginnings in Greece, rhetoric brought with it the danger of misuse. Wilson argued that *affected* rhetoric should be abolished (T4/80), whereas Sprat (T17/13–15), using arguments put forward in ancient literature, pleaded for a complete ban. Its misuse is also Shakespeare's topic in T31D (see Cordelia's "I want that glib and oylie Art, / To speake and purpose not", *Lear* I.1.246–7), and Milton's in *Paradise Lost*, where he contrasts Satan's persuasiveness (2.226 "with words cloath'd in reasons garb make appear the worse the better reason") with true rhetoric.

2.8.2 *Style*

t11   STile is a conftant & continuall phrafe or tenour of fpeaking and writing, extending to the whole tale or procefle of the poeme or hiftorie, and not properly to any peece or member of a tale: but is of words fpeeches and fentences together, a certaine
5   contriued forme and qualitie, many times naturall to the writer, many times his peculier by election and arte, and fuch as either he keepeth by skill, or holdeth on by ignorance, and will not or peraduenture cannot eafily alter into any other .   1589

Style is the (usually deliberate) characteristic selection of linguistic means of expression made by an individual or a group from the alternatives that the linguistic system or the norm allows. The term 'style' is most frequently applied to written expression, and mainly to vocabulary and syntax (cf. OED's definition, s.v. *style*: "those features of literary composition which belong to form rather than to the substance of the thought or matter expressed"). Style is inadequately defined as deviance from an expected norm. The imitation of the prose styles of Latin or French authors by English writers during the Renaissance shows that stylistic traditions need not be confined to a particular language but can – with the restrictions imposed by differences in grammatical structure – be an international phenomenon.

Style is subject to changing fashions to an even greater degree than other aspects of the language. Such change appears to have been especially rapid in the last decade of the sixteenth century – a fact which gave Shakespeare ample opportunity for the criticism of various stylistic excesses (in *Love's Labours Lost*, 1595?, cf. Carroll 1976), and which made Hoskins remark in his *Directions for Speech and Style*:

> I have used and outworne six severall
> styles, since I was first fellowe of
> newe Colledge, and am yet able to
> beare the fashion of writing Companie.
>
> (*c.* 1599; quoted from Partridge 1969: 213)

Change of style is particularly obvious where old texts are re-phrased in a new style. A good example of the verbose style of the late sixteenth century is Batman's re-phrasing (1582) of Trevisa's Prologue to his translation (*c.* 1390) of Bartholomæus Anglicus (t12, p. 30).

Attempts to refine English style, and thereby make English more respectable, are reflected in the increasing use of rhetorical devices of various types, such as long and neatly structured periods in deliberate imitation of Cicero (T7, 6.8.2), the short-lived euphuism (T25) or the more moderate use of rhetorical figures to achieve 'beautiful' language in Sidney's *Arcadia* (T26).

t12

THE PROLOGVE
of the Tranſlator.

Rue it is,that after the
noble ꝭ expert doctrine
of wiſe and well learn-
ed Philoſophers,lefte ꝭ
remaining with vs in
wꝛiting,we knowe that
7 the pꝛoperties of thinges followe and
enſue their ſubſtaunce . Wherfoꝛe it is,
that after the oꝛder and the diſtinction
10 of ſubſtaunces,the oꝛder and the diſtinction of the pꝛoperties of things ſhall be
and enſue. Of the which things , this
woꝛke of all the bookes enſuing , by the
grace,helpe and aſſiſtaunce of Almighty
15 God,is compiled and made.Peruaile not
ye wittie ꝭ eloquent readers,that J thin
of wit,and void of cunning, haue tranſ-
lated this booke from latin into our vulgar language , as a thing pꝛofitable to
20 me, and peraduenture to manye other ,
which vnderſtand not Latine, noꝛ haue
not the knowledge of the pꝛoperties of
things,which things be appꝛoued by the
bookes of great and cunning Clearkes,
25 and by the experience of m ˜ wittie ꝭ
noble Philoſophers.All theſe pꝛoperties
of things be neceſſarie and of great ba-
lew,to them that will be deſirous to vnderſtand the obſcurities oꝛ darkneſſe of
30 holy Scriptures,which are giuen to vs
vnder figures,vnder parables ꝭ ſeblance
oꝛ likelihoods of things naturalls ꝭ ar-
tificialls. S.Denis that great philoſopher
and ſolempne Clearke,in his booke na-
35 med, The heauenly Hierarchies of An-
gells, teſtiſieth and witneſſeth the ſame,
ſaiꝫng in this manner : Whatſoeuer a-
ny man will coniect,fainte,imagine, ſup-
poſe,oꝛ ſay: it is a thing impoſſible,that
40 the light of the heauenly diuine bꝛight-
neſſe couered and cloſed in the Deitie oꝛ
in the Godhead, ſhould ſhine vpon vs :
if it were not by the diuerſities of holy

conertures.

Trevisa c. 1390, ed. Seymour

(7) For þe propirtees of
þinges folewyth þe sub-
staunce, þe ordre and
distinccioun of propir-
tees schal be ordeyned
to ordir and distinccioun
of þe substaunce þerof.

(13) By help of God þis
werk is compiled, profit-
able to me and on cas to
oþir þat knowith nouȝt þe
kyndes and propirtees of
þinges þat beth toschift
and isprad ful wide in
bokes of holy seyntes
and philosophris

(28) to vndirstonde redels
and menynges of scriptures
and of writinges þat þe
holy gost hath iȝeue
derkliche ihid and wrapped
vndir liknes and fygures
of propirtees of þinges
of kynde and craft,

(33) as seint Denys schew-
eth in *Ierarchia angelica*,
and seith þat þe beme of
God ȝeueth to vs no liȝt
but iveyled and ihid by
dyuerste of holy veyl-
ynges and wrappinges.

FINIS PROLOGI.

The stylistic devices used by Lyly are particularly conspicuous; they are summarized by Holzknecht (1954: 346) as:

1   balanced parallel sentence structure, often accompanied by alliteration or assonance;
2   repetition and strained antithesis;
3   rhetorical questions and exclamations, either alone or in combination with (1) and (2);
4   *exempla*, anecdotes, or other illustrations from history or literature, or the author's invention;
5   proverbs, pithy sayings, wise saws, and *sententiae*;
6   puns and word-play;
7   fantastic similes drawn from mythology, science or pseudo-science, recondite lore, especially the fabulous habits and qualities of plants and animals ("unnatural natural history") and seldom used singly.

Criticism of stylistic excesses started in the sixteenth century; thus Peacham, s.v. *Periergia*:

t13   (writers) that doe fondly couet coppy, and take greater
      care to paynte their speech with fyne fygures, then to
      expresse the truth plainly.   1577

Or Lever, who writes in "The Forespeache" of his book:

t14   As for Ciceronians & suger tongued fellowes, which labour
      more for finenes of speach then for knowledge of good
      matter, they oft speake much to small purpose, and shak-
      ing foorth a number of choise words, and picked sentences,
   5 they hinder good learning wyth their fond chatter.   1572

From early on, Protestants felt the need to defend the plain language of the Bible (see T8/142 – but this did not stop rhetorical excesses in sermons); Fulwell 1575 and Becon 1564 are typical of such defensive attitudes:

t15   I confesse I haue not the gifte of flowing eloquence,
      neyther can I enterlace my phrase with Italian termes,
      nor powder my style with frenche Englishe or Inkhorne
      Rhetoricke, neyther cowche my matter vnder a cloake of
   5 curious inuentions, to feede the daintie eares of deli-
      cate yonkers. And as I cannot: So if I could, I woulde
      not. For I see that manye men are so affected with these

premisses, that manye good matters are obscured, the
Aucthors encombred, the woorkes but meanely commended,
10 and the Reader deceaued. For while he coueteth to come
to the purpose, he is lead amasked in the wylde Desert
of circumstance and digression, seeking farre and finding little, feeding his humor on pleasant woordes of
slender wayght, guyded (or rather giddyed) with plau-
15 cible eloquence.   1575

t16 But they obiect, that I (i.e. the Bible) am rude, grosse,
barbarous, impolite, vntrymmed, vnpleasaunte, vneloquent,
&c. I aunswere, If this be the true eloquence, as all truly learned menne do define, to expresse a matter with
apte, open, and euident wordes, and euen with suche ter-
5 mes as be most fytte to make the thyng, whereof it is
entreated, playne and manifest to them, that either rede
or heare it, I dare boldly affirme than, that the true
and pure eloquence is onely founde in me ...
my doctrine doth beyonde al mesure excell all humayne
10 teaching, seme it neuer so ornate, venuste, eloquent and
paynted with all ye coloures of Rhetoryke.   1564

Criticism of styles such as euphuism or Arcadianism, of
imitation of Spenser or Petrarch, or of copiousness in general,
became widespread in the seventeenth century, when discontent
found its classic expression in Bacon's definition of 'delicate'
learning (T13). His destructive criticism of the 'old' style is complemented by the formulation of his own aims in the Latin
revision of his book in 1623 (cf. the translation quoted by Croll in
Fish 1971: 14).

In the Restoration period a further reaction was the advocation
by the members of the Royal Society of a plain style as the ideal
(Sprat, T17). This is convincingly illustrated by the text of the
three editions of Glanvill's *Vanity of Dogmatizing* (1661, 1664,
1676), in which the author proceeds from a flowering to an
austere and plain style (cf. the parallel passages printed by Jones in
Fish 1971: 66–9). Compare, too, his re-definition of 'wit' (1664:
lxv) and his appreciation of Sprat's work (quoted from Jones in
Fish 1971: 64):

t17 'Tis none of the least considerable expectations that
may be reasonably had of our Society, that 'twill dis-
credit that *toyishness* of *wanton fancy*; and pluck the

misapplyed name of the *Wits*, from those conceited
5   Humorists that have assum'd to bestow it upon the more
manly spirit and *genius*, that playes not tricks with
words, nor frolicks with the *Caprices* of *froathy imag-*
ination.   1664

t18 That the *Style* of that Book hath all the *properties* that
can recommend any thing to an *ingenious relish:* For 'tis
manly, and yet *plain; natural* and yet not *careless:* The
Epithets are *genuine*, the *Words proper* and *familiar*, the
5   *Periods smooth* and of *middle* proportion: It is not *broken*
with *ends* of *Latin*, nor *impertinent Quotations;* nor made
harsh by *hard* words, or *needless terms* of *Art;* not ren-
dred *intricate* by long *Parentheses*, nor *gaudy* by *flant-*
ing Metaphors; not *tedious* by *wide fetches* and *circum-*
10 *ferences* of *Speech*, nor *dark* by too much *curtness* of
Expression: 'Tis not *loose* and *unjointed*, *rugged* and
uneven; but as *polite* and as *fast* as *Marble;* and briefly
avoids all the *notorious defects*, and wants none of the
proper ornaments of Language.   1664

Bacon's call for plainness was also made a requirement for sermon
style by some. John Wilkins demanded in *Ecclesiastes*:

t19 It must be plain and naturall, not being darkened with
the affectation of scolasticall harshnesse, or Rhetoric-
all flourishes. Obscurity in the discourse is an argument
of ignorance in the minde ... And it will not become the
5   Majesty of a Divine Embassage, to be garnished out with
flaunting affected eloquence ... It must be full, without
empty and needlesse Tautologies, which are to be avoided
in every solid business, much more in sacred. Our expressions should be so close, that they may not be obscure,
10 and so plain that they may not seem vain and tedious ...   1646

But not all authors achieved the self-imposed stylistic ideal.
Thus Day (reminding one of Polonius, 2.8.3) demanded "breuity
of speach" (T43/18), but his love of the copious style diverted him
away from his stated aim (cf. T43/55–69).

2.8.3 *Idiolect/individual style* (Brook 1976, Blake 1983, Scheler 1982)

The problems inherent in the reconstruction of any idiolect of
EModE can be exemplified with reference to the language used to

characterize personae in Shakespeare's plays. These texts are, of course, in 'the language of Shakespeare', but as a dramatist the poet plays various roles; he also makes characters describe incorrectly their own language use (cf. Polonius' "since Breuitie is the Soule of Wit ... I will be breefe", *Hamlet* II.2.96), or combines characterization with criticism of fashionable styles. To name a few other instances: Gower, in *Pericles*, uses appropriately archaic language, but Armado in *Love's Labours Lost* ("That hath a mint of phrases in his braine", I.1.165) uses an affected form of speech which mingles archaisms with neologisms and poetical compounds with synonyms in order to achieve copiousness of style; Mistress Quickly (*2 Henry IV*) and Dogberry (*Much Ado*) are characterized by their use of malapropisms and folk etymologies (7.3.6), such as *honey-suckle* for *homicidal*; and finally Falstaff, when playing the King (*1 Henry IV*, II.4.444–65), parodies euphuistic extravagance.

Individual style as linguistic criticism is evident in Ben Jonson, where parodies of courtly speech and dated literary styles are contrasted with a positive norm; cf. the detailed investigation by King, who states (1941: xxii): "I believe Jonson's preoccupation with linguistic mannerisms to be unique in the Elizabethan period."

However, the extent to which poetic diction should be permitted to diverge from common usage (see Görlach 1985a) remained a matter of dispute. Ben Jonson (cf. *custom*, T14), who criticized Spenser for writing "no language", formulated his ideals in accordance with Quintilian's *Institutio oratoria* 2.12.11 and 2.5.10:

t20 The true Artificer will not run away from nature, as he
     were afraid of her; or depart from life, and the like-
     nesse of Truth; but speak to the capacity of his hearers.
     And though his language differ from the vulgar somewhat;
  5 it shall not fly from all humanity, with the *Tamerlanes*,
     and *Tamer-chams* of the late Age, which had nothing in
     them but the *scenicall* strutting and furious vocifera-
     tion to warrant them to the ignorant gapers ... hee ...
     hath auoyded faint, obscure, obscene, sordid, humble,
 10 improper, or effeminate *Phrase*; which is not only prais'd
     of the most, but commended (which is worse) especially
     for that is naught.   1640

2.8.4 Poetic diction

A form of language that is intentionally divergent from the general usage must be given a description reflecting this deviance. The generally approved means of achieving poetic style are subject to the fluctuations of taste (see the changes in prose, 2.8.2). Thus poetry before 1550 was often Latinized (T18A/21–8) and Spenser's diction intentionally made archaic. Different types of word-formation were preferred in different periods (7.5.2). A comparison of parallel translations of Virgil's *Aeneid* (T21) reveals such changes: Stanyhurst preferred compounds, Waller and Dryden descriptive adjectives (notably those ending in *-y*).

How the principle of decorum influenced the choice of words is possibly best illustrated from Milton's works: a large proportion of his vocabulary is either restricted to his poems (e.g. 'hard words'; the use of existing lexemes with meanings adapted from Latin equivalents) or found only in his prose writings (e.g. the 'low' words used in the political and religious conflicts of the Civil War). It is perhaps correct to say that Milton and the Civil War period represent the decisive stage in the process leading to the sharp distinction between poetic diction and non-literary language, thereby anticipating the tenets of classicism (Davies in Watson 1970: 175–93).

For the grand style of the epic particularly strict demands were made in the name of decorum; thus Addison, modelling himself closely on Aristotle, in his 1712 review of Milton:

> t21   It is not ... sufficient, that the Language of an Epic
>   Poem be Perspicuous, unless it be also Sublime. To this
>   End it ought to deviate from the common Forms and ordinary
>   Phrases of Speech. The Judgment of a Poet very much dis-
> 5   covers it self in shunning the common Roads of Expression,
>   without falling into such ways of Speech as may seem
>   stiff and unnatural; he must not swell into a false Sub-
>   lime, by endeavouring to avoid the other Extream.   1712

Even when poetical language is re-written as prose, it ought to retain its poetical character (T29, 47–51). In general, it should not be forgotten how dependent the choice of linguistic features is on rhyme and metre. Such constraints can explain many syntactical selections (such as word order or frequency of *do*), and especially lexical preferences, aphaeresis (e.g. *'gainst*) and ornamental prefixes (often *a-*, *en-*, *y-*, cf. 7.5.2). Foreign or national traditions and models also greatly influenced poetic diction, as the vocabulary and word order of T34, patterned on Homer and Virgil, illustrates.

Archaisms and neologisms present a special problem. The poet was advised to choose a middle way, avoiding both too recent and too archaic words; cf. T14/11–12, and E. Phillips' statement in his preface to *The New World of English Words* (1658):

> it being an equal vice to adhere obstinately to old words, as fondly to affect new ones.

But this advice was not taken seriously until the eighteenth century, when Pope repeated it: "Alike fantastic, if too new, or old" (*Essay on Criticism* 334).

2.9 The status of English (Jones 1953)

2.9.1 The emancipation of English

The precarious position of English in the fifteenth and sixteenth centuries was similar to that of other European vernaculars. Latin, the international language of education, rediscovered in its classical form, was well ordered, prestigious and dominant in many fields of written communication; by contrast, the vernacular was deficient in vocabulary and syntax, imperfect by standards of rhetorical beauty and copiousness, lacking obligatory rules of spelling, pronunciation, morphology and syntax, unsupported by any respectable ancient literary tradition and, finally, subject to continuous change. For all these reasons it was obvious that the vernacular was ill-equipped for many of the needs of written communication. Indeed scholars often enough claimed that it was deficient in principle and incapable of attaining the grammatical orderliness and copiousness of Latin.

However, many of the early humanists believed in the value of education in the vernacular. Despite the fact that good Latin was vital to Thomas Elyot, he also stressed the importance of good English style in a child's education, and as a consequence, of the proper choice of a nurse:

t22   hit shall be expedient/ that a noble mannes sonne in his
infancie haue with hym continually/ onely such/ as may
accustome hym by litle and litle to speake pure and elegant latin. Semblably the nourises & other women aboute
5   hym/ if it be possible/ to do the same: or at the leste
way/ that they speke none englisshe but that/ whiche is
cleane/ polite/ perfectly/ and articulately pronounced/
omittinge no lettre or sillable/ as folisshe women often
times do of a wantonnesse/ wherby diuers noble men/ and
10   gentilmennes chyldren (as I do at this daye knowe) haue
attained corrupte and foule pronuntiation.   1531

In a similar vein, Palsgrave claimed that many teachers were not
well suited to teaching proper English, because they

t23   canne wryte an Epistle ryght latyne lyke, and therto
speake latyne, ... they be not able to expresse theyr
conceyte in theyr vulgar tonge, ne be not suffycyente,
perfectly to open the diuersities of phrases betwene our
5   tonge and the latyn.   1540

That such demands were only partially effective is evident from
the fact that similarly critical statements are found up until the
end of the EModE period and beyond, as in Locke's *Some
Thoughts Concerning Education* or in Defoe's *Compleat English
Gentleman* (see passages quoted in Rusch 1972: 129, 138).

From 1476 onwards, printing made books more easily access-
ible, and better education and the increasing confidence of the
middle classes led them to question the earlier educational privi-
leges of the upper class. Such pressures, combined with a growing
national pride, slowly removed doubts about using English – or
Scots (cf. T51) – for *all* purposes.

In the early sixteenth century many authors still felt called upon
to justify writing in English, as R. Ascham did at the beginning of
Toxophilus (1545):

t24   And althoughe to haue written this boke either in latin
or Greke (which thing I wold be verie glad yet to do,
if I might surelie know your Graces pleasure therein)
had bene more easier & fit for mi trade in study, yet
5   neuerthelesse, I supposinge it no point of honestie,
that mi commodite should stop & hinder ani parte either
of the pleasure or profite of manie, haue written this

Englishe matter in the Englishe tongue, for Englishe
men.   1545

Such arguments are also found in the prefaces of scientific
treatises. A comparatively late statement of this kind appears in
Skeyne (T45/22–8, from Scotland); Mulcaster's provocative question "Why not all in English?" (T8/163) was thus still highly
pertinent in 1582.

The process of securing acceptance of the vernacular was difficult and slow in many European countries. Dante had pleaded for
the use of Italian in *De vulgari eloquentia* (itself written in Latin!)
and felt that writing the *Divina Commedia* in Italian was justified
by the fact that it was *not* a tragedy, and Ariosto used Italian in
opposition to Bembo's objections (T33/14). In sixteenth-century
France, the Pléiade poets and Malherbe demanded that French
should have the same status as Latin.

In the early sixteenth century, English interest concentrated on
how to spread knowledge among those without Latin and how to
translate Latin terminologies. Arguments here are concerned
with the privileged position of doctors and, in the case of Bible
translations and homiletic literature, of the Roman church, which
claimed that reading religious matter in the vernacular stimulated
heresy. From 1550 to 1570 onwards the pursuit of classical knowledge through translations of Latin and Greek authors and the
enrichment of English poetic and rhetorical diction came to be
the chief concerns.

2.9.2 The continuance of Latin

Latin remained the linguistic ideal, ordered as it was by grammatical rules and beautified by rhetoric, unchanged and
unchangeable and therefore the safeguard of an author's lasting
fame, the authoritative language of the Bible and ecclesiastical
tradition – and the international language of scholarship, ensur-
ing fame beyond the British Isles (see Milton in T33/23–4). Even
many grammars of English, usually intended for foreign learners,
were written in the international *lingua franca*, Latin.

The short list of Anglo-Latin books below illustrates how
incomplete the cultural history of Britain is if works in Latin are
ignored – consider the consequences for a selection of texts such
as that in the present volume:

Literature	T. More, *Utopia* 1515ff.; Milton, early Latin poems
History	Boetius, *Chronicles* (cf. T36 and T36A); W. Camden, *Britannia*
Sciences	W. Gilbert, *De magnete* ... (1600), W. Harvey, *Exercitatio Anatomica de Motu Cordis et Sanguinis in Animalibus* (Frankfurt, 1628), I. Newton, *Principia* (1689)
Philosophy	F. Bacon, *De augmentis scientiarum* (1623, cf. T13), T. Hobbes, *De cive* (1642)
Grammars, etc.	T. Smith, *De recta et emendata linguae anglicae scriptione* (1542, printed 1568), A. Gil, *Logonomia Anglica* (1619/21, cf. t34), J. Wallis, *Grammatica Linguae Anglicanae* (1685, English version 1687)

It was also quite common to write in either language, the choice frequently being motivated by topic and intended readership; this is illustrated by the works of Thomas More, of Milton and of the philosophers Bacon, Hobbes and Locke. It is only with the late English writings of Newton (*Opticks* 1704) and Locke that Latin can be considered definitely passé as the language of learning. (Its use lingered on until much later in several European countries.)

The decline of Latin in the seventeenth century is explained by Jones (1953a: 308–12) as the result of the following factors:

1   The grammar schools increasingly adopted English-medium education; the use of Latin declined sharply as soon as it began to be learnt only for reading texts (Latin classics, etc.).

2   Bacon and the 'New Science' looked more critically at classical and humanist concepts and their rhetorical forms; their demand for plain language strengthened the vernacular (T13, 15–17).

3   The influence of Puritanism increased, and Puritans tended to equate Latin with Roman Catholicism.

4   The upheavals of the Civil War disrupted the old traditions of the schools.

In spite of Latin's gradual retreat the question whether English was adequate for *all* functions remained unanswered until late in the period. Milton claimed that even a national epic could be written in English (T34/16 "Things unattempted yet in Prose or Rhime"), but critics were divided on the success of his attempt at achieving sublimity in English, and Addison (1712) even said:

> t25   if his *Paradise Lost* falls short of the *Æneid* or *Iliad*
> ..., it proceeds rather from the Fault of the Language in which it is written, than from any Defect of Genius in the Author. So Divine a Poem in *English*, is like a stately Palace built of Brick.
> 1712

2.9.3 *Contemporary opinions on the prestige of English*

The status of English and its expected future was described in terms of the same or similar characteristics all through the EModE period, but the tenor changed *c.* 1570–80 from apologetic self-consciousness to confidence. Previously classified as "uneloquent/inelegant (rude, gross, barbarous, base, vile)" and lacking in "grace and majesty", English was re-evaluated, the same qualities now being interpreted positively as "plain, honest, serviceable, unadorned", and writers frequently stressed the improvement of English in the sixteenth century.

Contemporary arguments claiming that English was equal (or even superior) to Latin (or French) are summarized by Rusch (1972: 212ff.):

1   English is more sonorous (as a consequence of Romance influence on the vocabulary).
2   It has a more copious vocabulary owing to its mixed lexicon.
3   It exhibits linguistic economy owing to its Germanic component (with words of one or two syllables).
4   It has a simple grammar.
5   It is of great age and noble descent.

The arguments are distributed as follows: Harrison 1577 (1, 2, 5; cf. T10); Bullokar 1580 (1, 2, 3, 4, 5; cf. T7); Mulcaster 1582 (2, 3; cf. T8); Carew 1595 (1, 2, 3, 4; cf. T12); Verstegan 1605 (5); Camden 1605 (5); Lisle 1621 (3, 5); Gil 1621 (5); Butler 1634 (2,

5); Vindex 1644 (1, 2); Wharton 1654 (4); Phillips 1658 (1, 2, 5); Cooper 1685 (1, 2, 3, 4); Miège 1688 (1, 2, 3); Defoe 1728 (2); Johnson 1747/55 (2, 3).

(In their extreme forms 1 + 2 contradict 3, and each was also sometimes used in censure; 4, too, is more frequently mentioned as a defect than as a positive quality. The distribution of criteria also reflects (apart from the interdependence of the authors) changing attitudes towards English over two centuries.

Study questions

Q1   What reasons are there for saying that the EModE period extended to 1800?

Q2   What elements give Spenser's literary dialect in T23B a 'northern' flavour?

Q3   Describe how attitudes to the geographical expansion of English changed within the EModE period. Compare the statements made by Mulcaster (T8/108–17), Daniel (t6), and Milton (T33/23–6) and the attitude underlying T58.

Q4   Compare Bellenden's Scots text with Harrison's 'translation' (T36 and T36A). Which grammatical levels (orthography, inflexion, syntax, vocabulary) exhibit the more drastic differences?

Q5   To what extent is James' language in his letters to Elizabeth (T42) mixed? Can adaptation to her EModE speech have played a part in this?

Q6   What reasons cause the language of artisans to be evaluated quite differently by Puttenham (T11/34) and Sprat (T17/78)?

Q7   Explain the causes which Evelyn sees effective in language corruption (T16/16–23). Is he representative of his period?

Q8   What does "his dewe obseruing of Decorum" in T23A/15 refer to, and what does Milton mean by "That with no middle flight intends to soar" (T34/14)?

Q9   What are, according to T31D, the qualifications required for a rhetor? Are the expressions used technical terms? To what extent can one here speak of an 'abuse' of rhetoric?

Q10   Categorize the figures of speech used in T18F and T26.

Q11   Interpret the arguments put forward for and against biblical translation (T18C and T18D), placing them in their historical and linguistic context (cf. T37A).

3 Writing and Spelling

3.1 Levels of analysis

The analysis of written documents can be undertaken on various levels, not all of which are relevant to linguistics.

1 The individual features of the original manuscript.
2 Individual handwriting described on the basis of recurring features (problems of ascription, graphology as a means of interpreting character traits, etc.).
3 Geographically or chronologically restricted writing conventions attributable to certain schools/traditions (dating and localization of manuscripts, transmission of manuscripts, palaeography).
4 Letter types, such as EModE secretary script vs. italic (see t27–t29) or (in the printed book) typefaces of varying size and shape, as in the T20 facsimile (cultural history, palaeography).
5 The writing system, i.e. its distinctive features and their distribution determined by the analysis of minimal pairs (linguistics).
6 Type of writing system, such as alphabetic or syllabic, ideographic or logographic, or various mixtures (linguistics, the history of writing).

3.2 Manuscripts and prints (Petti 1977: 15ff.)

We normally read EModE texts in edited form. Editing entails the transliteration of manuscript texts, which means that often widely varying graphs must be identified as realizations of the appropriate graphemes, in accordance with the writer's intention.

This is not always easy, especially with texts written in sixteenth-century secretary script (compare t27 in Elizabeth I's own handwriting with the transliteration beneath).

Secretary script predominated (at least in private writing) until 1630, but from 1550 *italic* gained ground. This script was based on Italian humanist printing types and it was, accordingly, at first restricted to Latin texts written by scholars. Italic is beautiful, easy to read and quick to write (see t28, James VI's poem in his own hand). It was also considered easy to learn, a fact that, so Billingsley says in *The Pen's Excellencie*, made it especially appropriate for women:

t26   it is conceiued to be the easiest hand that is written
      with Pen, and to be taught in the shortest time: There-
      fore it is vsually taught to women, for as much as they
      (hauing not the patience to take any great paines, be-
  5   sides phantasticall and humoursome) must be taught that
      which they may instantly learne?   1618

From 1600 on, mixed scripts appeared, replacing secretary script after 1630 and italic after 1650 (see Milton's holograph, t29).

The graphemic interpretation of a printed text is of course much easier, as a consequence of the invariant shape of the letter forms. A typical feature, found in sixteenth-century books in particular, is the use of more than one typeface, often to distinguish between main text and comment, or a Latin text and its English translation, or to set off Latin quotations inserted in an English text (T20). In the seventeenth century important terms were often capitalized and printed in a different typeface (t18, T57, T58, cf. modern italicization).

3.3 Graphemes and allographs

Looking at the forms of ⟨s, r⟩ in early prints, one soon becomes aware that each has two different lower-case shapes; ⟨s⟩ is ſ at the beginning of words but *s* elsewhere, while ⟨r⟩ (only in textura) is ꝛ following *o* and other letters ending with a curve, such as *bdhpwy*, but *r* elsewhere. There were, then, strict rules regulating the occurrences of the two letter forms; no *s* or *r* could be re-

t27   Happy to muche the formar Age
      With faithful fild content
   Not Lost by sluggy Lust
      that wontz the Long fastz
5   to Louse by son-got Acorne

t28   till at the last i chancet to call to minde
   hou that hir nature did resemble neir
   to that of phœnix quhilk i redd: hir kind
   hir heu hir shape did mak it plane appeir
5   sho uas the same: quhilk nou uas lichtit heir
   this maid me to esteeme of hir the moire
   hir name & rarenes did hir so decoir.

t29   By the rushie-fringed banck
   where grows the willow, & the osier danck
   my sliding chariot stayes
   thick set wth Agat, and the azurne sheene
5   of [turquis] turkis blew, & [emrald] emrauld greene

placed by the alternative form and vice versa. This meant that their distribution was complementary and predictable – they were allographs of one grapheme, ⟨s⟩ or ⟨r⟩ respectively.

In texts printed before 1630 a comparable distribution of *u* and *v* is found: *v* was used only initially, *u* elsewhere, independently of the phonetic value of each as /u/ or /v/: T11/1–3 has *naturall, sauing, vtter, voyces*. Bullokar (T7/5) consequently arrived at a total of twenty-four 'graphemes' 'with their paiers', i.e. upper-case forms, counting *u/v* as one (and omitting non-existent *j*). (Italic scripts also had *vv* ('double u') for *w*, T23A; there was of course no such letter provided for in Latin or Italian alphabets.)

The allographic distribution of ⟨r⟩ was lost in the sixteenth century and that of ⟨s⟩ in the eighteenth, neither having served a necessary function. The letters *u* and *v* came to be used according to their phonetic value (i.e. as graphemes) after 1630; and a similar distinction was introduced for *i:j* between 1630 and 1640.

Latin influence was responsible for the additional graphemes ⟨æ⟩ and ⟨œ⟩ found in a few words in some texts (T23A). Medieval practice was continued in the use of abbreviations (Petti 1977: 22–4) such as *y*ᵉ and *y*ᵗ for *the* and *that*, *&* (ampersand), *9* as a marker of genitive or plural, ~ for nasals, and abbreviations for the Latin prefixes *con, per, pro*. Accents were occasionally used, but without lasting success (in T7 and, in the form of a proposal, in T16/37–43).

3.4 The historical foundations and EModE developments

3.4.1 Features inherited from late ME

ME spelling is somewhat variable and unsystematic, as the result of a mixture of native and Anglo-Norman traditions, and the lack of a written norm. More consistent conventions emerged in London scriptoria in the late fourteenth century, and these formed the basis for Chancery documents after 1430 and for the manuscript production flourishing in fifteenth-century London. Most features of this tradition found their way into early printing, but spelling is often more variable in early prints than in 'good' manuscripts.

Scragg (1974: 64–6) believes that this is due to the fact that most of the early printers were foreigners. Even Caxton had worked abroad most of his life and when he returned to England he may have lacked insight into recent English spelling conventions, and his compositors were all foreigners. A succession of laws in 1515, 1529 and 1534 finally curbed the activities of foreign printers, which led to a return to pre-Caxton conventions, a typical feature being the increasing use of the digraph *ea* (e.g. *meat(e)* for earlier *mete*).

Fifteenth-century spelling conventions exhibit the following characteristics: vowel length was indicated by doubling the vowel, *ee, oo* (rarely *aa, ij*; cf. *ou/ow*), or by post-consonantal *e*, as in *name, mete, rise, nose, lute*, the *-e* having been retained after such words had become monosyllabic in the fifteenth century (3.4.2). These spelling conventions still suffered from a great number of defects, however, such as the multiple representation of a single phoneme (/eː/ spelt *ee, ie, e*; /ɛː/ spelt *ea, ei, ee, e*) or the ambiguity of some graphemes or grapheme combinations (/u(ː), ɔu/ both spelt *ou*). The representation of consonants was less diverse and inconsistent: every consonant pronounced was also written, and almost every written consonant was pronounced – at least in 1430 (*wrought, knight*).

Though phoneme:grapheme relations were settled (however imperfectly) in the fifteenth century, there were still many variant spellings for individual words: throughout the EModE period there was some choice among possible spellings (e.g. *an-, in-, ynough(e), enoff, yenough, eno', enouch, enufe*, etc., OED). By 1700 one of such variant spellings had become conventional – but not always the most 'logical' one. By contrast, spelling in private letters, diaries (T54) and texts like the Salem depositions (T64) remains quite variable until the end of the EModE period. The mixture of English and Scottish spelling conventions, particularly in the seventeenth century, created variability of a specific kind (T53, T55, and see Devitt 1989).

The orthographic differentiation of *meet/meat* and *boot/boat* word pairs, a problem still unsolved in Chaucer's time, was achieved by the sixteenth century, a period when the Great Vowel Shift (4.3.3) had, obviously, made the distinction appear more urgent. In the fifteenth century ⟨ea⟩ was introduced and was well established by 1520–50, when ⟨oa⟩ was introduced by analogy.

Both have the alternative spelling VC*e* (as in *complete*, *nose*), but because ⟨oa⟩ is more recent than ⟨ea⟩, it is much less frequent. In the fifteenth century ⟨ie⟩ was taken over from French to represent ME /eː/; it is found, not unexpectedly, mainly in words of French provenance (*chief*, though also *field*).

3.4.2 *Functions of final* -e

The loss of the final /-ə/ in bisyllabic words made the -*e* spelling appear to be arbitrary and optional from around 1400, as is evident from scribal practice in the fifteenth century. However, final -*e* came to be interpreted as functional in the EModE period – though its functions, of which there were at least three, overlapped and thus added new ambiguities:

1 Final -*e* indicated that the vowel in the (historically) open syllable was long (*name*, *mete*, *nose*). This -*e* was interpreted as an indication of vowel length and transferred to words such as *case*, *life* (cf. fourteenth-century spellings *ca(a)s*, *li(j)f*). This, however, produced new ambiguity in words like *writen*, which accordingly came to be spelt with -*tt*- to indicate the shortness of the preceding vowel (cf. *ridden*, *glad*:*gladder*, *rot*:*rotted*:*rotten*, but not double *v* in *driven*). This development also explains the alternative spellings *sonne*, *potte* (for *son*, *pot*), which were a welcome aid to compositors before 1640 in adjusting right-hand margins.

2 The ambiguity, then as now, of some consonantal graphemes (*c* = /k, s/; *g* = /g, dʒ/; *th* = /θ, ð/) favoured the retention of -*e* to mark the second consonantal quality (*prince*, *plunge*, *breathe*).

3 Final -*e* also came to distinguish inflexional -*s* from word final /s/ in *dens* + *s* ≠ *dense*, and to prevent *i*, *u*/*v*, *z* and sometimes *o* from occurring at the end of words (*lie*, *toe*, *glue*, *love*, *freeze*).

Occasionally -*e* carries two functions at once (as in *grace*, *mice*, *oblige*, *drive*, *haze*); it produces homographs (in *live*, *use*) and serves different functions in similar words (*love*, *grove*, *move*). Also, there are a few cases of functionless -*e* surviving from the time when it was optional (*come*, *infinite* and homographs of the *separate* type).

3.4.3 *Graphemes representing consonants*

⟨u/v⟩: there had always been variant forms to make reading easier, but the systematic distinction of *u/v* as allographs (3.3) was made only in the fifteenth and sixteenth centuries. Proposals in the sixteenth century to distinguish between them phonetically (t31) were not successful at first, but the distinction became common practice after 1630 (though the upper-case letter was always *V* until 1700). Also note double *v* ('double u') for *w* in the sixteenth century (T23A).

⟨i/j⟩: the functional distinction also dates back to 1630–40. New ⟨j⟩ = /dʒ/ replaced older ⟨i⟩ (as in *iolly* T11/87, *iudge* T11/93), but appeared for older *g* in only a few words; *g* thus remained ambiguous, which in turn led to *gu* or *gh* spellings in accordance with French or Dutch models (cf. older *goost* T19A/16, *gesside* 'guessed' T19B/17).

⟨s/z⟩: all attempts to distinguish between voiced and unvoiced qualities were inconsistent; thus ⟨z⟩ always stood for /z/, but /z/ could also be represented by ⟨s⟩. This produced homographs (*house*, *use*) or alternative spellings, as in *-ise/-ize* words.

EModE sound changes did not normally affect the spellings, though we have *draught* (old spelling) vs. *draft*; *light* vs. *lit*.

By 1630–50 teachers and printers had generally settled in favour of *one* spelling for the individual word, usually the shorter one (*sonne:son*). The fact that compositors had more urgent things to do in the upheavals of the Civil War than to worry about adjusted margins may have contributed to this development. However, it is more plausible to assume that the immensely popular spelling books (which allowed only one spelling per word) speeded up the process (Scragg 1974: 73–7). Their preferred spellings were obviously largely the same as those prevalent in the Bible (AV). Since correct spelling enjoyed high prestige, there is much less variation in seventeenth-century private letters and diaries than there was in the Elizabethan period (see Elizabeth I, T20/42).

Apart from such general tendencies, particular conventions developed in individual printing houses. Poetry sometimes stood apart since rhyming words were often also made to look alike in their spelling: *tong*; *seele*; *straict*, rhyming with *pourtraict*; *despight* in T24 were possible, but certainly not the most common spellings in EModE, and it is likely that they were deliberately selected for their rhyming function by Spenser.

3.4.4 *Capitalization* (Partridge 1964: 75–7; Osselton 1985)

The early history of the printing of Shakespearean texts extends from 1593 (*Venus and Adonis*) to 1623 (the First Folio). Conspicuous changes happened during this time with regard to capitalization. In 1593 (as throughout the sixteenth century) capitalization affected certain classes of nouns only: personifications, names of animals and plants, minerals, the arts and sciences, religions and their institutions, cosmological and geographical terms, expressions relating to royalty and the state, occupations, kinship terms, and foreign words not yet anglicized.

In the First Folio of 1623 capitalization was extended (possibly owing to the influence of books printed on the Continent) so that any noun, verb or adjective might be capitalized. However, capitalization in individual instances is difficult to account for: emphasis cannot always be held responsible. The heyday of capitalization was to follow after the Civil War (1660–1750). There are some eighteenth-century books in which *all* nouns are capitalized, but there was a rapid decline in this practice after 1750 (Osselton 1985).

3.4.5 *Dating*

The developments and tendencies sketched above can be used to date EModE texts in accordance with the following criteria (some of these criteria are only applicable where the amount of continuous text is considerable).

1   The consistency of the *ee* (*ie*):(*eCe*), and *oo*:*oa* (*oCe*) distinctions (early texts).
2   The use of lower- and upper-case *u, v, w* and *i, j, y*.
3   The frequency and functions of *-e* (especially of functionless *-e* not found in PrE).
4   The frequency and functions of capitalization.
5   The number of alternative spellings for the same words.
6   Spellings based on Latin or Greek etymology.

3.4.6 *Shorthand* (Kökeritz 1935)

It deserves mention that from 1600 various proposals were made to facilitate faster writing through omission of letters and use of contractions and symbols (cf. Pepys' diary in Petti 1977: 121). These symbols also stimulated various attempts at producing logographic writing systems, such as Wilkins' of 1668.

3.5 Spelling reform (Dobson 1968)

3.5.1 *Reasons for EModE interest*

The need for a spelling reform and the question of loanwords were among the central problems of sixteenth-century grammarians and men of letters. The earliest proposals for a reform were made by scholars like Smith and Cheke, who were humanists and philologists. They did not find, in contemporary English, the values of the vowel graphemes of Latin, French and Italian and of ME before the Vowel Shift, such as $a = $ /a(:)/ etc., nor did they find the one-to-one relation between phonemes and graphemes that occurred almost consistently in Latin and Italian. It was also obvious that the spelling must be regulated before the syntax and the lexicon could be tackled (consider the alphabetical ordering of dictionary entries, and cf. T6/49–50).

3.5.2 *Spelling reformers 1551–1621*

Five reformers deserve to be singled out for the quality of their suggestions and their (relative) importance:

The ideas of John Cheke (1514–57; cf. Dobson 1968: 43–6) on the reform of English spelling grew out of his reflections on the correct pronunciation of ancient Greek. His suggestions, which can be reconstructed from the spelling employed in his unfinished translation of the Gospels (cf. t30), were, however, not well thought out, and his practice was inconsistent. He frequently marked vowel length by duplication (cf. T5).

John Hart (†1574; cf. Dobson 1968: 62–87) is commonly regarded as the most important phonetician in sixteenth-century England. His aim was an international phonetic alphabet which would make it easier for English speakers to read their mother tongue, for dialect speakers to acquire the standard, and for anyone to learn foreign languages. He found English spelling deficient in many ways (T6). In particular he deplored the insufficient number of graphemes, the writing of letters (in some words) that had no equivalent in pronunciation, etymological spellings (loanwords ought also to be integrated orthographically, t36) and unnecessary distinctions in the writing of homophones, where the context should be enough to prevent misunderstandings (as it did in spoken discourse).

Hart, then, saw that the number of graphemes must be enlarged, but objected to the use of digraphs for single phonemes. He therefore argued that *ai, ei, ea, ee, eo, oo* for /ɛː, iː, uː/, and the use of final -*e* to mark the preceding vowel as long (3.4.2) ought to be avoided. However, the use of digraphs to represent diphthongs was considered legitimate (*teim* for /təɪm/). As for consonants, *th*, and *g* for /dʒ/ ought to be abolished and the phonemes /k, g, tʃ, dʒ, θ, ð, ʒ/ represented unambiguously; he therefore created five

Cheke, *c.* 1550	Hart, 1570	t31

t30   Our faẏer which art
     in heaven halowed be
     ẏ name, ẏ king-
     doom come, ẏ wil be doon
5   in earth as it is in heven.
     give vs ẏis daí our daílí
     breed. And forgive vs
     our detts as we
     forgive yᵉᵐ yᵗ
10   be our dettors, and lead
     vs not into tempting,
     but deliver vs from yᵉ evel.
     For thijn is yᵉ kingdoom,
     yᵉ powr and glorie
15   for ever and aí. Ameen.

Bullokars Booke at large, for the *Amend-ment* of *Orthographie* for English speech: wherein, a most perfect supplie is made, for the wantes and double *sounde of letters in the olde Orthographie, with Examples for the* ⁵ same, with the easie conference and vse of both Orthographies, *to saue expences in Bookes for a time, vntill this amendment grow to a generall vse, for* the easie, speedie, and perfect reading and writing of Englilh, (the speech not changed, as some vntruly and malicioufly, or at the least ignorantlie blowe abroade) by the which amendement the same Authour hath also framed ¹⁰ a ruled Grammar, to be imprinted heereafter, for the same speech, to no small commoditie of the Englilh Nation, not only to come to easie, speedie, and perfect vse of our owne language, but also to their easie, speedie, and readie entrance into the secretes of other Languages, and easie and speedie pathway to all Straungers, to vse our Language, heeretofore very ¹⁵ hard vnto them, to no small profite and credite to this our Nation, and stay therevnto in the weightiest causes. There is also imprinted with this Orthographie a short Pamphlet for all Learners, and a Primer agreeing to the same, and as ²⁰ learners shall go forward there- in, other necessarie Bookes shall spedily be proui- ded with the same Orthographie.

²⁵ Heerevnto are also ioyned written Copies with 'the same Orthographie.

Giue God the praise, that teacheth alwaies.

When truth trieth, errour flieth.

Seene and allowed according to order.

³⁰ *Imprinted at London by* *Henrie Denham.* 1 5 8 0.

43   The amendment of ortography.

Aa:Bb:Ćć:Çç: Ꟁꟁ ch: Dd: Eea: Éé: Ff: GꟅ Ig:
Cg: Hh: I i y : Ʀk : Ll : Ł: Ꟁm : ꟁ: Nn: ꞑ: Oo: ꝏ: Pp:
Ꟁꟁ: Qq: Ʀr ʒ : ŕ: Ss ʒ : ſſ : Tt : Th th : Ꟁh ch : Vbu:
Vy y ꝏ ꝏ: Vʼvu̇ : Ww: Ꟁꟁ wh: Xr: Py: Zʒ. ad ꝏ thæ ʒ, e.

Paterʒ of
letterʒ.

Of the xl. letterʒ befōr hewed, xxviiȷ. of them, and their paterʒ   5
ár caled consonantʒ, ꟙhich ár thæʒ: b. ć.c. ch. d. ḟ. ġ. g. h. k. l. m. n.
p. ꟙh. q. r. ſ. h. t. th. ꟙh. ꞑ. w. ꟙh. r. g. ʒ.

Other, viiȷ. a. e. e̊. i. o. ꝏ. v. y. ár caled voꟙelʒ, ꟙith their paterʒ.

Other, iiȷ. Ł. ꟁ. ꞑ. ár caled half voꟙelʒ: ad ꝏ thæʒ: ŕ: and ſoyn-
ded aʒ this ſillabl: er: and ſo naméd alſo.   10

Thæʒ voꟙelʒ: a. e. i. y. o. h. y. ꝏ. ꝏ: ár alꟙay of hoʒt ſound:
except: a. e. i. be dobled thus: aa. ee. iy. yi: oʒ that on of thæʒ accent
pointʒ: ʹ :ʺ :ˆ: be ſett ouer: a: e: y: o: for then be thæʒ of longer
ſound, ꟙrytn thus: á: áʺ: áˆ: and ſo of the reſt, for help in eqiuocy.

I cal the firſt, á: a, ꟙith accent: the ſecond, áʺ:a, ꟙith dobl accent: 15
the third, áˆ: a, ꟙith forked accent: and ſo of other voꟙelʒ ſo nóted,
bicauʒ it may help much in eqiuocy.

And thæʒ, e̊. ꝏ. v. u. ár alꟙay of long ſound, ad ꝏ thæʒ, æ, and alſo
the half voꟙelʒ, Ł. ꟁ. ꞑ. ŕ. ár of longer ſound, then any voꟙel of hoʒt
ſound.   20

Ꟁhen tꟙo voꟙelʒ (oʒ half voꟙelʒ) com together in on ſillabl, they
ár caled a diphthong, ꟙhar-of ther be in number, viȷ. ei. ay. ei. ey. oi.
ow. oy: ading hær-vnto: ui: ſeldom in ve.

So ading thæʒ ſeuin mixt ſoundʒ (caled diphthongʒ) befōr ꟙrytn,
ther ár in engliſh ſpech, xliiiȷ. ſeuerak ſoundʒ in voice, ynder ꟙhom ak   25
engliſh ꟙordʒ and ſillablʒ ár ſounded and ſpókn: ading hær-vnto
the rár diphthong: uy.

Thæʒ diphthongʒ hau paterʒ in ſound, and ther be alſo other diphthongʒ, but they hau the ſound of on of the voꟙelʒ befōr ſaid, ak
ꟙhich hak be ꟙrytn together in ſqárʒ next onder: but for the tým in   30
ak thæʒ, not that euery diphthong iʒ of aʒ long tým oʒ longer, then
any long voꟙel: ad hær-vnto that hake voꟙelʒ may mák a diphthong after, a, oʒ o, ꝶ ár paterʒ tꟙo the ſillablʒ in their ſqárʒ foloꟙing.

And hær-in iʒ tꟙo be nóted, that for later iioʒʒ, ther iʒ e hak be a Pamphlet imprinted, conteining brekly the effect of this bꝏk, ſeruing alſo   35
for conference ꟙith the old oʒtography her-after.

                    Diph-

rxviiȷ. cõ-
ſonantʒ
ꟙith their
paterʒ.

viiȷ. voꟙ-
elʒ.

iiȷ. half
voꟙelʒ,
ŕ. thær-
vntꝏ ad-
ed.

voꟙelʒ
of hoʒt
ſound, ex-
cept, ꝛc.
The námʒ
of thæʒ
accentʒ.
voꟙelʒ
of long
ſound.

viȷ. diph-
thongʒ.

xliiiȷ. diui-
ʒionʒ in
voice, for
engliſh
ſpech).

new letters for them by modifying existing ones (t31). Hart made no use of the letters *c*, *q*, nor of *y*, *w* (since he classified /j, w/ as vowels), nor of the allographs of ⟨s, r⟩. Vowel length was indicated by a subscript dot.

Hart's proposal was the most consistent attempt at reforming sixteenth-century English spelling, but it was much too radical to stand a chance of being accepted.

William Bullokar (*c*. 1530–1609; cf. Dobson 1968: 93–117) in his *Booke at large* (t32–t33, T7) opposed the introduction of new graphemes as proposed by Hart. For the necessary distinction of the forty-four 'sounds', he preferred modifications of existing letters by accents, ligatures (*ph*, *th*, *ch*, *wh*, *sh*), modified letter forms for syllabic /l, m, n, r, s/ and *æ* for *ea*. Although the system proposed was quite complicated (t33), he did not succeed in rendering all the phonemic and allophonic distinctions, nor in freeing himself from traditional spelling.

Richard Mulcaster (1530–1611; cf. Dobson 1968: 117–28) was one of the greatest pedagogues of his day. The title of his book (T8) itself shows that spelling and its reform were planned as the first part of a comprehensive handbook on education. Mulcaster did not see any urgent need for a reform, since, he felt, it was possible for the learner to cope with ambiguous letters or with others whose English value diverged from that encountered in other languages – arguments that miss the point the reformers were trying to make.

Mulcaster's importance lies in the impact that the spellings used in his book had on contemporary spelling books: each word was given one spelling, used consistently, and this was usually the one that passed into PrE (with the exceptions of those affected by later systematic changes such as those involving *u/v* and *i/j*).

Alexander Gil (1564/5–1635; see Dobson 1968: 131–55, t34) was Mulcaster's successor as headmaster of St Paul's School, London. He wrote his great grammar of English *Logonomia* (1619, second edition 1621) in Latin, the language also used by Thomas Smith before him (1568). In the 1619 edition he tried to use a consistently phonemic spelling for the passages quoted in English, adding letters from other alphabets and also using red ink to change existing letters as the system required in every copy printed. Finding this procedure too time-consuming, he decided

to use digraphs and diaeresis for vowel length in the second
edition of 1621 (t34b):

t34

Fair laundz,tu täk 'ðe sun in sezn dvs
Sajt spriyz, in ẃid'a ɦouzand nimfs did plai ş
Soft rumbliy brvks,'ðat ʒentl slumbtr drv ;
Hjh rẽrd mounts, 'ðe landz about tu'vv ;
Lǫu lvkiy dälz,disloin'd from kommon gäz ;
Deljtful bourz,tu solas luvtrz trv ;
Fair labtrinɦs,fond runtrz tiz tu däz :
Al'ẃid'bj nätvr mäd, did nätvr self amäz
And al wiɦout,&c.   1619   10

Fresh shadöuz,fit tu shroud from suni rai;
Fair laundz,tu täk 'ðe sun in sezn dv;
Swit springz,in wich à thouzand nimfs did plai;
Soft rumbling brüks, 'ðat ʒentl slumber drv;
5 Hjh rẽrd mounts,'ðe landz about tu vv;
Lǫu lüking dälz,disloin'd from komon gäz;
Deljtful bourz, tu solas luvers trv
Fair laberinths,fond runerz eiz tu däz:
                                 1621

Gil's system is meant to be phonemic (based on the pronunciation of educated speakers), but it is made slightly inconsistent by
the retention of etymological spellings, the distinction of
homophones, and certain features taken over from traditional
spelling. Thus he devised a workable system close to existing
usage: "His venture deserved to succeed, and it is to our loss that
it failed" (Dobson 1968: 154). The only impact Gil had in his
teaching was his influence on the spelling conventions used by his
greatest pupil, John Milton.

With Gil a series of proposals in which attempts were made to
base spelling systems consistently on pronunciation came to an
end. Later grammarians and lexicographers (including Dr Johnson and Noah Webster) were content with comparatively minor
adjustments. In the period 1550–1620, with the awakening interest in linguistic matters and a clear conception of the defects of
existing spelling (with variability still common), reform could
have been successful. However, as early as 1582, Mulcaster had
judged the situation realistically: "The vse & *custom* of our
cuntrie, hath allredie chosen a kinde of penning" (p. 98). After
1630–40 the stabilized conventions of printers succeeded where
scholarly effort had failed: they established in practice a set of
rules, though not of course the kind of consistent system the
reformers had hoped for.

3.5.3 *Later corrections*

What orthographical changes there were as EModE developed
into PrE concerned the spelling of suffixes (EModE *-all*, *-ick*, *-or*,

etc.) and individual words. The latter were affected by the following factors:

1   Etymological influences (3.5.4).
2   The distinction of homophones. Although the value of such distinctions is uncertain, modern spellings became common in a few homonymic pairs such as *waste/waist* and *whole/hole* and (etymologically) polysemous pairs such as *flower/flour* and *metal/mettle* in the seventeenth and eighteenth centuries.
3   Uniformity within groups of etymologically related words. In some instances, such as *deceit/receipt*, this principle was not carried out consistently, which made Johnson admit in 1755: "I have been often obliged to sacrifice uniformity to custom; thus I write, in compliance with a numberless majority, *convey* and *inveigh*, *deceit* and *receipt*, *fancy* and *phantom*..."
4   Phonetic spelling. The power of ever more firmly established orthographic conventions limited the number of such instances to a few, such as *stud* (ME *stood*) or *jail* (earlier only *gaol*) and loanwords, especially from 'exotic' languages.

3.5.4 Etymological spellings

A great number of loanwords had been introduced from French in ME times; many of these had been subject to French sound changes but still remained recognizable as descending from Latin words. The prestige of Latin being what it was in the Renaissance, it was only natural that many of these loans were 'corrected' from the Latin etymon (cf. T47/32 *explaning of my conceipt*). Since such corrections had started in fourteenth-/fifteenth-century French, it is not always clear whether a Latinized form is due to French or to 'native' English humanistic efforts.

There occur, particularly in the early texts included in my selection, many specimens of 'uncorrected' forms: *auantage* T1/32, *marchaunt* T2/31, *descryue* T45/59 (also cf. the various spellings of instances of *perfect* and *doubt*). A comparison of biblical translations of 1525 and 1611 is especially rewarding, the AV showing much more markedly the impact of Renaissance Latinization.

However, the new spelling was not, in all cases, the one that was historically more correct. ME *autour* (<Latin *auctor*) is represented by EModE *autour, aucthor* and *author* (T37B/7), the modern form being 'incorrect' in spelling and pronunciation.

There was evidently little resistance to such etymologizing. Mulcaster, who argued for the full integration of loans, was an exception:

> t35   the verie nature of *enfranchisment* doth enforce obedience
> to the *enfranchisers* lawes, not to be measured by his
> bare person, but by the *custom, reason & sound*, of his
> cuntries speche. And as vnaduised cunning, or not suf-
> 5 ficientlie aduised, doth plaie to much vpon the foren
> string, being verie loth to leaue out anie one letter,
> as *eleemosinarie*, for *amner, hospitall* and *victuall* for
> *spitle vitle* and such other.   1582

When there are two standard languages, as was the case with English and Scots in the sixteenth century, the results of etymologizing may be expected to vary; this is illustrated by Hart's comparison:

> t36   Some thinke Scottish speach more auncient Englishe than
> as we now speake here in England, yet there is no liuing
> English man, so much affected to write his English as
> they doe Scottish, which they write as they speake, and
> 5 that in manye wordes, more neare the Latine, from whence
> both we and they doe deriue them, as fruct for fruit, and
> fructfull for fruitfull, disponed for disposed or distrib-
> uted, humely for humbly, nummer for number, pulder for
> pouder, saluiour for sauiour, and compt for account, and
> 10 diuerse others, wherein we pronounce not those letters
> which they do, & therfore write them not as reason is.
> Yet in others we do excéede with them, as the b in doubt,
> c and h in aucthoritie, l in souldiour, o in people, s in
> baptisme, p in corps, and in condempned, and certain like.
>   1569

3.6 Punctuation (Salmon 1988)

Punctuation reflects intonation, to some extent, as well as the syntactical-logical structure of the sentence and of larger units (cf. 6.8); formally, it is convenient to treat it as part of spelling. The interrelation of page lay-out and punctuation can be studied in facsimile volumes (cf. T11, T23A, etc.).

The virgule, colon and full stop or period (/ : .) are the only marks found in early books printed in England, but from 1520–40 the comma replaced the virgule. The structuring reflected by these marks was in the main rhetorical, until the use of logic-based punctuation increased in the seventeenth century (though it never achieved the logical consistency of, say, German punctuation). The phases leading from rhetorical to logical punctuation and the reasons for this development are not quite clear. The transition is possibly related to the changing communicative functions of written English as it developed further and further away from being merely a representation of spoken English (or of texts meant for oral delivery) towards greater autonomy as a system. Most striking is the re-interpretation of the colon (:), which originally was a mark indicating a pause of medium length, but which developed into an indicator of text coherence expressing logically consecutive or adversative relations ('therefore'; 'on the other hand'). This change is clearly related to the introduction of the *semi*colon (or comma-colon) from 1580–90, which more or less assumed the syntactical function of the earlier colon, that of separating two closely connected main clauses.

The question and exclamation marks did not become common until the seventeenth century. In addition, the paragraph sign (¶) was used in several rather vague functions, and by no means only to introduce a paragraph (T20/24ff., T30). Parentheses ( ) and square brackets [ ] often functioned like modern inverted commas (found from the eighteenth century), as in T11, or they marked translation equivalents (T11/101).

The function of the apostrophe was purely phonetic at first, marking the omission of a sound (T11/57, 77), and was therefore frequently used in drama texts, where it indicated that inflexions were not intended to be syllabic ('*st*, '*d*). Its specifically morphological function to mark the genitive came later; it became obligatory for the singular in the seventeenth century, and for the plural in the eighteenth.

3.7 The Scottish system

A full interpretation of Scottish spelling would only be possible in the context of a history of the Scottish language, which is beyond the scope of this book: it would presuppose some knowledge of the divergent phonological developments of Scots and EModE from northern and southern OE respectively, of the differences between the two in the correlation of spelling and pronunciation, of chronological and dialectal differences within Scots and, finally, of spelling interferences from English in sixteenth-century Scottish texts. For example, the spelling *quhose hayme* alone would need the following comments:

1.   Word-initial /xw/ was preserved in Scots (conventional spelling *quh*).
2.   Most *i*-diphthongs merged with long monophthongs in fourteenth-/fifteenth-century Scots; hence, *i/y* could be used as an indication of vowel length.
3.   OE /aː/ developed into southern English /ɔː/ but into Scots /ɛː/ (the joke in t8 is based on this divergence).
4.   The *o* in *quhose* indicates the southern sound; the *i/y* marker of vowel length (see 2) is here missing in this anglicized form.

As such detailed explanations cannot be provided for the whole system here, a few common characteristics of Scots spelling are merely listed below:

quh corresponds to EModE *wh*;
w/u/v are largely interchangeable;
þ, ȝ are often found in manuscripts (see T36), but in printed books ⟨ȝ⟩ is replaced by ⟨z⟩;
ch represents /x/ (a sound more commonly preserved in Scots), and corresponds to EModE *gh*;
sch is widespread for /ʃ/, EModE *sh*;
i, y can indicate vowel length.

Study questions

Q12   What functions do changes of typeface have in t32 and T20; how is italicization used in the texts by Dryden?

Q13   What orthographic and typographic differences are to be found in the two versions of Bacon's *Essay* (T30)?

Q14   Apply the criteria listed in 3.4.5 (Dating) to the *Hamlet* text (T31B).

Q15   Compare Hart's arguments in support of a reform of EModE spelling with those commonly mentioned in twentieth-century discussions.

Q16   Compare Cheke's and Hart's suggestions for a reformed spelling with regard to their consistency and practicability, basing your arguments on their transcriptions of the Lord's Prayer (t30, t31). In which words did the pronunciation used by the two reformers apparently diverge?

Q17   Analyse the syntactic structure, and its relationships to the punctuation, in T7, T17, T32.

Q18   Compare the punctuation of T31D and T31E with that used in the corresponding passages of a modern edition of Shakespeare.

4 Phonology

4.1 The reconstruction of the phonological system

4.1.1 Sources (Horn and Lehnert 1954: 69–117; Görlach 1982: 44–5)

The following aids are available to anyone attempting to reconstruct the EModE sound system – or rather its chronological, geographical and social subsystems.

1 Statements made by grammarians and spelling reformers, and their transcriptions. In the interpretation of such evidence, the grammarian's provenance, his attitude (his views of correctness, the influence on him of written English) and the vague terminologies used to describe sounds must be taken into account. From the seventeenth century onwards, shorthand manuals permit a few phonological conclusions to be drawn. Language-teaching manuals intended to teach English to foreigners (and foreign languages to Englishmen) contain valuable comparative information.

2 Rhymes and rhyming dictionaries. It must first be established how precise a poet's rhyming practice is: the material will be of dubious value if assonances, eye rhymes or traditional rhymes have been used (Wyld 1923).

3 Puns, which are based on phonetic similarity or identity. They rarely provide reliable information on actual pronunciation, however.

4 Metre, which can be used where regular patterns allow assumptions to be made about the number of syllables in a particular word.

5 Spelling. Since correspondences between phonemes and graphemes are not clear-cut, the criterion cannot always be applied with success. However, the widespread variation within

EModE permits more conclusions than are possible in languages with fully regulated orthographies. Where distinctions are consistently preserved in EModE spelling, phonological contrasts can be assumed. 'Naive' or 'inverse' spellings (such as T20/99 *righmes*, T46/13 *in waight*, T64/2 *their aboughts*), are important because they can reflect a sound change already completed or in progress (here: loss of /x/). T64/4 *forting* 'fortune' indicates [ə n] in this word and in regular -*ing*.

6 Conclusions arrived at by synchronic investigation of features of the system (oppositions, gaps).

7 Conclusions drawn from diachronic investigation of the provenance of sounds or their later development. Dialect forms can be useful where they preserve older stages of the language or reveal independent development, as in the case of the London standard transferred to Scotland after 1603, or of certain features of AmE, which can be explained as independent developments of BrE sounds by the eighteenth century.

8 Loanwords. The transfer of a loanword and its integration permit certain conclusions about the sound system of the recipient language.

4.1.2 Sociolect and language history (Horn and Lehnert 1954: II, 1197–9; Leith 1983)

The multiplicity of forms described as co-existent within the sound system in 4.2–4.6 reflects social variation in EModE far more impressively than written texts alone can do. The geographical and social expansion of the spoken standard was a much more difficult process than that of the written, and language norms, when accepted, were not as easily stabilized. Gaps in the historical sources prevent us from reconstructing gradual shifts of pronunciation to the extent that is desirable (and necessary) in Labov's view (cf. Harris 1985, Görlach 1988). Determining what the significant variables were, exploring the historical source of the prestige model and its gradual acceptance and spread is in many cases a matter of shrewd guess-work rather than cogent sociolinguistic evidence, even though the main tendencies are clearly discernible – partly, of course, because we know what they led to.

Phonetic changes which resulted from 'sloppy' articulation and diverged from the written standard, and which can therefore be assumed to have had their origin in colloquial and popular speech, often took a long time to find general acceptance against the traditions of the schools. This often resulted in delayed adoption of an innovation or, in the case of phenomena such as the reflexes of ME /au/, in pronunciations that differ from word to word; all this points to the co-existence of various forms in sixteenth-century spoken London English.

It would, then, be misleading to mistake the following as specimens of sound changes that occurred within the standard language; what happened was that 'educated' pronunciations were replaced by more popular ones. It is hardly a matter of chance that many of these replacements occurred after the upheavals of the Civil War (cf. details in 4.2–4.6).

1   Consonants exhibited assimilatory simplifications in the fifteenth century, which were accepted into standard speech only in the seventeenth.

2   Vowels were affected by conditioned changes (influences from neighbouring sounds) and by mergers, some of them early in colloquial speech but not accepted until later by the educated.

4.1.3 Levels of phonological analysis

Phonological levels cannot all be reconstructed with the same degree of certainty and accuracy. Phonemes, as distinctive sound segments, and their distributions can be deduced quite reliably, and even allophonic variation is sometimes reconstructible, especially where we have available contemporary accounts such as Ben Jonson's remarks on /r/: "It is sounded firme in the beginning of the words, and more liquid in the middle, and ends; as in *rarer*, *riper*" (quoted from Horn and Lehnert 1954: 915).

Data relating to word and sentence stress are also available in sufficient quantity, whereas other prosodic/suprasegmental factors such as intonation, speed or pitch are almost impossible to reconstruct.

4.1.4 *Stress* (Dobson 1968: 445–64, 838–78; Ekwall 1975: 5–10)

Word stress can normally be reconstructed, but some doubts remain about some words or types of words. However, the following generalizations can be made:

1   The degree of integration of French and Latin loanwords (as shown by their frequency and spread through sociolects) was of greater consequence then than it is now. Whereas the frequent words (or all words, in the speech of the less educated) had initial stress (with corresponding weakening of the other syllables), rarer words occurring only in the sociolect of the educated classes often preserved the original stress. This frequently meant, especially in poetic and careful, educated pronunciation, secondary stress on syllables which are unstressed in PrE. Even more conspicuous is the retention in EModE of secondary stress in words of four or more syllables, a stress pattern still occurring in many words in AmE.

2   There was some uncertainty about where to place the main stress in a word; this is evident even today in some contradictory patterns of word stress.

3   Level stress in compounds etc. was apparently rarer in EModE than it is today (only Gil comments on this feature).

4   Two different pronunciations, depending on sentence stress, are frequently found side by side, especially with prepositions, pronouns and auxiliary verbs (cf. 4.5).

Further uncertainties (also apparent in contemporary grammarians' statements) might be the result of analogy with other members of the same word class and of special conditions in fixed idioms.

4.2 The phonological system of EModE
(conservative speakers, 1570–1620)

In view of the amount of variation there was in the pronunciation of EModE, it is best to start with a well-defined subsystem before co-existing subsystems or later developments can be described. The subsystem here chosen, that of the conservative pronunciation of the educated, was described in detail by phoneticians from Hart (1570) to Gil (1619). It also appears to have been comparatively stable: Gil's severe criticism of certain features of Hart's speech shows that grammarians were anxious to preserve this subsystem as the norm of 'correctness'. There is evidence (4.8) that similar attitudes were adopted by teachers in grammar schools, for whom spelling pronunciation in particular seems to have played an important role. The list of vowels and diphthongs in this subsystem of educated EModE is as follows:

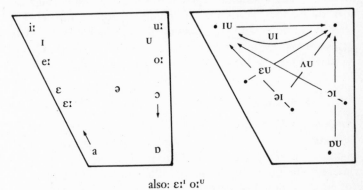

also: ɛːᴵ oːᵁ

Fig. 1 Conspectus of EModE vowel phonemes and diphthongs, *c.* 1600

As for the EModE consonant inventory, it lost the phoneme /x/ by 1600, but on the other hand it expanded to include /ʒ/ and /ŋ/, creating a system which has remained unchanged to the present day.

	bi-lab.	lab.-dent.	dent.	alv.	post-alv.	pal.-alv.	pal.	velar	glott.
plosive	p, b			t, d				k, g	
affricate						tʃ, dʒ			
spirant		f, v	θ, ð	s, z		ʃ, ʒ			h
nasal	m			n				ŋ	
lateral				l					
approximant	w, ʍ				r		j		

Fig. 2 Table of EModE consonant phonemes, *c.* 1600

4.3 Types of phonological change
(in the vowel system in particular)

4.3.1 Terminology

Sound change is said to be 'unconditioned' ('spontaneous') when it applies regularly in all environments. This definition is a working hypothesis which allows one to contrast it with conditioned change (happening only in specifiable environments) and with sporadic change (found in a few words only). Sound change can alter the system, i.e. it may be phonemic, or be restricted to variation in the realization of phonemes, in which case it may be termed subphonemic or allophonic. Types of phonemic change (Görlach 1982: 48–50) are: phonemic split, shift, merger and loss.

4.3.2 Phonemic split

Phonemic split occurs when two allophones conditioned by the phonetic context cease to be positional variants of a single phoneme, becoming functionally contrastive and therefore two different phonemes. Thus the ME allophone [ŋ] of the phoneme /n/ occurred only before /g, k/, but became phonemic in the late sixteenth century after /g/ was lost in words like *sing*, as minimal pairs such as *sin:sing* /[sɪn:sɪŋg] > [sɪn:sɪŋ]) clearly show.

Similarly a new opposition /ʊ/ ≠ /ʌ/ developed from the allophones of /u/, namely [ʊ, ɣ], in words like *book:buck*.

When allophones are re-distributed among existing phonemes, there is of course no split: the divergent pronunciations of older /a/ = [æ, ɔ] in words like *cat:what*, for example, led to the velar variant joining the phoneme [ɔ] as in *cot* in about 1600.

4.3.3 Phonemic shift: the Great Vowel Shift and its consequences

The causes of EModE variation among long vowels and of the rift between spelling and pronunciation go back to ME times. According to Dobson (1968) the shift that took place among the long vowels in the course of the so-called GVS arose in the strongly stressed variants, whose allophonic space of articulation widened. Lass (1976: ch. 2) sees Luick's assumption of a push chain – i.e. that the GVS began with an upward movement of tense /eː/ and /oː/ – confirmed by northern English developments: since ME /oː/ had moved to [øː, yː] in these dialects, there was no /oː/ in the GVS to move up to /uː/ and to push /uː/ into diphthongization. The consequence is that words like [huːs] in northern dialects remained what they were, whereas *all* BrE dialects have diphthongization of ME /iː/ in words like *time*.

The social reasons for these innovations are unexplained but, according to an interesting (if speculative) hypothesis put forward by R. Le Page (in Samuels 1972: 145, n. 3), the upper classes, whose socially distinctive competence in French petered out in the fifteenth century, may have substituted a 'refined' pronunciation of English. An early centralization of the first elements in the new diphthongs is part of an old and still unresolved controversy. Among others, Lass (1976: ch. 2) argues against the reconstruction of ME /iː/ > [ɪi] > [əi] and ME /uː/ > [ʊu] > [əʊ], finding no evidence for this in the orthoepists' descriptions, which in the sixteenth century rather point to the alternative development of /iː/ > [ei] and /uː/ > [oʊ], with centralization of the first element to follow in the seventeenth century.

The major fifteenth-century shift in the system of long vowels can be diagrammatically displayed as follows (? indicates slower movement, there being no pressure towards differentiation).

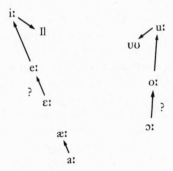

Fig. 3 The Great Vowel Shift (traditional model)

Samuels (1972: 42) expanded this model by including the later consequences of the GVS for diphthongs, and interpreting the complete process as cyclic, in which formal/tense (__) and colloquial/lax (_ _ _) variants co-exist.

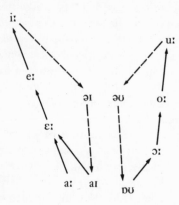

Fig. 4 The Great Vowel Shift (expanded model)

The GVS and its after-effects, then, shifted the long vowels without merging them with neighbouring vowels; such mergers among long vowels did not occur until later (see 4.3.4).

4.3.4 Phonemic merger

The GVS did not change phonemic boundaries – at least in careful, conservative pronunciation. However, [ɛː] merged with [aː > æː > ɛː] in progressive speech so that a mixture of sub-systems resulted in homophonous pairs of the *great:grate*, *break: brake* type, a marginal merger of little consequence for standard EModE and the subsequent history of the language. Other conflicts arose from the monophthongization of the reflex of ME [ai], which in the late sixteenth century merged with the reflexes of either ME /ɛː/ or /aː/. In the standard language the merger of the *tail:tale* words became established in the early seventeenth century.

The opposition between ME /ɛː/ and /eː/ had been lost in many ME dialects and also been levelled in London ME in certain environments. From the beginning of the EModE period, the merger of *meet:meat* words must accordingly be assumed for most forms of lower-class or informal speech. The schools, stressing the distinction preserved in spelling, insisted on the distinction as [iː] vs. [ɛː] in educated speech until the second half of the seventeenth century.

Samuels (1972: 147) provides an alternative explanation, namely that there were three co-existing subsystems and that the one which resulted in the smallest number of homophones finally became dominant. I here add to his table Hart's idiolect, which represents a fourth variant possible in sixteenth-century London:

	I	II	III	Hart	t31
meed	iː	iː	⎱ iː	bi̠	[iː]
mead	eː	⎰	⎰	le̠d	[ɛː]
made	⎰ ɛː	⎰ eː	⎰ eː	nam	[æː]
maid	⎱	⎱	⎱	de̠li	[ɛː]

Fig. 5 Four different mergers of long front vowels/diphthongs in the sixteenth century

Relations among EModE back vowels are simpler: apart from conditioned change (such as non-diphthongization of /uː/ in a labial environment and following [w, j], as in *room*, *wound* (n.), *you*), the most remarkable development was the merger of the reflexes of ME /ɔː/ and /ɔu/ as EModE /oː/ in the early seventeenth century (*sole:soul*).

4.3.5 *Phonemic loss*

Only one phoneme was lost in EModE times, namely /x/ with its allophones [x, ç]. Its realizations were replaced by a lengthening of the preceding vowel except after /u/, where they were redistributed as allophones of /f/ as in *laugh*, *enough* etc.

me.		1500	1600	1700	1800	1900	
/aː/	æː						name
	ɛː						
	eː				eɪ		
/ɛː/	ɛː						sea
	eː						
	iː						
/eː/	iː						see
/iː/	ɪɪ		əɪ	ɑɪ			time
/ɔː/	ɔː						boat
	oː				oʊ	əʊ	
/oː/	uː						boot
/uː/	ʊu		ʌʊ	ɑʊ			foul
/ai/	ʊɪ/æɪ/ɛɪ						way
	ɛː						
	eː				eɪ		
/au/	ɒʊ						cause
	ɒː			ɔː			
/ɔu/	oʊ		oː		oʊ	əʊ	blow

conservative ———————— and progressive ———————— pronunciation according to Dobson (1968). Broken lines indicate transitional periods with coexisting variants.

Fig. 6 Conspectus of the developments of long vowels and diphthongs, 1450–1900

4.4 Conditioned change: vowels

4.4.1 Developments among short vowels

The short front vowels /ɪ, ɛ/ remained unchanged in standard speech, but [ɪ] was frequently lowered to [ɛ] in some dialects such as London speech as represented by T40 (4 *menysters*, 15 *cete*, 16 *ennes*, and especially before [r]: 5 *consperacy*, 30 *sterope*). The short back vowels were lowered in the sixteenth century [ʊ > ɣ], [ɔ > ɒ]. This lowering did not always take place after labials and before [tʃ], [ʃ] so that a new phoneme resulted from the split of /ʊ/ in the early seventeenth century. Later restored in BrE was [ɔ], but [ɒ] remained in AmE; with a few words, this seventeenth-century development went further and [ɒ] became [a], especially in fashionable pronunciation (*plot/plat, God/Gad*). The lowering of [ɔ] narrowed the space available for /a/, which was restricted to front allophones [æ], except after [w] unless followed by [g, k] where it was velarized and merged with /ɔ/: *cat, what, wag* = [kæt, ʍɔt, wæg]. These developments were described by grammarians around 1640, but must have been widespread in colloquial speech by about 1600.

4.4.2 *Changes in vowel quantity: 'shortening'*

Earlier (OE and ME) changes in vowel quantity were often, though not always, reflected in the spelling (*kept, fed, husband*, against *wilderness, southern*), but developments occurring after 1430 did not normally show up. Whenever the modern spelling of vowels is in conflict with the expected pronunciation, two explanations are possible:

1   in *heaven, weather* etc. the spelling reflects older bisyllabic forms with long (first) vowels, the pronunciation trisyllabic (inflected) forms with a short vowel;
2   in *dead* etc. (originally a long vowel in all forms) a new short form was introduced after 1400.

Such short vowels reflecting ME long vowel quantities are most frequent where ME has /ɛː, ɔː/ before /d, t, θ, v, f/ in monosyllabic words, but even here they occur only in a minority of possible words. It is likely that the short vowel was introduced on the pattern of words in which the occurrence of a short or a long vowel was determined by the type of syllable the vowel appeared in (*glad* vs. *glade*). When these words became monosyllabic in all their forms, the conditioning factor was lost and the apparently free variation of short/long spread to cases like (*dead*). That such processes must have continued for some time is shown by words ending in -*ood*: early shortened forms (*flood*) are found side by side with later short forms (*good*) and those with the long vowel preserved (*mood*).

4.4.3 Lengthening

EModE lengthening of vowels was conditioned by certain post-vocalic consonants. Vowels preceding [r] were lengthened in OE in [-rd, -rð, -rz]. Elsewhere, lengthening of the vowel is a compensation for the increasingly weaker articulation of [r] in postvocalic position; however, the ultimate loss of [r] (merging with [ə]) in southern BrE was not complete until about 1800.

In the late seventeenth century, [æ] and occasionally [ɔ] were lengthened if they preceded [s, f, θ] in words like *staff, glass, path, off*. New [æː] became [aː] in southern BrE, a development not shared by AmE. New [ɔː] was not stable, so that short [ɔ] is common in modern BrE *off, loss*, etc.

4.4.4 Development of vowels preceding [r]

Postvocalic [r] tends to round and lower the preceding vowel; as far as the development of long vowels is concerned, this meant that the effect of the GVS was retarded. The development of [ɛr] to [ar] was common in the fifteenth century (*star*); [eːr] became [ɛːr] also in the fifteenth century, this development partly overlapping with [aːr] > [æːr] > [ɛːr]. Unlike other distributions, in which reflexes of ME /ɛː/ and /eː/ commonly merged, the development of vowels preceding [r] was not uniform:

/ai/	fair	pair	hair			PrE /ɛə/
/aː/	fare	pare	hare	bare	tare	
/ɛː/		pear		bear	tear	
	fear		hear		tear	
/eː/		peer	here	beer		
		pier		bier	tier	PrE /iə/

Fig. 7 Conditioned change: development of vowels preceding [r]

[ɔːr] was preserved; about 1600, however, it merged with [uːr] (from ME [uːr] and shifted [oːr]) to give us [ɔːr] for both: *bore, boar, board; whore; mourn, floor, pour*. However, ME [oːr] could also exhibit the 'regular' development to give EModE [uːr] (*poor*),

Phonology

and ME [uːr] to produce EModE [auər] (*shower, sour*). In BrE dialects and AmE there are a great number of developments diverging from standard BrE.

Of the short vowels preceding [r], [ɪr, ur, ɛr] merged to give [ər] about 1600. Since old [ɛr] words had [ar] from the fifteenth century, words containing ⟨er⟩ = [ər] must be more recent loans or words in which *er* was re-introduced (*perfect, merchant*, 3.5.4), or they are words in which short forms earlier alternated with [ɛːr], as in *earth* (t31/5).

4.4.5 Development of vowels preceding [ɫ]

A glide [ʊ] developed between velar vowels and word-final [ɫ], or [ɫ] + consonant in the fifteenth century: [a > aʊ], [ɔː, ɔ > oʊ], [oʊ, ʊ > uː] as in (*all, call; doll; colt, told*). This [ɫ] was completely vocalized if it preceded velars or labials: [aʊɫ] > [ɒʊ] > ModE [aː] in *calf, calm*; unconditioned [aʊɫ] developed into ModE [ɔː] as in *chalk, talk*. ME [oʊɫ] > EModE [oᵘː] > ModE as *folk, yolk*.

4.5 Unstressed vowels

Vowel differences in syllables with secondary stress or in unstressed position, if reflected in spelling at all, are important as the only indication (apart from grammarians' statements) of certain prosodic features in EModE. Unstressed vowels occur in polysyllabic words and (often as alternative forms) in certain positions in the sentence. However, in syllables which did not carry the main stress in polysyllabic words, the reduction of the affected vowels was not nearly as far advanced as it is in PrE.

Vowel length was sometimes preserved in secondary stress in the final syllable of words such as *openly* [əɪ], *emperour* [ʌur], *captain* [ɛɪ]; alternating quantities are found in *certain* [ɛɪ/ɛ], *capital* [aʊ/a], *history* [əɪ/ɪ], *purpose* [ɔː/ɔ] and *glorious* [ʌʊ/ʊ]. Even historically short vowels often remained distinct (i.e. were not merged to give [ə]): *countenance, village* [a], *kingdom, seldom* [ʊ].

Naive spellings and later developments show, however, that [ə] must have been widespread already, especially in less careful pronunciation. Further reduction resulted in syllabic consonants: see

Hart's transcriptions for *father*, *heaven* and *evil* (t31) and the new graphemes suggested by Bullokar (t33, 19). Loss of medial vowels is found in words with the stress pattern v́(x)x: *cent(u)ry = sentry*, *courtesy = curtsy*, *phantasy = fancy*; *bus(i)ness*, *med(i)cine*, *reg(i)ment*, *marr(i)age*, *mill(i)ons*.

Alternation of fully stressed and weak forms according to position in the sentence was particularly common for certain prepositions, pronouns and auxiliaries; the most frequent pairs are:

and	[ən/and]	*have*	[(h)əv/hæːv]	*there*	[ðɛr/ðeːr]
are	[ar/ɛːr]	*he*	[(h)ɪ/hiː]	*their*	[ðɛr/ðeɪr]
as	[az/as]	*his*	[(h)ɪz/hɪs]	*thou*	[ðʊ/ðuː]
be	[bɪ/biː]	*my*	[mɪ/məɪ]	*through*	[θrʊ/θrʌʊx]
been	[bɪn/biːn]	*me*	[mɪ/miː]	*thy*	[ðɪ/ðəɪ]
could	[kʊd/kuːld]	*of(f)*	[əv/ɒf]	*to*	[tʊ/tuː]
should	[ʃʊd/ʃuːld]	*other*	[ʊðər/uːðər]	*we*	[wɪ/wiː]
would	[wʊd/wuːld]	*shall*	[ʃəl/ʃaʊl]	*who*	[wə/huː]
do	[dʊ/duː]	*so*	[sə/soː]	*with*	[wɪð/wɪθ]
doth	[dʊð/duːθ]	*the*	[ðə/ðɛː, ðiː]	*you*	[jʊ/juː]

Fig. 8 Frequent stress alternants (weak vs. full forms)

4.6 Consonants (Dobson 1968: 927–95)

As far as conclusions can be drawn, it appears safe to say that the articulation of consonants has remained more or less the same from OE times, with the exception of /r/, which was articulated initially as a tremulant, elsewhere as an alveolar fricative (see Jonson 4.1.3).

The EModE consonant system was enlarged by two phonemes (4.3.2): /ʒ/, which developed from /zj/, was considered 'foreign' by sixteenth-century grammarians, but became more frequent in the seventeenth century, when it was also found in words like *measure*. Though /ʒ/ is still the least frequent phoneme in PrE, its correlation with voiceless /ʃ/ gives it a firm place in the PrE phonemic system (for /ŋ/ see 4.3.2).

New instances of /ʃ/ developed from earlier /s + j/: naive spellings show that *profession* and *position* must have had /ʃ/ as early as the fifteenth century, but sixteenth-century grammarians insisted on [sɪ, sj], as Hart did in his transcription of *temtacion* (t31/11). The corresponding voiced phoneme [dj] > [dʒ] was frequent from the seventeenth century in words like *Indian*, but later looked upon as vulgar and therefore replaced by the spelling pronunciation [dj].

Reduction of initial clusters continued OE and ME simplifications: [wr > r] occurred from the fifteenth century but did not become fully acceptable until the seventeenth; [gn, kn > n] was largely established by the late seventeenth century. As regards word-final clusters, [-mb] was widely reduced to [-m], though sometimes reintroduced from the spelling, while the reverse development is found in *soun(d)* (not accepted in *tounde* T50/46); cf. *ancien(t)*, *agains(t)* and *whils(t))* from ME on.

The phoneme /x/ was lost in standard speech (4.3.5). From the thirteenth century on, words were frequently spelt without ⟨ʒ, gh⟩, especially where *t* followed, but only after the fifteenth century were all positions affected, especially in dialect and colloquial speech. The sound was replaced by vowel length, as in *ought* or (word-finally after /ʊ/) merged with /f/ as in *rough*. In careful speech [x, ç] were apparently preserved well into the seventeenth century, and grammarians insisted on them being pronounced, partly because of their written presence. In particular the [f] pronunciation was objected to, but was common from at least 1625.

Vocalization of consonants is found with [ɫ] preceding labials and velars (4.4.5); to pronounce [ɫ] in such words was considered pedantic (T31F/24). In ME [w] had already been lost before [u, oː] (*sword*, *two*, cf. *who*, *whose*, *whom*) and before unstressed vowels (*Southwark*, *Greenwich*, *conquer*, *answer*). On the other hand, unetymological [w] developed before [ɔ, u] in some dialects (*whotest* T23B/67, *howsswold* T40/23). Scottish and southern scribes frequently mixed up *wh*, *w*, *v*, which suggests that the sounds represented must have been merged at least partially (T40/17 *whent*, and T40/41 *vomen*; frequent in Scots texts).

Loss of initial [h] was typical of dialect and 'vulgar' speech (T40/28 *yt* 'hit'; cf. the hypercorrect spelling T40/39 *hes* 'is'), but it was not stigmatized as strongly as it was from the nineteenth century onwards. Although *h* was historically mute in French loanwords, it has increasingly been pronounced as a consequence of the spelling.

Alternation of [d] and [ð] is found in a few words such as *murthering/murdering* (T46/11, 32), *burthen* (T3/9), *togyder* (T35/20), *althermen*, *odur* (T40/8–9). Metathesis of [r] is recorded in *thrid* 'third', *thurst* 'thrust' (T46/21).

4.7 Transcriptions of specimen passages

T3/48–55 (1549)

ðə fɪrst ən tʃiːfəst pɔɪnt ɪz ðət ðə dɪlɪdʒɛnt
mæɪstər mæːk nɔt ðə skɔlər hæːst tu mʊtʃ
bʊt ðət hɪ ɪn kɔntɪnvans ən dɪlɪdʒens əv
tɛːtʃɪŋ mæːk hɪm rɪɛ(ː)rs sɔː ðət mɑɪl hɪ
hæːv parfɪtlɪ ðat ðət ɪz bɪhɑɪnd hɪ svfr
hɪm nɔt tʊ goː fɔrward fɔr ðɪs poːstrɪŋ
hæːst ɔːvərθrʊvəθ ənd vrtəθ ə greːt sɔrt
əv wɪts ən kastəθ ðəm ɪntʊ ən əmæːzədnəs
mɛn ðæɪ knɔʊ nɔt hʌv ðæɪ ʃavl əɪðər goː
fɔrward ɔr bakward

T8/107–14 (1582)

bʊt ɪt mɛˑɪ biː rɪplɑɪd əgeˑɪn ðət ʌvr ɪŋglɪʃ
tʊŋ dvθ niːd noː svtʃ prɔɪnɪŋ ɪt ɪz əv smavl
reːtʃ ɪt stretʃəθ noː ferðər ðɛn ðɪs əɪlənd əv ʌvrz
neˑɪ nʊt ðɛːr oːvəravl mat ðoː jet ɪt reˑɪnəθ
ðɛːr ənd ɪt servz vs ðɛːr ənd ɪt wuːld biː
klɛːn brʊʃt fɔr ðə weːrɪŋ ðɛːr ðoː ɪt goː nʊt
bɪjɒnd seː ɪt wɪl serv ʊn ðɪs sɑɪd ənd biː nʊt
ʌvr ɪŋglɪʃ foːˠks fɪnɪʃ az wɛl az ðə forən

T15/4–10 (1672)

ɛnɪ mæn hu: ri:dᴢ ðo:ᴢ ɛksəlɛnt po:ɪts ən
kɒmpe:rᴢ ðe:r læŋgwədʒ wɪð mɒt ɪᴢ nʌv rɪtn
wɪl sɪ: ɪt ʋ:lmo:st ɪn ɛvrɪ lɑɪn bʌt ðət ðɪs ɪᴢ
ən ɪmpru:vmənt əv ðə læŋgwədʒ ʋr ən ʋ:ltəre:ʃən
fʊr ðə betər wɪl nɒt so: ɪ:zɪlɪ bɪ græntɪd fʊr
mɛnɪ ær əv ə kɒntrærɪ ʋpɪnjən ðət ðɪ ɪŋglɪʃ
tʌŋ wɒᴢ ðɛn ɪn ðə hɑɪt əv ɪts pɛrfɛkʃən

T36/39–47 (Scots, 1531)

fʊr xwɛn ðɪs tɑɪrən pɛrse:vɪt al mɛn havənd
hɪm ɪn drɛ:d hɪ bɪgan tø dre:d al mɛn ɪn ðə
se:mɪn manər ənd bɪ ðat we: grɪv me:st
o:dɪvs tø ɪs svbdɪts sle:ɪn ɪᴢ no:bɪlᴢ bɪ vɛ:n
kʋ:ᴢɪᴢ fʊr brɛ:kɪn ɔf ɪᴢ nɪv lʋ:ᴢ ɔr ɛls ɛstʃe:tɪn
ðɛr gø:dᴢ ənd xwɛn hɪ had gɔtɪn grɛ:t prɔfɪt
bɪ slʋ:xtɪr ənd prɔskrɪptɪu:n ɔf ɪᴢ no:bɪlᴢ
hɪ bɪgan tø pvt ɪᴢ handᴢ me:r pɛrtlɪ ɪn ðɛr
blø:d bɪkʋ:ᴢ ðə prɔfɪt ðerɔf ape:rɪt ɪlk dɛ:
mo:r swɪ:t

Fig. 9 Transcriptions of specimen passages

4.8 Spelling pronunciation

Since written English was considered 'more correct' and had a
higher prestige than spoken forms in general, teachers began
early on to insist on pronunciations modelled on the written
form. In particular, many demanded that *all* letters be pronounced, an attitude satirized in Holofernes (T31F). This
requirement had consequences, especially in the case of words
whose spelling was corrected by reference to the Latin etymon

(3.5.4): in most of these words (but not in all) spelling pronunciations slowly came to predominate (*perfect*, *servant*, but *doubt*, *receipt*). Hart still considered *c* and *h* in *aucthoritie*, *l* in *souldiours* and *s* in *baptisme* superfluous, since there was no equivalent in pronunciation. With polysyllabic words, the written form supported careful 'unclipped' pronunciations (*marriage*, 4.5, cf. AmE *secretary*). As shown above, spelling influence can even reverse sound changes, as it has done in *Indian* (4.6). Vachek (1962, following Luick) even believes that modern [ɔɪ] in *point*, etc., is due to spelling influence after [əɪ] from former [ʊɪ] had merged with reflexes of ME [iː] as in *pint*; it is claimed that the [ɔɪ] pronunciation was intended to stress the foreign provenance of these words.

Study questions

Q19   Which words in the transcriptions of Hart (t31) and – where determinable – of Cheke (t30) have a different vowel quantity from the one expected for the PrE word?

Q20   What information about seventeenth-century pronunciation can be drawn from Ogilby's and Dryden's rhymes (in T21) *gate:state:wait*, *hair:bear*, *souls:poles*, *got:hat*?

Q21   Continue the transcription of T3 (in 4.7 above) as far as T3/66.

Q22   Compile a full list of Scots vowels and diphthongs from the transcription of T36/39–47 (in 4.7 above) and compare the set with the sixteenth-century EModE system.

Q23   When (and in which sociolect) did the following pairs become homophonous: *seam:seem*, *write:right*, *sale:sail*, *sloe:slow*? Are *waist:waste*, *draft:draught* also specimens of homophony resulting from sound changes?

5 Inflexional morphology

(Only inflexions will be discussed in this chapter; word-formation, which can be considered the second main branch of morphology, is treated in chapter 7, "Vocabulary".)

The range of EModE inflexions is almost identical with that of PrE. This fact was particularly striking for grammarians who compared English with the highly inflected Latin language (T27/78–9, "it wanteth Grammer"). Whereas inflexion had a great number of forms and functions in OE and ME, continuous levelling and loss of endings now made it necessary to express some syntactical functions by other means (cf. 6.4).

5.1 Nouns: pluralization (Graband 1965: 39–102)

The EModE system is almost identical with that of PrE. The unstressed [ə] of the [əz] ending was lost (except after sibilants) in the fifteenth century; this, along with subsequent assimilation to preceding voiceless consonants, resulted in the modern allomorphs of the regular plural morpheme {s} = [ɪz, z, s]. However, Hart's careful transcriptions (1570) show that there was still a great deal of variation, and the modern regularity of phonemically conditioned allomorphs of {s} – and in {d} of the regular past tense formation (5.6.2) – came about only in the seventeenth century (cf. Lass, forthcoming).

As in PrE, allomorphic variation of fricatives was restricted to a few words: /f ~ v/, as in *loaf*, alternated in a dozen frequent words, some six had /θ ~ ð/ alternation, but /s ~ z/ is found only in *house*. Whether such alternations were stable right into the modern period appears to have depended on frequency of occurrence,

79

especially of plural forms: if a word was mainly used in the singular, 'regular' pluralization (base form + *s*) was likely to become established (*beef* + *s*).

Other plural forms were rare (as they are in PrE): *-en* in *oxen*; *been*, *eyen*, *hosen*, *housen*, *peasen*, *shone* (t51/11) – but these (apart from *oxen*) were more common with the regular plural inflexion; *-en* forms were criticized by grammarians, and cultivated as archaisms by Spenser; also consider *brethren* (*brothers* is common from Shakespeare onwards), *children*, *kine* ('cows', cf. *oxen*). Umlaut plurals (*mice*, *men*, etc.) were the same as in PrE. Zero inflexion was especially frequent in words where 'plural' could be redefined as 'collective', as in *deer*, *horse*, *swine*, *folk*, *year*, *pound*; the feature was also transferred to words of similar meaning (*fish*, *fowl*) and loanwords such as *cattle*.

Classification according to the EModE 'countable':'uncountable' distinction can differ from PrE in individual words; the texts have plurals such as *those . . . learnings* (T8/84), *stealthes* (T31A/28) or *moneys* (Bacon in 7.6.1), which sound unusual today.

5.2 Case

5.2.1 Introductory

Since English had, by the late fifteenth century, lost all case markers in articles and adjectives, and retained only the genitive singular in noun inflexion, EModE cannot be considered a fully inflected language. The individual NP's role in the sentence in EModE was determined by functional word order, prepositions and, in spoken English, by stress and intonation. Grammarians of the sixteenth and seventeenth centuries, then, found themselves in a dilemma: most tried to find in English the formal category 'case', setting up paradigms such as *the man*, *of the man*, *to the man*, *a man*, *o man*! (as Gil did in 1619 – a tradition that Churchill still remembered from his own school days). Ben Jonson was one of the first grammarians to explain 'case' not as a matter of form but of syntactic function, thus establishing *functional* equivalences between Latin and English.

5.2.2 *Genitive* (den Breejen 1937, Altenberg 1982)

The genitive of the singular was the only form marked for case in EModE. Plurals were marked as 'possessive' by position only, as were most singular nouns ending in sibilants (t37); this feature extended to other words as well as some dialects (T40/1 *y^e quen grace*, T40/39 *master Hall cronnacull*). As regards meaning, the genitive alternated to some extent with *of*-phrases and the so-called 'possessive dative': *the kings palace = the palace of the king = the king his palace*, as can be illustrated by the following passage from Ben Jonson's *Alchemist*:

t37   I haue a peece of IASONS fleece, too,
       Which was no other, then a booke of *alchemie*,
       Writ in large sheepe-skin, a good fat ram-vellam.
       Such was PYTHAGORA's thigh, PANDORA's tub;
5   And, all that fable of MEDEAS charmes,
       The manner of our worke: The Bulls, our fornace,
       Still breathing fire; our *argent-viue*, the Dragon:
       The Dragons teeth, *mercury* sublimate,
       That keepes the whitenesse, hardnesse, and the biting;
10   And they are gather'd into IASON'S helme,
       (Th'*alembeke*) and then sow'd in MARS his field,
       And, thence, sublim'd so often, till they are fix'd.
       Both this, th'*Hesperian* garden, CADMVS storie,
       IOVE'S shower, the boone of MIDAS, ARGVS eyes,
15   BOCCACE his *Demogorgon*, thousands more,
       All abstract riddles of our *stone*. How now?

Whereas, from quite early on, the genitive tended to predominate for the expression of 'possession' as against prepositional phrases for other functions (apart from phrasal lexemes such as "a day's journey"), the possessive dative did not become frequent until the fifteenth century in written English. It is likely to have been a popular feature which was introduced into written and printed texts at a time when the number of texts and their readers dramatically expanded. In the sixteenth century the construction appears to have spread into 'respectable' prose, but was largely restricted to the form *his* following words ending in sibilants, in which the possessive would have otherwise been without a formal marker (t37 *Cadmus*, *Argus*; cf. *highnes* in

T37B/18, 20, 30; T48/13, 31). It was possibly also preferred to the cumbrous construction of the group genitive ("James VI his poem"). Other possessive pronouns (*her, their*) were used very rarely (*his* and *-s* being phonetically identical in most environments). The use of the possessive dative was unanimously condemned by grammarians, including Ben Jonson, who – while he saw in it a useful means of distinguishing between singular and plural genitives – nevertheless preferred his own solution: *princis* (sg.) vs. *princes* (pl.). However, *his* is found in his plays (t37); indeed, it even occurs in the title of *Seianus His Fall*.

As regards spelling, the use of the apostrophe (*boy's*) was optional from 1500, frequent in the seventeenth century and fully established by 1690–1700 – the plural marking (*boys'*) was to follow only in the eighteenth century. These innovations appear to have been sparked off by a desire to achieve unambiguous marking at least in the written medium. After *'s* had been established for the genitive, this spelling was also used for /z/ in *fox's*, and thus became a grammatical convention. That it was this new function that determined the retention of the apostrophe is evident from a comparison with other inflected forms that frequently made use of the apostrophe in the seventeenth and eighteenth centuries, but gave it up later, such as *'d* in weak preterites and participles.

After [ə] had been lost in inflexions (5.1), the alternation of /f ~ v/ became opaque in *wife:wives*. Since number distinction in nouns had taken priority from ME on, the genitive singular was re-analysed ([wiːvəz > wəɪf + s]).

Group genitives: the sixteenth century showed a rapid decline in the number of 'split' attributives in NPs: for *the kinges wif of England* (ME) either *the wife of (the king of England)* or *(the king of England)'s wife* became the preferred forms. My bracketing is to indicate that the constituent was marked as a whole, whether by *of* or by *'s*. There was no grammatical restriction, as far as the available evidence goes, on where group genitives could be used, but longer groups do not seem to have been acceptable.

Two types of genitives without accompanying head became established in EModE, one avoiding repetition of the head, as in T48/55 "an other shippe of her Maiesties (shippes)", and one in which the head can be supplied from the context, as in T40/12–13 "vnto powlles" (to St Paul's Church/Cathedral).

Unambiguous marking of the categories 'genitive' and 'plural' was not achieved in EModE. Ways in which the problems involved were tackled can be summarized in four types.

1   There was no distinction between 'genitive' and 'plural', i.e. 'genitive' was not marked in plural nouns, as is still the case with most nouns in spoken PrE, and was the rule in EModE written texts as well: *kinges* = 'kings', 'king's', 'kings''.

2   The genitive was always marked by *'s* which made plural marking impossible; see Bunyan's *their mother's wombs*, and *hound's* (pl.) in T21/67.

3   The genitive and the plural were marked independently (as in written PrE). This was Bullokar's intention when proposing *bridgis, bridges, bridgeses; earis, earz, earz's*. Similar marking is found in some modern dialects: *the farmerses cows*.

4   The genitive was indicated by position only (frequent since ME in some dialects): *the bishop palace* vs. *the bishops palaces*.

5.3 Adjectives (Graband 1965: 156ff.)

After the fifteenth century, adjectives were no longer inflected for case, number and gender: gradation was the only inflexional category that remained. The types *cold:colder:coldest, old:elder:eldest* and *great:gretter:grettest* were inherited from OE, as were some suppletive paradigms from stems unrelated by etymology (*good:better:best*).

Most paradigms with vowel alternation were regularized in ME times, *longer* replacing older *lenger*. Alternative regular forms (*older:oldest, later:latest*, and *nearer:nearest*) came to be used in EModE, often without semantic differentiation.

Periphrastic gradation (*more, most*) became common in ME for all adjectives. In EModE there were three ways of expressing a comparative: *easier, more easy, more easier*. The choice depended on the particular word, text type and metrical/rhythmical context. *More, most* appear to have been commoner in written or educated language. Gil (1619: 12) claimed that *stonier, famouser* were acceptable in spoken English, but should be avoided in writing;

English dialects still prefer *-er/-est* gradation with *all* adjectives. The choice was still optional around 1600 (reflecting style or sociolect at most), but by the late seventeenth century the *-er/-est* comparison had been established for monosyllabic words. The complicated rules holding for bisyllabics in PrE clearly show these to have been formulated by eighteenth-century grammarians.

Double gradation was frequent in colloquial speech, in which it could serve to express emphasis. Such forms became more frequent in the sixteenth century and were accepted in respectable prose, too. Ben Jonson praised them as a special virtue of the English language. Specimens from the texts include: *more easier* (t24/4), *more solemner* (T18C/124), *most ryfest* (T25/92), *the most vnkindest cut of all* (T31D/15, cf. Franz 1939: 210–11) and *moste ancientest* (Verstegan in 7.1.5). When rationalism came to prevail in the late seventeenth century, these forms were condemned as being illogical (T15/141–2, cf. 6.1.6); they were removed consistently from Shakespeare's texts in the editions prepared by Rowe (1709) and Pope (1725).

5.4 Articles and pronouns (for uses, see 6.2)

5.4.1 *Articles* (Graband 1965: 207ff.)

The undeclinable article *the* had become established by the end of the ME period (the plural *tho* survived in a very few early prints, see T19A). The spelling was *þe* until the fifteenth century and later in some manuscripts; it was printed as ye before 1630 because the letter forms of *þ* and *y* had been conflated. The forms *a/an* of the indefinite article were in complementary distribution as in PrE; occasional variation is found before initial *h-* or *u-* (*an hundred*, t1/3; *an union*).

5.4.2 *Personal and possessive pronouns*

In PrE personal pronouns, unlike nouns, are marked not only for number but also for (subject vs. object) case and, in the third person singular, for gender. The exception is *you*, which is not even marked for number: the communicative situation must here

make up for the lack of the number distinction. Since case function has been expressed by word order since ME times, case
marking in pronouns is redundant. This permitted the substitution of one form for another without endangering communication. The EModE system was as follows:

I (ich)	thou	he	she	it	we	ye	they
me	thee	him	her	it	us	you	them (hem)
my/mine	thy/thine	his	her	his	our	your	their

Fig. 10 EModE personal and possessive pronouns

The EModE second-person forms differed conspicuously from
PrE, the four EModE forms having been reduced to one. This
development was brought about by phonological and sociolinguistic factors: from the fifteenth century, *ye* and *you* had the
weakly stressed form [jə] in common, which combined with
redundant case marking to produce incorrect generalizations
(possibly partly influenced by the reverse vowel pattern in
thou/thee). From around 1600 *ye* was a rare alternative to *you* and
had ceased to carry any case distinction.

The decline of *thou/thee* was the result of the social uses of the
pronouns (cf. Barber 1976: 208–13; Finkenstaedt 1963): the
polite use of the plural pronoun had been introduced from French
in the fourteenth century, restricting *thou* to use among equals or
as a mode of address for people of lower status. Use of the 'polite'
form increased continuously until it became the common,
unmarked form of address around 1600, leaving for *thou* the
function of affective address (familiar, in the positive or negative
sense) for a short period of transition. Eventually, *thou* became
confined to biblical quotations and church prayer, to Quaker
speech (T50), some forms of religious literature (Bunyan,
T60/59–65) and archaic use in dialects from the late seventeenth
century onwards.

Possessive pronouns: conventions were similar to those for personal pronouns, especially in the second person. As for the forms,
mine/thine became restricted to positions preceding vowels (like
PrE *an*) and before pauses, but attributive /-n/ forms became
quite rare in the seventeenth century. Pronouns used predi-

catively received more stress and were often placed before pauses; these generally retained /-n/. These facts led to the originally phonetically conditioned distribution of forms being re-interpreted in grammatical terms in the seventeenth century. (It is possible that -*n* was also interpreted as a reduced form of *one*, but whether this was indeed the case is difficult to determine.) Other pronouns adopted this -*n* (*hisn*, *hern*, etc., in particular in southern dialects, a feature generally criticized by grammarians), or they added -*s*, which is obviously a transfer from 'free' genitives in identical position: *a ship of her Majesty's ~ of hers*.

The possessive *its* (Graband 1965: 256–60) is the only EModE innovation; *his*, common for neuter reference until after 1600 (T10/14), did not reflect the distinction 'human':'nonhuman' found elsewhere in the pronominal system. This is likely to be the reason for the possessive form *it* (T18E/50), which is found from the fourteenth century, and the less equivocal forms *of it* or *thereof*, which are common in the sixteenth and seventeenth centuries (T48/112). But *its* (first recorded in 1598; T18F/8 and 38 contain some of the earliest occurrences) obviously fitted the system ideally, as can be deduced from its rapid spread in the first half of the seventeenth century.

5.4.3 *Reflexive pronouns* (Graband 1965: 263ff., cf. 6.3.3)

Traditionally, the personal pronouns were used to express reflexivity, but obvious ambiguities (*he killed him*) led to the increasing use, after 1500, of *self* compounds: *self* was either added (*him self*) or used as a noun with preceding possessive (*his self*). Although this duplication of forms was eliminated in the course of the EModE period, selection was not consistent (cf. *myself* but *himself*). Since *self* is marked for number, a number distinction is possible for the second person (*yourself* vs. *yourselues*, T18E/66). A new form, *oneself*, was first recorded in the sixteenth century, but only became established in the eighteenth.

5.4.4 *Relative pronouns* (Graband 1965: 276ff.)

There are a great number of EModE relative pronouns whose functional and stylistic distinctions (where they exist – most relatives appear to be in free variation) are not always quite clear (6.8.3). ME relative pronouns ceased to be inflected; this accounts for the transference of the interrogative forms *whose*, *whom* to the relative pronoun system from the fourteenth century, and for their greater frequency in comparison with later relativized *who*. The relative *quhilk* could be pluralized in Scots (T36/2 *quhilkis*), possibly by analogy with French and Latin patterns.

5.4.5 *Demonstrative pronouns* (Graband 1965: 289–96)

EModE forms are identical with those of PrE; variants still common in earlier ME had been given up by 1500. *This/these, that/those* are different from most other pronouns in that they have number distinction even when they precede nouns, where this marking is redundant. EModE developed away from ternary (*this: that:yon*) to binary deixis, though in ME *yon* had already been rare and not always distinguished from *that*. From the seventeenth century, *yon* was poetic-archaic – or Scots (T21/111, T42/57).

Demonstratives could be intensified by *ilke* or *self* in the fifteenth century, by *same, selfsame* in the sixteenth and seventeenth (note archaizing *thilke same* in T23B/1), but after 1650 almost exclusively by *very* in the written standard (*here/there* in spoken non-standard language).

Relatives were also used for demonstratives in the construction of Latinate periods (6.8.4).

5.5 Verb inflexion for person

5.5.1 *Introductory*

The use of verb inflexion for person is bound up with personal pronouns: languages, in which person and number are obligatorily marked on the verb by inflexion (such as Latin), tend to have optional personal pronouns, which then are used for emphasis. The reduction of ME and EModE inflexion can, then, be explained as a combination of sound laws (reduction or loss of unstressed vowels and final /-n/) and loss of function (with the increasing obligatoriness of pronouns).

5.5.2 Early Modern English forms

EModE has the following forms (rarer variants, often regarded as dialectal or archaic, are bracketed):

Pres. Ind. Sg. 1	Ø	Pl. Ø (en, eth, es)
2	(e)st, (es, t)	
3	eth, (e)s, (Ø)	
Pres. Subj. Sg.	Ø	Pl. Ø (en)
Imper. Sg.	Ø	Pl. Ø (eth)
Infin.	Ø (en)	
Pres. Part.	ing	
Pret. 1, 3 Sg.	Ø	Pl. Ø (en)
2 Sg.	(e)st	
Past Part.	ed/e(n)	

Fig. 11 EModE verb inflexion for person

-es in the 2nd pers. sg. ind. pres. is northern (T23B/34), but was occasionally used to reduce consonant clusters elsewhere (T31B/36); -t is found in some modals (wilt, shalt) and in wast, wert. The loss of -est in the seventeenth century is obviously concomitant with the loss of thou (5.4.2).

The development and distribution of EModE forms of the 3rd pers. sg. is complex. Ø occurs with modals and occasionally after sibilants (T48/120), but in all other cases -eth (from southern ME) and -es (from northern dialects) are in competition. In the six-teenth century -(e)s was preferred in colloquial speech and in poetry. This distinction between prose and metrical poetry is found even in texts by the same author (figures are from Franz 1939: 156–7): Lyly's prose Euphues (T25) has only 4 per cent s, but his play The Woman in the Moon has 85 per cent; compare Sidney's prose Apologie (T27) with 14 per cent and Marlowe's plays with 92 per cent. These statistics may have been slightly distorted by compositors: many an s in manuscript is certain to have been printed as eth.

In general, -eth appears to have been the more formal variant; it predominated in official documents and biblical translations, including the AV of 1611, but is rarer in private letters and diaries. In poems, -(e)s is more frequent in end rhymes than medially; the variation of monosyllabic loues and bisyllabic loueth could be profitably employed (*that hateth thee and hates vs all*) to achieve regular metre. Phonological preferences may have been important in the prose of a period of transition around 1600; Samuels (1972: 174) shows that monosyllabic verbs, apart from those ending in /s, z, tʃ, dʒ, ʃ/, favour -*(e)s*: *runs, liues*, but *riseth, preacheth, intendeth*. Rhythmical, stylistic and semantic factors must also have played a part, so that the reasons for the choice of inflexion cannot be reconstructed in many cases. Use of -*(e)th* declined rapidly in the seventeenth century; how much frequency of occurrence depends on the time factor has been convincingly shown from the Shakespeare corpus (which spans the 'critical' years) by Taylor (1976). It was largely preserved in *doth* and *hath*, but was considered biblical/archaic with other verbs. Some seventeenth-century grammarians consider -*eth* a purely *graphic* variant.

The present plural (ind. and subj.) was still frequently indicated by -*en* in fifteenth-century texts (T1/16–17, 22, 42); it is found in letters written by Elizabeth I and in an archaizing function in Lyly and Spenser (T23B/40, 46). Also used well into the seventeenth century were -*eth* and -*(e)s/z*; they came from dialects or were transferred from the singular (T42/17 *Your commissionars telz me*; T44/136 *dothe*).

Variants were especially numerous with the auxiliaries and modals. The negated short forms *an't, in't, arn't*; *shan't* and *won't* only became frequent in the seventeenth century. *Be/beest* were quite common in the sixteenth, but rare in the seventeenth century and are dialectal (south-western) today.

1 Sg. Pres.	2 Sg.	Pl.	Pret.	2 Sg.
am (*be*)	*art* (*beest*)	are (*be*)	was/were	*wert/wast*
can	*canst*		could	*couldst*
dare	*darest*		*durst*	
			(17th c: dared)	
may	*mayst*	*mowe*	might,	*mightst*
			mought	
shall	*shalt*		should	*shouldst*
will, *wolle*	*wilt*		would	*wouldst*

Fig. 12 EModE forms of auxiliary and modal verbs
(forms not surviving in PrE are in italics)

5.5.3 The Scottish system

Verb forms in Scots are conspicuously different from those in EModE. An analysis of T28 (with a few additions) provides the present-tense forms *I, we, ʒe, thay luf; þow, he lufis* if the pronoun precedes the verb, but *-is* throughout if it does not (see T18A/5–8). The imperative is unmarked in the singular; the plural form is often *-is* for the first verb, but invariably Ø for successive verbs (contrast T18A/2 with 3). The participle ending *-and* is clearly distinct from that of the verbal noun or gerund (*-yng*). Although English influence was so early that all the Scots texts here included exhibit both *-and* and *-yng* for the participle, the ratio of *-and* to *-yng* tokens can be taken as an indicator of the Scottishness of sixteenth-century texts.

5.6 Tense formation

5.6.1 Strong verbs (Ekwall 1975: 98–113, Brunner 1960–2: 194–252)

Verbs are designated 'strong' if they indicate tense by vowel change (ablaut) and do not have a dental segment added. In a synchronic description of EModE the traditional classification of strong verbs in seven ablaut classes makes little sense, but it is useful for diachronic comparisons. The numbers of strong verbs inherited from OE were decimated in ME: many verbs, in particular rare ones or those confined to poetic registers, disappeared or were used with regular (weak) tense forms (see figures in Baugh and Cable 1978: 163).

The paradigms of ME strong verbs surviving into EModE exhibit extensive regularization. The following tendencies, apparent in EModE variation, are especially conspicuous:

1   Loss of the functionless alternation of two past forms (1st and 3rd sg. as against the plural) of the *was:were* type. Only traces remain of this alternation in early EModE texts (*foond:founden*, etc.).

2   Levelling of consonantal alternants; compare the voiced fricative in PrE *rose, gave* with the earlier *roos* (T19B/3) and

3af (T19A/16). Vestigial alternation is found in EModE *seethe:sod:sodden, leese:lorn (cf. was:were).*

3   The tendency often led to a two-form system in which the preterite was brought into line with the participle (less often vice versa) *get:got < got* vs. *hold:held > held.* T2 retains older *vnderstande:-stod:-stonden/-stande*; t39 the participle *holden.*

These tendencies were influenced by various factors that differ from one verb to the other (frequency, rhyming analogies, influences cutting across verb classes, and stigmatization of some forms by grammarians). Moreover, no consistent selection was made from the existing variants, which means that the EModE standardization process bequeathed a heterogeneous set to the eighteenth-century grammarians (see Lowth 1762: 64–90).

It is especially remarkable that, despite grammarians and the written tradition in general, many verbal paradigms nevertheless adopted new weak forms. The following strong forms were still common in EModE, even though weak forms came to predominate as time went on: *glide, glode; creep, crope, cropen; seethe, sod, sodden; leese, lorn; climb, clomb; help, holp, holpen; delve, dolve, dolven; melt, moulte, molten* T49/20; *carve, corve; thresh, throshen; yield, yolden; wash, washen; wax, wox, waxen.*

Certain historically weak verbs also had strong forms: *snow, snew; crow, crew; row, rown* (all patterned on *blow, grow, etc.*); or *sew* and *show*, which still have mixed paradigms. A much smaller number of verbs exhibited the opposite development, adopting strong forms on the basis of analogy; apart from those above, *dig, spit* and *stick* changed over to the strong class as late as the sixteenth century.

The forms of *write* may serve to exemplify EModE variation. The regular preterite was *wrote*, which co-existed with *writ* (from the past participle) and *wrate* (patterned on *gave, brake*, etc.). The regular participle was *written* or *writ*; it co-existed with *wrote* (from the preterite).

In paradigms of the *bear* type, the regular preterite *bare* (t51/1) lost its phonetic distinctiveness as a consequence of the GVS and was in consequence replaced by *bore* (from the past participle), a form which may have been stigmatized as colloquial (Samuels 1972: 172–3). Hypercorrection would then have led to *a* also in *wrate* though *o* was the form historically justified in this paradigm. Even though *spake*, etc., were familiar from the Bible (cf. T60/68), *bore, spoke* established themselves after 1600, and the analogical forms *wrate, drave* were discontinued. (*Wrate*, etc., cannot be explained as northern/Scots forms; in Scots the vowel was regular, cf. *wrait* T51/24, *abaid* T36/88.)

The past participle: two forms merged in fourteenth-/fifteenth-century London English, southern *ibore* and northern *boren*. After loss of unstressed *i-*, many verbs wavered between -*(e)n* and Ø endings. Again, it is hardly possible to state the rules of selection according to which, in later EModE, one form came to be accepted as standard for each verb. In most cases, the phonological make-up appears to have been decisive – thus -*(e)n* is frequent after stops (*written, spoken*), but Ø after nasals (*run; found* – EModE also *founden*, t39). Isolated PrE adjectives derived from past participles are often witnesses of EModE alternatives (*bounden, drunken, sodden*).

5.6.2 Weak verbs

The distinctive feature of weak verbs is that the preterite and past participle are formed by the addition of [d ~ t ~ əd] (Ø in the case of a few verbs ending in a dental), with or without a change of stem vowel. In ME, weak verbs can be classified as either regular (with [-əd-] or [-d-]) or irregular. After [ə] was lost in these environments in the sixteenth century, the following new allomorphic types developed: ME [haːtəd] > EModE [hæːtəd]; ME [luvəd] > EModE [luvd]; ME [pasəd] > EModE [past] with assimilation of [d] to [t] after [s] (but note that Hart documents widespread variation as late as 1570; cf. Lass, forthcoming). The spelling of these regular verbs varies in EModE; phonetic spellings (*ed, 'd, d, 't, t*) are frequent, but some texts have *ed* throughout (as in PrE).

Ø is found in verbs ending in a dental, which have no inflexional marking in PrE either, e.g. *cast*, but also in the participle *lifte* (T19A/32), *up-lift* (T34/28). On the other hand, there are regularizations such as *puttide* T19B/22, which were not accepted into the later standard. The Ø class was temporarily enlarged by verbs of Latin provenance, first borrowed as participles (cf. the Scots participles *direct* T53/34 and *educate* T53/40) and later also used as base forms until inflexion patterned on the *hate* type became common (7.3.3).

The number of irregular weak verbs was almost identical with that in PrE (of the type *brought, sold, sent, dealt*), but there were also forms such as *wrought* 'worked' (T30/65); *caught* was common, but regular *catcht* also occurred.

Other variants of the preterite, which had not yet been functionally defined (*he ate/was eating, did eat*, see 6.5), were more or less equivalent to the simple form. Such alternatives could be used when tense marking was otherwise unclear or the correct form of the simple preterite in doubt. Thus the forms *did eat* and *did lift* were the only forms used in the AV; cf. also the frequent occurrence of the type *did separate* (T48/58–9, cf. 6.6).

In early Scots a phonological rule barred word-final clusters of stop + /t/ so that the preterites of verbs like *stop* or *lack* were unmarked. (This rule also applied to early loans such as *suspeck, obieck* in T36/8, 31.) Tense marking was achieved by transference of *it* from the *hatit* 'hated' pattern, and later extended to the majority of preterites/participles (except those with an /-s/ or /-ʃ/ stem such as *purchest; nurist, banyst, opprest, wincust* in T36).

Study questions

Q24 Are the Scots personal pronouns used in T28, T29, T36, T45 and T51 identical with those of EModE?

Q25 Give a list of the forms of pronouns used in T31B; concentrate on second-person forms and make use of further Shakespearean texts.

Q26 Analyse the arguments relating to the use of *thou* in T50, contrasting it with usage in other seventeenth-century texts (Finkenstaedt 1963).

Q27 Test the frequencies of *-eth* vs. *-(e)s* for the verbal ending of the third person singular in the present tense in texts of various genres dating from 1570 to 1620. Can the distribution of the two forms in T26/43–68 be explained?

Q28   Compare the forms of strong verbs used by Spenser and Shakespeare and in the AV (Sugden 1936, Franz 1939).

Q29   Comment on the Scots participle forms *delicat, insert, cuttit* (T28) and *cumd* (T29/9).

6   Syntax

6.1 General problems of description

6.1.1 Introductory

The ModE system of inflexional morphology was already present in outline by 1430 and reached its final form by 1630. By contrast, syntactical developments occurring in the EModE period were so fundamental that it has rightly been claimed that "Modern English syntax begins with Dryden". Though there were many reasons for these changes, they were chiefly connected with the emerging standard's need for functional expansion and stylistic differentiation in new written forms of communication in English and in the expression of complex thought in various fields of scholarly discourse. This meant that new patterns developed:

1   to make up for inadequacies in the linguistic system that had arisen in ME;
2   to provide an adequate mode of expression for various topics, stylistic levels and fields of discourse;
3   to imitate (and from the seventeenth century also to rival) the beauty and flexibility of the Latin language.

In syntax, as in the expansion of the vocabulary, the primary aim of the sixteenth century was first to overcome the inadequacy, and then the inelegance, of the vernacular.

If T2, Caxton's original text (which displays the parataxis so characteristic of ME syntax), is compared with texts after 1580 (e.g. T7), the increase in complex sentence structures becomes apparent. This is evident in sentence length and depth, in the more specific use of prepositions and participles, and also in stricter adherence to the sequence of tenses and accuracy in the use of

95

mood. Most of this is demonstrably due to the influence of Latin, whose function as the language of scholarship was now being taken over by EModE and which provided the model of flexibility and precision English needed in order to be able to function as a modern standard language.

6.1.2 State of research and model of description

There is no adequate model available which could be used to describe synchronically the wide range of EModE syntactic structures on sentence and text levels, and which is capable of taking account of the great number of textual varieties and the social differences between individual authors and intended audiences, and also of dealing diachronically with the drastic changes in syntactic conventions as well as the rapid succession of literary styles in the period between 1500 and 1700. Pilot studies have so far investigated only small, specific areas of EModE. Synchronic differences in sentence and text structure are (*inter alia*) determined by the following factors (cf. 6.9.2):

1   the subject matter (T6 vs. T49);
2   the degree to which rhetorical conventions have been adopted (T7 vs. T2, T48);
3   whether a text was meant for publication (T40, T42, T50) and whether indeed it was originally a written text at all (T39, but also T31);
4   the function of a text (e.g. instructions in T49, a public address/proclamation in T37, T38);
5   formal differences (metrical, rhymed, prose);
6   differences between various literary genres such as lyric poetry, epic poetry, the drama, expository prose, and the related question of stylistic levels;
7   differences between an original text and a translation;
8   the influence of certain stylistic traditions (types of rhetorical elements and structures used; archaisms and quotations, etc.).

Geographical differences, so conspicuous in a comparison of the orthography and lexis of English and Scottish texts, appear to be negligible in the field of syntax.

Certain very important features which first appeared in EModE and gave rise to PrE patterns remain to be investigated. They are outlined below.

1   Part-of-speech classification was syntax-based rather than morphological in EModE, i.e. it depended increasingly on the position and function of an element within the sentence. This created new ways of filling certain positions such as the premodifier slot between determiner and noun. The chronological development of the new possibilities and restrictions (e.g. that of premodifying participles) is not at all clear.

2   The replacement of a verb by a verb + noun group (*to swim – to have a swim*) appears to have first become moderately frequent in EModE.

3   Participial, gerundial and infinitival clauses increasingly replaced finite adverbial and relative clauses – an economy more apparent than real since it involves the loss of tense and mood marking. The origin of such stylistic features (in the language of chanceries and lawyers' documents? cf. T37) and the history of their spread remain obscure.

4   The greater rigidity of word order in EModE created the necessity for alternative means of topicalization (at least in written English, in which intonation cannot serve to clarify the meaning) such as passive transformations and cleft constructions. Were these devices fully developed in EModE or are they features of more recent English?

5   The basic functions of aspectual contrast appear to have been established by the end of the EModE period. To what extent were the greater refinement and the obligatory use of the aspect system developments of the eighteenth century?

6   How far can modern methods of text linguistics be applied to individual EModE texts, and also to establishing text types diachronically?

The following discussion will be based on a model that is structuralistic in that syntactic units are identified and classified and the function of each within the higher unit is described. This model involves a hierarchy of levels in which the 'sentence' is particularly important (even though it is not always easy to determine what constitutes a sentence in EModE and to delimit it, separating it off from the surrounding paragraph (T7)).

However, EModE lacks many firmly established syntactic rules of a modern type. It is therefore necessary to describe tendencies and frequencies, giving due consideration to those that developed into obligatory rules in the eighteenth century and also accounting for those that obviously diverge from PrE and are thus specific to the period.

6.1.3 *The value of contemporary descriptions* (Michael 1970, Padley 1985)

> t38 Now the English speech though it be *rich, copious* and
> *significant*, and that there be divers Dictionaries of it,
> yet under favour, I cannot call it a regular language in
> regard though often attempted by som choice wits, ther
> 5 could never any Grammar or exact Syntaxis be made of it.
>
> 1630

The tradition of grammars of English (with those for foreigners often written in Latin) started in 1582 with Mulcaster and slowly increased during the seventeenth century, reaching a peak in the eighteenth. For his survey Michael used 2 grammars dating from the sixteenth century, 9 for the period 1601–50, 25 for 1650–1700, but 9 + 17 + 35 + 81 + 93 for periods of twenty years in the eighteenth century. Since grammarians of the time were chiefly concerned with classifying parts of speech (and parsing), it would appear natural to base a description on their categories, methods and materials. However, their descriptions should not be adopted uncritically – for the reasons named above (4.1.1), but also because their purposes were different from ours.

The medieval division of the *trivium* into grammar, rhetoric and logic, passed on to Renaissance grammatical theory by Petrus Ramus (2.8.1), meant that 'grammar' was largely identical with the grammar of the word (its inflexion, congruence and government; see Michael 1970).

Grammar was the *ars recte dicendi*, but rhetoric the *ars bene dicendi*, "bene" including "recte": the numerous rhetorical rules comprised advice on 'wrong' grammar, but also formulated deviances permitted by poetical licence.

Moreover, most grammarians relied on Latin categories, a dependence that did not lessen until after the Civil War. This meant that existing EModE forms were incorrectly interpreted because they were equated with Latin structures (as, obviously, in the case of the emergent vernacular distinction between preterite and perfect). It also meant that forms not paralleled in Latin were tacitly omitted, possibly because grammarians were not really aware of them (as in the case of the developing functionalization of *do*, 6.6, or the nascent aspectual differences between the simple and expanded forms). Moreover, most early grammarians did not include a chapter on what is now called 'syntax'; Gil and Ben Jonson are praiseworthy exceptions to the rule.

Many EModE writers' great dependence on Latin structures also makes it legitimate to consider whether certain constructions, such as absolute participles, 'accusative and infinitive' and some types of relative clauses are not best described with Latin terms since they are deliberate transfers by writers who were competent bilinguals and in whose usage English and Latin syntax may have merged to some extent.

6.1.4 *The problems of parts of speech*

Since inflexion and the number of word forms – for EModE writers the central concern of grammar – vary according to the parts of speech, their classification became an important topic of EModE grammar. In these attempts, the Latin-style classification according to morphological criteria was slowly giving way to definitions based on syntactic functions, with all possibilities occurring in different degrees of mixture:

(a) formal (morphological) classification;
(b) syntactic classification, based on the function of the element in the sentence;
(c) semantic classification, which relates parts of speech and categories of meaning.

The problem had become urgent in EModE because of:

1 the loss of most inflexions and homonymic clashes between many of those that remained, so that not only base forms but also most inflected tokens became

homonymous (*work*, *works*, but *worketh*, *worked*, *working*);
2 the great number of new zero derivations (7.5.6) which considerably increased the number of those inherited from OE and ME;
3 the expanded range of syntactic functions (determined only by position in the sentence) that a part of speech may have without change of word class, e.g. the increasing uses of nouns or adverbs as premodifiers. (T33/20 *choycest* and T3/48 *chieffest*, with change of word class, are exceptions.)
4 the neutralization of the transitive:intransitive distinction in many verbs – the core meaning being common to both functions, position in the sentence must clarify the syntactic meaning.

The loss of inflexions made the distinction between nouns and adjectives also largely a matter of syntax. A noun became obligatory as the head of an NP in EModE, especially in the singular (6.2.1); at least a dummy (*man*, *thing*, *one*) is necessary. Adjectives, incapable of number distinction, could from EModE on occur as heads only in certain expressions (*the poor*, *the sublime*).

A contrary development, however, is observable in the case of adverbs: in English, unlike German (in which adverbs are defined syntactically), marking gradually became obligatory for derived adverbs, most slowly where they modified adjectives or adverbs (*exceeding well*, cf. 5.3).

6.1.5 Syntactic interference from Latin

Transfers from Latin were only natural in a period in which Latin grammar was the foundation of all linguistic instruction in the grammar schools. Such influences are found on all syntactic levels; however, they are most frequent and most conspicuous in the verb phrase (government), at clause level (use of participles and gerunds), at sentence level (tense sequence, cohesion) and finally in the rhetorical structure of the text as a whole. It is sometimes difficult or impossible to decide whether or not a syntactic feature was deliberately borrowed from Latin, especially if there were similar native constructions.

Milton provides a good example of how thoroughly a style can be moulded by the deliberate use of Latinisms. His early English poems and political prose exhibit little Latin influence, but his *Paradise Lost*, in which he emulated Virgil, is full of it (T34, specimens complemented from other texts):

1   The use of 'absolute' participles (Latin *abl. abs.*): *Satan except* (T34/75).
2   Word order (such as fronted object with verb in end position): *which filching* Cicero *with a large discourse in his booke* de Oratore *defendeth* (T12/102–3).
3   The use of adjectives as nouns.
4   Relative connectives: *Which when Beelzebub perceiv'd* (T34/74).
5   Double negation as emphatic affirmation.
6   The absolute comparative: *Her prouder steed* 'very proud' (T21/70); *Thy weaker Novice* 'too weak' (T24/30).
7   A noun in the genitive (represented in EModE by *of*) as the complement of a present participle to describe a permanent quality (cf. Latin *patriae amans*): *most loving of Antiquity* (T14/20).
8   The most extraordinary borrowing is that of the syntactic rule which makes it impossible to have a relative clause dependent on a superlative. Milton's imitation reads: *Beelzebub ... then whom ... none higher sat* (T34/74).

It is these syntactic borrowings, with which he intended to achieve a truly epic style, together with his use of the 'Latin' meanings of certain older loanwords (e.g. *aspect* for 'mien, expression', T34/76) that give his work its Latinized character – all without excessive numbers of Latin loanwords.

6.1.6 *The influences of rationalism*

The later seventeenth century brought to the English language a greater regularity and logical clarity. All levels of grammar were affected, ranging from spelling to text-syntax, and this without any clear indication that the grammarians and school teachers were responsible for the change. There were tendencies to introduce etymological spellings, to differentiate between homophones in writing, to avoid 'unnecessary' words, hybrid word-formations (such as *unperfect*) and homonyms and excessively polysemous words. However, syntax is most affected by endeavours to achieve unambiguous clarity, as is illustrated by Sprat's goals in T17 and Dryden's criticism of Elizabethan dramatists in T15. They can be summarized as follows (Knorrek 1938):

1 Stricter regulation of number and concord.
2 Precise delimitation of the genitive and the *of* paraphrase; final banishment of the 'possessive dative'.
3 Consistent morphological marking of derived adverbs.
4 Functionalization of the use of *do*.
5 Obligatory inversion following a sentence-initial negative adverb.
6 Stigmatization of double negation.
7 Proscription of the double comparative and superlative.
8 Differentiation between the uses of *who* and *which*.
9 Avoidance of redundant pronouns (anaphoric or cataphoric).
10 Regulation of the distinction between *will* and *shall*.
11 Stricter use of tenses, including differentiation between past and present perfect.
12 The introduction of an obligatory distinction between the simple and progressive aspects.
13 A decline in the occurrence of the subjunctive following *if*, *though* (the conjunction alone being sufficient marking).

Note that these developments started in the later seventeenth century, but continued all through the eighteenth. In consequence, they were much less influential in America, which means that some important differences in usage between BrE and AmE can be acccounted for by the historical facts described here.

6.2 The noun phrase (NP) (Barber 1976: 225–35)

6.2.1 The head of the NP

In EModE the constituents of an NP and their sequence were more or less the same as in PrE; however, the following differences deserve mention.

A noun (marked for number) became obligatory as head in

EModE: adjectives, except in certain idiomatic expressions required a dummy head (*man/men, thing(s)*) or (from 1500) pronominal *one(s)* (T18D/3–5, though the plural was attacked as 'illogical' in the seventeenth century, T15/99. *One* came to have the double function of avoiding repetition of nouns (with persons and countables) or of being an independent dummy. Jespersen (1909–49: II.248) mentions the pun directed at newly married couples: "May all your troubles be little ones."

Which adjectives were permitted as heads and in which special functions was not as firmly regulated in EModE as it is in PrE; therefore EModE usage is sometimes surprising: *this last sort of ambitious and enuious* (T7/41); *the learned foren* (T8/150); *naturall* 'the vernacular' (T8/158); *originals* 'origins' (T10/115, T11/16). More frequent were EModE uses of the generalized singular (for things) or plural (for persons). However, for the latter, plural marking varied; cf. Jespersen's quote (II, 234) from Fielding: "We moderns are to the ancients what the poor are to the rich." From the sixteenth century, the addition of *-one, -body, -thing* was obligatory with singular uses of *some, any, no* and *every*, too.

6.2.2 Articles and pronominal determiners

From 1500 the use of *a(n)* became common in phrases such as *It is a custom* (*folly, honour, labour, pity, pleasure, shame, wonder*) and *He is a lawyer*.

The definite article was used (in contrast to PrE usage) with parts of the body; cf. the alternation of articles and possessive pronouns in T46/19–31.

Different types of pronominal determiner could co-occur freely in EModE: *this your handiwork* (T5/34; cf. T5/36, T6/81, T10/30, T18C/105); *euerie his preface* (T8/80); *such his purpose* (T23/53); *all and euery his subiectes* (T37/56); also cf. *this her Maiesties commaundement* (T38/25) and *other some* (T23A/65). But the usual modern construction is also found: *This period of mine* (T8/1).

6.2.3 Types of attributes and their positions

Nouns were commonly modified by adjectives and participles; these normally preceded the noun, but postposition of a single adjective was more common in EModE than today, and not confined to legal and poetic registers: *a thyng excusable* (t39/14); *profe reasonable* (T3/45); *Epistle Dedicatory* (T23); *towne corporate* (T38/8). As in PrE, expanded constructions normally followed the head: *Things unattempted yet in Prose or Rhime* (T34/16); *with Head up-lift above the wave* (T34/28).

Split constructions were rarer (and were becoming even more so towards the end of the EModE period): *the translated Bibles into the vulgar tonges* (T18C/40–1); *with fixed Anchor in his skaly rind* (T34/41). As is shown by the translation of Matthew 13.47 (in Görlach 1982: 164), this construction is already found in OE.

The fact that the position before the noun was commonly reserved for simple adjectives meant that the use of premodifying expanded participles could be combined with other elements of poetic diction to create a poeticism of expression as in *night-founder'd Skiff* (T34/39; cf. 7.5.2).

If there was more than one adjective, one could be postponed (without addition of *one(s)*): *a rare younge man and a wise* (T41/85).

Freer use of nouns as premodifiers increased in EModE, but it was infrequent in comparison with PrE; compare, however, *neighbour* (T17/104) used in this position, where the corresponding adjective would be obligatory today.

Genitives preceded the head; if they were expanded, a split construction was common in ME (Chaucer: *of euery shires ende of Engelond*) and possible as late as Shakespeare (*the Archbishops grace of York*). However, from the fifteenth century continuous constructions became regular, premodifying as group genitives, or appended as *of* + NP (5.2.2). Prepositional attributes and clauses followed the head; relative clauses were, however, more often separated from their antecedent than in PrE.

Poetic language must again be treated separately: postposition of adjectives was more frequent and non-use of the article a popular stylistic feature of sixteenth-century poetry.

6.3 The verb phrase (VP)

6.3.1 Government

Verbs are traditionally classified on the basis of their complements: as transitive if a direct object is obligatory, otherwise as intransitive or absolute. This distinction is not possible with poly-functional verbs such as some inherited from OE (*break, burst, bow*) and a few French loans (*cease, join*). The existence of these verbs and the growing importance of sentence structure (cf. 6.1.4) meant that in the fifteenth and sixteenth centuries many transitive verbs acquired an intransitive function, too (*breed, bend, compare, close, divide, drop, fill, open*).

Transitive uses of traditionally intransitive verbs were rarer; they are found with verbs of motion, where the locative comple-ment is the direct object: *if ye designe were ariv'd thus far* (T16/128); *walke the night* (T31B/93); cf. *depart* (*this life*), *banish* (*the court*). Some of these uses are likely to have been literary (*waite the Queen*, T21/69); they are frequent in Milton's *Paradise Lost*, where the syntax is often modelled on the corresponding Latin structures.

6.3.2 Intransitive verbs

In OE and ME, intransitive verbs (especially those of motion) formed perfect and pluperfect forms – where already recorded – with the auxiliary *be*, but from ME onwards, *have* encroached upon *be*, a change that was far advanced by 1700 but not com-pleted before 1850, *go* and *come* being among the last verbs to be affected (cf. Rydén and Brorström 1987, and T18D/25, T15/150, T17/60). Shakespeare still normally uses *be* with *flee, retire, enter, meet, creep, go, ride, run* (Franz 1939: 513–15). The selection of *be* or *have* was partly determined by whether the action or the resultant state was to be stressed, but was also influenced by a great many other factors (Fridén 1948, cf. Barber 1976: 262).

6.3.3 Reflexivity

The reflexive relation between the action and the actor-subject was often expressed in EModE (as in OE, ME and in French, which may have served as a pattern) even where the marking is redundant, as after verbs of motion and of feeling (*come, go, hie, return, run; despair, doubt, fear, repent, wonder*). After 1700, reflex-ive pronouns went out of use not only with these verbs; reflexives also became rarer where they were in contrast with a direct object (*tourne hym* (T3/57) = PrE *turn*), though cf. deviant use in *rots it selfe* (T31B/118).

6.3.4 'Impersonal' verbs (Trnka 1930: 54ff.)

A person not looked upon as actor can be made object complement, the subject position being filled by *it/there*, the name of a thing or an infinitive (*if it would like you to extend*, T4/56). The loss of noun inflexion had made constructions of the type *the king liketh the crown* ambiguous, or rather the increasing frequency of SVO order had led to a re-interpretation of *the king* as the subject of the sentence. In the sixteenth century unambiguous sentences with a pronoun in first position (type *me thinketh*, T25/9) were adapted to the SVO pattern so that impersonal constructions with the verbs *ail, chance, list, please* and *think*[2] sounded archaic by 1600, and were obsolete by 1660. The transition phase is illustrated by T25/6–7, where both constructions are used with *need*: "there needeth no Iuie-bush. The right Coral needeth no colouring". Accordingly, Spenser uses the impersonal construction as an archaizing feature in forms such as *me behoueth, me liefer were, was him loth, it pitties me* and *her listed*; T43/55 "it shall ... behoue him ... to ..." could be an instance of hypercorrect formal style.

6.3.5 Phrasal verbs

In ME the original alternation of prefixed or postposed adverbs (*outride*: *ride out*) was regularized in favour of postposition. This development also tended to level the distinction between adverb (part of the phrasal verb) and preposition (introducing an NP): *he went up/the hill = he went/up the hill*. The earlier type quickly declined in EModE: the last survivors of the type *outride* 'ride out' were replaced by verbs of the class *outride*[2] 'to ride faster than' from 1580. Postposition also became more frequent in derivation (as in *looker-on, come-at-able*).

The following uses exemplify EModE postposition:

1   use with the passive (possible from the fourteenth/fif-
     teenth centuries, cf. Brose 1939 and 6.5.7): *vnlookt for Age*
     (T20/107); *long taried for answer* (T42/16); *spoken against*

(T17/59); *to be excepted against* (T18D/5); *wondred at of the best* (T23A/13);

2   with gerunds/verbal nouns: *so the sho holde the plucking on, nor I, so my labours last the running ouer* (T25/53–4);

3   with agent nouns: *a priar in at the chinks* (T41/20, colloquial use?);

4   with fronted object (topicalization): *Stories I delight in* (T41/68–9);

5   with relative clauses (necessary with *that* and Ø). Alternative solutions were possible (preposition + *which*, or *whereof, -at, -by*, etc.), which makes late seventeenth-century criticism of the 'postponed preposition' possible. Compare Dryden's self-criticism attached to his comment on Ben Jonson's *frighted from* and *reach unto* (T15/73–82).

Pre-position was regarded as archaic or poetic from the late sixteenth century: *she vp gan reare* (T24/101, in combination with archaic *gan* and obsolescent meaning of *reare*); *with Head up-lift* (T34/28).

6.4 Case, word order and prepositions

6.4.1 Case-marking and word order

With the exception of the genitive singular, there was no case-marking of nouns in EModE; the historical functions of case had long been taken over by word-order and prepositions. However, there were many more deviances from SVO word order and variant uses of prepositions than in PrE.

SVO had become the normal word order in affirmative statements by 1500; a few types of deviant structure had, however, not been fully adapted to the dominant pattern:

1   After sentence-initial adverb (*then, now; here, there; so, yet;* etc.) the verb (or auxiliary) came second in most cases in Chaucer (compare German word order). In EModE the frequencies of SVO and VSO order vary greatly with author and text type (cf. Jacobsson 1951: 96–7): Roper, More and Sidney prefer inversion (85–67 per cent), other authors have equal proportions (Puttenham, Deloney, Nashe, Lyly), but Caxton's 8 per cent almost corresponds

to modern practice. Inversion became very rare in the seventeenth century (with the exception of Browne, Raleigh and Bunyan, cf. T60/8, 12, 61, etc.); the modern state of affairs was arrived at with Dryden.

1a   The above remarks relate to prose; much greater freedom is found in EModE poetry.

1b   After long sentence-initial adverbials the length of con-stituents (i.e. the rhythmical factor) often plays a part (T15/178); inversion sounds natural in T10/1 but more forced in T10/2.

2   If the initial adverb was (semantically) negative or restric-tive, inversion became obligatory in the seventeenth century.

3   Fronting of objects (OSV, more rarely OVS, T44/184ff.) was common in ME and not unusual until Dryden (T15/146), Bunyan and Swift (Jacobsson 1951: 135), though specific reasons for the position (such as topicaliza-tion, actuality; euphony, rhythm) cannot be discovered in all individual cases. Frequently fronting was used for tex-tual coherence (*this, that, such*; compare *which* in Latinized relative construction, T7/27).

3a   Alternative means of topicalization, such as passive trans-formations or cleft constructions, were possible in EModE, but used more rarely: *But it is not their Plots which I meant, principally to tax* (T15/45); cf. *And for my Soule, what can it doe to that?* (T31B/53). But *Him hath God exalted* (T19A/70) corresponding with modern *He it is whom God has exalted* (T19A/90).

6.4.2 *Prepositions*

Prepositions serve to express various syntactic relations between constituents of the sentence, especially within expanded NPs (most frequently *of*, but other prepositions are also found) and as part of VPs, where they introduce obligatory complements and optional adverbial phrases.

Two tendencies are evident in EModE as a consequence of the increasing importance of prepositions in written communication: the semantic range of existing prepositions was becoming restricted, and more specific prepositions were being newly formed or borrowed.

The development of EModE *of* can be seen as representative of the restriction of meanings:

1   In ME *of* was the most frequent preposition used to mark the agent in passive constructions; it dominated well into the late sixteenth century. Phrases such as *A terme borrowed of our common lawyers* (T11/113) were ambiguous, but *by* already predominated in this function in Puttenham (compare the variation in *allowed of/by* in T11/100, 128).

2   *of* was used without difference in spelling for PrE *off*, but was replaced in this locative function by *from* or *out of*.

3   From the seventeenth century, *about* frequently replaced *of* following *say, tell*, etc. and meaning 'about, with regard/reference to', etc. This made *about* less useful with locative meaning so that it was widely replaced in turn by *(a)round*.

4   It follows that *of* became restricted to uses equivalent to Latin genitives (apart from certain idiomatic expressions) and itself came to contrast with the English genitive in the course of the seventeenth century (cf. 5.2.2).

Other prepositions exhibit similar changes, which means that a comparison with PrE usage reveals many differences (see the list in Partridge 1969: 100–10).

In view of the fact that the class of prepositions is now a relatively closed one, the increase in prepositions and prepositional phrases in EModE is quite remarkable: the explanation for this phenomenon is again most likely to be the need for greater precision in increasingly written communication. New units came from the following sources:

1   Former participles, developing from Latinized absolute constructions, such as:
    14th century *considering, during*
    15th century *according to*
    16th century *concernynge* (T19A/35), *touching* (T7/47, T12/63), *sauing for* (T11/1)
    17th century *pending*
    18th century *respecting, regarding*
    19th century *including, excluding, owing to*

2   Phrases of the structure prep. + noun + prep. (mostly *of*). Since the semantic content of the noun remained transparent, it is difficult to determine exactly when the phrase in question achieved preposition status. As with no. 1, many of the phrases listed below were, and still are, restricted to written English, or took some time to become established in speech:

14th century *for the sake of, in respect of, by reason of, because of, apart from*

15th century *in spite of, in/with regard to*

16th century *in consideration of, in place of, in/with reference to*

17th century *on account of, in front of, in advance of*

18th century *on (the) occasion of*

The intended precision could be endangered by such innovations becoming polysemous themselves, as evidenced by *in respect of*, which added to its old meaning 'in comparison with' (T7/73) the new ones 'with reference to', 'in view of/because of', 'considering/since that', 'in case' (all sixteenth century; source: OED).

A similar expansion took place in the case of conjunctions, and indeed many of the newly coined prepositions were also used as conjunctions, sometimes in combination with *that*, just as *after, until, till, since, before* and *because* had come to be so used in ME.

6.5 Tense, mood and aspect

6.5.1 Introductory

The range of EModE forms was still being reduced as regards mood on the one hand, and on the other had not been fully expanded as regards tense and aspect, nor had the functional distinctions found in PrE been fully established: many forms were still in free variation (i.e. could be selected in accordance with stylistic, rhythmical, metrical, semantic or other personal preference) and had not become fixed by usage and the prescriptive efforts of grammarians.

6.5.2 Tense

EModE was progressing towards the PrE tense system, which reflects three time points: the point of the event, the point of speech and the point of reference. In EModE, not all the necessary forms were available, and the Latin model (whose tense system is structured quite differently) was a hindrance rather than a help in the setting up of descriptive categories by EModE grammarians or in imitations of Latin style.

The EModE present tense served to refer to present time, timelessness, and also future time: *as long as letters endure* (T7/76); *When the age ... is dead ..., there will another succeede* (T8/18). It was used instead of the past tense (as the so-called 'historic present') in popular styles, as in the alternation of present and preterite in T32 (*got ... gets ... goes ... quoth*, 10–21), or in imitation of Latin models in translations of Virgil's *Aeneid* (T21, translation of Book IV, 129–34). It could also express the perfect time relation, stressing the result of the action, as in *He that cometh lately...* (T4/14–15).

Tenses referring to past time: the distinctions made in PrE were not yet obligatory. Thus use of the preterite was still possible for past-before-past time (especially following *after*, T7/55), the present perfect was common instead of the very rare future perfect (*till Custome has made*, T15/156), and the semantic distinction of past:perfect was not fully established (cf. Fridén 1948: 27–37). The co-existence of these two *forms* (and misleading classifications by contemporary grammarians on the basis of Latin distinctions) made erroneous interpretations possible. Although there are indications of a system evolving towards that of PrE (see Visser 1963–73: II, 751), the very low frequency of perfect forms, and the compatibility of preterites with *since* and *never* (and, more rarely, compatibility of the perfect with adverbs indicating actions completed in the past), show that regularity had not been achieved. Sometimes hypercorrect marking of 'past' is found (T31A/20–1); unreal *scripsisse* is even rendered as *to had vrytin* in T45/24.

Only after a strict semantic differentiation of past: perfect had been established in the early eighteenth century, did the sequence of tenses (especially in subject and conditional clauses) become possible: present/perfect/future as against preterite/pluperfect/second future (see Brunner 1960–2: II, 305).

Future time: It is uncertain whether 'future' existed as a 'pure' tense in ME or whether all instances of *shall/will* should not be classified as modals (statements with future reference always being accompanied by desire, expectation, obligation, fear, etc.), but the semantic weakening of *will* (originally 'wish') and *shall* (originally 'be obliged to') throughout ME is uncontested. *Shall* appears to be the more frequent choice in unmarked position in the sixteenth century; it also predominates in biblical style. The distinction between *will* (3rd and 2nd person) and *shall* (1st and 2nd person) was required by some seventeenth-century grammarians, but was fully enforced in written standard BrE only in the eighteenth-century prescriptive tradition. However, since all tokens can be explained as expressing modality, the interpretation of individual passages remains problematic.

Note the expression of 'immediate future' (before *be about to* or *be going to* became established) in T27/25 *when he was to driue out Catiline*, or T49/12 *when it is to be eaten*.

6.5.3 *Modality* (Visser 1963–73: 789–95)

Modality expresses the speaker's attitude to the propositional content of a statement; in EModE this could be expressed by intonation and by a variety of complementary markers (sometimes used pleonastically, T32/38–9):

1   inflexion (indicative vs. subjunctive, possibly also tense);
2   conjunctions with modal content (*as, though, if*);
3   introductory formulae (*I wish/I hope that*...) or other contextual markers;
4   modal adverbs (*possibly, probably*);
5   modal verbs (*may, might, should*...);
6   deviation from the sequence of tenses (in direct speech).

A further reduction of inflexional marking (the indicative:subjunctive contrast) became possible, since functional distinctions could be expressed by so many alternative means. The greatly reduced list of subjunctive forms in EModE even caused grammarians to neglect or misunderstand them. On the other hand, calquing of Latin rules led to some expansion of the use of subjunctives in certain texts.

6.5.4 *The subjunctive* (Franz 1939: 521–35)

The subjunctive forms remaining in EModE are: 3rd person present *he take* (as against *he taketh*); 1st–3rd person present *I, thou, he be* (vs. *am, art, is*). Subjunctives were used in EModE main clauses to express 'desire' (alternative: *may*). In subordinate clauses, mainly conditional and concessive but also temporal ones expressing uncertainty about the future (*till, before*), it was also possible to substitute a modal verb (*should, might, may*).

Before 1650 the frequency of the subjunctive varied from one author to the next; no regular distribution according to type of text or style can be determined. Among sixteenth-century texts, T8 and T10 have many specimens: *till decaie ensew* (T8/2), *if lak ... be* (T8/60–2), *tho he be dead* (T8/75), *if ... were* (T8/98), *tho it go, ...* (T8/112). Use declined in the seventeenth century, in particular owing to the influence of the rationalists (6.1.6/13), who argued that modality was sufficiently expressed in the conjunction. Use of the subjunctive remained possible all through the seventeenth century: *If it tempt* (T31B/56), *though ... court it* (T31B/138), *Least that ... take* (T31C/3). Specimens from the late seventeenth century (*if, ... there happen not*, T15/171–3; *though it be*, T16/4) show that Milton's uses in *Paradise Lost* need not be classified as Latinisms: *till ... restore us, and regain* (T34/4–5); *if ... delight* (T34/10–11).

Fronting of subjunctive verbs/auxiliaries (*were, had*) also occurred as an alternative to the *if*-clause: *were I Brutus* (T31D/57); *gyue shee onz but an ey* (T41/52); cf. T15/136, T41/55.

6.5.5 *Modal verbs*

Modal verbs in EModE became restricted to auxiliary function; use as a 'full' verb was continued only with expressions of direction (*you shall along with me*) and with *can* 'know': *lerne no frenssh ne can none* (T1/34). Other rare constructions are not to be found any later than the early sixteenth century (specimens quoted from OED, *s.v.* MAY):

infinitive   *that appered ... to mow stande the realme in great stede* (1533)

present participle   *Maeyinge suffer no more the loue...* (1556)
past participle   *Ye haue mought oftentimes & yet maie desceyue me* (1510)

With the loss of non-finite forms new quasi-modals were introduced or their frequency increased (*to have to, be able to, be going to,* etc.). The PrE marginal modals *dare* and *need* were closer to the central modals in EModE.

The two existing forms of most modals have always had various functions in accordance with the semantics of these verbs. They can play purely tense roles (as they do in the sequence of tenses), but the remote form is also used in polite, less direct statements and requests. The decline of the subjunctive caused an increase in the frequency of the modals in the sixteenth century.

After *mote* was lost from EModE in the early sixteenth century (preserved slightly longer in Scots, T45/36), the system consisted of five pairs (*can, could; dare, durst; may, might; shall, should; will, would*) and three single forms (*must, need, ought*) – plus poetical *list* 'desire', which quickly declined with the loss of the impersonal construction. *Mun, man* is restricted to the north (T29/14), and is anglicized as *must* in T29/29.

A semantic comparison shows that the modals have also changed their meanings since EModE times. EModE *may* means 'is able to', while *can* could not be used to imply permission; *will/would* were volitional, whereas *shall* could signal obligation – not only in biblical texts.

6.5.6 *Aspect* (Nehls 1974; Brunner 1960–2: II, 366–79)

Aspect was the latest verbal category to be developed in English (even though the *expanded form* = EF is already found, as a form, in OE); it is difficult to ascribe a central (or 'core') meaning to it. It is possible that more specialized uses of the EF developed from notions such as 'stressing the duration and intensity of the action as such'; since such early marking would have been optional, it is difficult to pin down. The EF also appears to have had a certain affinity with uses of *do* in the sixteenth century before the two forms were differentiated for individual functions. The restriction of the EF to 'progress of an action' may have been influenced by the gerundial construction of the type *he is a-praying* (*Hamlet* III.3.73), which was very similar in form.

The EF's low frequency in EModE and its incomplete paradigm suggest that the wide range of modern functions cannot have developed yet in EModE. Nehls counted 40 tokens of the EF per 100,000 words in Shakespeare, 120 tokens in Restoration Comedy, but 837 tokens in twentieth-century drama. Not unexpectedly then, specimens in the texts are few and far between: T19A/58 *are standing* is likely to have been patterned on the Latin source (cf. the more literal translation in T19A/39–40); T39/7 *let your plough therfore be going and not cease* could be intended to intensify the action. Intensifying, too, were uses with the imperative, as in T12/141–2 *Bee going … be faring*. (This form was replaced by *do go* in the seventeenth century.) The EF is quite rare until Dryden: *I was thinking of it* (T18H/13).

The total absence from the corpus of instances of the EF indicating 'actual present', its most frequent modern function, is particularly striking.

Complementation of the set of forms was quite slow, too, partly because future-time marking was still optional, as was the past vs. perfect distinction; non-finite forms (including the participle contained in EF) were neutral regarding tense and voice; this produced the following development:

he shows	is -ing	-ed	was -ing
is shown	**is being -n**	was -n	**was being -n**
will –	*will be -ing*	would –	*would be -ing*
will be -n		would be -n	
has -n	*has been -ing*	had -n	*had been -ing*
has been -n		had been -n	
will have -n		*would have -n*	
WILL HAVE		WOULD HAVE	
BEEN -N		BEEN -N	

(Middle E, *Late ME*, EMODE, **1700–1900**)

Fig. 13 The development of aspectual forms, ME–nineteenth century

An apparent dislike of forms which were too long and the existence of alternative ways of expressing aspectual meaning have stood in the way of a complete set of expanded forms to this day.

6.5.7 The passive

Non-finite forms can still be neutral as regards voice, so that the 'passive' need not be marked: *It is easy to see* = 'it is easily seen'; *the book is printing* = 'is being printed'. This was even more common in EModE, even if some authors, following Latin distinctions, were led to mark voice extremely carefully.

The passive transformation was often used to topicalize the object/goal of an action; it is also frequently found in cases in which the agent cannot be expressed, or was intentionally left out. The indefinite agent *me*, *men* had become obsolete by the fifteenth century, and other expressions (such as *people*, *you*, *they*) never became firmly established in all styles, possibly because they remained ambiguous. All this strengthened the passive, especially in types of text in which an impersonal style was preferred, as in scholarly prose: thus the omission of the agent is deliberate in T31B/96–7. *But that I am forbid / To tell the secrets...* and T31B/120 *It's giuen out*. A specific agent is unimportant in T30/47–52 *Some Bookes are to be Tasted*, whereas the choice of the passive is purely stylistic as the agent can be easily supplied in T31A/19, 22: *a thing ... worthie to haue bene wished* [by us] and *it hath bin ordain'd* [by God]. The tendency to mark the passive in participles and infinitives (following Latin patterns) is obvious: *being aduertised ... he came* (T36A/78); *Makbeth ... caused the wife ... to be slaine* (T36A/84).

The frequency of passive constructions was also increased by attributive use in *my long-taried-for answer* (T42/16) and *one thing, not to be passed by* (T17/80). The great freedom with which EModE passive constructions could be used is also demonstrated in *there ought no regard be sooner had* (T33/9).

Since the EF did not occur with passives in EModE, and quasi-modal *get* + participle did not develop until later, and the type *the house is building* was comparatively rare, action and state were not normally distinguished in the passive: *their necks are broken* (T46/19).

6.6 Functions of 'do' (Ellegård 1953; Barber 1976: 263–7)

EModE *do* has a variety of functions well known in PrE: as proverb and operator (*Doe not my Lord*, T31B/50; T3/43, T19B/77, T30/23); and as the result of topicalization of the lexical verb (*& pay it wee did*, T50/54). It can also be a full verb with a wide range of meanings ('make, produce, affect', etc.): *doe wrong* (T19B/74).

Two new functions of *do* arose in the fourteenth/fifteenth centuries, first as a causative verb, then as an optional tense operator. Occasionally the two are found in combination in the late fifteenth century: *(he) ded do shewe to me* (T2/13) 'he had it shown to me'.

Its obvious usefulness for rhyme and metre made this expletory *do* very popular in metrical poetry from the late fifteenth century onwards, replacing synonymous *gin, gan*. 'Empty' *do* is frequent in all sixteenth-century poets: Spenser has eighteen instances in T24/37–108, apart from six of archaizing *gan*. In second-rate poets (but also in Preston's translation, T20/189–212), it is found up to the end of the EModE period.

Do was found in all types of sentences, except when another auxiliary was present (but even then, on occasion, in the fifteenth century). Also note the peculiar Scottish use as a participle: *Had he done wryt* 'had he written' T51/28, cf. T51/51). Its frequency in fifteenth-century prose is, however, below 10 per cent. After that it rose conspicuously, depending on sentence type (declarative:interrogative:imperative; affirmative:negative), as the following graph from Ellegård (1953: 162) shows (based on a representative sample of prose texts; verse is omitted because of the distorting factors mentioned above):

Per cent *do*-forms in various types of sentence

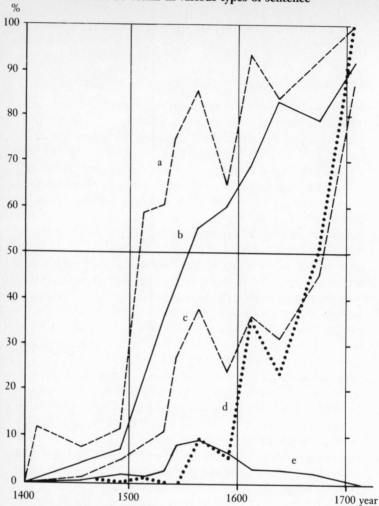

a negative direct questions
b affirmative direct questions
c negative declarative sentences
d negative imperatives
e affirmative declarative sentences

Fig. 14 The development of functional *do*, 1400–1700

These figures show the increasingly functional distribution of *do*, which is likely to be connected with the increasing rigidity of fixed word order in the sixteenth/seventeenth centuries. In questions, two types of construction were found:

Seest thou these things? or feare we thee in vaine V S O V S O	T21/128
Or do those flames … vs affray Aux S O Vb	T21/130
Do we feare in vain / Thy boasted Thunder Aux S Vb O	T21/246–7
Doeth wit reste in straunge wordes, or els standeth it in … Aux S Vb AdvP V S AdvP	T4/70
is not the tongue geuen Aux S Vb	T4/73
Will ye saie it is nedelesse? Aux S Vb O	T8/57

Object questions:

What should we doe? What may this meane? O Aux S Vb O Aux S Vb	T31B/40, 34
What say you to … O V S	

The optional use of *do* c.1500 had two advantages over inversion of the full verb: it made the structure identical with that of sentences containing an auxiliary/modal – possibly the majority of instances – and it preserved the sequence SVb(O) which was important for sentence semantics. It is no surprise, then, that *do* came to be preferred in these patterns, a process that was completed only some two hundred years after it began.

Two other EModE developments appear to be closely related to this: inversion after sentence-initial adverb (6.4.1) was found in 44 per cent of relevant sentences in the years 1370–1500 (Jacobson 1951), but the figure declined to 34 per cent in the sixteenth century and 7 per cent in the seventeenth: again the order preferred was SVO. It is significant that the percentage of inversions is higher with sentence types containing an auxiliary or intransitive verb.

The development of historically impersonal verbs (6.3.4) may also be considered in this connection: here re-interpretation of the initial complement led to SVO order.

In sentences negated by *not* two options were available:

if then you doe not like him ≠ if you need them not
   S Aux N Vb O   S   V   O   N

(T31A/42, 45)

Or, if O is not a personal pronoun: *(he) seeth not the vse* (T3/36); *I say not this* (T11/51). Contrast sentences containing an auxiliary: *I wil not force any man* (T4/36); *I haue not dedicat this ... treatise* (T28/1). This shows that the *do* structure was preferable on three counts: it was identical to the structure of sentences containing an auxiliary; it preserved the contact position Vb–O, and it unambiguously indicated sentence negation (rather than object negation).

The use of *do* remained optional as long as it was not grammaticalized. This does not mean that the distribution of *ate*: *did eat*: *was eating*: *has eaten* was arbitrary or random, but that uses were not obligatory and therefore not fully predictable. Metre, rhyme and a great number of other factors could determine the choice (cf. Samuels 1972: 174).

The use of *did eat*, *did set* throughout the AV is likely to have been influenced by uncertainty in tense formation. *Do* also made the integration of -*ate* verbs from Latin easier (7.5.5); *doth illuminate* avoids the clumsy form *illuminateth* (but cf. *insinuateth*, T31F/26), and *did illuminate* avoids the problem of whether a preterite suffix can be attached to a word form originally a participle. *Do* facilitated inversion in certain circumstances (e.g. with sentence-initial adverbs) and thereby permitted rhythmical variation (e.g. in T13), giving long and complex sentences harmonious and logically transparent balance. Finally, it *could* be used to add emphasis, as in the correction *stung ... did sting* (T31B/121–4) – but far from all occurrences are emphatic. Only after *do* had become the norm in questions and negative sentences, and its optional use in affirmative statements abolished, did the use of *do* for contrastive emphasis become regular in the eighteenth century. Note, however, that the use of non-functional *do/did* lingered on in informal writing to some extent (six instances of *did* in T64/24–57; and cf. Tieken-Boon van Ostade 1987).

6.7 Concord (Franz 1939: 565–75)

After most inflexions had been lost, problems of concord were reduced to a few uncertainties: can the verb be inflected for the singular with two singular subjects forming a logical unit or if a plural subject *follows*, or is a plural verb admissible after a collective noun (formally singular) or after *each, every, either, none, many a* in the subject NP?

EModE use varied – not unexpectedly in a language whose niceties had not been regulated by grammarians; but often content rather than form decided the construction to be used. Stricter attitudes towards concord were adopted by the editors of Shakespeare's *Second Folio*: they removed every single verbal -*s* with plural subjects.

6.8 The syntax of the complex sentence

6.8.1 Introductory

A compound sentence consists of two or more co-ordinate clauses; a complex sentence has at least one main and one subordinate clause, which can be finite or non-finite (infinitival, participial, etc.). Dependent clauses or participial, gerundial and infinitival clauses can appear in subject and object position, and as complement in a prepositional phrase.

How greatly sixteenth-century English syntax needed refining, was felt strongly by the humanists who compared their English prose with that of classical Latin writers such as Cicero. To us, too, it is evident in the clumsiness and imperfect structure found even in authors praised for their style by contemporaries, such as Sir Thomas More in his *Apologye*:

t39   Now then as for other fautes of lesse weyght and toler-
       able, I nothynge douted nor do, but that euery good
       chrysten reader wyll be so reasonable and indyfferent,
       as to pardon in me the thyng that happeth in all other
  5   men, and that no suche man wyll ouer me be so sore an
       audytour, & ouer my bokes suche a sore controller, as to
       charge me with any great losse, by gatherynge to gether
       of many such thynges as are wyth very fewe men aughte re-
       garded, and to loke for suche exacte cyrcumspecyon and
 10 sure syght to be by me vsed in my wrytynge, as exept the

prophetis of god, and Cryste and his apostles, hath neuer
I wene be founden in any mannes elles byfore, that is to
wit to be perfyte in euery poynte clene from all manner
of fautes, but hath alway ben holden for a thyng excus-

15 able, though the reader in a longe worke perceyue that
the wryter haue as Horace sayth of Homere, here and there
some tyme fallen in a litle slomber, in whyche places as
the reader seeth that the writer slept, so vseth he of
courtesy yf he can not slepe, yet for company at the leste

20 wyse, to nappe and wynke with him, and leue his dreme
vnchekked.   1533

6.8.2 *Adverbial clauses* (Franz 1939: 427–73)

EModE exhibits increasing use and intensified semantic differentiation of the subordinating conjunctions in structuring longer
and more complex sentences; this development was particularly
evident in sixteenth-century prose, where imitation of Latin
models was clearly intended. The following conjunctions are
found in EModE (classified semantically):

Semantic relation	Conjunction (italics indicate frequent use with subjunctive)
resultative	(so) that
purposive	*so that, to the end*; *least*
concessive	*(al)though*, albeit, however, for all
comparative	as … as, so … as, as (if)
adversative	whereas
temporal	while(s), when (as), as, *(un)til, before, ere, after*, since
conditional	*if, an(d), so*; *unless*, without, but
causal	as, sith, since, because, for, now, for why, in that
modal	how, as, in that

Almost all conjunctions could be combined with *that*, a practice
which was given up almost entirely, as superfluous, in the late
seventeenth century.

Hypotaxis is especially difficult to handle in cases like T7,
where subordinate (finite) clauses, participial and infinitival
clauses form hierarchies of subordination which reach the seventh
degree of syntactical depth:

Line	Connective	Type of sentence and syntactical depth	Contents/ argument
9	Continuative Clause (CC)	Main Clause (MC)1	A: Causes of the deficiency
10	*for*	MC2	
	then	2/comparative C1	
	and	2/comparative C2	
13	CC	MC3	B1: emergency
13	infinitive	2/infin.C	solutions (internal
14	participle	3/partic.C	consequences)
15	infinitive	4/infin.C	
16	*how*	5/object C	
17	*when*	6/adverb.C	
18	CC	MC4	B2a: external
18	*though*	2/adverb.C	consequences (for the learner)
20	word order	MC5	
21	participle	2/partic.C	
21	*when*	2/adverb.C	
24	CC	MC6	B2b: foreign judgements
25	*whereas*	MC7	C: excuse
26	(specification)	2/parenthesis	
27	CC	MC8	
28	word order	MC9	
28	*when*	2/adverb.C	
29	participle	3/partic.C	
29	∅	4/object C	
30	participle	3/partic.C2	
31	participle	3/partic.C3	
32	participle	4/partic.C	
32	infinitive	4/infin.C	
33	*because*	5/causal C	
34	*if*	6/condit.C	
35	*as*	7/relat.C	
36	*and*	MC10	
36	*so ... that*	2/consec.C	
37	*and*	MC11	
37	*and*	2/consec.C1	
38	∅	2/consec.C2	
39	participle	3/partic.C1	
39	participle	3/partic.C2	

Fig. 15 The structure of a complex sentence (T7/9–40)

6.8.3 Relative clauses

Although the use of various other types of finite and non-finite clauses was on the increase, the relative clause (which was supported by the Latin model) remained the most important type of subordination, especially the non-restrictive relative clause in loose, descriptive writing; cf. Sugden's statement (1936: 55):

> On the evidence of syntax alone, it is quite clear that Spenser's fondness of descriptive clauses, for picturesque details, and elaborations, is much greater than his desire for the purely defining or restrictive clause. His style is revealed as loose, discursive, diffuse, highly-coloured and emotional.

(This statement does not seem applicable to non-literary texts; moreover, the relations between the two types of relative clause changed in the course of the seventeenth century.)

The most frequent EModE relative pronouns were: *(the) which*, *that*, *who(m)* and *∅*; rarer alternatives: *as* (almost exclusively after *such*); *but* (following negation, T22A/1, T26/43); and – in avoidance of clumsy combinations of preposition + *which*, or postposed prepositions – *where*-combinations (-*about*; -*against*; -*at*; -*by* T13/2, T17/84, T18E/15, 17; -*fore* T18E/49; -*in* T13/17, T18C/25, T26/28, T31B/8; -*into*, -*of* T13/66, T18D/44; -*to* T27/42, 74; -*unto*; -*upon* T18E/65; -*with(al)*). Note that the latter were used with non-personal antecedents, and were not restricted to formal style, as are those still in use today. Other relatives were *(the time) when*, *(the cause) why*, *(the way, manner) how*, *(the place) where*, *whence*.

The frequencies of these slowly changed in EModE. Exclusively sixteenth-century are *(the) whiche* + repetition of the antecedent (following Latin patterns): *whiche olde englysshe wordes and vulgars* (T22A/6); *win credit ... which credit, is the neerest step to perswasion: which perswasion ...* (T27/49–50).

Whom was used besides *which* with personal antecedents in the sixteenth century, but the relative *who* was rare before 1550 (not found in Tyndale, and consequently rare in the AV); in the seventeenth century *who*-forms slowly replaced *which* if the antecedent was personal. Since there is no genitive of *which* or *that*, the form *whose* became common with non-personal antecedents at an early date (T3/6).

Which predominated in all types of relative clauses in early sixteenth-century texts, especially in translations, but was only rarely used for persons after the AV of 1611.

That appears to have been preferred in restrictive clauses; its use increased greatly in the AV and in post-Shakespearean drama. Its frequent occurrence in the latter is an indication of its colloquial flavour – which provoked Steele's "Humble Petition of Who and Which" (1711) against the upstart *that*. A typical EModE feature is the use of *that* for 'that which' in nominal relative clauses (T3/35–6, 64), but *that, whyche* is found in the same text (T3/11), as is *that, that* (T3/51). *What* did not become frequent until the seventeenth century.

Ø is rarely found in the sixteenth century. In the text corpus it is relatively frequent only in Sidney: *the matter it works vpon is nothing* (T26/55); *so is the hiest ende it aspires vnto* (T26/60); *for the matter we speake of* (T26/63). In EModE, Ø could be used as subject after *there* or superlatives: *there were an Antony would ruffle...* (T31D/58); *theres noe bodye holdes you* (T12/149); *which is one of the greatest beauties can be found* (T27/90).

Exhaustive investigations and reliable statistics on the distribution of the relative pronouns in EModE are available only for the earliest period (Rydén 1966): at that time, the distribution of *who:which:that* appears to have varied from one author to the next without any regularity. (For Scots, see Romaine 1982.) For the seventeenth century the selective counts quoted by Graband (1965: 288) and Barber (1976: 216, 218) do not provide a satisfactory description.

The syntax of the relative clause was affected considerably by Latin models, as the following features clearly show:

1   the great frequency of relative clauses in the early sixteenth century;

2   the widespread acceptance of the rule that prepositions ought to precede relatives;

3   rare cases of *than* preceding a relative: *then whom ... none higher sat* (T34/74; cf. 6.1.5);

4   the choice of a relative instead of a demonstrative in sentence-initial position (cf. 6.8.4);

5   the occasional telescoping of two relative clauses, a construction susceptible of misunderstanding;

6   the combination of relatives with absolute participles: *which being once vnderstood* (T36A/37), or with 'accusative and infinitive' (T48/40–1).

6.8.4 Continuative clauses (Reuter 1938)

The use of a relative for a demonstrative pronoun introducing a main clause in imitation of a widespread Latin construction ought, strictly, to be treated under text grammar (6.9), but since the distinction between new main clause and relative clause is often uncertain, it is here discussed after relative clauses. (An additional problem is that what constituted a 'sentence' was different in EModE – and Latin – from what it is now; for instance, in T7 the complete treatment of a complex argument is set out within the confines of a single sentence/paragraph.) The CC was particularly frequent in early translations, and then spread to other kinds of formal prose (T7). Spenser made excessive use of it, especially to link individual stanzas (T24/47, 74, 88, 92). Even more remarkable are the occurrences in a private letter (*wiche whan bothe you way*, T42/37) and in the popular jest T32, where the construction contrasts with various colloquial features (T32/19, 20, 59; 7 and 25 are probably better regarded as loosely appended relative clauses). Does this indicate an editor who favoured this stylistic feature without being competent to handle it?

Especially conspicuous, since in conflict with traditional English syntax, is the frequent use of a relative preceding a conjunction: *Which when that warriour heard* (T24/47, cf. Latin *Quae cum miles audivisset*); *Whom when (he) did behold* (T24/74); *which default when as some endeuoured to salue* (T23A/60). The relative can also occur as part of a participial clause: *Which he perceiuing greatly gan reioice* (T24/92); *which being noted by . . . hee was quickly in* George *his pocket: which he perceiuing, wrings . . .* (T32/19–20).

6.8.5 Participial clauses (see Brunner 1960–2: II, 379–83)

The following section deals with clauses containing non-finite verb forms; their use appears to have increased in EModE because of their frequency in Latin and their apparent economy, but their range of use continued to develop down to modern times.

The increase in concision is often achieved at the price of greater obscurity because some syntactical relations tend to become opaque in non-finite forms. This loss of syntactical information is particularly obvious in nominalizations: *the shooting of the hunters* can be used in context to mean 'the hunters shoot'/'the hunters are shooting'/'the hunters shot'/'the hunters are shot'/, etc.

Participles can become members of other word classes as prepositions (*sauing, except = outtaken*), conjunctions (*provided*) or adjectives (*interesting*). They may be constituents of complex verb forms or of non-finite participial clauses, which can be related to relative or adverbial clauses. Distribution of the various types of participial clause varies considerably according to text type, but it appears safe to say that the range of uses was greater in EModE than it is today.

Most of the following specimens are taken from T36A, a text which does not depend on a Latin source, and in which therefore – as comparison with T36 will show – the frequent use of PCs must be interpreted as peculiar to Harrison's stylistic intention. However, there are also a few counter examples, such as that in T36/80 vs. T36A/116, where Bellenden's PC *Thir tythingis comin in Scotland drew þe nobillis* is paraphrased as *After these newes were spread abroad*. Specimens from *Hamlet* (T31B) show how frequent PCs could be even in a dramatic text. The occurrences in the texts can be classified as follows, some of them according to categories of Latin grammar on which they were patterned:

1   Modifiers
    (a) The participle precedes the head (normal, if not expanded or modified): *a prepensed deuise* (T36A/28); *the contriued slaughter* (T36A/57); *Canoniz'd bones* (T31B/30); *forged processe* (T31B/122). The distinction between premodifying participles and 'full' adjectives is fuzzy: T36A/50, 53; also cf. *smiling damned Villaine* (T31B/189).
    (b) Postposed (rare unless expanded): *Goblin damn'd* (T31B/23); *hill called D., situate in G.* (T36A/76).
    (c) In combination with *have* 'let, cause': *haue his house slandered* (T36A/17).

    (d) Following a verb of perception (alternating with bare infinitives): *persauit all men havand him in dreid* (T36/39).

2   Adverbial participial clauses (cf. 1(b)) – the construction can be used with any constituent in Latin, but in English the participle must be related to the subject of the head clause or have its own subject (absolute construction).

    (a) *Being aduertised ... he came ... trusting to haue found* (T36A/78; cf. T36A/2, 14, 23, 52, 54, 83, 101, 103, etc.; T31B/19, 157, 187, etc.).

    (b) In non-finite adverbial clauses with subordinating conjunction: *So Lust, though to a radiant Angell link'd* (T31B/139).

    (c) The participle unrelated to the subject (avoided as 'dangling' or 'misrelated' in PrE): *that sleeping in mine Orchard A Serpent stung me* (T31B/120; cf. T31B/142, T36A/49).

3   The absolute participle, frequent in OE and again from the late fifteenth century in imitation of Latin and French structures. In EModE common in a few lexicalized expressions, but mainly in written use: *which being ... vnderstood* (T36A/37) (*quibus rebus cognitis*); *no reckoning made* (T31B/161); compare in a more Latinized text: *al these thinges had, ... is a man ... by speculation. And speculation obtayned...* (T44/59–60); or T44/137–8, where *than* expresses the temporal/conditional relation.

It ought to be stressed that complex verb forms of the types *having seen, being seen, having been seen*, which were increasingly formed in EModE to express tense and aspect in the non-finite participles as well, have no formal equivalent in Latin.

6.8.6 *The infinitive* (Brunner 1960–2: II, 339–51)

The infinitive could be used in subject and object position (alternating, in particular, with *that* clauses, but it increasingly also replaced clauses of purpose and result, relative clauses and co-ordinated main clauses of the types *time that will come = time to come* (ME); *the first (man) that saw = the first (man) to see* (fourteenth century); *he went and never returned = he went never to return* (seventeenth century).

The perfect infinitive was used in EModE (unlike PrE) to express a possible, intended or unreal action (Brunner 1960–2: II, 348; *for to haue sayled* (T2/25–6). Clauses of purpose were often introduced by *for to* (T1/22, T2/27) until the sixteenth century, by *to the end to* in the sixteenth/seventeenth, and by *in order to* after 1650.

From EModE on, phrases of the type (*it was good/easy/dangerous for him*) (*to leave*) were re-analysed as (*good*) (*for him to leave*), and use of the second constituent was extended to new contexts. Its modern frequency is, however, quite a recent development (compare *the time approached for God to fulfil the promise* in T19B/80 with earlier translations T19B/1, 27, 54).

Another new use of the infinitive was the imitation of the Latin accusative and infinitive construction, which became common with more types of verbs in EModE and frequently occurred in the passive: *showes the Matine to be neere* (T31B/172); *which your selues confesse by vse to be made good* (T18E/65).

6.8.7 *The gerund and verbal noun* (Brunner 1960–2: II, 351–61)

The already existing verbal noun came to be complemented (possibly on the Latin pattern) by a gerund with verbal government: English now had two constructions of similar meaning but different syntactic behaviour, which could be formed from practically any verb. The homonymy of these forms and their virtual interchangeability led to various 'mixed' forms in EModE, which often makes it impossible to classify specimens found in the texts. In particular, the gerund was often followed by *of*: *For easye learning of other Languages by ours* ... (T12/47); *as in reciting of playes, reading of verses, &c, for the varying the tone of the voice* ... (T16/41).

The increasing use of these constructions was possibly stimulated by chancery language, compare *A proclamation ... for dampning of erronious bokes and heresies, and prohibitinge the hauinge of holy scripture* (T37A/3–6) and occurrences in the formal style of T17. Again, their modern frequency is a recent phenomenon, as can be illustrated by a comparison of the *New English Bible* with earlier translations: *avenged the victim by striking* (T19B/95); *but without using force for fear of being stoned by the people* (T19A/80–1); *we ... ordered you ... to desist from teaching* (T19A/83); *whom you had done to death by hanging him* (T19A/89).

One particular use of the gerund is functionally related to the progressive aspect of the verb (EF), and was largely interchangeable with it in EModE: *he was a-hunting of the hare = he was hunting the hare* (cf. Nehls 1974: 66–72). Such gerunds are found especially in seventeenth- and eighteenth-century texts, but were minority forms even then: there are 14 instances in Shakespeare (as against 348 EFs); no specimen is found in the appended texts.

6.9 Text syntax and rhetoric

6.9.1 Text and sentence

Classical Latin texts, especially Cicero's, helped EModE writers to structure complex arguments in often excessively long sentences or periods – a unit can correspond to the modern 'paragraph' (see T7/9–40 and cf. the analysis in 6.8.2). Problems of the definition of 'sentence' also occur in analysing seventeenth-century texts and are not confined to written texts intended to be read:

> though Milton's prose was obviously intended to be printed and read, it is nonetheless difficult to escape the conviction that he composed with an audience rather than a reader foremost in his mind. Certainly much of the difficulty and awkwardness of his prose, particularly that associated with the length and complexity of his sentences, is greatly diminished if we attend to him as to spoken discourse – as to an oration...
>
> (Hamilton, in Emma and Shawcross 1976: 321–2)

> Milton's sentences are often closer to the paragraph than to the sentence in modern usage: that is, they are at times less a single, closely integrated and self-contained idea or complex of ideas than a means of holding together all that he wished to say on a particular point.
>
> (Hamilton, in Emma and Shawcross 1976: 318–19)

6.9.2 Coherence (De Beaugrande and Dressler 1981, Halliday and Hasan 1976)

'Coherence' best describes the features that make a conglomeration of sentences into a structured text. Coherence is the product of various factors:

1   the non-linguistic cultural knowledge of speakers/ listeners;

2   linguistic markers, such as:

  (a) intonation features (sentence stress, intonation, emphasis and contrast);

  (b) syntactic features (anaphoric reference, selection of articles, word order, pronouns and adverbs, sequence of tenses);

  (c) semantic features (various forms of text-internal reference, including metaphors, 7.6.8).

Such features are not, of course, confined to one individual language, but their selection, distribution and consistency depend on factors such as text type, audience, etc., and typical patterns are discernible for specific languages and individual periods. The choice of markers to achieve coherence in EModE texts depended on various factors (cf. 6.1.2):

1   Medium: was the text meant to be read or to be delivered? Does, therefore, written or oral (oratorical) style predominate?

2   Dependence on certain traditions (e.g. on Cicero or on Tacitus in expository prose).

3   Intended level of style (grand, medium, low).

4   Predominance of either logical argumentation or progression.

5   Relevance of symmetry and rhythm; length and complexity of constituents on different syntactic levels.

6   Relevance of purely ornamental form and frequency of specific rhetorical figures.

7   Predominance of either parataxis or hypotaxis.

8   Explicitness of relations between constituents of the sentence and beyond (in particular, choice of prepositions, conjunctions, tense and mood).

9   Transfer of Latin patterns (such as continuative clauses, 6.8.4)?

10   Delimitation of the sentence as a syntactic unit, and means of integrating sentences into higher units (paragraph).

11   Typographical lay-out (titles, marginalia, sizes and forms

of typefaces used, paragraphs, numberings, graphics and other forms of illustration and punctuation).

12 Consistency in points 1–11 or specific variations, and naturalness of expression.

Other structural distinctions, partly determined by narrative style and found in various mixtures in the texts, can be classified into several types (a classification overlapping with others such as the one above).

1 Chronological. The principle of arrangement here is the sequence of events in time by which causal relations can be implied or be made explicit; diaries, travelogues, chronicles – and cookery books (T40, T41, T48, T49, T50). Cohesive features: time adverbs, dates, temporal clauses.

2 Descriptive. When there is no natural, obvious sequential order in the object of description, the arrangement of constituents and their coherence is often loose (unless there are fixed traditional patterns): descriptions of pictures, countries, characters, etc. (parts of T1, T14, T29, T45).

3 Defining-concluding. Parts of the arguments are defined, enumerated and arranged so as to lead to a logical conclusion: scholarly prose, legal pleading and sermons (T3, T6, T7, T8, T13, T39), often structured by means of very explicit linguistic and typographic features.

4 Rhetorical 'artificial' prose. Explicitly formulated on the principles laid down in classical rhetoric, linguistic structuring (e.g. in the form of parallels, antitheses, etc.) can outweigh content (cf. Bacon's criticism in T13). The form is dependent on fashion rather than type of text (T25, T36, T43).

5 Dialogic. Complementary linguistic forms are required by the speech roles characteristic of the interaction of persons in drama, letters and other forms of question and answer structures. The type also occurs as a rhetorical device used in type 3 in texts where arguments are put forward as replies to fictitious questions (T8).

It is easy to see that the impact of rhetorical rules was greatest in EModE texts of types 3–5, rules practised in Latin exercises being transferred to EModE compositions. This was, however, rarely made explicit as it is in T43/143–217, where Latin terms show the reader which stage in the rhetorical structure of the letter he has reached. Where such reference is lacking, it can be easily supplied.

6.9.3 *Stylistic change* (cf. 2.6.2; Croll, in Watson 1970: 84–110)

Stylistic change in EModE resulted in most cases from the substitution of one tradition for another as stylistic model; a style can be described in terms of features that make it distinctive (in contrasting it with other texts). Thus the change from the long and complex Ciceronian sentences of the later sixteenth century to styles of the seventeenth such as those modelled on Seneca and the ideal favoured by the Royal Society (T17) is reflected not only in sentence length but also (in the curt style):

1   in the absence of conjunctions and adverbs linking clauses and sentences. These were largely replaced by punctuation, and sometimes by deliberate asymmetry (changes of subject, of word order and of tense, loose co-ordination of sentence structure and rhyme, and grouping incomplete argumentation).

2   in the perspicuous shortness of units between punctuation marks. Coherence is established here not by linguistic means, but by the contextual knowledge and presuppositions shared by writer and reader.

The alternative to curt style was loose style with long, but lightly structured sentences loosely strung together. Such strings are intended to look spontaneous, following in a natural manner the line of speakers' and listeners' thoughts, with digressions, parentheses, anacolutha and uncertain sentence boundaries (as seen in T. Browne's style). This pattern is in marked contrast to the Ciceronian period, which builds up to a climax and comes to a well-rounded finish.

The two styles reflect, then, the disintegration of logical construction. These tendencies were, however, checked by the philosophical schools of the late seventeenth century, which brought to the English language:

> the study of the precise meaning of words; the reference to dictionaries as literary authorities; the study of the sentence as a logical unit alone; the careful circumscription of its limits and the gradual reduction of its length; the disappearance of semicolons and colons; the attempt to reduce grammar to an exact science; the idea that forms of speech are always either correct or incorrect; the complete subjection of the laws of motion and expression in style to the laws of logic and standardization – in short, the triumph, during two centuries, of grammatical over rhetorical ideas.
>
> (Croll, in Watson 1970: 109)

Study questions

Q30 Did Harrison retain the syntactical structures of his source text in T36A?

Q31 What is the meaning of 'grammar' in T12/42–6, T16/28 and T44/47?

Q32 Discuss word order in sentences starting with an adverb, using data from the texts (especially T41 and T75). Do sentences with initial *then* (T10/26; T13/50, 51, 55, 58, 61, etc.), *there* and *here* (T25/60, 62, 67, etc.), *so* (T26/77; T27/2, etc.) and *yet* (T25/2; T35/19, etc.) exhibit the expected patterns?

Q33 How can the patterns found in *And such Readers we wish him* (T31A/46), *and them we toke* (T48/105), *& on their tops grow nuts* (T48/108) and *Of this opinion was...* (T18H/9) be accounted for?

Q34 Interpret the uses of the preterite in T1/8; T7/55; T10/19, 69 and those of the perfect in T2/41 and T10/71–2. Look for examples where the use of tenses does not conform with PrE grammar (or is at least doubtful).

Q35 Is the alternation of *will* and *shall* in T6/8–11, 25–9 a matter of modal meaning? What additional meanings do *will* and *shall* have in other texts (e.g. in T4/10–27; T3/55, 67–70)?

Q36 Which forms in T31B would have to be in the expanded (progressive) form in PrE, and which could be, depending on interpretation?

Q37 What use did translators of T20 and T21 make of expletive *do*? Does analysis of a longer passage from Dryden's *Aeneid* confirm the impression that he avoids the construction? Are all uses of *do* in T31B expletive?

Q38 List the texts in which continuative clauses are used. Is the construction found in any seventeenth-century texts printed here?

Q39 The Roman Catholic translation of the Bible (Rheims/Douai) is said to be especially close to the syntax of the Latin original. Is this claim confirmed by the use of participles in T19A and B? Compare these data with material from AV.

7   Vocabulary

7.1 General problems

7.1.1 *Lexical structure* (Görlach 1982: 101–4)

The vocabulary of an individual language is (synchronically) structured in various ways. The description may be organized according to:

1   form (by similarity, rhyme, etc.)
2   content (synonyms, antonyms, homonyms, 7.6)
3   subject/fields of knowledge (encyclopaedic fields)
4   collocational potential and frequency in texts
5   dialectal, sociolectal, ideolectal distribution
6   etymology (especially if speakers are aware of it (cf. 7.1.5–7))

The great number of possible classifications makes statistical approaches a particularly important aid to the description of the lexicon (Finkenstaedt *et al.* 1973; Wermser 1976).

7.1.2 *The growth of the EModE vocabulary*

The EModE period (especially 1530–1660) exhibits the fastest growth of the vocabulary in the history of the English language, in absolute figures as well as in proportion to the total. This emerges clearly from a list of the numbers of new words per decade and half-century based on the *Chronological English Dictionary* (*CED*, 1970):

	–10	–20	–30	–40	–50	–60	–70	–80	–90	–00
15..	409	508	1415	1400	1609	1310	1548	1876	1951	3300
16..	2710	2281	1688	1122	1786	1973	1370	1228	974	943

	[1]16 (5341)	[1]17 (9587)	[1]18 (3651)
[2]15 (2716)	[2]16 (9985)	[2]17 (6488)	[2]18 (4678)

Fig. 16 The growth of the EModE vocabulary, 1500–1700

It must be admitted that determining the first occurrence of a word is problematic. In the first place, the data used in compiling the *OED* were incomplete: cf. *contemplate* (T4/54 of 1553), first *OED* occurrence in 1592; *gaiety* (T8/69 of 1582), first *OED* occurrence in 1634. Also, very many words must have been in spoken use for centuries before they were first written down – and even then the texts need to have survived into our times (for a discussion of the whole problem, see Schäfer 1980).

That peak figures for first recorded words coincide with the publication dates of important dictionaries is not only the result of the lexicographer's tendency to coin new words to provide equivalents, but also of the fact that the dictionaries included sections of the vocabulary that had previously been in exclusively spoken use. It is easier to decide whether a first occurrence is a true neologism when it appears in a literary work which reflects its author's active concern for his language. Explicit notice of a word's novelty (as far as the author was informed on this point) can be found in the case of Elyot's borrowings (t48, t49), in Puttenham's discussions (T11/77ff.), in Holofernes' *peregrinat, as I may call it* (T31F/15–16), or in Dryden's comment on his new coinage *witticism* ("A mighty Wittycism, (if you will pardon a new word!)...", *OED*, 1677).

However uncertain the dates of first occurrences (including the CED dates quoted above) may be, the general tendencies of development are quite obvious: an extremely rapid increase in new words especially between 1570 and 1630 was followed by a low during the Restoration and Augustan periods (in particular 1680–1780). The sixteenth-century increase was caused by two factors: the objective need to express new ideas in English (mainly in fields that had been reserved to, or dominated by, Latin) and, especially from 1570, the subjective desire to enrich the rhetorical potential of the vernacular.

Since there were no dictionaries or academies to curb the number of new words, an atmosphere favouring linguistic experiments led to redundant production, often on the basis of competing derivational patterns. This proliferation was not cut back until the late seventeenth/eighteenth centuries, as a consequence of natural selection or as a result of grammarians' or lexicographers' prescriptivism.

The additions were almost exclusively borrowings from foreign languages and new coinages (7.5), apart from the expansion of the meanings of existing words (7.7). The rapid increase in the lexicon and the sources of the new words were repeatedly commented upon in the EModE period, and succinctly summarized by Wilkins (1668: 8) at the end of the great expansion:

t40 Since Learning began to flourish in our Nation, there
     have been more than ordinary Changes introduced in our
     Language; partly by new artificial *Compositions*; partly
     by *enfranchising* strange forein words, for their elegance
5   and significancy, which now make one third part of our
     Language; and partly by *refining* and *mollifying* old words,
     for the more easie and graceful sound: by which means
     this last Century may be conjectured to have made a
     greater change in our Tongue, then any of the former, as
10   to the addition of new words.
                                                              1668

That borrowing was a major factor in this growth is apparent from the figures provided by Wermser (1976: 40), who compared the number of loanwords with that of new coinages (but misleadingly did not count coinages on foreign patterns as loanwords):

	loanwords	coinages
	%	%
1510–24	40.5	53.5
1560–74	45.3	49.4
1610–24	50.5	47.2
1660–74	47.9	47.8
1710–24	37.6	58.3

Vocabulary

The extent to which the domains of English expanded in the sixteenth–seventeenth centuries emerges from the thematic groupings of loanwords below (Wermser 1976: 126–8; the first figures represent new words in periods of fifteen years, the second those not accepted into the *general* vocabulary):

	1510–	1560–	1610–	1660–	1710–
theology	12/ 2	60/21	124/73	42/25	17/10
philosophy, rhetoric	2/ 0	11/ 6	28/19	18/13	12/10
architecture, art	7/ 2	60/41	56/24	58/35	64/42
law	21/13	20/11	44/28	12/ 9	6/ 2
navigation	11/ 2	11/ 3	46/30	21/15	11/ 6
trade, commerce	12/ 0	19/ 1	33/ 7	12/ 1	17/ 3
crafts, technology	19/ 2	26/ 7	96/57	80/59	47/27
biology	28/18	102/65	125/89	224/189	72/62
medicine, anatomy	12/ 4	46/32	141/100	84/75	53/44

Fig. 17 The growth of EModE terminology according to domains

7.1.3 *Obsolescence* (Visser, 1949; Görlach 1982: 107–9)

Although neologisms are a more conspicuous feature of EModE, the contrary development, the obsolescence of words, can also be found. However, loss of words was much more typical of the fifteenth century, when the emerging standard apparently stigmatized many lexemes as belonging to regional or socially less acceptable dialects, and thus caused their obsolescence. This selection process must be obvious to anyone who considers the large number of ME words which, after 1500, became restricted to Scots or northern dialects (see Görlach 1987).

The frequency of certain pairs of partial synonyms in the works of Chaucer, Spenser and Shakespeare may serve to illustrate lexical change in the transition from ME to EModE: the disappearance of many Chaucerian words is evidence of the fifteenth-century watershed. The effects of archaizing fashions (with borrowings largely taken from Chaucer, 7.1.4) are also made evident by the figures below. However, straightforward word counts can produce misleading results since polysemy makes it impossible in most cases to use word *pairs* to illustrate obsolescence. This excludes such specimens as *folk:people*, *host:army*, *cheer:face*, or *fowl:*

bird from consideration – such words must be analyzed on the basis of developments within their lexical fields (7.6). For *elde/age*, cf. T20/31, 33, etc.; for Spenser, see the occurrences in T23B/33–4, 49.

	Chaucer	Spenser	Shakesp.	other (partial) synonyms
swink n/v	6n + 19v	9	–	*toil, travail, work*
labour n/v	73n + 10v	100+	x	
wone	22	19	–	*live, abide*
dwell	240	100+	x	
siker(ly)	48	11	–	*forsooth, soothly*
iwis	180+	4	3	*in faith*
certes	++	54	5	
certainly	77	2	29	
elde	28	15	2	
age	83	62	224	
delve	10	–	3	
dig	1	3	10	
clepe	300+	12	2	*cry, shout*
call	150+	250+	958	
sweven	25		–	
dream n	42		x	

x   dominant (or competing with lexemes not mentioned)
++   not counted by the concordances; 180+ indicates approximate figures

Fig. 18 Obsolescence and revival of selected lexical items

Apart from such general causes of obsolescence, a few more specific (internal and external) causes can be discerned. It must, however, be admitted that the number of concurrent factors involved often makes it difficult or impossible to reconstruct the specific causes that have led to the loss of an individual word.

The reason for a word's disappearance is obvious in cases where its referent went out of use: since lexemes are not normally transferred to the new entities that replace the old (though this did indeed happen in the cases of *paper* and *match*), some loss of words is inevitable in fields such as dress, food/cookery or weaponry, as any thematically arranged word-list dating from an earlier period will show; cf. 'weapons' in Wilkins (1668: 278–9):

t41   **V.** The Proviſions neceſſary for Offence and Defence are ſtyled by the general name of AMMUNITION, *Magazin, charge, diſcharge, Arcenal.*
     To which may be adjoyned the word BAGGAGE, *Impediments, Luggage, Lumber.*

5   They are diſtinguiſhable according to their Shapes, and thoſe ſeveral Uſes for which they are deſigned, into ſuch as are more

   { *General; denoting the common names belonging to things of this nature; whe-*
   {   { WEAPON, *Arms offenſive.*   (*ther ſuch as are* || *offenſive:or defenſive.*
   { 1. { ARMOUR, *defenſive Arms, Mail, Headpiece, Helmet, Scull, Gorget, Gaunt-*
10   { *Special; for*   (*let, Habergeon,* &c. *Armorer, Armory.*
   | *Offence.*
   | { *Comminus,* near hand; being either for
   | {   { *Striking* chiefly; whether || *bruiſing* : or *cutting.*
   | {   {   { CLUB, *Bat, Batoon, Battle-ax, Mace, Pole-ax, Cudgel.*
15 | { 2. { SWORD, *Scimitar, Hanger, Rapier, Tuck, Ponyard, Stilletto, Dag-*
   | {   *ger, Fauchion, Glave, Cutler.*
   | {   { *Thruſting* chiefly; of which the latter is ſometimes uſed for *ſtriking.*
   | {   { SPIKE, *Spear, Launce, Javelin, run at tilt.*
   | { 3. { HALBERT, *Partizan, Trident.*
20 | *Eminus,* at a diſtance; whether
   | { *Ancient and leſs artificial; denoting either the*
   | { *Inſtrument giving the force,* being of a curved figure and elaſtical
   | { *power; to be held in the hand, either* || *immediately* : or *by the ſtock to*
   | {   { BOW, *ſhoot, Archer, Fletcher.*   (*which it is fixed.*
25 | { 4 { CROSS-BOW, *ſhoot.*
   | { *Inſtrument or Weapon projected; whether* || *immediately out of the hand:*
   | {   { DART, *Javelin, Harping-iron.*   (*or mediately from ſomething elſe.*
   | { 5. { ARROW, *Shaft, Bolt.*
   | *Modern and more artificial,* (i.) fire-Arms; denoting either the
30 | { *Veſſels giving the force; according to the name of* || *the whole kind* : or *of the bigger kind.*
   | {   { GUN, *ſhoot, Snaphance, Fire-lock, Musket, Carbine, Blunderbuſs,*
   | { 6. { *Piece, Arquebus, Petronel, Piſtol, Dagg, Potgun, play upon.*
   | {   { ORDNANCE, *Cannon, Artillery, Saker, Minion, Baſilisk, Drake,*
35 | {   &c. *ſhoot.*
   | *Utenſils; ſignifying the thing* || *enkindling* : or *enkindled.*
   | 7. { MATCH, *Tinder, Touchwood, Spunk.*
   | { POWDER, *Gunpowder.*
   | *Things diſcharged;* either || *ſolid* : or *hollow.*
40 | 8. { BULLET, *Ball, Pellet, Shot.*
   | { GRANADO, *Petard.*
   | *Defence.*
       9. BUCKLER, *Shield, Target.*

Psychological causes of obsolescence include factors such as the weakening of emphasis through overuse, a factor which is likely to have contributed to the loss of many intensifiers (*wondrous*; ME/EModE *al*, *ful*, *right* and *wel* exemplifying restrictions of meaning). Euphemisms (i.e. cover terms for referents considered offensive) can lead to successive losses, as is illustrated by designations for 'toilet' (cf. Barber 1976: 156–7, T44/208, T45/80) or, for example, for 'prostitute': Wilkins (1668: 273) lists under FORNICATION: *courtesan, concubine, harlot, trull, leman, punk, quean, drab, strumpet* – to which one might add EModE *wench, whore* (t47/30–1) and *minion, mistress, prostitute, stale, vizard*, etc. Though for reasons different from those affecting the field of 'weapons', the disappearance of individual words has greatly reduced the number of the synonyms listed above.

As far as internal causes are concerned, conflict between homonyms (or homophones) is the most convincing factor, but even this is rare and difficult to establish in individual cases. Words belonging to the same class and sharing syntactical and semantic features are most likely to be affected since they are easily confused in many contexts, which leads to misunderstandings and, in consequence, reduced frequency.

Ile make a Ghost of him that lets me (T31B/70) may serve to illustrate the phenomenon of homonymic clash (cf. Samuels 1972: 69, T8/149). The two ME verbal paradigms [lɛːtən] pres., [leːt] or [lɛttə] past – 'to let', and [lɛttən, lɛttə] – 'to hinder' came into conflict after the weak past (ME) and the short present tense vowel (fifteenth/sixteenth century) had become established in the paradigm of 'let'. Even though the two verbs remained distinct in a number of syntactic patterns (*that lets me/ do it ≠ from doing it*), ambiguity was inevitable in others. Since enough synonyms were available for 'hinder', *let* quickly became obsolete in this sense in the seventeenth century. In a similar way, PrE *cleave* 1 'split' 2 'stick' are differentiated syntactically (cf. *claue asunder* T19A/37), but they are affected by homonymy; although not obsolete in PrE, the use of both words has declined in favour of their synonyms *split* and *stick* (both available in EModE, cf. T3/56). The most famous example in the history of the English language is, however, the pair *queen:quean* 'prostitute', the members of which became homophonous in educated speech in the seventeenth century, creating a 'pathological' situation. It certainly contributed to the loss of *quean* that it was already endangered as a taboo word and that many substitutes were readily available.

Similar ambiguities can result from polysemy, but these normally lead to the obsolescence of individual sememes rather than to lexical loss so that the word involved remains but with fewer meanings. The opposite tendency, namely to drop redundant lexical items, usually leads to erstwhile synonyms becoming semantically differentiated, though it may also contribute to the loss of a word. This may have been a factor in the disappearance of *nim* from London speech; the verb had been replaced by *take* in general use by the time of Chaucer, but it survived into the seventeenth century in cant ('to steal', cf. *a notable nimmer*, T32/19).

Other factors contributing to word loss are even more difficult to establish. Phonic inadequacy (as in phonaesthemes containing clusters such as *sl-*, *fl-*) may have a part in causing obsolescence (and change of meaning; cf. Samuels 1972: 45–8). Words can also disappear if their type of word-formation no longer conforms with productive patterns (cf. the neutral meaning of *-ish* in *soulish* T8/6). Many uncertain cases, however, remain. Thus the loss of *neat* 'cattle' (T49/1) cannot be fully explained by the shift of *cattle* to a similar meaning, since unlike *neat* the word is uncountable (cf. T49/1 *neates tongue* with **cattle's tongue*); moreover, its being homonymous with *neat* adj. can hardly have caused a conflict (though Samuels, 1972: 73, thinks it did).

The disappearance of dictionary words (7.2) should not, however, be classified as obsolescence; great numbers of such words were coined, by Cockeram for instance, but they were not accepted by later lexicographers or indeed the speech community. They are consequently not to be counted as ever having formed part of the English lexicon (in consequence, the *OED* editors omitted many of these items).

7.1.4 *Archaisms and poetic diction* (Barber 1976: 96–100)

The use of archaisms, borrowed from earlier stages of the language, was considered a possible means of filling gaps in the

English vocabulary without having recourse to foreign languages (the archaizers' and purists' aims overlap in this respect, see 7.3.7). However, the revival of obsolete words, though making possible a form of poetic diction in the Chaucerian tradition, did not provide a solution for the major problem: the expansion of scientific and technical vocabulary.

Caxton (T2/8ff.) had been very cautious with regard to revivals, but Berthelette (T22A/5–26) explicitly justified his new edition of Gower's works by drawing attention to the older English words that the texts made available. There are many sixteenth-century comments on the great popularity of archaic diction and Chaucerisms. Some writers, biased by nationalistic fervour, overlooked the fact that the charge of obscurity and affectation made against foreign words also applied to archaisms, a point made by P. Ashton:

t42   throwghe al this simple and rude translation I studyed
       rather to vse the most playn and famylier english speche,
       then either Chaucers wordes (which by reason of antiquitie
       be almost out of vse) or els inkhorne termes (as they
5   call them) whiche the common people, for lacke of latin,
       do not vnderstand.

                                      1556

The chief proponent of archaisms in the sixteenth century was, of course, Edmund Spenser. His friend E.K. (T23A/1–46) stressed this aspect of Spenser's style, justifying it by pointing to Cicero's practice. The tables in 7.1.3 above, however, clearly show that Spenser had no intention of using old words exclusively, but that he skilfully introduced them side by side with modern expressions in order to give his poems an archaic flavour without endangering their intelligibility.

Outside the 'Spenserian school', attitudes towards archaisms remained negative (as in Puttenham's remark in T11/40–2) or divided – as with Ben Jonson, who avoided archaisms in his plays and attacked Spenser for his conglomerate style ("Spenser, in affecting the ancients, writ no language"), but who adopted a lenient attitude where he followed Quintilian (T14/6–14).

The seventeenth-century literati lost interest in archaism and the related problem of purism; the very fact that Dryden *translated* Chaucer, justifying the undertaking as necessary in view of the unintelligibility of the texts, demonstrates the new attitude of the Restoration period. Note that the attitude of lexicographers remained divided (T59/49–57).

7.1.5 Etymology (Jones 1953: 214–71; Schäfer 1973: 1–25; cf. 3.5.4)

Awareness of the etymology of individual words was important in EModE times in two respects. First, knowledge of the Latin or Greek provenance of many words affected by sound changes in French (whence they were borrowed into ME) prompted restitution of their classical 'correct' spellings. Spellings were Latinized in increasing numbers in the fifteenth to seventeenth centuries (e.g. *avowtery* replaced by *adultery*), and sometimes respelt on the basis of historically incorrect 'etymologies' (*sithe* replaced by *scythe* as if from *scindere*; *abhominable* T31F/25 as if from *ab homine*, and not from *omen*). The meaning of loanwords was also affected when the original classical meanings were added to the English ones (semantic loan), and syntactic behaviour (such as government in the case of verbs) was also sometimes changed to conform with classical etymons.

On the other hand, the Germanic roots of English came to be regarded as more and more important. Whereas knowledge of OE mainly served ecclesiastical purposes in the sixteenth century (thus, in Parker's view, helping to prove the historical independence of the English church), the appearance in 1605 of books by Camden and Verstegan (who had adopted his Dutch grandfather's name) prompted a wave of Teutonism. The ancient Germanic language was regarded as being the equal of Latin (since of equal age):

> Yf the Teutonic bee not taken for the first language of the world, it cannot bee denied to bee one of the moste ancientest of the world.　　　　　　　　　　　　　　(Verstegan 1605: 192)

It is easy to see how close such attitudes are to purism and archaism. They disappeared in the late seventeenth century when French influence became dominant during the Restoration.

Even though etymological research had made great progress in the sixteenth/seventeenth centuries in comparison with the Middle Ages, it still cannot be called a modern linguistic discipline. Fancy often replaced philological knowledge, the biblical explanation of the original language and its "confounding" at Babel still prevailed, and belief in a natural connection between form and content in the original words often led lexicographers astray.

Many of the older words were (and still are) of uncertain etymology, but this also applies to more recent words first recorded in the sixteenth/seventeenth century, as a look at the words for 'mock' listed in Wilkins (1668: 273) will show: MOCK-ING, *deride, flout, jeer, scoff, twit, gibe, quip, gird, frump, bob, taunt, wipe, jerk,* etc., where the etymology is clear for *deride* (Latin) and *twit* (OE), and shifts of meaning are plausible for *bob, gird, jerk* and *wipe,* but where there remain seven of uncertain etymology: *scoff* v 1380, *taunt* v/n 1500, *quip* n 1532 /v 1584, *flout* v 1551 /n 1570, *gibe* v 1567 /n 1573, *jeer* vi 1577 /vt 1590, *frump* v 1587 /n 1589.

The desire to explain unintelligible words by analysing them on the basis of known morphemes led to folk etymology (cf. malapropisms such as *honey-suckle* 'homicidal', 2.6; 7.3.6). This is possibly also the case with *barberry* (T49/26 from *berberis*) – but it would be rash to assume that author or compositor was guided by folk etymology (or antigovernment attitudes) when spelling *Moanarchie* in T8/140.

7.1.6 *Regional differences in vocabulary: Scots* (cf. 2.4–5)

EModE texts in dialect are very rare (T61), and even word collections such as Ray's (t5) are poor substitutes for authentic dialect texts. Therefore discussion will here be restricted to a comparison of EModE and Scots, since the availability of original texts and their translations (T29, T36 vs. 36A) facilitates a straightforward contrast. The texts yield a great number of lexical pairs that are obviously translation equivalents (i.e. heteronyms): *traisting – trusting, wrangwis – vnrighteous, gudeserr – grandfather, compere – appeare* (*in the kings presence*), *subdittis – subiects, biggitt – builded, fretis – prophecies.* We also find idioms with their equivalents, such as *put him to þe horne = proclamed him traitor* (T36/60, T36A/87).

However, while polysemy makes it unlikely that any two lexemes will be absolutely identical in meaning (cf. synonymy, 7.6.9), partial overlap = partial heteronymy is frequent: cf. Scots *child* (as in T36/20) and *barn* (T36/58, 64) corresponding to EModE *child* (T36A/36, 84, 92).

7.1.7 *The social structure of EModE vocabulary* (cf. 2.4.3; Barber 1976: 37–47)

Sociolectal differences between EModE words become apparent in texts specifically addressed to different audiences, in occasional warnings against colloquial or 'low' words (t10), in special-purpose language and, in particular, cant (T9), and in lexical differences to be found in the usage of religious communities (T18C, T18D, T50).

T9 presents a text in which cant heteronyms for most nouns and many verbs replace EModE ones. (To what extent such a text is authentic can no longer be determined. One may, however, assume that the equivalence of the individual words is exact, i.e. that they form proper heteronymic pairs.) Linguistic differences between Protestants and Roman Catholics were especially conspicuous in conflicts concerning sixteenth-century biblical translation. Pairs such as *baptism – washing*, *grace – love*, or *azymes – shewbread* were shibboleths of religious denominations and, in consequence, heteronyms, or heteronymic for the specific meaning.

Such characteristic linguistic features (found in addition to extralinguistic ones such as the refusal to kneel or to doff one's hat in front of worldly authorities) were even more striking among Quakers (cf. T50), and they consist of:

1   new coinages (restricted to internal use or reference to Quakers): *steeplehouse, to thee/thou*;
2   restricted meanings: *convince(ment)*, *church* (= 'community');
3   use of idiomatic (biblical) expressions: *come to y^e light y^t Christ had enlightned him withall.*

7.1.8 *Special vocabulary*

Although the problems of special terminologies are not identical with those of foreign words (some special *meanings* of common words can cause even greater difficulties of understanding), they were often equated at the time of the Renaissance. Specimens come from fields ranging from cookery (*parboyle*, T49/28) to astrology (*sygnes ... attractyue, recentyue, expulsyue, dygestiue,* T44/104–6), from rhetoric (T43/145ff.) to biblical translation (*Azimes, Holocausts, Præpuce,* T18D/42ff.), from arms (t41) to pharmacy (T44/160–9, 185ff.) and alchemy (*argent-viue, mercury sublimate, alembeke,* t37), and from law to medicine (T44–T45) and sailor's language (T56).

The two latter fields can be regarded as typical as far as EModE lexical expansion is concerned. The language of the law had been exclusively French until the late fourteenth century, which caused a great number of French law terms to be borrowed when usage shifted to English in the fifteenth and sixteenth centuries. Since the field was of great importance in everyday life, many of these loans entered the common vocabulary (in colloquial speech often developing meanings much vaguer than those of the original terms). The tension between special and general meaning is reflected in Shakespeare's *Sonnet* 46 (T31G), which employs legal metaphors throughout (a device quite often found in Renaissance poetry, as is the argument between eye and heart):

> *defendant OED* 3: the party in a suit who defends, ≠ plaintiff. 1400–
>
> *plead* 2: to maintain or urge the claim of a party to a suit. 1305–
>
> *plea* 2a: an allegation formally made by a party to the Court. 1381–
>
> *bar* 5a: to arrest or stop (a person) by ground of legal objection from enforcing some claim. 1531–
>
> *title* 7: legal right to the possession of property. 1420–
>
> *impannel*: to enter (the names of a jury) on a panel or official list; to enrol or constitute (a body of jurors). 1487–
>
> *quest* 2: the body of persons appointed to hold an inquiry. 13..–
>
> *verdict*: the decision of a jury in a civil or criminal cause upon an issue which has been submitted to their judgement. 1297–
>
> *moiety* 1: a half, one of two equal parts (in legal use). 1444–

A reading of T45 and T44 will illustrate the difference between a highly popularized and a more 'scientific' presentation of medical problems. T44 in particular makes it obvious that the help to the uneducated intended through the use of English is rendered largely ineffective by the Latinate terminology (cf. T44/195ff.: *for I nor no man els can nat in theyr maternall tonge expresse the whole termes of phisicke*):

> *insycyon* T44/92: cutting into some part of the body in surgery. 1474–
> *scaryfycation* T44/92: making ... slight incisions in a portion of the body. 1400–
> *flebothomy* T44/92: venesection, blood-letting, bleeding. 1400–
> *adusted* T44/151: supposed state of the body ... of dryness, heat, deficiency of serum... 1430–
> *congellacion* T44/179: process or state of freezing, paralysis. 1536–

An aid to comprehension was occasionally provided by word pairs, with the foreign terms followed by common equivalents or interpretations: *corrode & eat, corodyng or eatynge* (T44/146, 148), *putryfy & corrupt* (T44/148).

Medical terminology was used metaphorically even more frequently than legal terms were. The problems treated in expository prose in T44/95–9 appear in metaphoric use in *Hamlet* III.4 (First Folio: 2530–2).

> It will but skin and filme the Vlcerous place,
> Whil'st ranke Corruption mining all within,
> Infects vnseene.   (See Waldron 1978: 185)

If a technical term enters the common vocabulary, its meaning will normally be generalized. This is obvious with words like *humour* (7.7), or *moiety* (see above), which signified 'claim to one half' in legal terminology (1444), was first used in a more general sense in 1475, and had finally acquired the meaning 'small portion' by 1593.

7.2 The tradition of the dictionaries (Starnes and Noyes 1946, cf. Barber 1976: 106–11)

7.2.1 The sixteenth century

Considering how much attention EModE vocabulary, especially the loanwords, received from sixteenth-century writers and grammarians, it comes as a surprise that there does not appear to have been any demand for an *English* dictionary until the late sixteenth century.

Mulcaster (1582) pointed out how useful such a dictionary would be and himself compiled a list of 8,000 entries, without definitions. For Bullokar (1580) an English dictionary would have formed part of a comprehensive description of the language, which was not, however, realized since he never proceeded beyond the treatment of spelling. Sixteenth-century lexicography is therefore limited to bilingual (mostly Latin) dictionaries, which makes Puttenham's statement in T11/57 enigmatic.

There were some more specialized compilations, such as Paul Greave's *Vocabula* (1594), glossaries to accompany scholarly texts, explanations of archaisms (E.K.'s glosses in T23B, Speght's editions of Chaucer, 1598/1602, cf. T22B) or E. Coote's list of 1596, a precursor of the hard-word lists, all important as sources for the first English–English dictionaries.

7.2.2 *The seventeenth century*

Inspired by Coote's list and Thomas' Latin–English dictionary of 1588, Cawdrey published his first dictionary (still of modest size with its 2,500 entries) in 1604; it contained (like all its successors in the early seventeenth century) only a part of the English lexis, namely the 'hard words'.

t43   A Table Alphabeticall, conteyning and teaching the true
       writing, and vnderstanding of hard vsuall English wordes,
       borrowed from the Hebrew, Greeke, Latine, or French, etc.
       With the interpretation thereof by plaine English words,
   5   gathered for the benefit & helpe of Ladies, Gentlewomen,
       or any other vnskilfull persons. Whereby they may the
       more esilie and better vnderstand many hard English
       wordes, which they shall heare or read in Scriptures,
       Sermons, or elswhere, and also be made able to vse the
  10   same aptly themselues.   1604

The character of hard-word lists became even more obvious in John Bullokar's *An English Expositor* of 1616, which was twice the size of Cawdrey's work. H. Cockeram's *English Dictionarie* of 1623 first introduced a highly dubious innovation: apart from borrowing heavily from his predecessors, he also took over large parts of Thomas' Latin–English dictionary, anglicizing the Latin and thereby creating 'new' English words, a method which greatly increased the number of his entries. Even more questionable is his part II, in which he supplied learned equivalents for common words, apparently reacting to his customers' desire not only to understand difficult expressions, but also to refer to everyday topics using Latinate terms:

t44   The first Booke hath the choisest words themselues now
        in vse, wherewith our Language is inriched and become so
        copious, to which words the common sense is annexed. The
        second Booke contains the vulgar words, which whenso-
5   euer any desirous of a more curious explanation by a more
        refined and elegant speech shall looke into, he shall
        there receiue the exact and ample word to expresse the
        same: Wherein by the way, let me I pray thee to obserue,
        that I haue also inserted (as occasion serued) euen the
10   *mocke-words* which are ridiculously vsed in our Language,
        that those who desire a generality of knowledge, may not
        bee ignorant of the sense, euen of the *fustian termes*,
        vsed by so many, who study rather to be heard speake,
        than to vnderstand themselues.   1623

His letter B includes the following monstrosities:

t44a	TO BABBLE	Deblaterate
	A BABLER	Inaniloquos
	MUCH BABLING	Dicacity, Vaniloquie
	LOUE OF BABLING	Phylologie
5	BAKED	Pistated
	TO BARKE	Latrate, Oblatrate
	TO BOYLE	Elinate, Ebullate
	TO PLAY THE BOY	Adolescenturate
	A FOSTER BROTHER	Homogalact
10	TO BUILD A NEST	Nidulate
	TO BURY	(Con)tumelate, sepulize
	TO BURN LIKE A COAL	Carbunculate
	HALFE BURNT	Semiustulated
	TO BUY AND SELL	Nundinate
15	AT FAYRES	

                                                    1626

The inkhorn terms of the sixteenth century, which had been confined to certain groups of people and in particular criticized as university jargon (T11/31, t51), were here spread among the common people, who may have regarded Latinate speech as an indicator of linguistic emancipation (also cf. Coles, T59/58–62). But it is easy to foresee that the consequence was bound to be incorrect use of foreign words (cf. malapropisms 7.3.6).

Later dictionaries were further expanded by the inclusion of encyclopaedic material (in particular, explanations of Roman and Greek antiquities), of archaisms, of dialect and cant, and increasingly of etymologies. A comprehensive compilation of the complete vocabulary, though projected on the French pattern (cf. Evelyn, T16/44ff.), was not achieved in the EModE period.

Phillips' *The New World of Words* (1658) started the critical reaction to Latinized dictionary words, which were branded as to be avoided; as he put in his preface to the 5th edition of 1696:

t45 Errors for which *Blunt* and *Cole* are justly to be condemned, as having crouded the Language with a World of Foreign Words, that will not admit of any free Denization; and thereby misguiding the Ignorant to speak and write
5 rather like conceited Pedants and bombastic Scriblers than true Englishmen.   1696

However, there was no consistent rejection of unusual (and unused) Latinate words before J.K's *New English Dictionary*, which promised on the title page:

t46 a Compleat Collection of the Most Proper and Significant Words, Commonly Used in the Language; with a Short and Clear Exposition of Difficult Words and Terms of Art ... omitting ... such as are obsolete, barbarous, foreign or
5 pecular to the several Counties of England.   1702

7.2.3 EModE dictionaries of living languages

French, Spanish, Italian and Dutch dictionaries of English (and vice versa) deserve special attention because they were meant to aid everyday communication and therefore presented the vocabulary of the languages concerned (including English) on a wide range of subjects and with comprehensive lists of translation

Vocabulary

equivalents. Accordingly, they are a mine of information on
synonyms and on colloquial speech (Palsgrave 1530; Florio 1598,
1611; Cotgrave 1611). The following excerpts from Cotgrave
illustrate his desire not to leave out a single translation equivalent,
to keep apart the EModE equivalents of the various meanings of
polysemous French headwords and occasionally to include
encyclopaedic information:

t47 ADVENIR. To happen, chance, betide, come to passe, fal
out, befall.
ELEGANT. Elegant, eloquent, fine-spoken, choice in words,
neat in tearmes; also, compt, quaint, spruce, trimme,
5   daintie, delicate, polite.
ELLEND. Th'Elke; a most fearefull, melancholike, strong,
swift, short-neckt, and sharp-houued, wild beast;
much troubled with the falling sicknesse, and (by
reason of the extraordinarie length of his vpper lip)
10   euer going backward as he grazeth; (some report, that
his forelegs are ioyntlesse, and his flesh good veni-
son; but *Vigenere* (vpon Cæsar) denies th'one, and
Gesner dislikes th'other.
ENNUY. Annoy; vexation, trouble, disquiet, molestation;
15   sorrow, griefe, anguish; wearisomenesse, tediousnesse,
irkesomenesse, importunitie; a loathing, or sacietie,
of; a discontentment, or offence, at.
FILLE. A daughter; also, a maid; girle, modder, lasse,
wench.
20   FIN. Wittie, craftie, subtile, cunning, wilie, fraudulent,
cautelous, beguiling; also, fine ...
FOL. A Foole; asse, goose, calfe, dotterell, woodcocke;
noddie, cokes, goosecap, coxcombe, dizard, peagoose,
ninnie, naturall, ideot, wisakers ...
25   FOL. Foolish, fond, simple, witlesse, foppish, idle, vaine.
FOLIE. Follie, simplicitie, foolishnesse, fondnesse, vn-
aduisednesse, foppishnesse, indiscretion, ideotisme ...
FORT. Strong; tough, massiue; hardie, sturdie, lustie,
able-bodied; mightie, forcible, powerfull, effectuall ...
30   GARÇE. A wench, lasse, girle; also, (and as wee often
meane by the first) a Punke, or Whore.
GARÇON. A boy, lad; youth, stripling.
LATINISEUR. One that writes, or speakes Latine; also, an
inkhorniser; one that vses inkhorne tearmes.

35   FAIRE DU LATINISEUR. A dunce, or ignorant fellow to counterfeit
        Schollership.
      MAL. An euill, mischiefe; hurte, harme, domage, wrong,
        displeasure, annoyance; also, a griefe, paine; sick-
        nesse, disease.
40   MAL. Ill, bad, naughtie, lewd; scuruie, mischieuous, hurt-
        full, harmfull, shrewd; vnseemely; vncomely, vndecent;
        sicke, diseased, crazie, pained, sore, ill at ease.
      RUSTIQUE. Rusticall, rude, boorish, clownish, hob-like,
        lumpish, lowtish, vnciuill, vnmannerlie, home-bred,
45   homelie, sillie, ignorant.
      SPHINGE. The Sphinga, or Sphinx; an Indian, and Ethyopian
        beast, rough-bodied like an Ape (of the kind whereof
        he is) yet hairelesse betweene his necke, and breast;
        round, but out, faced; and breasted like a woman; his
50   vnarticulate voice like that of a hastie speaker; more
        gentle, and tameable then an ordinarie Ape, yet fierce
        by nature, and reuengeful when he is hurt: hauing
        eaten meat ynough, he reserues his chaps-full to feed
        on when he feels himselfe hungrie againe.   1611

7.3 The problem of loanwords

(illustrated mainly from the Latin influence on EModE)

7.3.1 Language contact and language mixture

If two linguistic systems (whether dialects, sociolects or two different languages) are in contact in a more or less bilingual
speaker, one system is likely to influence the other. The extent of
this influence and the resulting forms depend on a number of
factors, among which the following are most frequently mentioned (Weinreich 1959; Görlach 1982: 129–30):

1   Internal: similarities and differences in the structures of
        the two languages in contact.
2   External: size and homogeneity of groups of speakers, pro-
        portion of bilinguals, length of contact, extent of com-
        munication between groups; degrees of competence,
        domains of the two languages and frequency of use;

method of acquiring second language, relative status of the two languages, and the community's evaluation of individual bilingualism and of interference.

The high prestige of Latin meant that it had considerable influence on all Renaissance vernaculars; Latin can in consequence be adduced to illustrate borrowing in EModE even if Latin, as an almost exclusively written language restricted to certain domains and registers, cannot be considered representative of all forms of language contact.

Different from borrowing (although sometimes preparing the ground for the borrowing process) is code-mixing from playful, careless or ostentatious motives. Where such mixtures occur in texts the foreign elements remain clearly unintegrated; an extreme example is Pepys' sentence "Here did I endeavour to see my pretty woman that I did baiser in las tenebras a little while depuis". It was probably such code-mixing (and not the borrowing of individual words) that was criticized as 'oversea language' or 'Ingleso Italiano' (T4/14–17) in the sixteenth century.

By contrast, snatches of Latin, mostly in the form of quotations, were not objectionable in EModE, as is indicated by their frequent use in 'respectable' texts (T14, T15) – the occurrence can even be typical of literary genres aiming for the *auctoritas* of classical tradition, especially in theory-oriented texts on rhetoric and literary criticism.

7.3.2 Types of loans

The influence of Latin can be found at all levels of EModE grammar (with the possible exception of phonology). It is especially conspicuous (and significant) that EModE syntax was so thoroughly affected. As far as the lexis is concerned, the number of loanwords was incomparably higher than that of coinages formed on Latin patterns (loan translations, etc.). Latin influences can be classified as affecting:

1   the writing system (import of graphemes such as <æ, œ>, (cf. 3.3)
2   the syntax

3   the vocabulary
Influences affecting the vocabulary can be subclassified according to:

(a) the rank of the item affected (morpheme, compound/derivation)

(b) whether the item is a transfer or a calque, and formal exactness in calquing

(c) whether only the form, only the content, or form + content is affected

(1) form only: *parfit* replaced by *perfect*; hypercorrectness in *prophane* (T18C/95)

(2) content only (i.e. the acquisition of an additional meaning by an existing word; semantic loan, cf. 7.7.2h):
wit on the pattern of *ingenium*, *washing* = 'baptism' (T18D/40), *poetike flouris* (T29/50); cf. the title of T14, *Timber* on the pattern of *silva* 'dense mass, sketch book'

(3) form + content:

(a) loans with varying degrees of integration and at various ranks:
foreign: *Pasche* (T18C/129); *indiuiduum* (T12/16), *Logodædali* (T16/67); *Cymini sectores* (T30/74); *Ne sutor vltra crepidam* (T28/44); even longer units are found in, e.g. the quotation from Horace (T11/134–6) = T15/157 = T18H/19–21)
integrated: *conspicuous* (T17/102); *letters patentes* (T4/88)

(b) calquing:
loan translation: *maker or Poet* (T11/25); *shew bread* (T18C/131, from Luther's *Schaubrot*); *forespeache* (Lever); *consent of the Learned* (T14/18 = *consensus eruditorum*)
loan rendition: *ouerreacher* (= *hyperbole*, Puttenham); *witcraft*, *naysay* (= *logica, negatio*, Lever)
loan creation: *dry mock* (= *ironia*, Puttenham); *backset* (= *praedicatum*, Lever); *fleshstring* (= *muscle*, Golding)

7.3.3 *The integration of loans*

In ME times it was common for loanwords from French and Latin to spread from upper-class use to lower-class speech, becoming variously adapted in the process. Such integration was much less effective with loans from contemporary languages from the sixteenth century on. Many words, in particular those derived from French and Italian, appear to have been left unadapted because they were regarded as shibboleths of educated speech. (This attitude did not, of course, apply to loans from the exotic languages of America, Africa and Asia, whose pronunciation and unrecognized morphology were often altered beyond recognition.)

Morphological integration presented serious problems, especially with verbs. In ME, there had been inconsistencies in deriving the base form of verbs from French (*obeischinge* T19A/17, but *obey* T19A/36; *nurischide* T19B/10 = PrE *nourish*). From the fourteenth century, similar problems occurred with Latin loans (the following data are from Reuter 1936). It would seem natural to derive English base forms from the Latin present stem, as were the Chaucerian verbs *appropre, calcule, confeder, dissimule, encorpore,* etc. Loans derived from Latin participles were originally participles in ME – but Chaucer already used forms such as *determinate, exaltate, preparate,* etc., both as base forms and as participles. Uncertainty as to what Latin forms ought to be chosen for deriving English verbs continued all through the subsequent centuries, as shown by Reuter's figures based on the works of individual authors: Chaucer used some 200 foreign verbs derived from the present stem, as against 37 from the participle, but the ratio is 300/100 for Caxton, 400/200 for Shakespeare, 175/200 for Cawdrey and 250/850 for Cockeram (who has a distorted proportion because of his craze for forming -*ate* verbs, 761 of his 850 coming from Thomas' Latin dictionary, 7.2). In ME, the co-occurrence of two forms often indicates French vs. Latin provenance, as is the case with Caxton's *conduyse/conduct; corrige/correct; possede/possess.* It sometimes also happened that EModE selected one form, and Scots another: *conquer* vs. *conquess* (T36/3); *dispose* vs. *dispone* (t36/7).

More than 800 of these verbs had two forms at one time or another. Where only one form survived, this was the one based on the present stem in 238 cases (mostly borrowed before 1450) and on the participle in 264 cases. Doublets (175) survived, mostly with differentiated meanings, and often with one of the pair obsolete in PrE: *administer/administrate, conduce/conduct, confer/col-*

*late, confound/confuse, convince/convict, esteem/estimate, refer/
relate, repel/repulse, transfer/translate* represent a small selection
from the better known pairs.

7.3.4 Augmentation: lexical expansion by means of loanwords

Sir Thomas Elyot can be considered a typical writer of the early
sixteenth century. One of the most active mediators of classical
knowledge, he was forced by the gaps in EModE vocabulary to
introduce many loanwords. He did so quite systematically, as he
stated himself in the preface to his *Of the knowledg which maketh a
wise man*:

> t48 His highnesse benignely receyuynge my boke/ whiche I
> named the Gouernour, in the redynge therof sone perceyued
> that I intended to augment our Englyshe tongue/ wherby
> men shulde as well expresse more abundantly the thynge
> 5 that they conceyued in theyr hartis (wherfore language
> was ordeyned) hauynge wordes apte for the pourpose: as
> also interprete out of greke, latyn/ or any other tonge
> into Englysshe, as sufficiently/ as out of one of the
> said tongues into an other. His grace also perceyued/
> 10 that through out the boke there was no terme new made
> by me of a latine or frenche worde, but it is there de-
> clared so playnly by one mene or other to a diligent
> reder that no sentence is therby made derke or harde to
> be vnderstande.   1553

The explanation of new words is common elsewhere, too: *commixtion and medling* (T1/11–12); *counterfete & likene* (T1/21);
foundacion and groundewoorke (T3/7–8); *rotation and circling*
(T16/103–4); *Stond or Impediment* (T30/64); *the primogenitiue, and
due of Byrth* (T31E/32) – but some instances are likely to be due to
the desire for 'copiousness'. Few authors took the pains to provide
detailed explanations as Florio did in T18F/61–4, or Elyot in his
defence of the neologisms *modestie* and *mansuetude*.

> t49 In euery of these thinges and their semblable/ is
> Modestie: whiche worde nat beinge knowen in the englisshe
> tonge/ ne of al them which vnderstode latin/ except they
> had radde good autours/ they improprely named this vertue

5 discretion. And nowe some men do as moche abuse the worde
   modestie/ as the other dyd discretion. For if a man haue
   a sadde countenance at al times/ & yet not beinge meued
   with wrathe/ but pacient/ & of moche gentilnesse: they/
   which wold be sene to be lerned/ wil say that the man is
10 of a great modestie. where they shulde rather saye/ that
   he were of a great mansuetude: whiche terme beinge semblably before this time vnknowen in our tonge/ may be by
   the sufferaunce of wise men nowe receiued by custome:
   wherby the terme shall be made familiare.   1531

Translations played an important role in the integration of
loanwords. Many sixteenth-century scholars were against the
greatly increasing numbers of translated texts (their arguments
are summarized in Hoby's statement "Our learned menne for the
most part hold opinion, to haue the sciences in the mother tunge,
hurteth memorie and hindreth lerning"), but most writers saw
their practical usefulness, as argued by Hoby in the same text, in
the preface to his translation of *The Courtier*:

t50 translations open a gap for others to folow their steppes,
    and a vertuous exercise for the vnlatined to come by
    learning, and to fill their minde with the morall vertues,
    and their body with ciuyll condicions, that they may
5   bothe talke freely in all company, liue vprightly though
    there were no lawes, and be in readinesse against all
    kinde of worldlye chaunces that happen, which is the
    profite that cometh of philosophy.   1556

Many reasons were given to justify the introduction of new
loanwords. Most frequently it was claimed that lexical gaps and
insufficient differentiation in the existing vocabulary made the
new words indispensable: thus Boorde with regard to medical
terms in T44, the translator Florio in T18F, and even Evelyn,
who strongly supported cultivation of the mother tongue, with
regard to non-technical loans from French (T16/112–15).

The Romans, too, it was also reasoned, borrowed from Greek;
moreover, the strangeness of new words would soon be lost with
frequent use.

The penchant for loanwords was enhanced by the stylistic ideal
of *copiousness* (*copia verborum*), apparent in English texts from the

fifteenth century, but especially noticeable in the sixteenth. Such *copia* relies on large numbers of (partial) synonyms, which could easily be supplied by loans from French and Latin. The procedure is glaringly obvious in the early text T35 of 1523, which juxtaposes

1   largely synonymous expressions such as *shewe, open, manifest, declare*;

2   synonyms, arranging them in the form of a climax: *eschewe, auoyde, vtterly flye*;

3   serial actions: *enquere, desyre, folowe*.

Even when the loanword discussion had lost much of its heat in the late sixteenth century, authors still felt called upon to justify their use of them. The arguments put forward were often not very clear or convincing, as is seen from Puttenham's defence of loanwords in T11/59–131: he accepted, as valid reasons for borrowing, not only lexical gaps, but also use in courtly speech and euphony; but condemned synonyms that provided neither semantic differentiation nor harmonious sound. In particular, the grand style of the epic could not do without linguistic ornament, and most poets were convinced that this could only be achieved by the use of choice Latinisms. (This attitude is found as late as Dryden, who discussed the question in his *Dedication of the Aeneis* in 1697 (ed. Ker 1961: 234–5).)

7.3.5 *Inkhorn terms* (Barber 1976: 81–90)

It was not primarily the Latinate terminology necessary for the anglicization of the sciences or moderate attempts at copiousness that provoked mockery and resistance, but rather the sixteenth-century fashion for using Latinate expressions (loanwords or words newly formed from Latin elements) as indicators of elevated style. In particular, many writers objected to the use of Latinisms in inappropriate contexts and for concepts for which an English word was easily available, i.e. for common objects in everyday communication. This craze, criticized by Puttenham as *peeuish affectation* and widespread in the universities, is illustrated by the conduct of an Oxford student in *A Hundred Mery Talys*:

t51   *Of the scoler that bare his shoys to cloutyng.*
      In the vnyuersyte of Oxonford there was a skoler yᵗ de-
      lytyd mich to speke eloquent english & curious termis/
      And cam to yᵉ cobler wyth hys shoys whych were pikid
5   before as they vsyd yᵗ seson to haue them cloutyd &
      sayd thys wyse/ Cobler I pray the set me .ii. tryangyls
      & .ii. semy cercles vppon my subpedytals & I shall gyue
      the for thy labor/ This cobler because he vnderstode hym
      not half well answerid shortly & sayd/ Syr youre elo-
10   quence passith myne intelligence/ but I promyse you yf
      ye meddyll wyth me/ the clowtyng of youre shone shall
      coste you .iij. pence. ¶ By thys tale men may lerne yᵗ
      it is foly to study to speke eloquently before them that
      be rude & vnlernyd.   1526

The joke is fully understood only if it is realized that *semicircle*, not yet well known from geometry lessons, is first recorded by the OED from this text, and *subpeditals* is *only* found here.

From the mid-sixteenth century such exaggerated borrowings were derided and opposed as *inkhorn terms* (an expression still new enough to require the remark "as they call them" in t42). The classic passage illustrating the fashion is Wilson's *ynkehorne letter* (T4/40–66). It shows what types of Latinisms were opposed, and indicates that they were just one feature of an exaggerated pleonastic style which only becomes intelligible, then as now, after translation into plain English. (See the analysis in Barber 1976: 264.) That such Latinization was used in a supplicatory letter (however fictitious) may well reflect the view that this elevated style was appropriate for use in communication with "the better brought vp sort" (T11/38). Wilson added the far-sighted warning that further Latinization must lead to the breaking up of the English language into mutually unintelligible sociolects (T4/76–81).

Contemporary criticism of Boorde's verbose Latinized style (T44) is found in Day in 1586 (cf. T43):

t52   was there euer seene from a learned man a more preposter-
      ous and confused kind of writing, farced with so many and
      such odde coyned termes in so litle vttering? ... diuers
      to whome I haue showed the booke haue very hartily laughed
5   in perusing the parts of his writing.   1586

Objections to such excesses continued until 1600, even though increasing confidence in the value of English made people feel less concerned about the fashion.

However, *inkhornism* remained a popular term of abuse in literary controversies, as is illustrated by Nashe's and Harvey's criticism of each other's styles. Ben Jonson put Marston on the stage (as Crispinus in *Poetaster*) and ridiculed him by making him, after an emetic had been forced on him, spew out the following stream of Latinisms (mixed with a few vulgarisms):

> Retrograde, reciprocall, Incubus, glibbery, lubricall, defunct, magnificate, spurious, snotteries, chilblaind, clumsie, barmy froth, puffy, inflate, turgidous, ventosity, oblatrant, obcaecate, furibund, fatuate, strenuous, conscious, prorumped, clutch, tropologicall, anagogicall, loquacity, pinnosity, obstupefact.

"You must not hunt for wild outlandish terms, To stuff out a peculiar dialect" is Virgil's comment (*Poetaster* V, iii).

7.3.6 *Malapropisms*

   t53 CACOZELON, an ill imitation or affectation, that is;
         when words be vsed ouerthwartly, or contrarily, for want
         of iudgement, vsed of foolish folk, who coueting to tell
         an eloquent tale, doe deface that which they would fain-
    5 est beautie, men not being content to speake plaine eng-
         lish, doe desire to vse wordes borowed of the latine
         tongue, imitatyng learned men, when they knowe no more
         their signification, then a Goose, and therfore many
         tymes they apply them so contrarily, that wyse men are
  10 enforced to laugh at their folly, and absurditie.

1577

One consequence of the flood of new Latin words was that a language barrier was erected *within* English in the sixteenth century. The proper use of the Latinate portion of English came to replace knowledge of the classical languages alone as the marker of social class and education. In popular speech many foreign words were used imprecisely, thus acquiring a larger, more general range of meaning (perceptible *post hoc* as instances of language change, i.e. as generalization of meaning). Such uses could be caused by erroneous equation of the range of meaning of the foreign term with that of its native partial synonym: thus *old*, *ancient* and *antique* became largely synonymous in the sixteenth century, partly as a consequence of the desire to replace the common *old* by more refined expressions (T4/50; cf. T2/46, and cf. Cockeram's equations, 7.2).

Even more conspicuous are distortions of the forms of foreign words, reinterpretations by folk etymology, or confusions of similar words (T41/7 *prezidents* 'presence'). Hart was one of the first to comment on this danger:

t54   as to say for temperate, temporall: for surrender, sul-
      lender: for stature, statute: for abiect, obiect: for
      heare, heier: certisfied, for both certified, and satis-
      fied: dispence, for suspence: defende, for offende:
 5ʹ surgiant, for surgian: which is the French term *chirur-*
      gian, which is flesh clenser.   1570

Such mistakes are indicators of widespread (but only partly successful) attempts at linguistic emancipation, attempts which were frequently caricatured by Elizabethan dramatists, as Shakespeare did with Mistress Quickly or Dogberry (cf. Schlauch 1987). To judge by the success of Cockeram and his imitators (7.2.2), there was a large market in the seventeenth century for dictionaries translating common expressions into elevated diction. This indicates how difficult it must have been to limit loanwords to a moderate number. The issue was obviously not the objective need to fill lexical gaps for the sake of unambiguous reference, but the pairing of common words with their Latinate equivalents, the implication being that use of the elevated term was more prestigious – even if it was unintelligible and therefore useless for communication.

7.3.7 *Purism* (Barber 1976: 90–100; Gray 1988)

Purism, understood as resistance to foreign words and as aware-ness of the possibilities of the vernacular, presupposes a certain level of standardization of, and confidence in, the native tongue. It is no surprise that puristic tendencies are unrecorded before the end of the Middle Ages – wherever native expressions were coined to replace foreign terms, they served a different purpose: to help the uneducated understand better, especially sermons and biblical paraphrase. Tyndale's striving for the proper English expression was still motivated by the desire to enable the plough-boy to understand more of the Bible than the learned bishops.

A puristic reaction was, then, provoked by fashionable eloquence, as is evident from aspects of fifteenth-century *aureate diction* and sixteenth-century *inkhornism* (7.3.5). The humanists had rediscovered a classical form of Latin instituted by Roman writers who fought against Greek technical terms as well as fashionable Hellenization, but who could not do without terminologies for the disciplines dominated by Greek traditions. Ascham, Wilson and Cheke (all counted among the 'purists' in a loose application of the term) behaved exactly as Cicero had done: they wrote in the vernacular (no obvious choice around 1530–50), avoided fashionable loanwords and fanciful, rare expressions, but did not object to the borrowing of necessary terms.

Cheke was as inconsistent a 'purist' as he was a reformer of EModE spelling (3.5.2). On the one hand, he went further than most of his contemporaries in his efforts to preserve the English language "vnmixt and vnmangeled" (T5/14), but on the other hand he also borrowed beyond what was necessary and what his own tenets seemed to allow. (The problem of untranslatable terms, as in his renderings of biblical antiquities, was solved by marginal explanations.) The practice (and historical ineffective-ness) of other 'purists', too, who attempted translations of Latin terminologies – Golding for medicine, Lever for philosophy and Puttenham for rhetoric (cf. 7.5.3) – demonstrates that there was no such rigorous puristic movement in sixteenth-century England as there was in many other countries during the eighteenth and nineteenth centuries. The purists' position and their influence on EModE has often been exaggerated; it is more to the point to speak of "different degrees of Latinity" as Moore (1910) did.

The anti-rhetorical position of Protestant–Puritan traditions (2.8.2) might lead one to expect purism in biblical language and theological terminology in particular. However, the ME Bible and Wycliffite writings around 1380–1400 had created a tradition of religious language which made neologisms in this field less urgent. Even Bishop Gardiner's demand that ninety-nine religious terms should be left untranslated in the English Bible (cf. the full list in Partridge 1969: 51) was prompted not by linguistic but rather by dogmatic considerations: which central concepts should be left to be interpreted by the church. The translators of the Roman Catholic (Rheims–Douai) Bible strove to avoid possible charges of diverging from the exact phrasing of the Latin original, and thereby of giving rise to hereticism. Their text is, then, highly Latinized in its vocabulary, idiom and syntax (T18C/105–21; cf. T19). Their efforts were a pre-emptive strike in anticipation of charges that were bound to come: A. Marten in 1583 referred to the ninety-nine terms as "new inkpot terms" for concepts perfectly familiar in the vernacular. The implicit accusation was that the Catholic authorities were actually barring the laity from what they professed to be providing – however grudgingly – in their translation.

The craze for foreign terms and puristic reactions to them remained a problem, though to a lesser degree, in the seventeenth and eighteenth centuries. After 1600, puristic tendencies united with nationalistic-antiquarian sentiments in favouring Saxon monosyllables. A last extreme representative of uncompromising purism was Fairfax, who in 1674 tried to do without foreign terms in his description of the sciences:

t55　That thinking with my self, how I an English man would
　　　write a Book in English tongue, I made it now and than a
　　　little of my care, to bring in so many words of that
　　　speech, that the Book might thence be call'd English,
　5　without mis-calling it. And indeed however our smoother
　　　tongued Neighbours may put in a claim for those bewitch-
　　　eries of speech that flow from Gloss and Chimingness;
　　　yet I verily believe that there is no tongue under heaven,
　　　that goes beyond our English for speaking manly strong
　10　and full. And if words be more to teach than tickle, as I
　　　reckon they are, our Mother tongue will get as much by
　　　speaking fit and after kind, as it can loose by faring
　　　rough and taking up the tongue to utter, and more than
　　　any else can gain by kembing better and running glibber.

15 Where I thought an outlandish word would be better taken,
I have often for the Readers sake set an English by it,
as thinking it unmeet to free my *words* upon another, in
such a piece as where I was to leave all free, as to the
things I spake about. Only I thought it not amiss, after
20 I was once in, for the taking off that charge that some
have too heedlesly layd upon our speech, of a patcht up
Tongue from Lands and kinreds round about, to shew, that
a Book of thus many sheets, might be understandingly and
roundly written, in hail and clear English, without tak-
25 ing from abroad, so much as twice so many words ...

                                                        1674

t56 either to fetch back some of our own words, that have
been justled out in wrong that worse from elsewhere
might be hoisted in, or else to call in from the fields
and waters, shops and work-housen, from the inbred stock
5 of more homely women and less filching Thorps-men, that
well-fraught world of words that answers works, by which
all Learners are taught to do, and not to make a Clatter ...

                                                        1674

From the late seventeenth century, criticism focused on the
fashionable adoption of vocabulary from *French* (cf. 7.4.2). This
explains Dryden's taunts and Dr Johnson's oversensitive reactions
to 'Gallicisms' – and his curious opinion that to go back to the
language of the classical authors of the Elizabethan period meant
returning to the "wells of English undefiled" (1755: C 1).

7.4 Loans from living languages

7.4.1 Introductory

European and non-European languages are represented unevenly
among sixteenth/seventeenth-century loanwords, but the statistics reflect the cultural position of England between 1500 and
1700, her economic relations, widening horizons and finally her
rise to the position of a world power.

Wermser (1976: 45) has found the following percentages
among loanwords, basing his statistics on periods of fifteen years
with data taken from the *CED*:

	Lat.	Greek	French	Ital.	Span.	Dutch	Other Euro.	Overseas
1510–24	47,8	0,6	40,7	0,9	0,9	3,4	5,3	0,3 = 322
1560–74	54,4	3,8	31,8	2,4	1,4	1,8	2,8	1,7 = 953
1610–24	60,7	5,2	19,3	2,3	2,6	1,3	1,7	6,9 = 1725
1660–74	57,7	5,9	22,5	3,1	1,4	1,4	3,4	4,6 = 974
1710–24	37,9	6,9	25,7	14,2	1,7	1,7	6,6	5,2 = 346

Fig. 19 Provenance of EModE loanwords

7.4.2 Borrowing from French

The predominance of Latin can mislead one into overlooking the continuing French influence in the EModE period. Lambley (1920) has competently summarized the causes of this impact; they can be listed as follows:

1   Even after French had lost its standard (official) functions in England between 1350 and 1450, it was still possible or even common for it to be used in some types of documents and as the language of the law (Law French) well into the seventeenth century.

2a   French was not found in the curricula of grammar schools, but knowledge of it was widespread amongst the nobility (much in advance of Italian and Spanish), thanks to a great number of French tutors, many of them Huguenot emigrants. Emigrants also ran important private schools. Many French grammars were published quite early on (A. Barclay 1521; Palsgrave 1530; Duwes 1533; etc.).

2b   French was more frequent in Scottish elementary and grammar schools, as a subject, but also as the teaching medium and in conversation.

3a   French emigrants, mostly Protestants, came in great numbers, especially in the late sixteenth century (when, it is claimed, 5 per cent of the population of London was French or Flemish) and after the revocation of the edict of Nantes in 1685.

3b   When English Royalist emigrants returned after 1660,

Gallomania reached its climax in England (French culture was the model elsewhere in Europe, too). Among those famous literati returning were Waller, Denham, Cowley, Hobbes and Fanshawe, and at a later date, Rochester, Wycherley and Vanburgh.

4   Literature written in French (especially romances) was popular in England. This included many translations of the Greek and Latin classics, which were, at least before 1550, commonly translated from French into English (as Caxton did a French prose version of the *Aeneid*, T2; for a later famous case, cf. Sir Thomas North's translation of Plutarch's *Lives* from the French of Amyot).

There is no straightforward correlation between the number of loanwords and speakers' reactions to borrowings, as attitudes from the sixteenth to eighteenth centuries show. Purism was directed against Latinisms in the sixteenth century, but it largely neglected the problem of French loans (even though attacks on fashionable forms of "oversea language", T4/14, include French). On the other hand, the French wave of 1660–1760 provoked reactions disproportionate to the number of loans. Still, French adoptions of the time do read like a chapter in the history of English civilization, as can be illustrated by a selection of *CED*'s entries for the years 1673, 1676 and 1699:

1673 *billet-doux, dishabille, double entendre, minuet, naiveté, ridicule, suite*
1676 *chicane, couchee, faux pas, pis aller, routine*
1699 *atelier, bijou, bureau, fiacre, tableau*

Much of this appears to have been courtly jargon, taken up (and often caricatured) by Restoration dramatists, who gave lasting currency to many French words – it is no surprise that these entries are concentrated in the year 1673, when Dryden's *Mariage à la Mode* and Wycherley's *Gentleman Dancingmaster* first appeared, and in 1676, the year Wycherley's *Plain Dealer* and Etherege's *Man of Mode* were published.

The changing (sociolectal, stylistic) function of French loans, ranging from necessary terms used by all classes of society to foreignisms indicating membership of a prestigious and educated

Vocabulary

elite, is also mirrored in declining degrees of adaptation to English phonological structure (and spelling conventions) after 1550.

7.4.3 Loans from other living languages

The number of loanwords from the other European languages is much smaller than that from French and Latin – and they are more concentrated in specific fields. Thus Italian terms were borrowed for military matters, architecture, painting, music and commerce; Spanish for Iberian objects and customs; and naval, commercial and military terms came from Dutch. Although Spanish and Italian were quite widespread as foreign languages in sixteenth-century England, many words from these languages were not borrowed directly but adopted in a French form.

Loans from other languages were almost exclusively indirect, such as Arab items (transmitted through French or Spanish) or those from America, Africa and Asia (mostly through Spanish) – but the foundation of the East India Company in 1600 gave rise to the first direct loans from Indian languages, just as the first permanent settlement in the New World in 1607 and the Pilgrim Fathers' voyage in 1620 provided the first opportunities for direct contacts with North American languages. The dates, sources and meaning of the following loanwords are significant: *racoon* (1608), *opossum* (1610), *mocassin* and *pemmican* (1612) and *moose* (1613).

Travelogues and geographical descriptions, such as Hortrop's (T48) or Blome's (T58), were highly popular EModE reading matter. Misleading information (T48/116–23) apart, they contributed to a great expansion of knowledge, which was also reflected linguistically. It is possible to compile long lists of loanwords designating foreign plants, animals, customs, buildings or officials (cf. Serjeantson 1935: 213–58). Words for 'delicacies', all dating from 1598, illustrate the point nicely: *ananas*, *cashew*, *coffee*, *curry*, *papaw* and *sardelle* (*CED*).

7.5 Word-formation

7.5.1 Introductory (Görlach 1982: 73–7; Bauer 1983)

Word-formation can be distinguished from both inflexion and syntax by the concept 'word'. Formal difficulties of classification arise, for instance, in making distinctions between zero-derivation and functional expansion (7.5.6), or between compounds and fixed combinations (type: *stone wall*).

In particular, it is important to decide whether word-formation is to include only the additive processes and patterns in which words are composed of smaller signs, such as compounds (free + free morphemes), synthetic compounds (free + free + bound morphemes) and derivations (free + bound morphemes, the latter including Ø), or whether the following types ought to be covered as well: back formations, clippings, portmanteau words (blends), phonaesthemes, acronyms and formations with unanalysed portions such as blocked morphemes (in names of weekdays or some berries), those formed on foreign bases (*ex* + *orc* + *ist* 1382, + *ism* 1450, + *ize* 1546) or loanwords showing superficial anglicization (such as Cockeram's neologisms in *-ate*, 7.2). The specimens quoted in T1/14 and in the following list from Wilkins illustrate phonaesthetic formations in EModE:

t57   Sensible Quality perceptible by the Ear, together with the Priva-
       tion of it, is styled by the name of *SOUND, Noise, resound, Report,*
       Coil, Rout, Racket, blow, loud, dinn, quetch, Echo, Euphony. To which
       may be adjoyned those natural words (fictitia à sono) *bounce, buz,*
       chatter, chink, clack, clap, clash, clatter, click, clink, crash, crush, ferk,
       hum, hiss, jar, jingle, jerk, knock, rattle, ruffle, rumble, russle, clutter,
       lash, pipe, ring, scream, shriek, snap, squeak, squall, roar, thump, toot,
       twang, thwack, tinkle, wheez, whimper, whip, whine, whistle, yell.
                                                              (1668: 216)

A historical analysis of word-formation poses specific problems; the following appear to deserve special attention in EModE:

1   How far can the analysability of words be determined?
2   Is it possible to determine how productive individual pat-
       terns were, and is frequency of occurrence the only
       criterion?

3   Can the phonological, morphological, syntactic and semantic restrictions effective in EModE be established?

4   Are certain types of word-formation typical of, or more frequent in, individual styles or authors?

5   How did competing patterns, and lexemes formed in accordance with them, develop within EModE (or on into PrE)?

6   What was the relevance of etymological considerations (or others proposed by grammarians) in the selection process, for instance in forming and accepting hybrids?

7   Are diachronic statements possible about the changing status of morphemes (for instance from 'free' to 'bound', thus changing the compound into a derivation)?

Analysability and productivity. The majority of composite loanwords were analysable for the educated speaker immediately on adoption: *agree*, + *able*, + *ment*. However, new coinages with foreign suffixes were rare in ME – the type *faithful* came much earlier than the type *lovable*. Prefixes and suffixes of Latin, Greek and French origin started being productive mainly in the sixteenth century, and even then etymological restrictions made it quite unusual to combine foreign affixes with a native base.

Productivity in historical stages of a language can be measured chiefly by the number of new coinages and their frequency in texts; such judgements are unreliable because first occurrences of words are difficult to establish with any certainty (7.1.2). That analysability and productivity must be determined afresh for each individual period is evident from the fact that words may still be transparent although the patterns on which they were formed are no longer productive (type PrE *full – fill*), and old compounds or derivations have become opaque: *halfett* 'temple' (T21/120) < OE *healf* + *heafod*; *sterope* 'stirrup' (T40/30) < OE *stig* + *rap*.

Word-formation also differs from inflexion in that not all formations permitted by the system are also acceptable – but such judgements presuppose a linguistic norm. Since there was no fixed standard in the sixteenth century nor any effective control imposed by grammarians or dictionaries, the acceptance or rejection of new coinages could only be tested by the speech community – which was much readier to accept experiments in the sixteenth century than in the eighteenth. As a consequence, there are many perfectly transparent EModE coinages in the texts that are no longer found in PrE, words illustrating the great freedom – and uncertainty – characteristic of EModE word-formation:

> *yongth* T1/20, *bestnesse* T3/25, *vnperfight* T5/22, *perfectness* T7/61, *nedefull* T8/57, *ouermuchnesse* T14/79, *wordish* T27/67, *likesum* T41/69, *thieflie* T45/47, *vnhonest* T46/54, *semblable* t49/1, *disciplinable* T11/8, *deceyuable* T20/93, *steadable* T42/133, *feuerable* T45/49.

As regards derivation, the greatest productivity documented in EModE appears to be in verbal nouns (verb + *ing*) and, increasingly, *-er* derivations, supplementing older occupational names (*baker*) with terms for 'doers' of individual actions:

> *ouerstraight a deemer of thinges* T5/32, *causers of our present maner of writing* T6/76, *the English vtterer ... foren vtterer* T8/168–9, *a great welwiller* T8/171, *sinistar whisperars, nor busy troblars of princis states* T42/46–7, *a priar in at the chinks* T41/20 (6.3.5).

An earlier, well-established word normally blocks a new competing coinage even when the system permits the latter (**warmness* because of *warmth*). With the lack of a norm in EModE and with a climate favouring linguistic innovation, this economy principle was largely ineffective, cf. *to glad* (vi. OE, vt. OE), *gladden* (vi. 1300, vt. 1558), *englad* (vt. 1523), *engladden* (vt. 1874), *beglad* (vt. 1617). (The synonymy of competing derivations in EModE may have become obscured in PrE if the redundancy was later exploited to achieve semantic differentiation, as is the case with PrE *to light/lighten/enlighten*.)

In the same way, existing loanwords can block new coinages that would be synonymous. There is no **housy/**housely* because of *domestic*, no **springly* because of *vernal*, etc., and *fleshly/carnal*, *bodily/corporeal*, *heavenly/celestial* co-exist because they differ in meaning. (It should be added that patterns for deriving adjectives from nouns have not been fully productive since OE times; from EModE onwards, nouns frequently function as premodifiers in attributive position – therefore the cumbersome adjectives in T4/40–66 *dominicall, scholasticall, pastorall* are, in the meaning here intended, un-English (since *school fellow*, and not *scholasticall panion*, represents the native pattern).)

Vocabulary

7.5.2 *Poetic diction and word-formation*

Literary traditions have also affected stylistic options with regard to word-formation; the consequence is that specific word-formations occur exclusively or predominantly in certain types of text. What is regarded as poetic diction will be re-defined from one generation to the next, and for each individual genre. Three EModE patterns may serve to illustrate the phenomenon:

1   Sidney (T27/88–9) praised the English language for its capacity for compounding. His own practice in the *Apologie* shows that he must have had in mind mainly adjectives used as epithets in the Homeric fashion (transmitted through Ronsard and the poets of the Pléiade); cf. from T27: *honny-flowing* (3), *Curtizan-like painted* (3), *winter-starued* (9). Lewis' translation of the *Aeneid* (T21/83ff., 262ff.) has *fine-meshed, keen-nosed, high-spirited* and *foam-flecked,* which indicates that such words are still considered appropriate to an epic style (also cf. Milton's *rushie-fringed banck,* t29). The compounds quoted above are poetical because they were novel, or because they varied literary models and occurred in semantically and syntactically unusual collocations. Besides this, the same type occurred in everyday use – also with increasing frequency in EModE: *a stiffe nekkit people* (2.5.1, quote from James VI); *a short-neckt, and sharp-houued wild beast* t47/7; *rough-bodied* t47/47; *our smoother tongued Neighbours* t55/5–6.

2   From Spenser onwards verbal derivatives with the prefix *em-/en-* became frequent, often duplicating existing verbs or varying an earlier verb by replacing the stem (7.5.5).

3   From the seventeenth century it became common in some types of poetry to use *-y* epithets of the type illustrated by *forky lightnings* (T21/248). In Dryden's translation of the *Aeneid* the following combinations are found in Book IV alone (selection): *tusky boar, wintry deluge/winds, airy race/quarrel, starry skies, piny forest, fishy food, wreathy spear, sulphury flame, watery war, snowy fleeces, snaky locks, cloudy front, balmy sleep, downy wings, rosy skies.*

7.5.3 Foreign influences in word-formation

It is difficult to evaluate foreign influence in more general types, since this becomes apparent only in growing frequencies; such is the case with adjectives derived from nouns, a type more common in Latin than in ME/EModE (T4/40–66). Easier to document is Latin influence in derived verbs (Trnka 1930: 14); these calques did not, however, stop the adoption of the loanwords themselves:

> *ineye* (1420–1708, *inoculate* 1420–); *innew* (1432, *innovate* 1548); *in/-embreathe* (1382, 1529– , *inhale* 1725); *inbread* (1547, *impane* 1547); *embody* (1548, *incorporate* 1398); *enoil* (1420–1647, after French *enhuiler*).

The possibilities of compounding and derivation were, then, employed more frequently from the sixteenth century; they were also seen as alternatives to borrowing: Cheke coined *hunderder* for *centurion*, and *biwordes* for *parables* (*c.* 1550); Lever attempted to write a handbook of logic (*The Arte of Reason, rightly termed, Witcraft*, 1573, written *c.* 1550), using English terminology throughout; Golding, completing a translation begun by Sidney, suggested *fleshstrings* for *muscles*; and Puttenham, writing for a non-specialist readership, used various paraphrases to assist them in understanding the Latin/Greek terminology of rhetoric:

> *cooko-spel* (epizeuxis), *crossecouple* (synesiosis), *dry mock* (ironia), *false semblant* (allegoria), *misnamer* (metonymia), *ouerlabour* (periergia), *ouer-reacher* (hyperbole), *redouble* (anadiplosis), *rerewarder* (hypozeugma), *ringleader* (prozeugma), *single supply* (zeugma), *turn tale* (apostrophe).

These authors must have been aware of the strangeness of the proposed coinages, but they rightly assumed that the strangeness of the words, if they were accepted, would wear off quickly, and their greater transparency might facilitate their acceptance. It appears that Cheke's and Hart's calques were patterned on the form of the Latin word (loan translation), whereas Lever, Golding and Puttenham normally adopted freer renderings (loan creation as in *fleshstring*).

7.5.4 *Competing patterns and the problem of hybrids*

In EModE foreign derivational morphemes became moderately productive – but most were predominantly or exclusively used with foreign bases. In consequence, a great number of redundant coinages arose from the co-existence of foreign and native patterns of derivation. The following alternatives were productive in five frequent types alone:

(a) adj → n (abstract): *-th, -head, -hood, -ness, -ship; -ment, -esse, -ity/acy, -ion, -ure*, etc.

(b) n/v → adj: *-y, -ish, -ful, -ly, -like; -al, -ous, -ic*

(c) n/adj → v: *be- 0, en- 0, -0; -ize, -(i)fy*

(d) n/adj → v (privative): *-0, un-/dis- 0, dis- ize*

(e) adj → adj (negation): *un-; in-, dis-*

Comparing the resulting wealth of forms with PrE norms, one finds a great number of EModE words that have become obsolete as a consequence of:

1   the survival into PrE of (normally) *one* form from a group of synonyms: †*hardiesse* (1340–nineteenth century), †*hardihead* (1579 Spenser), *hardihood* (1634–), †*hardiment* (1384–1600), *hardiness* (1634–) and †*hardiship* (1240), unless

2   the meanings were or became sufficiently different: *height* (OE–), †*highth* (T34/24) vs. *highness* (OE–); *hardship* (1225–) vs. *hardness* (OE–).

How likely new coinages were to survive depended on a number of factors:

(a)   The productivity of the pattern employed (cf. the predominance of *-ness* in group (a) above).

(b)   The semantic development of the derivational morpheme: the restriction of *-ish* (in n → adj.) to negative concepts made *soulish* (T8/6), *wordish* (T27/67), etc., unacceptable from the seventeenth century.

(c)   The existence of a firmly established English rival (*freedom*).

(d)   Etymological factors; in particular, from the seventeenth century, the conformity of a formation to a Latin or Greek model; the tendency to avoid hybrids, i.e. the combination of morphemes from different languages, wherever alternatives existed, as in the case of *-ness* vs. *-ity/-ion*, or *un-* vs. *in-* negation.

(e)   Phonological or morphological restrictions, such as obligatory *un-/dis-* preceding *in-* (*unintelligent, disinterested*), or the obsoleteness of *to womanish* (T26/79) because zero-derivation became impossible with *-ish* adjectives.

(f)   Individual analogies or associations (e.g. being too close to taboo words).

(g)   Memorable use of a word by a famous author.

7.5.5 *Derivation: verbs formed with* -ate, -ize, be-, en-, dis-

The five types above may be selected as typical representatives of EModE verbal derivation. A count of first occurrences in the years 1598–9 (*CED*) arranged by author is shown in Fig. 20 (pp. 178–9).

-ate (Marchand 1969: 256; Reuter 1936; cf. 7.3.3)

-ate was rarely added as a suffix to an existing loanword (URIN- + ATE, COMPASSION + ATE): specimens from the above table will be quoted in upper case letters). More frequently it entered the language along with its Latin or Graeco-Latin base, first as a participle and after 1530 chiefly as the base form of an English verb. As early as Wilson's inkhorn letter (T4), *-ate* verbs made up a large proportion of the criticized Latinisms; they remained the most frequent type among the pseudo-loanwords of seventeenth-century dictionaries (Cockeram) and, in consequence, the most frequent object of criticism. In many cases, *-ate* verbs duplicated existing words (*attemptat* T11/130; following *-ize* in *pulverizate*, etc.) and became obsolete before 1700. The close connection between *-ate* and *-ation* does not permit one to decide which has priority in all cases – historically, a great number of *-ate* verbs are likely to be back-derivations from nouns.

-ize (Marchand 1969: 318–19)

Early loans could not usually be analysed (*baptize*), but from the late sixteenth century onwards *-ize* was increasingly used as a productive suffix by writers who were aware of the functions of Greek *-izein* and French *-iser* (thus, EModE *petrarchize* 'write like Petrarch'; GERMANIZE 'translate into German'). Such coinages quickly spread, especially in scholarly (literary, medical, scientific, theological) texts, where they conflicted with zero-derivations (*equalize* 1590 = *to equal* 1590, *civilize* 1601 = *to civil* 1591, MODELIZE/to model 1604, CHAMPIONIZE/to champion 1605 – the latter two pairs with divergent meanings). The bases of the derivations were foreign – but cf. *womanize* (1593). That fashion played a part in the spread of *-ize* verbs is shown by the controversy between Nashe and Harvey, which induced Nashe to defend these verbs for their greater euphony:

> (They) carrie farre more state with them then any other, and are halfe so harsh in their desinence as the old hobbling English verbs ending in R.
> (*Christs Tears*, second edition 1594; preface quoted from Jones 1953: 210–11)

The second-largest portion of seventeenth-century dictionary words is represented by *-ize* words – but most of them, especially the duplicates, had already disappeared by the time of the Augustans.

be- (*OED*, Franz 1939: 103–4; Marchand 1969: 146–8)
From OE and ME times the prefix had four main functions; but frequency was low before 1580, when the productivity of the type appears to have increased again as the result of literary fashion:

1(a)   'cover with, surround by' = BECLOUD, BEMIST, BE-ASH; *bedew* (T20/102)
 (b)   'supply with': BESHACKLE
2   'transitivizing': *bemock* 1607, BEDARE
3   'factitive derivation from adj.': *bedim* 'make dim'
4   'intensifying': BEBLESS, *bebaste* (T32/62, cf. T32/31), *besprinckle*

In addition, it acquired the specific meaning (an EModE innovation) of 'address as': *bemadam*, *bewhore* 1604, *belord* 1586.

Since many of these functions could be expressed by Ø alone, *be*-words often duplicated these; as a consequence, *be-* was increasingly looked upon as an empty, but metrically useful, additional syllable (BEBLESS?).

	BE-	DIS-
Shakespeare (Schäfer 1973)		-hearten
Ben Jonson		-cloak
		-gallant
		-title
Nashe, *Lenten Stuffe* 1599	-shackle	-terminate
Sylvester, *Du Bartas* 1598	-bless	-leaf
	-cloak	-pair
	-cloud	
	-hem	
	-rinse	
Florio, *Dictionary* 1598	-cacke	-acknowledge
	-flour	-adorn
	-meale	-enamour
	-lome	-entangle
	-smother	-establish
		-infect
E. Sandys, *Europæ – Speculum* 1599		-friar
A.M., trsl. Gaebelkhover's *Boock of physicke* 1599		
Others	-ash	-afforest
	-dare	-attire
	-gall	-encumber
	-mist	-live
	-wreath	-wit
	...	...
cf. 1580–9	9 (+20)	24
1590–9	11 (+30)	50
1600–9	15 (+16)	38

Figures in parentheses refer to items without a main OED entry (counted for *be-*, *en-/em-*).

Fig. 20 EModE verbal derivation, 1598–9

EN-/EM-	-ATE	-IZE
enschedule	*deracin-*	*diamond-*
entame		*model-*
enstyle	*remonstr-*	*diamond-*
engallant		*model-*
embarrel	*adequ-*	*document-*
endungeon	*decurt-*	*paralog-*
ensaint (+ 2)	*diluvi-*	
	releg-	
embright		*champion-*
		crystall-
		german-
		idol-
		polygam-
entrammel	*disintric-*	*art-*
enfree	*altern-*	*epitom-*
enfroward	*commemor-*	*histor-*
	specul-	
	decoll-	
	degust-	
	urin-	
	vulner- (+2)	
encoffin	*compassion-*	*humor-*
	concaten-	*polit-*
	exor-	*satan-*
	preponder-	*spaniol-*
15 (+4)	29	10
45 (+30)	65	50
31 (+20)	79	32

en-/em- (*OED*, Marchand 1969: 162–4)

Early verbs of this type (before 1450) were all loanwords from French; later on, three types became productive:

1   'enclose in' (*en* + n/adj + **0**); ENCOFFIN, ENDUNGEON, *embay* (T24/62)
2   'reduce to a certain state' (*en* + adj/(n) + **0**); ENSAINT, ENFREE, *embase* (T16/81)
3   'intensifying' (*OED*: "in poetry often merely to give an additional syllable"; *en* + v)

The form of the prefix (*en-/em-*) was phonologically determined; *in-* was increasingly introduced where the Latin etymon was obvious (*enclose* vs. *include*).

dis- (*OED*, Marchand 1969: 158–61)

Privative meaning (reversing the content of the base) is found in a few cases of zero-derivation (*to stone cherries*). In EModE, new words formed on the pattern of *un* + n/adj + **0**, later of *dis* + n/adj + **0**/*ize* appear to have been preferred for their greater perspicuity. Resulting duplicates (such as *disthronize* 1583, *disthrone* 1591, *dethrone* 1609 and *unthrone* 1611) reflect EModE uncertainty.

7.5.6 *Zero-derivation* (Marchand 1969: 359–89)

Loss of inflexion, continuing in EModE (5.1), made homonymous more and more word forms representing different parts of speech (*love/love, loves/loves*) so that classification increasingly had to be based on syntax rather than on morphology. Zero-derivation had been common in OE and ME, but in EModE semantic restrictions on it appear to have been reduced even further: what was new in EModE, then, was the syntactic and semantic freedom with which new words were formed in this way rather than increased frequency. Spenser's peculiar nominalizations *the adorn, detain, implore, repent, covetize, riotize* may serve as illustrations, as may Nashe's verbs derived from bases formally marked as nouns: *to exception, remembrance, supplication, intercession, commotion.* (These derivatives duplicated existing words, which shows that they were not coined out of linguistic necessity.) Nashe's new derivatives contradict Gil, who restricted the pattern to native bases (*nomen commune uere nostrum*). The first grammarian to mention zero-derivation was probably Carew (T12/110–13), who praised the type as a particularly fortunate feature of English (although he included foreign bases among his specimens). His example *to cross* illustrates the advantages and semantic drawbacks of the pattern; according to the *OED*, in Carew's time, the verb could mean (earlier and later meanings in parentheses):

(†1)   to crucify (last used by Cheke, 1550)
2   to make the sign of the cross (1430–)
4   to cancel by marking with a cross (1483–), contradict (T12/61)
5   to lay a thing across another (1489–)
6   to intersect (1391–)
(7c)   to write across a cheque (1834–)
8   to pass over (a line, a river) (1583–)
(10)   to meet in passing (1782–)
11   to encounter (1598–)
(13)   (~ one's mind) to occur suddenly (1768–)
(16)   to cause to interbreed (1754–)

Even if the polysemy of the word is disambiguated in most contexts, the multiplicity of functions can be problematic.

7.6 Meaning

7.6.1 *Introductory* (Baldinger 1980; Görlach 1982: 111–28; Lyons 1968: 400–81)

To interpret an utterance in the way the speaker intends it to be understood is a very complex task largely dependent on 'meaning'. Therefore only a brief sketch of the problems will be given here and a few specimens from the texts interpreted; for the theoretical and methodological foundations of semantics, readers are referred to the relevant handbooks.

Linguistic signs are composed of expression (*signifiant*) and content (*signifié*); the interrelation of expression and content is arbitrary, and it is conventional. Bacon explained this phenomenon by comparing speech with money (1605, cf. T13):

> Words are tokens current and accepted for conceits, as moneys are for values.

By contrast, Locke finds that "*Words* then are made to be signs of our *Ideas*" (T63/24). Speakers employ linguistic signs to refer to objects and states of affairs (referents).

The actual or intended meaning of words in an individual text is apparently the product of various factors:

(a) the denotative meaning

(b) evaluative and associative components which the hearer may or may not share with the speaker (connotative meaning)

(c) elements deriving from the individual context and context of the utterance

(d) information supplied by the situation, participant roles, and from paralinguistic features such as gesture, etc.

(e) the speaker's intention and the listener's reaction

A similar model was proposed by Bühler (1978), who distinguished between the symbolic (representational), symptomatic (expressive), and appellative (signalling) functions of language.

The meaning of a linguistic sign (mainly as in (a) and (b)) is always defined linguistically and is therefore bound to an individual language. Therefore it is not to be expected that the contents of two signs (in, say, Latin and EModE) should be equivalent in translation – or that this is the case with an EModE word and the PrE word descended from it. Gavin Douglas found himself in the typical translator's dilemma when he complained that an uncontroversial translation of *animal* and *homo* was impossible, the semantic structures of Latin and Scots not being equivalent (T18A/37–50). Accordingly, the Roman Catholic principle in biblical translation of rendering each Latin word by one invariable EModE equivalent in all contexts signals a naive misunderstanding of 'meaning': the Protestants realized (T18D/7–28) that this procedure distorted, rather than preserved, the content of Holy Writ. The various meanings of Latin *iudicium* and the EModE (or PrE) words needed to render them are enough to illustrate the point.

Particular concepts, however, are not restricted to individual languages. This fact makes translation feasible, though not, of course, on a one-to-one, word-for-word basis since the linguistic structures expressing concepts are indeed language-specific; it is also the basic idea behind onomasiology (7.6.3) and efforts to establish a universal language, a topic much discussed by seventeenth/eighteenth-century writers (Knowlson 1975; Slaughter 1982). However, in the models proposed in contemporary writings, meaning was frequently identified with 'concept', or even with the entities themselves.

7.6.2 Determining the meaning of a word

Meaning is defined by the paradigmatic and syntagmatic relations existing between linguistic signs, i.e. by the delimitation of the content of one linguistic unit from others from the same semantic field, and by the ability of a sign to collocate with others in meaningful texts. These relations can be described as forming part of the competence of speakers and listeners, who are aware of lexical alternatives and are also able to select from the range of meanings the one that combines with the context to produce an intelligible interpretation reflecting the speaker's intentions.

Since all interpretations of the historical stages of a language are based on texts, lexical meanings must be reconstructed from the sum of recorded collocations (syntagmatic relations). A paradigmatic approach is possible only where texts give definitions (most often in manuals and dictionaries): in t49, Elyot contrasted *discretion* and *modesty/mansuetude*; Boorde defined diseases by listing their symptoms in T44; less perfect definitions were provided by Hortrop in T48/107–16. A manual such as Peacham's in t53 defined terms and explained their use; dictionaries delimit the content of individual lexemes by genus/species definitions and partial synonyms (cf. T56/29–49), in bilingual dictionaries by partial translational equivalents = heteronyms (t47). The diagram below will make it clear, however, that data from dictionaries provide a certain measure of aid, but are no real substitute for competence in EModE:

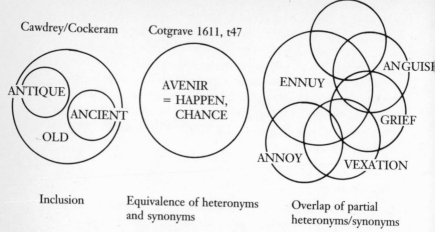

Fig. 21 Semantic relations in dictionary entries

Since partial overlap appears to be the rule, it follows that the data supplied by dictionaries require careful semantic analysis.

Translation can also provide considerable assistance, especially since skilful translators will not restrict equivalence to word rank. Although the value of translators' methodological reflections, often found in prefaces to the translated text, tends to be of varying quality (T18), they can help to explain the translators' practices. How valuable translations can be in semantic analysis depends on how precisely the meaning of the source text can be reconstructed, and to what extent the translator's comprehension of the original and the precise way in which he used his native tongue can be established. The utmost caution is, however, necessary when interpreting the semantics of EModE texts on the basis of competence in PrE – even if it includes archaic registers: since change of meaning is always possible, EModE/PrE 'equivalences' can prove to be dangerous *faux amis* (7.7.1).

Special difficulties arise from idiolectal uses. Thus, the number of lexemes available for the concept of 'modesty' ranges from one to three, depending on the individual (t49), and the number of words available to an individual speaker will, of course, determine their semantic range in his idiolect. In addition, poetic diction often deliberately diverges from accepted or usual meanings in order to avoid triteness of expression.

7.6.3 Semasiology and onomasiology

The semasiological approach attempts to establish the meanings of given lexemes, determining the distinctive sense components of each by a comparison with the similar contents of other lexemes, and the range of meaning by an account of all possible collocations. By contrast, the onomasiological approach presupposes universal conceptual structures and then attempts to find

t58   V. Such kind of *Utensils* as serve *to contain* other things, are usually called VESSELS, *Cask, Receptacle, Pan, Plate,* &c.

These are distinguishable by their Matter, Shapes and Uses, into such as serve

   Keeping and carriage of things ; being either   (*for the*

5   *Pliable to the things they contain* ; whether || *more loose :* or *more close.*

     BAG, *Sack, Budget, Pocket, Pouch, Purse, Sachel, Scrip, Wallet, Poke,*

   1.   *Male, Knapsack, Portmantue, Cloak-bag.*

     CASE, *Sheath, Scabbard, Shrine, Covering, Quiver, Tike, Pillowbear.*

   Stiff ; for

10   *Arids* ; being made either of || *bords :* or *twigs.*

     BOX, *Chest, Trunk, Ark, Coffer, Cabinet, Casket, Bin, Clapper, Cupbord,*

     Hutch, Locker, Safe, Spence, Press, Pyx, Coffin, Sumpter, Desk, Flash,

   2.   *Till, Drawer, Cap-case.*

     BASKET, *Flasket, Maund, Frail, Hamper, Pannier, Scuttle, Weel, Dorser.*

15   *Liquids* ; *in*

     Greater quantities ; either || *closed at both ends :* or *open at one.*

     BARREL, *Cask, Fat, Firkin, Keg, Hogshead, Kilderkin, Pipe, Tun,*

   3.   *Butt, Rundlet, Cooper.*

     TUB, *Bucket, Coul, Vate, Cistern, Pale, Piggin.*

20   *Less quantities* ; whether   (Earth, &c.

     Shallow ; being made either of || *Metal :* or *other materials,* Wood,

     DISH, *Platter, Pan, Charger, Voider, Bason, Laver, Patin, Plate, Por-*

   4.   TRAY, *Pan, Boul, Trough.*   (*ringer, Saucer.*

     Deep ; of || *a bigger :* or *lesser aperture.*

25   POT, *Flagon, Tankard, Jack, Jar, Pitcher, Jugg, Mugg, Noggin,*

   5.   BOTTLE, *Crewet, Jugg, Cruse.*   (*Postnet, Urne.*

Dressing or boiling of Meat ; either || *without :* or *with feet.*

   6.   KETTLE, *Caldron, Copper, Furnace.*

     SKILLET, *Pipkin.*

30   *Spending* ; either by

   Taking out, the Tube of effusion : to which may be adjoyned *the instrument*

     FAUCET, *spout.*   *tubulus.* (*for stopping it.*

   7.   TAP, *spiggot, Stopple.*

   Receiving in ; whether || *of a roundish :* or *oblong Cavity.*

35   SPOON, *Ladle, Scummer.*

   8.   SCOOP, *shovel, laving.*

   Laying on of Meat : or *pouring out of Drink.*

     TRENCHER, *Plate.*

   9   CUP, *Boul, Goblet, Beaker, Cann, Chalice, Mazer, Glass.*

out how these are reflected in the semantic structure of the individual language. Semasiological structure is, then, found in monolingual dictionaries and onomasiological in thesauruses such as Roget's (1962). In what follows, I will use examples from Roget's predecessor Wilkins (1668), which allows me to use EModE specimens and relations for a synchronic description of EModE and of the diachronic development of selected lexemes (7.7); compare the data for 'arms' (t41) and the list of 'vessels' (t58) above (Wilkins, p. 262).

7.6.4 Syntagmatic and paradigmatic relations

Every lexeme is defined by the combinations it can enter into (or, if the analysis is exclusively corpus-based, it is found in). Significant for semantic analysis are particularly close syntagmatic relations between words, such as implication (*stabb'd* in T31D/6, 8 presupposes the word *dagger*).

Paradigmatic relations hold between units that can be substituted for each other. Lists of lexemes whose senses are minimally distinct are especially helpful in describing semantic structure; compare Wilkins (p. 350) for the component [± adult] in words for domestic animals.

t59   By the firſt of theſe is meant the young ones or *brood* of any ſorts of Animals, for which we have no proper word in *Engliſh*.   So

Theſe words	will ſignifie	Theſe words	will ſignifie
Horſe	Colt,Foal,Filly	Dog	Puppy, Whelp
Cow	Calf	Cat	Kitlin, Chitt
Deer	Fawn	Cony	Rabbet
Sheep	Lamb	Hare	Leveret
Goat	Kid	Hen	Chicken
Hog	Pig	Frog	Tadpole
Bear	Cub	Herring	Sprat

5

Leaving the senses of homonyms, such as *calf* 'back part of the human leg', and possible cases of polysemy out of account, the sense of each of the lexemes listed consists of two distinctive components [zoological genus] and [± adult]. Words such as *mare, stallion, gelding, steed, jade, bay* for 'horses' show that more distinctive features are necessary for a full description of the semantic field – in both EModE and PrE. Thus the addition of [± male], [± castrated] provides the following description (in the form of tree diagram and matrix) – still leaving *steed*, *jade* and *bay* unaccounted for:

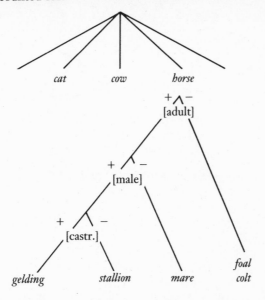

	horse	adult	male	castr.
horse	+	○	○	○
stallion	+	+	+	−
gelding	+	+	+	+
mare	+	+	−	−
foal	+	−	○	○
colt	+	−	+	−

Fig. 22 Representation of a semantic field by tree diagram and matrix

Both forms of description have *horse* as the generic term with fewer semantic features (*hyperonym*, *archilexeme*), whereas more specialized words with more features (*hyponyms*) are found further down the stemma. Where the sums of features are identical for two lexemes, further analysis will either yield additional distinctions or show that they are synonymous (7.6.9).

Arrangement of Wilkins' list of 'conveyances' (p. 257) in stemmatic form, retaining the distinctive features which he recognized, would produce the following diagram:

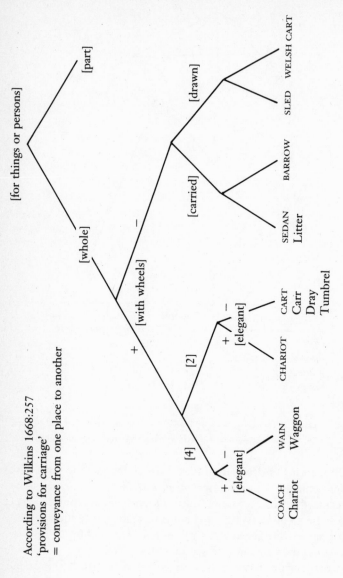

According to Wilkins 1668:257
'provisions for carriage',
= conveyance from one place to another

Fig. 23 Stemmatic representation of Wilkins' set of 'conveyances'

If such analyses were continued, the final result would (in theory) be an arrangement, on the basis of central semantic features, of *all* the EModE sememes (7.6.7) of *all* EModE lexemes in their semantic fields. These fields are part of the *semantic* structure of EModE, but they may largely coincide with encyclopaedic/notional fields ('arms', 'vessels'), which makes Wilkins' distinctions interpretable as semantic ones.

Polysemous lexemes necessarily have their places in more than one field, as is the case with *trade*, *conference*, etc., in the following table:

	traffic 1505–	trade 1375–	commerce 1537–	intercourse 1473–	communication 1382–	conference 1538–
'(commercial) exchange'	+1 1506– 1719		1	+1 1494– 1669	1?	
'sale, trading'	2 1568–	8	1			
'commodity'	+4 1555– 1778	11				
'traffic'	5 1825–					
'relations'	3?	+7b 1602–	2	2	5	+5 1565– 1651
'intercourse'			+3 1624–	2d		
'exchange of ideas'			+5 1634– 1757	+4 1570– 1692	+4 1462– 1605	4
'information'					2	

Fig. 24 The field of 'communication' of EModE: overlap and differentiation (senses according to *OED* classification)

In many cases, then, sense components established by semantic analysis correspond to features of extralinguistic classes and encyclopaedic components. The two must not, however, be confused: age and sex are encyclopaedic features of every living animal, but they are lexically distinguished in only a few species (possibly in different ones in different languages). Besides, the number of encyclopaedic features is unlimited, whereas the number of semes depends on the number of necessary semantic distinctions. Also note that the meaning of scientific terms differs from common meaning in that terminologies are defined on a notional basis and are intended to be non-ambiguous, non-contradictory and independent of any particular language.

In practice, it is often difficult to isolate semes unambiguously and to divide up the semantic content of a lexeme into discrete senses. Difficult problems of delimitation within a lexical field recur in distinguishing one field from another (see 'communication' above, or 'anger' in the list of partial equivalents of *ennuy* in t47). In particular, it must be pointed out that the structure of *OED* entries is not exclusively (or even primarily) semantic.

7.6.5 Lexical meaning

The morpheme may be defined as the smallest linguistic sign; it can occur as a free form (as a word) or as a part in composite lexemes (7.5). Morphemes have either lexical or grammatical meaning (function). The meaning of composite linguistic signs can usually be understood from the meanings of their components, but composite meanings are not always purely additive as many compounds or phrasal lexemes (idioms) prove. Straightforward compounds such as *horssebacke* (T47/80); *spoonefull*, *siluer spoone*, *Orange pill* or *Rye paste* (T49) are found along with others whose analysis is difficult without factual knowledge of the object itself (such as *moldwarp*, praised for its expressiveness by Carew in T12/25). Therefore, there is no alternative to the lexicographical practice of listing words rather than morphemes. Examples of phrasal lexemes at higher ranks (idioms, proverbs) are *put him to þe horne* 'outlawed him' (T36/60); *a shippe of salte for you, saue your credite* 'be gone' (T12/147–8); or such proverbial expressions used by Day as: *to caste pearles before swine* (T43/145–6 after Matthew 7.6) and *so long the pot goeth to the riuer, that at last it commeth broken home* (T43/195–6). Also compare a selection of EModE proverbs collected by Peacham under the entry *parœmia* (1577: sig. D iv).

If the discussion below concentrates on lexical meanings (chiefly of monomorphemic words), this is because lexicalizations at higher ranks are comparatively rare.

7.6.6 Denotative and connotative meaning

Even though denotative meaning predominates in the logical-semantic structure of the lexicon, associative and social meanings of individual speakers or groups are very important in actual language use and for successful communication. The affective associations of words are also factors in semantic change (not always easily detected in its early stages, 7.7.2).

7.6.7 Polysemy and homonymy

Many words have more than one meaning, not as a consequence of their syntactic ambiguity or of special speakers' intended meanings (as in irony). Rather, all languages contain a great number of words whose content must be described as a composite of various more or less distinct senses ('sememes'). These sememes may be related to each other, as is the case with most conventionalized metaphorical meanings. Often, however, sememes appear to be so heterogeneous that their having the same forms seems coincidental.

The distinction between the two categories of polysemy and homonymy is shown up by componential analysis. Polysemy holds between sememes if they have at least one sense component or feature ('seme') in common. In cases of homonymy there is no such semantic overlap. (Homonymy also holds if the relation can only be established by knowledge of a foreign language, as is the case with EModE *conference* from *conferre*, 7.7.2h.)

Since the distinction between polysemy and homonymy involves native-speaker judgement, classification becomes increasingly uncertain for historical stages of a language; diverging classifications are likely. The traditional (historical) definition of the two terms is quite different from the synchronic semantic classification sketched above: it is based on etymology, with the term 'polysemy' reserved for cases in which one original lexeme expanded its range of meaning (its number of sememes). This concept of 'polysemy' includes words which would be categorized as homonymous in a synchronic semantic analysis, the overlap between sememes having been lost in the process of semantic change (*game* 1 'play, sport, match'; 2 'trick or secret plan'; 3 'wild animals hunted or fished for food') – and even some now spelt differently (*flower*, *flour*).

Homonyms, according to the historical definition, result from the merger of the expression planes of two lexemes as a consequence of sound changes or borrowing. This includes a few cases which are interpreted as polysemous today, their different etymologies not being generally known (*pregnant* 'clear, obvious', 'ready, inclined' (in T25/9 *pregnant wit*), 'with child'). In this view, the distinction between polysemy and homonymy therefore depends exclusively on the etymologies being known.

For most users of a language such historical knowledge is normally neither interesting nor available. Since metaphorical uses (and a universal human desire to establish connections?) are common in speech, polysemy appears to be dominant in synchronic interpretation.

Lexicographers waver between synchronic-semantic and historical-etymological classifications in dictionary entries (but tend to prefer the etymological principle). However, for most words the two methods yield the same results, etymological distinctness normally surviving as semantic homonymy.

Polysemy and homonymy will normally be disambiguated by the context. Thus *foorm* is clearly to be understood as 'bench' in T41/23–4, 61 on the basis of the collocation with *sit dooun*, and *rheast* as 'seat' (the unusual spelling possibly intended to distinguish it from *rest* 'remainder' in the following line). *Stone* clearly refers to a gall-stone or nephritic stone in T30/66: *Bowling is good for the Stone and Reines*, but to the philosopher's stone in t37/16. Misunderstandings can occur, or deliberate puns be constructed, with polysemous words where the context does not properly disambiguate them, such as *capacities* in *depends vpon your capacities: and not of your heads alone, but of your purses* (T31A/3–4). In T18G/6–7, the ambiguity of *spirits* (1 'esprit'; 2 'courage';

3 'ghost'; 4 'alcoholic drink') is kept in balance by contradictory contextual elements: *wit* (1) *distilled* (4) *in one language, cannot be transferred without loss of spirits.* The more similar sememes are, the more difficult it is to disambiguate them contextually. The resulting linguistic pathology (Ullmann 1963) affects historical homonyms and homophones (such as *queen:quean*) as it does polysemous words (such as *copy*). The thus restricted usefulness of such words can lead, or contribute, to their loss (homonymy, 7.1.3) or at least to the loss of individual sememes (polysemy, 7.7.2g).

Polysemy was often considered an inadequacy in a language, especially in the late seventeenth century when the equation "one notion (or even one object) = one term" was considered the ideal to aim at (T17). On the one hand, Carew (T12/31–6) regarded polysemy as providing *significancye* ('abundance of meaning(s)'), which is matched, he claimed, on the expression plane by *Copiousnes* (11, 65) ('abundance of words') and is one of the positive characteristics of English.

The ultimate acknowledgement of homonymy are distinctive spellings, which make the separation into two signs unambiguous and irreversible. The original orthographic unity and polysemy of *travel/travail* is apparent from T48/31 (cf. the title and T48/36) – which makes it impossible to translate these instances as either PrE *travel* or *travail*. The modern distinctions between *human/ humane, discreet/discrete, flower/flour, mettle/metal* did not exist in EModE either.

7.6.8 *Metaphor and metonymy* (Lausberg 1967: 59–79)

Metaphorical use of a linguistic sign means that it is transferred, on the basis of one shared feature, whether semantic or encyclopaedic (the *tertium comparationis*), to a new referent.

Metaphors have therefore been characterized as abridged comparisons. The transfer does not affect the content of the lexeme. The clash between meaning and use is what makes a metaphor effective; thus some knowledge of the terminology of Elizabethan jurisdiction and of the techniques of court proceedings is essential for the understanding of T31G/1–14 (cf. T56/1–28, *lively set forth by an Allegorie of a Shippe under Sayle*).

This does not prevent metaphors from becoming conventionalized. *Thornes ... prick and sting* (T31B/170–1) had referred to 'conscience' in ME, and the expression in *from the Table of my Memory, / Ile wipe away all triuiall fond Records* (T31B/181–2) had been used metaphorically from antiquity. Transparent and conventional metaphors are also found in the description of the emancipation of the English language in T8/155–9 (*wean ... dry nurse ... milch nurse*), or in the equation of sweetness with pleasant style in T27/3, 20 (*honny-flowing; they cast Sugar and Spice, vpon euery dish*).

Finally, metaphorical uses can become habitual and thus lead to an expansion of meaning by creating new sememes (*foot* 'part of the leg', 'measure', 'bottom part of a ladder, of a page...'). This procedure is commonly used to fill linguistic gaps, but it also serves to provide new terms for colloquial speech (see t47, FOL).

Metonymy is related to metaphor (and cannot in all cases be properly distinguished from it). It is not based upon comparison, but on the extralinguistic connection between two referents in time or space: a part can be used to refer to the whole (synecdoche, T23B/89), the material to the object (*Dagger ... cursed Steele*, T31D/6, 9), the vessel to the content, etc. Here, too, use can become habitual – *tongue* has the sememes 'part of the body' in T11/5, but 'language' in T8/66; the two belong to two different semantic fields.

Metaphorical language in poetry is sometimes quite complex as a consequence of the intermingling of various fields. In T31E/35–6 there is not only the transfer of musical harmony to social relations (with the new word *vn-tune* coined for this context), but also the homonymy of *Discord* (as if from 'heart' and 'string', cf. *dischorde* in T23A/51). Metaphors can also be extended to permeate through complete poems (T31G) or longer texts such as complete plays (sexuality and disease in *Hamlet*). Also compare the function of allegory as in Spenser's *a continued Allegory, or darke conceit* (T24/3–4), which can be understood at text rank only.

Frequency and types of metaphors vary according to individual authors, periods and types of text. Authors of the late seventeenth century tended to regard metaphorical language very critically (in spite of a wealth of biblical metaphors in T50), because it was thought to lead to obscurity (T17).

7.6.9 Synonymy

The term was used in EModE in at least three ways:

1   A naive concept of the linguistic sign, and therefore of synonymy, underlies the statement in T18D/33–4 which equates synonymy and identity of reference: *hee vsing diuers words . . . and indifferently for one thing in nature.* Such synonymy may be employed for variation, to enrich the language of a text creating as it does *copie* of speech (*copie or store,* T18D/36).

2   Synonymy as identity of denotative meaning is what Carew had in mind in regarding his translational equivalents of *fortis* in T12/150–3 (the verb *Synnonomize* denotes 'translate').

3   Synonymy appears to be equated with substitutability in a given text or situation (including paraphrases) in Carew's equivalents of 'be gone' in T12/140–50.

On the basis of my definition in 7.6.1 above, two lexemes are here considered synonyms if their *signifiés* have the same descriptive meaning (cf. Carew, no. 2). Such complete identity of meaning is rare. Since most lexemes are polysemous, the identity of individual sememes is much commoner: one sememe of *copie* is synonymous with one sememe of *store* (T18D/36), but of course the two lexemes are not synonymous in the case of *copie* 'source text', 'text copies', or of *store* 'cattle, possessions'. Note that most (partial) synonyms had and have different connotative meanings – a possible source of semantic change (7.7.2–3).

Synonymy was an important stylistic device, creating *copie* of speech, in the forms of duplication (*copie or store*) or of variation which helped to avoid repetition (*ghost* T31B/20 and 86 vs. *spirit* T31B/23 and 92; *beckons:wafts:waues* T31B/42 vs. /46 vs. /55; cf. the combination in T39/54–6). Since most of the words quoted are polysemous, their synonymy can again be only partial.

The co-existence of partial synonyms can be very complex. In

particular, paradigmatic relations can become confusing if sociolinguistic distinctions (according to class, style, formality and age)
and the contrast between common words and special terminologies are also involved, or if diachronic considerations (old: new,
fashionable use) including changes of meaning are to be described. Two diagrams (Figs. 25 and 26) may illustrate the problem: the partial overlap of *gay/jolly/brave* and EModE *wit* and its
partial synonyms (cf. Barber 1976: 145–7 and the diachronic description in 7.7.2).

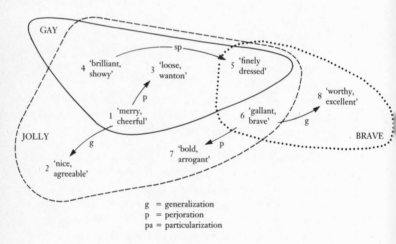

g = generalization
p = perjoration
pa = particularization

Fig. 25 Overlap and change of meaning in three EModE adjectives

Vocabulary

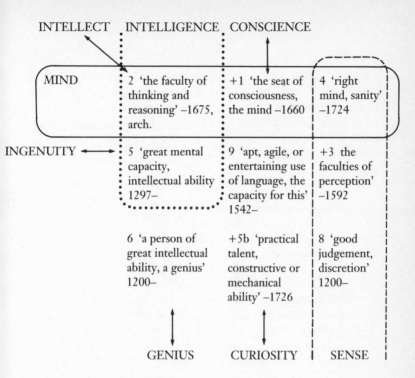

WIT and its partial synonyms (from the *OED*)

Fig. 26 Partial synonyms in the EModE field of intellect ('wit')

7.7 Change of meaning (Ullmann 1963: 171–257; Waldron 1978)

7.7.1 Introductory

Readers become aware of change of meaning when lexemes in older texts do not 'make sense' in context. Such 'semantic discomfort' (Lewis 1974: 1) should stimulate the reader to discover what sense the author intended and whether the misunderstanding (or deliberate ambiguity) results from original polysemy or later semantic change:

> We trauell in tongues (T8/66) 'we toil in the study of foreign languages'; haunt for traffike sake (T11/30) 'frequent in order to trade'; eager compounds (T31G/16) 'spicy dishes'; or stoutnesse of stomach (T36A/47) 'deliberate bravery' are as likely to be misunderstood by a modern reader, as is Milton's a singed bottom all involv'd / With stench and smoke... (T34/71–2).

Menner (1945) and Rudskoger (1952) investigated how quickly meanings change and what consequences extreme polysemy has for the survival of words. Reading Chaucer's General Prologue to the Canterbury Tales (c. 1390) leads one to suspect that – like the vocabulary in general – many meanings had changed drastically by the time Dryden felt that a translation of Chaucer was necessary (T18H); certainly semantic changes are less conspicuous in the next stretch of 300 years from Dryden to PrE.

It will only be possible to test this impression empirically within a larger framework (e.g. in the forthcoming Historical Thesaurus of the English Language). The following seven extremely polysemous words were selected at random, and the figures showing their 'senses' were taken from the OED, although the inclusion of technical senses further distorts the picture:

With the above reservations in mind, it appears safe to say that:

1   new meanings considerably outnumber obsolete senses – a result which may partly reflect the preservation of archaic styles in certain registers and the conservative bent of the OED compilers;

2   polysemy does not stop a lexeme from acquiring more new sememes, even in the form of semantic loans;

3   the EModE period was exceptionally productive not only
       in the overall growth of lexemes but also in the increase in
       their semantic ranges.

	draught	form	sense	set	stock
–OE					2–1
–1300	5–2	8–3			2–1
–1400	11–6	5–1	2–1	1	9–2
–1500	7–2	3–1		2–2	8–3
–1600	11–5	2	16–1	8–4	14–4
–1700	5	2	8–1	3–1	12
–1800	2	1	1	7	6–1
–1900	5		1	10	
Total	46–15	21–5	28–3	31–7	53–12

	trade	train	wit	Total
–OE			3–1	5–2
–1300			4–1	19–7
–1400	2–2	1–1	2–2	33–15
–1500	1–1	4–1	1	26–10
–1600	4–2	6–2	2	63–18
–1700	2	1	1	34–2
–1800	2–1	2		21–2
–1900	2	1		19
Total	13–6	15–4	13–4	226–56

Selected polysemous words of EModE: increase in the number of main senses and
losses of meanings by centuries (from the *OED*; doubtful and nonce meanings
excluded).

Fig. 27 Accretion and obsolescence of individual senses
         in selected polysemous words, 1200–1900

7.7.2 *Causes and conditions of semantic change*

A great number of factors, often specific for the individual word, may be involved in the conditions that make change of meaning possible, in the situation that actuates it and favours its spread, and in its acceptance by the speech community. All this makes a satisfactory description of the phenomenon and the classification of individual cases a difficult and largely unsolved problem for the history of the English lexicon. However, a number of factors initiating change should be mentioned (excluding the connotative ones mentioned in 7.6.1 above):

(a) Scientific and technological change and changes in society may be reflected in new designations (loanwords or newly coined words) or in changes in the meanings of old words acquiring new denotata – but it may remain without narrowly semantic effect if old words continue to be used, with the sum of their semantic features remaining constant. This is obviously the case with the generic terms *ship* ('vessel for navigation on water') and *house* ('building used for human habitation') whose material forms have greatly changed since OE *scip* and *hus*. Change of meaning has occurred where lexemes have changed their position within a semantic field as a consequence of new semantic contrasts caused by the addition of new words to the field and the resulting changes in the number and composition of the sememes of the older lexemes. For example, the field of 'vehicles used on land' (7.6.4) has seen, especially from EModE times onwards, rapid technological development *and* semantic differentiation, new encyclopaedic features becoming semantically distinctive as well (e.g. [on rails], [manner of propulsion], [for persons or goods], [number of wheels]).

(b) Psychological factors may initiate and favour semantic change, as in the case of euphemism. Social taboos in such areas as disease, death or sexual and excretory functions mean that these tend to be referred to by emotionally neutral and morphologically and etymologically opaque foreign words (*defunct* 'the dead woman', T42/59), or more general words are used, the specific reference being indicated by additional linguistic or situational information:

> *wench* 'young girl' > 'prostitute' (t47/30–1, cf. the development of *mistress* and *quean*); *sege* 'seat' > 'lavatory' (T44/208); *closettis* [*of*

ease] 'closed room' > 'toilet' (T45/80). Similarly disguising expressions result from metaphorical or metonymic uses (AmE *washroom* 'toilet').

Such new meanings with disguising functions can push out older ones (PrE *undertaker*); in such cases older texts can happen to become comical: *I passed away* (T50/1) 'went off', not 'died'; cf. Milton's *singed bottom* (T34/71).

Whereas euphemisms are meant to tone down, the expressive metaphors of colloquial speech illustrate the opposite tendency: the translational equivalents listed for FOL in t47 are mostly emphatic metaphors; a similar expressiveness underlies adverbs of the EModE type *wondrous, exceeding*.

Disguising and expressive functions become ineffective through frequent use, which results in shifts in the connotative (but often also in the denotative) range of meaning.

(c) Similarity of form or historical homonymy can also affect semantic context, causing the meanings of the respective lexemes to converge. This also applies to words containing submorphemic combinations (phonaesthemes) which come to be associated with certain (ranges of) meaning(s); cf. the specimens adduced by Samuels (1972: 45–8) to illustrate their effect on change of meaning in English words.

(d) The lexicon of common speech and special jargons continuously affect each other. This process can involve semantic expansion (generalization) when technical terms are adopted into the general vocabulary, a phenomenon especially frequent with legal (7.1.8) and medical terms (cf. *humour* below). The opposite process takes place with common words that are re-defined to function as technical terms.

Similar changes occur with other internal loans from social or regional subsystems: as in all borrowing processes, it is not to be expected that all shades of meaning and connotative features will also be transferred.

(e) Contextual restrictions or expansions change the collocational compatibility of lexemes, and hence possibly affect their meanings. The fact that the meaning of adjectives (in particular, as expressing evaluations) is more context-dependent than that of nouns or verbs tends to lead to more conspicuous semantic changes than in the case of other parts of speech, as Menner's

(1945), Lewis' (1974) and Rudskoger's (1952) studies have amply demonstrated.

The history of *nice*, *fond* and *silly* drastically shows how thoroughly expressive meanings can change in time. Pejoration is a shared characteristic of adjectives and related nouns in the semantic field 'clever' (with the single exception of *shrewd*): thus most uses of *cunning* (T8/90, 99, 124, 175), of *art* (T47/34–9), of *craft* and *craftie* (T30/9), and of *sle* 'sly' (T18A/4) are still neutral in their EModE contexts, but T31G/29–42 betray contextually negative connotations in *cunning* and *art*, which came to predominate in the former.

A negative connotation also came to be attached to neutral *vulgar* (T37A/6); *voluble* (T11/5, but *volubility* T17/47); *vitious* (T14/6); *impertinent* ('not pertinent', T11/59); *insolent* ('unusual', T18E/34, a Latinate meaning). Both *notorious* and *notable* being neutral, they can be found in uses and collocations highly unusual in PrE (T12/21; *a notable nimmer*, T32/19).

Another form of syntagmatical change is that found in ellipsis, which transfers the meaning of the complete phrase to one word: *closettis* [*of ease*], *fall* [*of leaves*], *private* [*soldier*].

(f) The differentiation of former synonyms starts with connotative features and contextual factors. *Ghost/spirit* are interchanged in T31B, but have become distinct in PrE, whereas there has never been a fully effective split between *liberty* and *freedom*. The history of *evil/ill/bad* illustrates the complex differentiation of three near-synonyms: statistics show that the central, unmarked word was *evil* in OE/ME, *ill* in EModE and *bad* in PrE (neglecting partial synonyms such as *wicked*, EModE *shrewd*, etc., that do not appear to have played any part in the differentiation):

	evil	ill	bad	total frequency
Chaucer	77%	7%	15%	163
Spenser	30%	50%	20%	351
Sidney	55%	27%	18%	98
Shakespeare	19%	54%	27%	500
West (1953)	24%	27%	49%	1551

Fig. 28 Relative frequencies of *evil:ill:bad*

Vocabulary

(g) Polysemous words tend to reduce their range of meanings, especially if the contexts in which they are normally used do not sufficiently disambiguate individual senses, and if the information transmitted is regarded as important: the great variety of meanings of *doom* was obviously intolerable in a field that demanded terminological clarity.

Reduction of the number of meanings also appears to be regular where sememes are particularized so that they become their own hyponyms so to speak, as happened to *meat* in the fifteenth to seventeenth centuries.

I ME   II Sixteenth century   III Seventeenth century

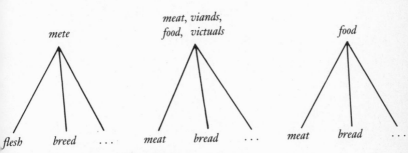

Fig. 29 Semantic development of *meat*

(h) Language contact can be responsible for semantic change in three ways (here illustrated from Latin: EModE, cf. 7.3.2):

1.   The meaning of a native word (or an earlier loan) is expanded by the adoption of a foreign sememe. This tends to occur when the native and the foreign word are partially synonymous, i.e. already have sememes in common, further sememes then being easily transferred:

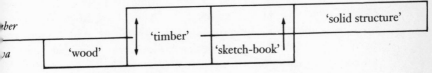

Fig. 30 Semantic calquing

203

2   The adoption of a loanword provides more precise denotation; this may reduce the semantic range of the earlier word by the meaning of the loan: *old* – (*antique* + *ancient*). It is, however, also possible for the new loans to acquire meanings from the earlier words (as happened with *antique* and *ancient*, which were widely used as more refined synonyms of *old* in the sixteenth century).

3   An earlier loanword may be borrowed afresh. Often it is difficult to decide whether a particular instance is better classified as a new loanword or as an expansion of the meaning of the earlier lexeme (1). The repetitive borrowing of individual sememes may be illustrated from the development of EModE *conference* and *copy*.

For *copy*, the *OED* lists among other meanings:

†1	'plenty, abundance'	(1375–1656)	
†1b	'fullness'	(1483–1500)	
†1c	'copiousness' (of words)	(1511–1637)	(T13/64)
2	'a transcript'	(1330–)	
3	'picture'	(1580–)	
4	'reproduction'	(1596–)	
†4b	'specimen'	(1641–55)	
6	'example' (of a book)	(1538–)	(T18C/50)
8	'original source'	(14..–)	(t9/4, T18C/108)

As a central term in stylistics and rhetoric, *copy* (1c) had the partial synonyms *store* (T18D/36), *plentye* (T12/68), *copiousness* (T12/65) and Scots *fowth* (T18A/16).

The diagram below illustrates the relationship between borrowed meanings (→) and those developed within EModE (–––):

All the borrowed meanings of *conference* (*OED* 1–5, only no. 4 surviving into PrE) are from before 1610: †3 'comparison, collation' (t2/6, t32/5) 1538; †2 'furnishing, supplying' 1545; †4 'conversation' (T30/19) 1555; †5 'communication, intercourse' (T8/34, 37) 1565; †1 'collection' 1610. As an EModE development, the modern meaning of *conference* arose from no. 4 around 1586. It is now difficult to decide whether the fact that the individual sememes of *conference* were semantically so wide apart may have contributed to their later loss.

Vocabulary

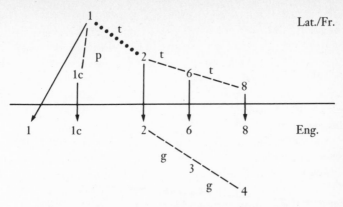

(p = particularization, g = generalization, t = metaphorical or
syntagmatic transfer)

Fig. 31 Borrowed meanings and independent developments: *copy*

The classification of semantic change suggested above ((a)–(h))
overlaps with other possible distinctions, namely deliberate vs.
chance, gradual vs. sudden. The factors ((a)–(h)) are not of equal
weight, but impossible to arrange in any hierarchical order, and
many co-occur, making the hypothetical causes of many particular changes very complex. A look at some monographs treating,
among other words, *wit*, *humour* and *conceit* shows the intricate
connections between such central terms and the history of ideas,
relations which can only be imperfectly described by the methods
of componential analysis.

Wit, the OE word for 'intellect', 'good sense' and 'conscience'
became increasingly polysemous in ME, being employed (in addition to the loanwords *science* and *sentence*, *sense*) to translate Latin
scientia and *sententia*. The further history of *wit* is complicated by
far-reaching overlaps with meanings of *mind*, *reason* and *fancy*; any
description of one of these in isolation appears to be almost
impossible. A comprehensive description of *wit* would also have
to take account of specific changes effected by medieval and
Renaissance philosophy and psychology. While some of the
medieval meanings became obsolete, new ones arose when *wit*
was transferred to the person having *wit* (*OED* 9) and, increasingly employed as a rhetorical term, *wit* came to mean the art of

witty conversation – and mockery. This development (as indeed the wealth of new verbs signifying 'to mock', cf. 7.1.5) appears to be typical of the sixteenth century. In the seventeenth century *wit* became associated with the comic, its meaning reduced to purely verbal *witticism*, while at the same time it became a central term in literary criticism ('poetic fancy') – a polysemic clash that led writers between 1660 and 1760 to distinguish between *false wit* and *true wit*.

The early history of *humour* illustrates the revolution taking place in physics and medicine and also the generalizations of meaning typical of technical terms adopted into common speech. The word meant 'moisture', 'juice', 'fluid' in ME, and was used from the beginning of medical writing in the vernacular as the generic term for the four cardinal humours of the body (blood, phlegm, choler, melancholy). Since their mixture (temperament) was thought to determine "a person's physical and mental qualities and disposition" (*OED* 2), thereby also affecting a person's mood (*OED* 5) or whims (*OED* 6), *humour* not unnaturally became a widely used fashionable word, with mushrooming meanings, developing a definite bias towards quaintness of behaviour (and finally "the quality of action, speech, or writing, which excites amusement", *OED* 7a, and "the faculty of perceiving what is ludicrous or amusing", *OED* 7b) after the 'medical' foundations of the word had been shattered by Harvey's discovery of the circulation of the blood in 1632.

The original meaning of *conceit* (*OED*: "What is conceived in the mind") has obvious connections with *wit*; its most frequent meaning in the sixteenth century, however, was 'concept', as it is in Bacon's explanation of the linguistic sign (7.6.1) and in similar uses in t23/3, T11/2, T12/203, T27/37, 86. It also signified 'imagination' (T43/204) or a mental faculty (T8/164), meanings which had largely been replaced by new Latin loanwords (*concept*, *conception*) by 1700.

A second line of development derived from *conceive* 'estimate' (*OED* II), but the neutral meaning of *conceit* 'opinion' was soon restricted to 'favourable opinion', and then (shortened from *self-conceit*) to 'conceitedness' after 1605.

However, the most fruitful development of *conceit* put it (like *wit*) in the same lexical field as *imagination* and *fancy* in the sixteenth/seventeenth centuries, when it was used for 'fancy or imagination' (*OED* 7), 'a fanciful, ingenious, or witty notion or expression' (*OED* 8, cf. T32/10), and as 'a whim' (*OED* 7). Some of these uses may come straight from the Italian *concetto* (certainly its use as a poetical term for 'unusual metaphor' does). Like *wit* (≠ *humour*) and *fancy* (≠ *imagination*), *conceit* was defined more precisely in eighteenth-century literary theory as 'pure ornament' and thus distinguished from *imagery*.

The three lexemes *wit*, *humour* and *conceit* have not disappeared from English, but they have retained little of their range of six-teenth/seventeenth-century uses. The reduction that took place from the seventeenth century on is not only a consequence of new scientific insights (*humour*), or of replacement by partial synonyms (*wit* ousted by *sense*, *conceit*, which is in turn replaced by *concept*), but also appears to express more general changes of outlook on life. Such changes in values, attitudes and knowledge are, however, obviously impossible to describe on a purely linguistic level.

7.7.3 *Classification of semantic change*

Processes of semantic change can be classified as expansions, reductions and transfers. A meaning (content) expands if it is generalized (by the neutralization of formerly distinctive features) or if the number of sememes increases (the lexeme becomes more polysemous). A meaning (content) is reduced if it is particularized (by the addition of new distinctive features) or if the number of sememes is reduced (the lexeme becoming less polysemous). A transfer, i.e. a new sememe created by the transfer of sense com-ponents onto an old sememe, is of course a form of expansion.

Historically, the wealth of newly formed or imported words appears to have worked towards reduced ranges of meaning in individual lexemes throughout the modern history of English; this was also supported by demands for precision in increasingly written communication and in the expanding field of technical writing. But there also appears to be a universal tendency to adopt metaphorical (or picturesque) ways of speech counteracting this trend – and many words (such as the adjectives mentioned above) do not seem to fit into neat categories at all.

Other classifications that have been proposed can be regarded as variations on the basic model: pejoration and amelioration obviously narrow the range of meaning; meanings specific to certain groups or registers are particularizations adding connotative factors.

Study questions

Q40   Which words listed in the *CED* for the year 1530 are likely to be in fact older, and which of these make their first appearance here because they are found in Palsgrave's French dictionary of 1530?

Q41   T31B has the following words first recorded from this text (*OED* spellings and reference numbers): *rouse* n3 (1.10), *cerement* (1.31), *impartment* (1.43), *beetle* v. (1.58), *unhand* v. (1.69) and *unaneled* (1.160); and T31E has *insisture* (1.13), *primogenitive* (1.32) and *oppugnancy* (1.37). To what extent can the originality of these words be determined? (cf. Schäfer 1980).

Q42   Which of the words listed in t41 are not found in college dictionaries? Do the *OED*'s definitions of these words make it clear that they refer to instruments no longer used? Also test Wilkins' list for 'vessels' (t58), and discuss the dictionaries' distinction between 'arch.' and 'histor.'.

Q43   Do the texts generally condemn the use of archaisms/Chaucerisms? (Use the index.)

Q44   Are the words *soldatis, allyae, hardiment, man* v., *spagnoll* (all replaced in the anglicized reprint in T29) Scotticisms? Did the reviser forget to replace *ualkeryfe* in T29/12, 27? Is T55 characterized as Scottish by *failzie, speir* and *taws* (lines 4, 45, 63)?

Q45   Are the *-ate* forms in T4/40–66 first recorded as participles or base forms? Also test the *-ate* words in the glossary appended to the Everyman edition of T. Elyot's *The Governour*.

Q46   Discuss Puttenham's examples of 'necessary' loanwords in T11/77–117. Are the words (or meanings) first recorded here, and were no other words available in EModE? Was Puttenham's criticism of *audacious* (T11/129) justified? Did Evelyn's examples in T16/112–15 represent lexical gaps (especially in view of Cotgrave's translations of *Ennuy* in t47)?

Q47   Translate T4/40–66 into intelligible English (omitting pleonastic expressions). Which of the 'hard words' are first recorded in the letter?

Q48 When are *machine*, *éclat*, *abandon* and *manœuvre* first recorded in English, and to what extent do they exemplify incomplete integration? What do the forms of *gentle*, *genteel*, *jaunty* (all from French *gentile*) tell us about when they were borrowed?

Q49 Does the *OED* list all the *-er* derivatives collected in 7.5.1? What reasons are there for selectiveness in lexicographic practice with *-er* nouns (as well as the very frequent EModE adjectives with the prefix *over-* and the compounds of Q50)?

Q50 Discuss the types of compounds used in translations of Virgil (T21), in particular Stanyhurst's *catch toyls*, *huntspears*, *quicksenting*, *galloper horsman*, *smocktoy* and *hearelocks*.

Q51 Which of Dryden's (N + y) N combinations are 'poetical' (on account of the semantics of the derivation or unusual collocation)? What makes *skaly rind* (T34/41) and *rushie-fringed banck* (t29) poetical?

Q52 What did *to air* and *to beard* (T12/110) mean in 1595? Discuss the function of zero-derivations in T39/30 and 43–4, and the advantages and drawbacks of the type, also using the other examples mentioned by Carew.

Q53 Describe the fields 'weapons' and 'vessels', using matrix and stemma and retaining the features explicitly provided by Wilkins (and interpreting them as semes). Which of the two forms of presentation is more adequate or easier to handle? Are Wilkins' distinctions sufficient for an exhaustive semantic description?

Q54 Classify Carew's examples (in T12/33–5) as instances of polysemy or homonymy, taking first a synchronic-semantic and then a diachronic-etymological view of the terms.

Q55 Are the words listed by Puttenham in T11/120–4 EModE synonyms?

Q56 What are the EModE meanings of *gay* (in *gaiety* T8/69), *iolly* (T11/87), *braue* (T8/23, 174, and in *brauerie*, T10/13, T25/20) and *wit* (T8/62, 82–3, T18G/6, T25/9, 85, T30/64–72, T31B/128–9, T33/20 and T42/13)?

Q57 What is the meaning of *ciuill* (T30/title, t3/17), *curious* (t15/5, T5/10, T13/52, T18D/31), *dainty* (t15/5, T25/1), *delicate* (t15/5, T13/10), *eager* (T31B/3, 152), *fond* (T31B/182), *foul* (T47/5), *mad* (T32/28, 68), *nice* (T8/72, 77), *sad* (t49/7) and *sillie* (T8/62) – and how is the PrE semantic development of the individual words to be accounted for?

Q58   Determine, with the help of the *OED*, whether the ambiguities of the phrases quoted in 7.7.1 (*we trauell in tongues*, etc.) were already existent in EModE (and which words in the wider context helped to disambiguate the expressions), or whether the ambiguities have been brought about by changes of meaning.

Q59   Determine the sememes (and their individual semes) of *car*, *coach*, *wagon* and *wain* in BrE and AmE. Which encyclopaedic feature of *coach* may have made the transfer from seventeenth-century to modern denotations possible?

TEXTS

Editorial principles

Wherever possible, texts are from originals or facsimile editions. Punctuation and spelling have been retained, in particular *u/v* and *i/j* and capitalization. However, the allographs of ⟨s⟩ (s, ſ) and of ⟨r⟩ (r,) are printed as modern *s*, *r*, and *vv* is *w*. If marginal headings are printed, they are inserted in the text.

There is no possibility of imitating the alternation of various fonts, a typical feature of EModE books. I have decided to use Janson to render the basic font, and italic for whatever contrasts with it. However, italic is used to indicate Trevisa's additions to his Latin source in T1, Surrey's borrowings from Douglas in T21, and Harrison's retentions of words from his Scots source in T36A.

Pre-1640 prints are full of abbreviations and contractions; some of these serve to justify the right-hand margins. These have normally been expanded (with the exception of *yᵉ*, *yᵗ* and *wᵗ*, 'the', 'that' and 'with' in a few texts). Obvious printer's errors (such as turned letters, *u* for *n*, etc.) have been corrected.

ON SPEECH AND LANGUAGE

1 W. CAXTON: THE DESCRIPTION OF BRITAIN (1480)

OF THE LANGUAGES OF MANERS & VSAGE
OF THE PEPLE OF Y^r *LONDE*

As it is knowen how many maner of peple ben in this jlonde
ther ben also so many langages and tonges/ Netheles walssh
& scottes that ben not medlid with othir nacions kepe neyh
yet their langage & speche But yet the scottes that were
somtyme confederate & duellid with pictes drawe somwhat   5
after their speche But the flemmynges y^t duelle in the
west side of wales haue lefte her straunge speche & speken
like to saxons/ also englisshmen though they had fro the
beginnyng thre maner speches/ southern/ northern & myddell
speche in the myddell of the londe as they come of thre   10
maner of peple of germania/ Netheles by commixtion and
medling first with Danes & afterward with Normans in many
thinges the contre langage is appaired/ for some vse strange wlaffing chitering harryng garryng & grisbyting/
   This appayring of the langage cometh of two thinges/   15
ones because that children y^t gone to scole lerne to speke
first englissh/ & than ben compellid to constrewe her lessons in frenssh & that haue ben vsed syn the normans come
in to englond/ Also gentilmens children ben lerned &
taught from their yongth to speke frenssh/ & vplondissh   20
men wyll counterfete & likene hem selfe to gentilmen/ &
arn besy to speke frenssh for to be more sette by wherfor
it is said by a comyn proveerbe/ Jack wold be a gentilman
if he coude speke frenssh/
   this was moche vsed to for ye grete deth/ but sith it   25
is somdele chaunged/ for sir Johan Cornewayll a maister of
gramer chaunged the techyng of gramer scole & construction
of frenssh in to englissh/ And othir scolemaisters vse the
same way now in the yere of our lord .M.CCC.lxxxv. the ix.
yere of kyng Richard the seconde/ & leue all frenssh in   30
scoles & vse alle construction in englissh/ wherin they
haue auantage one way that is that they lerne the sonner
their gramer And in anothir disauauntage/ for now they
lerne no frenssh ne can none/ which is hurte for them
that shall passe the see/ And also gentilmen haue moche   35
lefte to teche their children to speke frenssh/
   Hit semeth a grete wonder that englissh haue so grete

diuersite in their owne langage in soune and in spekyng
of it/ whiche is all in one jlonde/ And the langage of
normandie is comen oute of anothir lande/ and hath one   *40*
maner of soune among alle them that speketh it in englond/
for a man of kente/ Southern western/ & northern men speken frenssh all lyke in soune & speche/ but they can not
speke theyr englissh so/ *Netheles ther is as many diuerse*
maner of frenssh in the reame of fraunce/ as diuerse eng-   *45*
lissh in the reame of england/ Also of the forsaid tonge
which is departed in thre is grete wonder/ for men of the
eest with men of the west accorde better in sownyng of
their speche/ than men of the north with men of the south/
Therfore it is that men of mercij that ben of myddell   *50*
Englond as it were partiners with the endes/ vnderstande
better the side langages northern & southern than northern
& southern vnderstande eyther othir/ Alle the langages of
the northumbres & specially at york is so sharp slitting
frotyng & vnshappe/ that we sothern men may vnneth vnder-   *55*
stande that langage/ I suppose the cause be that they be
nygh to the aliens that speke strangely/ And also by cause
that the kyngis of englond abyde and duelle more in the
south contrey than in ye north contre/ is by cause that
ther is better corn londe more peple/ moo noble Citees/ &   *60*
moo prouffytable hauenes in the south contrey than in the
north.

2 W. CAXTON: PROLOGUE TO ENEYDOS (1490)

... And whan I had aduysed me in this sayd boke I delyber-
ed and concluded to translate it in to englysshe And
forthwyth toke a penne & ynke and wrote a leef or tweyne/
whyche I ouersawe agayn to corecte it/ And whan I sawe
the fayr & straunge termes therin/ I doubted that it sholde   *5*
not please some gentylmen whiche late blamed me sayeng y^t
in my translacyons I had ouer curyous termes whiche coude
not be vnderstande of comyn peple/ and desired me to vse
olde and homely termes in my translacyons. and fayn wolde
I satysfye euery man/ and so to doo toke an olde boke and   *10*
redde therin/ and certaynly the englysshe was so rude and
brood that I coude not wele vnderstande it. And also my
lorde abbot of westmynster ded do shewe to me late certayn
euydences wryton in olde englysshe for to reduce it in to
our englysshe now vsid/ And certaynly it was wreton in   *15*

suche wyse that it was more lyke to dutche than englysshe
I coude not reduce ne brynge it to be vnderstonden/

And certaynly our langage now vsed varyeth ferre from
that. whiche was vsed and spoken whan I was borne/ For we
englysshe men/ ben borne vnder the domynacyon of the mone.   20
whiche is neuer stedfaste/ but euer wauerynge/ wexynge
one season/ and waneth & dyscreaseth another season/ And
that comyn englysshe that is spoken in one shyre varyeth
from another. In so moche that in my dayes happened that
certayn marchauntes were in a shippe in tamyse for to   25
haue sayled ouer the see into zelande/ and for lacke of
wynde thei taryed atte forlond and wente to lande for to
refreshe them And one of theym named sheffelde a mercer
cam in to an hows and axed for mete. and specyally he axyd
after eggys And the goode wyf answerde. that she coude spe-   30
ke no frensshe. And the marchaunt was angry. for he also
could speke no frensshe but wold haue hadde egges/ and she
vnderstode hym not/ And thenne at laste a nother sayd that
he wolde haue eyren/ then the good wyf sayd that she vnder-
stod hym wel/ Loo what sholde a man in thyse dayes now   35
wryte. egges or eyren/ certaynly it is harde to playse
euery man/ by cause of dyuersite & chaunge of langage. For
in these dayes euery man that is in ony reputacyon in his
countre. wyll vtter his commynycacyon and matters in suche
maners & termes/ that fewe men shall vnderstonde theym/   40
And som honest and grete clerkes haue ben wyth me and desired me to wryte the moste curyous termes that I coude
fynde/ And thus bytwene playn rude/ & curyous I stande
abasshed. but in my Iudgemente/ the comyn termes that be
dayli vsed ben lyghter to be vnderstonde than the olde   45
and auncyent englysshe/ And for as moche as this present
booke is not for a rude vplondyssh man to laboure therin/
ne rede it/ but onely for a clerke & a noble gentylman
that feleth and vnderstondeth in faytes of armes in loue
& in noble chyualrye/ Therfor in a meane bytwene bothe I   50
haue reduced & translated this sayd booke in to our
englysshe...

3 W. LILY AND J. COLET: A SHORT INTRODUCTION OF GRAMMAR (1549)

TO THE READER

To exhort every man to the learnyng of grammar, that intendeth to atteyne to the vnderstandynge of the tungues,
(wherin is conteyned a great treasorye of wysedome and
knowledge) it shoulde seeme muche vayne and little nedefull:
for so muche as it is knowen, that nothynge canne surely   5
bee ended, whose begynnyng is eyther feble or fautye: and
no buyldynge bee perfecte, whan as the foundation and
groundewoorke is ready to falle, or vnable to vpholde the
burthen of the frame. Wherefore it were better for the
thynge it selfe, and more profytable to the learner, to   10
vnderstande howe he may beste come to that, whyche he
oughte moste necessaryly to haue, and to learne the gayn-
est waye of obteynynge that, whyche muste be his beste
and certaynest guyde, bothe of readyng and speakynge, than
to falle in doubte whether he shall more lamente that he   15
lacketh, or esteeme that he hathe it, and whether he shall
oftener stumble in trifles, and be deceaued in lyghte mat-
tiers, whan he hath it not, or iudge trewely and faythful-
ly of dyuers weyghtye thynges whan he hath it.

  The whyche hathe seemed to many verye harde to compasse   20
afore tyme, bycause that they, who professed this arte of
teachyng grammar, dyd teache dyuers grammars, and not one,
and yf by chaunce they taughte one grammar, yet they dyd
it dyuersly, and so coulde not doo it all beste, for so
muche as there is but one bestnesse, not onely in euery   25
thynge, but also in the maner of euery thyng.

  As for the diuersitees of grammars, it is welle and
profytably taken awaye, by the Kynges Maiestees wysedome,
who fureseeynge the inconuenience, and fauourably prouidynge the remedye, caused one kynde of grammar by sundry   30
learned men, to be diligently drawen, and so to be sette
out, onely euery where to be taught, for the vse of learners, and for the hurte in chaunge of schoolemaysters.

  The varietee of teachynge is dyuers yet, and alwayes
wyll bee: for that euery schoolemayster lyketh that he   35
knoweth, and seeth not the vse of that he knoweth not,
and therefore iudgeth that the moste sufficient waye,

whyche he seeth to bee the readyest meane, and perfectest
kynde to bryng a learner to haue a thorough knowledge
therin.   *40*

Wherefore it is not amysse, yf one seeyng by tryall, an
easyer and readyer waie, than the common sorte of teachers
dooth, wold saie what he hath proued, and for the commod-
itee allowed, that other not knowynge the same, myghte by
experience proue the lyke, and than by profe reasonable   *45*
iudge the lyke, not hereby excludyng the better way, whan
it is founde, but in the meane season forbyddyng the worse.
The first and chieffest poynte is, that the diligente
mayster make not the scholar haste to muche, but that he
in contynuaunce and dilygence of teachynge, make hym re-   *50*
herse so, that whyle he haue perfectely that, that is be-
hynde, he suffre hym not to go forwarde. For this postynge
haste, ouerthroweth and hurteth a greate sorte of wyttes,
and casteth them into an amasednesse, whan they knowe not,
howe they shall eyther goe forewarde or backewarde, but   *55*
stycketh fast as one plunged, that can not telle what to
dooe, or whyche waies to tourne hym, and than the mayster
thynketh the scholar to bee a dullarde, and the scholar
thynketh the thynge to bee vneasy and to harde for his
wytte, and the one hath an yll opinion of the other, whan   *60*
oftentymes it is in neither, but in the kynde of teachynge. Wherfore the best and chieffest poynte throughly to
be kept, is, that the scholar haue in mynd so perfectely
that he hath learned, and vnderstande it so, that not
onely it bee not a stoppe for hym, but also a lyght and   *65*
an helpe to the resydue that foloweth.

This shall be the maisters ease, and the chyldes en-
couragynge, whan the one shall see his laboure take good
effecte, and thereby in teachynge, the lesse tourmented,
and the other shall thynke the thynge easyer, and so   *70*
with more gladnesse readye to go about the same.

4 T. WILSON: THE ARTE OF RHETORIQUE (1553)

PLAINES WHAT IT IS

Emong al other lessons, this should first be learned, y^t
we neuer affect any straunge ynkehorne termes, but so speake
as is commonly receiued: neither sekyng to be ouer fine,
nor yet liuyng ouer carelesse, vsyng our speache as most

men do, & ordryng our wittes, as the fewest haue doen.　　　　5
Some seke so farre for outlandishe Englishe, that thei
forget altogether their mothers langage. And I dare swere
this, if some of their mothers were aliue, thei were not
able to tell, what thei say, & yet these fine Englishe
clerkes, wil saie thei speake in their mother tongue, if a　　　10
man should charge them for counterfeityng the kynges English. Some farre iorneid ientlemen at their returne home,
like as thei loue to go in forrein apparell, so thei wil
pouder their talke w^t ouersea language. He that cometh
lately out of France, wil talke Frenche English, & neuer　　　15
blushe at the matter. Another choppes in with Angleso
Italiano: the lawyer wil store his stomack with the prat-
yng of Pedlers. The Auditour in makyng his accompt and
rekenyng, cometh in with sise sould, and cater denere,
for vi.s. iiij.d. The fine Courtier wil talke nothyng but　　　20
Chaucer. The misticall wise menne, and Poeticall Clerkes,
will speake nothyng but quaint prouerbes, and blynd allegories, delityng muche in their awne darkenesse, especially, when none can tell what thei dooe saie. The vnlearned
or foolishe phantasticall, that smelles but of learnyng　　　25
(suche felowes as haue seen learned men in their daies)
will so latine their tongues, that the simple cannot but
wonder at their talke, and thynke surely thei speake by
some Reuelacion. I knowe them that thynke Rhetorique,
to stande wholy vpon darke woordes, and he that can catche　　　30
an ynke horne terme by the taile, hym thei compt to bee a
fine Englishe man, and a good Rhetorician And the rather
to set out this folie, I will adde here suche a letter,
as Willyam Sommer himself, could not make a better for
that purpose. Some will thinke & swere it to, that there　　　35
was neuer any suche thyng written, well I wil not force
any man to beleue it, but I will saie thus muche, and
abide by it to, the like haue been made heretofore, and
praised aboue the Moone.

An ynkehorne letter. Ponderyng, expendyng, and reuolut-　　　40
yng with my self your ingent affabilitee, and ingenious
capacitee, for mundane affaires: I cannot but celebrate
and extolle your magnificall dexteritee, aboue all other.
For how could you haue adepted suche illustrate prerogatiue, and dominicall superioritee, if the fecunditee　　　45
of your ingenie had not been so fertile, & wounderfull
pregnaunt. Now therfore beeyng accersited, to suche

splendent renoume, & dignitee splendidious: I doubt not
but you will adiuuate suche poore adnichilate orphanes,
as whilome ware condisciples with you, and of antique   *50*
familiaritee in Lincolne shire. Emong whom I beeyng a
Scholasticall panion, obtestate your sublimitee to extoll
myne infirmitee. There is a sacerdotall dignitee in my
natiue countrey, contiguate to me, where I now contemplate: whiche your worshipfull benignitee, could sone   *55*
impetrate for me, if it would like you to extend your
scedules, and collaude me in them to the right honorable
lorde Chauncellor, or rather Archigrammacian of Englande.
You knowe my literature, you knowe the pastorall pro-
mocion, I obtestate your clemencie, to inuigilate thus   *60*
muche for me, accordyng to my confidence, and as you
know my condigne merites, for suche a compendious liuyng. But now I relinquishe to fatigate your intelligence
with any more friuolous verbositie, and therfore he that
rules the climates be euermore your beautreux, your   *65*
fortresse, and your bulwarke. Amen.

   What wise man readyng this letter, will not take him
for a very Caulfe, that made it in good earnest, &
thought by his ynkepot termes, to get a good personage.
Doeth wit reste in straunge wordes, or els standeth it   *70*
in wholsome matter, and apt declaryng of a mannes mynd?
Do we not speake, because we would haue other to vnderstande vs, or is not the tongue geuen for this ende,
that one might know what another meaneth? And what
vnlearned man can tell, what half this letter signifieth?   *75*
Therfore, either we must make a difference of Englishe,
and saie some is learned Englishe, and other some is rude
Englishe, or the one is courte talke, the other is countrey speache, or els we must of necessitee, banishe al
suche affected Rhetorique, and vse altogether one maner   *80*
of langage…

   Now whereas wordes be receiued, aswell Greke as Latine,
to set furthe our meanyng in thenglishe tongue, either for
lacke of store, or els because wee would enriche the language: it is well doen to vse them, and no man therin can   *85*
be charged for any affectacion, when all other are agreed
to folowe the same waie. There is no man agreued, when he
heareth (letters patentes) & yet patentes is latine, and
signifieth open to all men. The Communion is a felowship,
or a commyng together, rather Latine then Englishe: the   *90*

Kynges prerogatiue, declareth his power royall aboue all
other, and yet I knowe no man greued for these termes,
beeyng vsed in their place, nor yet any one suspected for
affectacion, when suche generall wordes are spoken. The
folie is espied, when either we will vse such wordes, as   *95*
fewe men doe vse, or vse theim out of place, when another
might serue muche better. Therfore to auoyde suche folie,
we maie learne of that most excellent Orator Tullie, who
in his thirde booke, where he speaketh of a perfect Ora-
toure, declareth vnder the name of Crassus, that for the   *100*
choyse of wordes, foure thinges should chiefly be obserued. First, that suche wordes as we vse, shuld bee
proper vnto the tongue, wherein wee speake, again, that
thei be plain for all men to perceiue: thirdly, that thei
be apt and mete, moste properly to sette out the matter.   *105*
Fourthly, that woordes translated from one significacion
to another, (called of the Grecians, Tropes) bee vsed to
beautifie the sentence, as precious stones are set in a
ryng, to commende the golde.

5 J. CHEKE: LETTER TO HOBY (1557)

TO HIS LOUING FRIND MAYSTER THOMAS HOBY

For your opinion of my gud will vnto you as you wriit,
you can not be deceiued: for submitting your doinges to
mi iudgement, I thanke you: for taking this pain of your
translation, you worthilie deseru great thankes of all
sortes. I haue taken sum pain at your request cheflie in   *5*
your preface, not in the reading of it for that was plesaunt vnto me boath for the roundnes of your saienges and
welspeakinges of the saam, but in changing certein wordes
which might verie well be let aloan, but that I am verie
curious in mi freendes matters, not to determijn, but to   *10*
debaat what is best. Whearin, I seek not the bestnes hap-
lie bi truth, but bi mijn own phansie, and shew of goodnes.
    I am of this opinion that our own tung shold be written
cleane and pure, vnmixt and vnmangeled with borowing of
other tunges, wherin if we take not heed by tijm, euer   *15*
borowing and neuer payeng, she shall be fain to keep her
house as bankrupt. For then doth our tung naturallie and
praisablie vtter her meaning, whan she bouroweth no coun-
terfeitness of other tunges to attire her self withall,

but vseth plainlie her own, with such shift, as nature,   *20*
craft, experiens and folowing of other excellent doth
lead her vnto, and if she want at ani tijm (as being vn-
perfight she must) yet let her borow with suche bashful-
nes, that it mai appeer, that if either the mould of
our own tung could serue vs to fascion a woord of our   *25*
own, or if the old denisoned wordes could content and
ease this neede, we wold not boldly venture of vnknowen
wordes. This I say not for reproof of you, who haue
scarslie and necessarily vsed whear occasion serueth
a strange word so, as it seemeth to grow out of the mat-   *30*
ter and not to be sought for: but for mijn own defens,
who might be counted ouerstraight a deemer of thinges,
if I gaue not this accompt to you, mi freend and wijs,
of mi marring this your handiwork. But I am called awai,
I prai you pardon mi shortnes, the rest of mi saienges   *35*
should be but praise and exhortacion in this your do-
inges, which at moar leisor I shold do better.
From my house in Woodstreete the 16. of Iuly, 1557
            Yours assured Ioan Cheek

6 J. HART: AN ORTHOGRAPHIE (1569)

THE PREFACE

In any chaunge which is to be attempted in any peoples
maner of doings, there is requisite eyther excelling
authoritie, or a good perswasion of a common commoditie.
The first must be obeyed what chaunge of any inferior
purpose soeuer may come therof. And thother is at liber-   *5*
tie to be taken or refused, according as experience,
maye finde it profitable or hurtfull.
    Wherefore I will nowe signifie vnto such as haue not
wilfully professed them selues to be obstinate in their
custome, that the vse and experience of thorder of this   *10*
following English Orthographie, shall bring these commodities following.
    The first commoditie for the vnlearned naturall English
people. First it shall cause the naturall English knowing
no letter, to be able to learne to decerne and easily to   *15*
reade (whatsoeuer he may see before him so written or
printed) so soone as he were able to learne readily, and
perfectly to know and name, the number of figures or mem-

bers of the bodie and substance of our voice and speach,
& so obseruing the new or strange order hereafter written,   20
the learned may instruct any naturall English reasonable
creature, to read English, in one quarter of the time that
euer any other hath heretofore bene taught to reade, by
any former maner. And in what lesse time, and how much
more easie and readie, it will be for the writer or Print-   25
er, Reader and hearer, I will not write, but leaue it to
the iudgement of the Reader, of the sayd following treatise, and to the experience it selfe as occasion shall
serue.

   Secondly for straungers or the rude countrie English   30
man, which may desire to read English as the best sort
vse to speake it. Secondly, if anye man of one or other
nation, would gladly learne to pronounce any straunge
speach which is accustomed to be written so confusedly,
as it were (of necessitie) only to be learned by the   35
liuely voice, and not able to be red by any order of
their writing, as maye be sayde of the Welsh and Irish,
yet vsing thorder hereafter, he shall be able to write
eyther of them (or any other like) euen as iustly in the
least voice, sound or breath, as it shall be naturallye   40
spoken vnto him, and so read it againe perfitely, when and
where soeuer he may see it, though many yeares thereafter,
and though he vnderstoode no worde therof, and that by
the reason hereafter shewed. Whereas by our present dis-
order it often happeneth that a verye good iudgement, maye   45
doubt in what sound, many a word shoulde be pronounced,
vntill by reasan of the sentence it bée founde, and many
a man doth scantlye know how the writing of his owne name
should be sounded, by which disorders and confusions,
there can be made no perfite Dictionarie nor Grammer,   50
which are very commodious for any straunger that desireth
to learne our tongue by Arte, or for the rude to learne
to speake well, as euery childe that hath learned his
Latine Grammer knoweth.

   Thirdly, for cost and time saued. Thirdly, we should   55
not néede to vse aboue the two thirdes or thrée quarters
at most, of the letters which we are nowe constreyned to
vse, and to saue the one third, or at least the one
quarter, of the paper, ynke, and time which we now spend
superfluously in writing and printing.   60

   And last, for a helpe for the learned sort which desire

to pronounce other tongs aright. And last of all, English
Latinistes maye hereby vnderstand, the Italian and high
Dutch and Welshe pronounciation of their letters, which
by presumption is verie neare as the auncient Greekes and   *65*
Latines did, being according to thorder and reason of
their predecessors first inuention of them, whereby our
errors are the better perceyued, and in the ende of the
booke a certaine example how the Italian, high Dutch,
French, and Spanyard doe vse to pronounce Latine and their   *70*
owne languages. Truly the commodities aforesaid (which I
perswade my self may follow) and the hinderance and confusion wherein I see we are, doe cause me to put it into
light: to thend such as are able to be iudges, may be
occasioned to consider therof. Whose like (I meane the   *75*
learned sort) haue bene in times past, causers of our
present maner of writing, by turning their penne to adde
or diminish, alter or chaunge, as they thought méete into
other letters and Carrects, much differing from the olde
Saxon maner. And the liuing doe knowe themselues no fur-   *80*
ther bounde to this our instant maner, than our predecessors were to the Saxon letters and writing, which hath
bene altered as the speach hath chaunged, much differing
from that which was vsed within these fiue hundreth, I
maye say within these two hundreth yeares....   *85*

7 W. BULLOKAR: BOOKE AT LARGE (1580)

THE FIRST CHAPTER, SHEWING THE OLD A.B.C. AND CAUSE OF
AMENDMENT, AND THAT BOTH MAY BE USED FOR A TIME.
THE OLD A.B.C.

There are in the olde A.B.C. (for so I call the ortography
vsed before this amendment) xxiiij. letters, of xxiiij.   *5*
seuerall names, which are these following.
    A.b.c.d.e.f.g.h.i.k.l.m.n.o.p.q.r.s.t.u.w.x.y.z. with
their paiers.
    Which fower and twentie letters, are not sufficient to
picture Inglish spéech: For in Inglish spéech, are mo   *10*
distinctions and diuisions in voice, then these fower and
twentie letters can seuerally signifie, and giue right
sound vnto: By reason whereof, we were driuen, to vse to
some letters, two soundes, to some, thrée soundes, hauing
in them no difference, or marke, in figure or fashion, to   *15*
shewe how the same double, or treble sounded letters,

should be sounded, when they were ioined with other letters
in wordes: which was very tedious to the learner (though
he coulde speake and vnderstand perfectly Inglish spéech
by nature and continuall vse) much more tedious was it,   *20*
to them of another nation not aided by such vse: when our
writing and printing, nothing agréed, in the seuerall
names of our letters, vnto the sounding of them in our
wordes: whereby our spéech was condemned of those stran-
gers, as without order, or sensibilitie: whereas the   *25*
fault was in the picture, (I meane the letters) and not
in the spéech: which fault, the strangers did not perceiue, much lesse could they remedie it, when we our selues, some contented with a custome thought it could be no
better, some perceiuing some fault, knew not the remedie,   *30*
some knowing some remedie (as touching their owne iudge-
ment and contentation) thought it hard to be altered,
because that the great volumes alreadie in print, should
be more than halfe lost, if they could not be vsed, by
such, as learned first the amended writing and printing: *35*
and som are so enuious that nothing is well, but their
owne doings: and some are so ambitious, they would haue
no knowledge but in themselues, and haue dominion ouer
vertue, not vsing vertuous waies themselues, but hinder-
ing the vertue of others.   *40*
   Against this last sort of ambitious and enuious, I call
to my assistance (in this point of ortography) sir *Thomas*
Smith, and Maister *Chester*, for their painfull séeking
remedy herein: yet complaining greatly of enimies that
hindered their good meanings: which might much discourage   *45*
me, (being of simpler calling, knowledge, and experience)
had not my great paines, (in the like point touching ortography) brought to passe (as I thinke) an indifferent
perfect worke: not onlie for true ortography for Inglish
spéech, but also framing the same, so néere the old orto-   *50*
graphy, that the want and abuses in the old, are not onely
hereby plainly set foorth, but also, that the same old
writing, and printing, may be in vse for a time, to saue
expences, as were the written volumes in times past,
after printing first began: which art of printing began   *55*
in Germany, and found out by a Knight, in the yeere of our
Lorde .1457. as Chronicles testifie: which is sixe score
and thrée yéere agon, or there about: and at this day, the
written volumes are in fewe places to be séene, but almost

in no place in vse, through the fairenesse of the printed 60
volumes, and more perfectnesse therein: yet is not the
same so perfect, (for lacke of true ortography) but that
diuerse men write, and also print, diuersely: and not one,
truely as Inglish spéech requireth, (if ye will haue a true,
perfect, and plaine picture thereof) as shall plainly ap- 65
péere in this treatise following.

So that for lacke of true ortography our writing in
Inglish hath altered in euery age, yea since printing began, (though printing be the best helpe to stay the same,
in one order) as may appéere by the antiquities: and if 70
now be a time of the most perfect vse of the same, which
must be confessed for the great learning dispersed in this
land at this day (in respect of any time past to the knowledge of man) thinke it the great gift of God, if a perfectnesse be now surely planted, not to be rooted out as 75
long as letters endure.

8 R. MULCASTER: THE FIRST PART OF THE ELEMENTARIE (1582)

OF PREROGATIUE ... This period of mine, and these risings
to mount, as the dismounting again, till decaie ensew, do
giue vs to wit, that as all things else, which belong to
man be subiect to change, so the tung also is, which chang-
eth with the most, and yet contineweth with the best. 5
Whereupon it must nedes be that there is som soulish substance in euerie spoken tung, which fedeth this change,
euen with perceptible means, that pretend alteration. For
if anie tung be absolute, and fré from motion, it is
shrined vp in books, and not ordinarie in vse, but made 10
immortall by the register of memorie...

I take this present period of our English tung to be
the verie height thereof, bycause I find it so excellentlie well fined, both for the bodie of the tung it self,
and for the customarie writing thereof, as either foren 15
workmanship can giue it glosse, or as homewrought hanling
can giue it grace. When the age of our peple, which now
vse the tung so well, is dead and departed there will another succede, and with the peple the tung will alter and
change. Which change in the full haruest thereof maie 20
proue comparable to this, but sure for this which we now
vse, it semeth euen now to be at the best for substance,

and the brauest for circumstance, and whatsoeuer shall
becom of the English state, the English tung cannot proue
fairer, then it is at this daie, if it maie please our   25
learned sort to esteme so of it, and to bestow their
trauell vpon such a subiect, so capable of ornament, so
proper to themselues, and the more to be honored, bycause
it is their own.

THE PERORATION There be two speciall considerations,   30
which kepe the *Latin*, & other learned tungs, tho chefelie
the *Latin*, in great countenance among vs, the one thereof
is the knowledge, which is registred in them, the other is
the conference, which the learned of *Europe*, do commonlie
vse by them, both in speaking and writing. Which two con-   35
siderations being fullie answered, that we seke them from
profit & kepe them for that conference, whatsoeuer else
maie be don in our tung, either to serue priuat vses, or
the beawtifying of our speche, I do not se, but it maie
well be admitted, euen tho in the end it displaced the   40
Latin, as the *Latin* did others, & furnished it self by the
the *Latin* learning. For is it not in dede a meruellous bondage, to becom seruants to one tung for learning sake, the
most of our time, with losse of most time, whereas we maie
haue the verie same treasur in our own tung, with the gain   45
of most time? our own bearing the ioyfull title of our
libertie and fredom, the *Latin* tung remembring vs, of our
thraldom & bondage? I loue *Rome*, but *London* better, I
fauor *Italie*, but *England* more, I honor the *Latin*, but
I worship the *English*...   50

The diligent labor of learned cuntriemen did so enrich
these tungs, and not the tungs them selues, tho theie
proued verie pliable, as our tung will proue, I dare assure it of knowledge, if our learned cuntriemen will put
to their labor. And why not I praie you, as well in *Eng-*   55
lish, as either in *Latin* or anie tung else?

1. *It is not nedefull* Will ye saie it is nedelesse?
sure that will not hold. If losse of time while ye be
pilgrims to learning by lingring about tungs, be no argu-
ment of nede: if lak of sound skill, while the tung dis-   60
tracteth sense, more then half to it self, and that most
of all in a simple student or a sillie wit, be no argument
of nede, then saie you somwhat, which pretend no nede. But
bycause we neded not, to lease anie time onelesse we list-
ed, if we had such a vantage, in the course of studie, as   65

we now lease, while we trauell in tungs: and bycause our
vnderstanding also, were most full in our naturall speche,
tho we know the foren excedinglie well, methink *necessitie*
it self doth call for *English*, whereby all that gaietie
maie be had at home, which makes vs gase so much at the   70
fine stranger.

 2. *It is vncouth* But ye will saie it is vncouth. In
· dede being vnused. And so was it in *Latin*, and so is it
in ech language, & *Tullie* himself the *Romane* paragon,
while he was aliue, & our best patern now, tho he be dead,   75
had verie much ado, and verie great wrastling against such
wranglers, and their nice lothing of their naturall speche,
ear he wan that opinion, which either we our selues haue
now of him, or the best of his frinds did then conceiue
by him. Is not euerie his preface before all his philo-   80
sofie still thwakt full of such conflicts, had against
those cauillers? our *English* wits be verie wel able,
thanks be to God, if their wits were as good, to make
those vncouth & vnknown learnings verie familiar to our
peple, euen in our own tung, & that both by president &   85
protection of those same writers, whom we esteme so much
of, who doing that for others, which I do wish for ours, in
the like case must nedes allow of vs, onelesse theie wil
auouch that which theie cannot auow, that the praise of
that labor to conceiue cunning from a foren tung into a   90
mans own, did dy with them, not to reuiue in vs. But whatsoeuer theie saie, or whatsoeuer theie can saie to con-
tinew their own credit, our cuntriemen maie not think,
but that it is our praise to com by that thorough pur-
chace, and planting in our tung, which theie were so   95
desirous to place in theirs, and ar now so loth to forgo
again, as the farest flour of their hole garland, which
wold wither soon, or else decaie quite, if their great
cunning, were not the cause of their continewance: and if
our peple also, were not more willing to wonder at their   100
workmanship, then to work their own tung, to be worth the
like wonder. Our English is our own, our *Sparta* must be
spunged, by the inhabitants that haue it, as well as
those tungs were by the industrie of their people, which
be braued with the most, and brag as the best.   105

 3. *Our tung is of no compas for ground & autoritie.*
But it maie be replyed again, that our English tung doth
nede no such proining, it is of small reatch, it stretch-

eth no further then this Iland of ours, naie not there
ouer all. What tho? Yet it raigneth there, and it serues 110
vs there, and it wold be clean brusht for the wearing
there. Tho it go not beyond sea, it will serue on this
side. And be not our English folks finish, as well as the
foren I praie you? And why not our tung for speaking, &
our pen for writing, as well as our bodies for apparell, 115
or our tastes for diet? But our state is no *Empire* to
hope to enlarge it by commanding ouer cuntries.
What tho? tho it be neither large in possession, nor in
present hope of great encrease, yet where it rules, it
can make good lawes, and as fit for our state, as the 120
biggest can for theirs, and oftimes better to, bycause
of confusion in greatest gouernments, as most vnwildi-
nesse in grossest bodies.

    4. No rare cunning in English. But we haue no rare
cunning proper to our soil to cause forenners studie it, 125
as a treasur of such store. What tho? yet ar we not ignorant by the mean thereof to turn to our vse all the great
treasur, of either foren soil, or foren language. And
why maie not the English wits, if they will bend their
wills, either for matter or for method in their own tung 130
be in time as well sought to, by foren students for increase of their knowledge, as our soil is sought to at
this same time, by foren merchants, for encrease of
their welth? As the soil is fertile, bycause it is applyed, so the wits be not barren if theie list to brede. 135

    5. No hope of anie greatnesse. But tho all this be
trew, yet we ar in dispare, euer to se ours so fined, as
those tungs were, where publik orations were in ordinarie
trade, and the verie tung alone made a chariot to honor.
Our state is a *Moanarchie*, which mastereth language, & 140
teacheth it to please: our religion is *Christian*, which
half repines at eloquence, and liketh rather the naked
truth, then the neated term. What tho? Tho no English man
for want of that exercise, which the *Roman* had, & the
Athenian vsed in their spacious and great courts, do proue 145
a *Tullie* or like to *Demosthenes*, yet for sooth he maie
proue verie comparable to them in his own common weal and
the eloquence there...

    6. It will let the learned communitie. But will ye
thus break of the common conference with the learned foren,
by banishing the *Latin*, and setting ouer her learning to 150

your own tung. The conference will not cease, while the
peple haue cause to enterchange dealings, & without the
Latin, it maie well be continewed: as in som cuntries the
learnedder sort, & som near cosens to the latin it self   155
do alreadie wean their pens and tungs from the vse of
Latin, both in writen discourse, & spoken disputation,
into their own naturall, and yet no dry nurse, being so
well appointed by the milch nurses help. The question is
not to disgrace the *Latin*, but to grace our own. And why   160
more a stranger in honor with vs, then our own peple, all
circumstances serued? ...

   Why not all in English? But why not all in English,
a tung of it self both depe in conceit, & frank in deliv-
erie? I do not think that anie language, be it whatsoeuer,   165
is better able to vtter all arguments, either with more
pith, or greater planesse, then our *English* tung is, if
the *English* vtterer be as skilfull in the matter, which
he is to vtter: as the foren vtterer is. Which methink I
durst proue in anie most strange argument, euen mine own   170
self, tho no great clark, but a great welwiller to my
naturall cuntrie. And tho we vse & must vse manie foren
terms, when we deal with such arguments, we do not anie
more then the brauest tungs do & euen verie those, which
crake of their cunning. The necessitie is one betwene   175
cuntrie & cuntrie, for communicating of words, for vttering of strange matter, & the rules be limited how to
square them to the vse of those which will borow them.

9 T. HARMAN: A CAVEAT (1567)

THE UPRIGHT COFE CANTETH TO THE ROGE
THE UPRIGHT MAN SPEAKETH TO THE ROGUE

V: Bene Lightmans to thy quarromes, in what lipken hast
     thou lypped in this darkemans, whether in a lybbege or
     in the strummell? *God morrowe to thy body, in what*   5
     house hast thou lyne in all night, whether in a bed,
     or in the strawe?
R: I couched a hogshead in a Skypper this darkemans.
     I layd me downe to sléepe in a barne this night.
V: I towre the strummel trine vpon thy nabchet & Togman.   10
     I sée the strawe hang vpon thy cap and coate.
R: I saye by the Salomon I will lage it of with a gage

of bene bouse; then cut to my nose watch. *I sweare*
by the masse, I wull washe it of with a quart of good
drynke; then saye to me what thou wylt. 15

V: Why, hast thou any lowre in thy bonge to bouse?
Why, hast thou any money in thy purse to drinke?

R: But a flagge, a wyn, and a make.
But a grot, a penny, and a halfe penny.

V: Why, where is the kene that hath the bene bouse? 20
where is the house that hath good drinke?

R: A bene mort hereby at the signe of the prauncer.
A good wyfe here by at the signe of the hors.

V: I cutt it is quyer bouse, I bousd a flagge the last
darkmans. *I saye it is small and naughtye drynke.* 25
I dranke a groate there the last night.

R: But bouse there a bord, & thou shalt haue beneship.
But drinke there a shyllinge, and thou shalt haue
very good.
Tower ye yander is the kene, dup the gygger, and 30
maund that is beneshyp. *Se you, yonder is the house,*
open the doore, and aske for the best.

V: This bouse is as benshyp as rome bouse.
This drinke is as good as wyne.
Now I tower that bene bouse makes nase nabes. 35
Now I se that good drinke makes a dronken heade.
Maunde of this morte what bene pecke is in her ken.
Aske of this wyfe what good meate shee hath in her house.

R: She hath a Cacling chete, a grunting chete, ruff Pecke,
cassan, and popplarr of yarum. *She hath a hen, a pyg,* 40
baken, chese and mylke porrage.

V: That is beneshyp to our watche.
That is very good for vs.
Now we haue well bousd, let vs strike some chete.
Now we haue well dronke, let vs steale some thinge. 45
Yonder dwelleth a quyere cuffen, it were beneship
to myll hym. *Yonder dwelleth a hoggeshe and choyr-*
lyshe man, it were very well donne to robbe him.

R: Nowe bynge we a waste to the hygh pad, the ruffmanes
is by. *Naye, let vs go hence to the hygh waye,* 50
the wodes is at hand.

V: So may we happen on the Harmanes, and cly the Iarke,
or to the quyerken and skower quyaer cramprings, and
so to tryning on the chates. *So we maye chaunce to*
set in the stockes, eyther be whypped, eyther had to 55

prison house, and there be shackled with bolttes and
fetters, and then to hange on the gallowes.

R: Gerry gan, the ruffian clye thee.
     A torde in thy mouth, the deuyll take thee.

V: What, stowe your bene, cofe, and cut benat whydds,   *60*
     and byng we to rome vyle, to nyp a bong; so shall we
     haue lowre for the bousing ken, and when we byng back
     to the deuseauyel, we wyll fylche some duddes of the
     Ruffemans, or myll the ken for a lagge of dudes.
     What, holde your peace, good fellowe, and speake   *65*
     better wordes, and go we to London, to cut a purse;
     then shal we haue money for the ale house, and when
     wee come backe agayne into the country, wee wyll
     steale some lynnen clothes of one hedges, or robbe
     some house for a bucke of clothes.   *70*

By this lytle ye maye holy and fully vnderstande their
vntowarde talke and pelting speache, mynglede without
measure; and as they haue begonne of late to deuyse some
new termes for certein thinges, so wyll they in tyme
alter this, and deuyse as euyll or worsse...   *75*

10 W. HARRISON: "OF THE LANGUAGES SPOKEN IN THIS ILAND" (1587)

After the Saxon toong, came the Norman or French language
ouer into our countrie, and therein were our lawes written for a long time. Our children also were by an especiall
decrée taught first to speake the same, and therevnto
inforced to learne their constructions in the French,   *5*
whensoeuer they were set to the Grammar schoole. In like
sort few bishops, abbats, or other clergie men, were admitted vnto anie ecclesiasticall function here among vs,
but such as came out of religious houses from beyond the
seas, to the end they should not vse the English toong   *10*
in their sermons to the people. In the court also it
grew into such contempt, that most men thought it no
small dishonor to speake any English there. Which brauerie tooke his hold at the last likewise in the countrie
with euerie plowman, that euen the verie carters began   *15*
to wax wearie of there mother toong, & laboured to
speake French, which as then was counted no small token
of gentilitie. And no maruell, for euerie French rascall,

when he came once hither, was taken for a gentleman, onelie bicause he was proud, and could vse his owne language.
and all this (I say) to exile the English and British   20
speaches quite out of the countrie. But in vaine, for in
the time of king Edward the first, to wit, toward the
latter end of his reigne, the French it selfe ceased to
be spoken generallie, but most of all and by law in the
midst of Edward the third, and then began the English to   25
recouer and grow in more estimation than before; notwith-
standing that among our artificers, the most part of
their implements, tooles and words of art reteine still
their French denominations euen to these our daies, as
the language it selfe is vsed likewise in sundrie courts,   30
bookes of record, and matters of law; whereof here is
no place to make any particular rehearsall. Afterward
also, by diligent trauell of Geffray Chaucer, and Iohn
Gowre, in the time of Richard the second, and after them
of Iohn Scogan, and Iohn Lydgate monke of Berrie, our   35
said toong was brought to an excellent passe, notwith-
standing that it euer came vnto the type of perfection,
vntill the time of Quéene Elizabeth, wherein Iohn Iewell,
Bishop of Sarum, Iohn Fox, and sundrie learned and excel-
lent writers haue fullie accomplished the ornature of the   40
same, to their great praise and immortall commendation;
although not a few other doo greatlie séeke to staine
the same, by fond affectation of forren and strange
words, presuming that to be the best English, which is   45
most corrupted with externall termes of eloquence, and
sound of manie syllables. But as this excellencie of the
English toong is found in one, and the south part of this
Iland; so in Wales the greatest number (as I said) retaine
still their owne ancient language, that of the north part   50
of the said countrie being lesse corrupted than the other,
and therefore reputed for the better in their owne estimation and iudgement. This also is proper to vs Englishe-
men, that sith ours is a meane language, and neither too
rough nor too smooth in vtterance, we may with much fa-   55
cilitie learne any other language, beside Hebrue, Gréeke
& Latine, and speake it naturallie, as if we were home-
borne in those countries; & yet on the other side it
falleth out, I wot not by what other meanes, that few
forren nations can rightlie pronounce ours, without some   60
and that great note of imperfection, especially the

234

French men, who also seldome write any thing that sauor-
eth of English trulie. It is a pastime to read how Nata-
lis Comes in like maner, speaking of our affaires, dooth
clip the names of our English lords. But this of all the   *65*
rest dooth bréed most admiration with me, that if any
stranger doo hit vpon some likelie pronuntiation of our
toong, yet in age he swarueth so much from the same,
that he is woorse therein than euer he was, and thereto
peraduenture halteth not a litle also in his owne, as I   *70*
haue séene by experience in Reginald Wolfe, and other,
whereof I haue iustlie maruelled.

The Cornish and Deuonshire men, whose countrie the
Britons call Cerniw, haue a speach in like sort of their
owne, and such as hath in déed more affinitie with the   *75*
Armoricane toong than I can well discusse of. Yet in
mine opinion, they are both but a corrupted kind of British, albeit so far degenerating in these daies from the
old, that if either of them doo méete with a Welshman,
they are not able at the first to vnderstand one an   *80*
other, except here and there in some od words, without
the helpe of interpretors. And no maruell (in mine opinion) that the British of Cornewall is thus corrupted,
sith the Welsh toong that is spoken in the north &
south part of Wales, doth differ so much in it selfe,   *85*
as the English vsed in Scotland dooth from that which is
spoken among vs here in this side of the Iland, as I
haue said alreadie.

The Scottish english hath beene much broader and lesse
pleasant in vtterance than ours, because that nation hath   *90*
not till of late indeuored to bring the same to any perfect order, and yet it was such in maner, as Englishmen
themselues did speake for the most part beyond Trent,
whither any great amendement of our language had not as
then extended it selfe. Howbeit in our time the Scottish   *95*
language endeuoreth to come neere, if not altogither to
match our toong in finenesse of phrase, and copie of
words, and this may in part appeare by an historie of the
Apocrypha translated into Scottish verse by Hudson,
dedicated to the king of that countrie, and conteining   *100*
sixe books, except my memorie doo faile me.

Thus we sée how that vnder the dominion of the king of
England, and in the south parts of the realme, we haue
thrée seuerall toongs, that is to saie, English, British,

and Cornish, and euen so manie are in Scotland, if you 105
accompt the English speach for one: notwithstanding that
for bredth and quantitie of the region, I meane onelie
of the soile of the maine Iland, it be somewhat lesse to
see to than the other. For in the north part of the region, where the wild Scots, otherwise called the Redshanks, 110
or rough footed Scots (because they go bare footed and
clad in mantels ouer their saffron shirts after the Irish
maner) doo inhabit, they speake good Irish which they
call Gachtlet, as they saie of one Gathelus, whereby they
shew their originall to haue in times past béene fetched 115
out of Ireland...

In the Iles of the Orchades, or Orkeney, as we now
call them, & such coasts of Britaine as doo abbut vpon
the same, the Gottish or Danish speach is altogither in
vse, and also in Shetland, by reason (as I take it) that 120
the princes of Norwaie held those Ilands so long vnder
their subiection, albeit they were otherwise reputed as
rather to belong to Ireland, bicause that the verie soile
of them is enimie to poison, as some write, although for
my part I had neuer any sound experience of the truth 125
hereof.

11 G. PUTTENHAM: THE ARTE OF ENGLISH POESIE (1589)

CHAP. IIII.
Of Language.

SPeach is not naturall to man sauing for his onely habilitie to
speake, and that he is by kinde apt to vtter all his conceits with
sounds and voyces diuersified many maner of wayes, by meanes
of the many & fit instruments he hath by nature to that purpose,
as a broad and voluble tong, thinne and mouable lippes, teeth euē 5
and not shagged, thick ranged, a round vaulted pallate, and a long
throte, besides an excellent capacitie of wit that maketh him more
disciplinable and imitatiue then any other creature : then as to the

R ij

forme and action of his fpeach, it commeth to him by arte & teaching, and by vfe or exercife. But after a fpeach is fully fafhioned
to the common vnderftanding, & accepted by confent of a whole 10
countrey & natiõ, it is called a language, & receaueth none allowed alteration, but by extraordinary occafions by little & little, as it
were infenfibly bringing in of many corruptiõs that creepe along
with the time: of all which matters, we haue more largely fpoken 15
in our bookes of the originals and pedigree of the Englifh tong.
Then when I fay language, I meane the fpeach wherein the Poet
or maker writeth be it Greek or Latine, or as our cafe is the vulgar
Englifh, & when it is peculiar vnto a countrey it is called the mother fpeach of that people : the Greekes terme it *Idioma*: fo is ours 20
at this day the Norman Englifh. Before the Conqueft of the Normans it was the Anglefaxon, and before that the Britifh, which as
fome will, is at this day, the Walfh, or as others affirme the Cor-
nifh : I for my part thinke neither of both, as they be now fpoken
and ponounced. This part in our maker or Poet muft be heedy- 25
ly looked vnto, that it be naturall, pure, and the moft vfuall of all
his countrey : and for the fame purpofe rather that which is fpoken in the kings Court, or in the good townes and Cities within
the land, then in the marches and frontiers, or in port townes,
where ftraungers haunt for traffike fake, or yet in Vniuerfities 30
where Schollers vfe much peeuifh affectation of words out of the
primatiue languages, or finally, in any vplandifh village or cor-
ner of a Realme, where is no refort but of poore rufticall or vnci-
uill people : neither fhall he follow the fpeach of a craftes man or
carter, or other of the inferiour fort, though he be inhabitant or 35
bred in the beft towne and Citie in this Realme, for fuch perfons
doe abufe good fpeaches by ftrange accents or ill fhapen foundes,
and falfe ortographie. But he fhall follow generally the better
brought vp fort, fuch as the Greekes call [*charientes*] men ciuill
and gracioufly behauoured and bred. Our maker therfore at thefe 40
dayes fhall not follow *Piers plowman* nor *Gower* nor *Lydgate* nor
yet *Chaucer*, for their language is now out of vfe with vs : neither
fhall he take the termes of Northern-men, fuch as they vfe in dayly talke, whether they be noble men or gentlemen, or of their beft
clarkes all is a matter : nor in effect any fpeach vfed beyond the 45
riuer

riuer of Trent, though no man can deny but that theirs is the pu-
rer English Saxon at this day, yet it is not so Courtly nor so currant as our Southerne English is, no more is the far Westerne mās
speach: ye shall therfore take the vsuall speach of the Court, and
that of London and the shires lying about London within lx.   50
myles, and not much aboue. I say not this but that in euery shyre
of England there be gentlemen and others that speake but specially write as good Southerne as we of Middlesex or Surrey do, but
not the common people of euery shire, to whom the gentlemen,
and also their learned clarkes do for the most part condescend, but   55
herein we are already ruled by th'English Dictionaries and other
bookes written by learned men, and therefore it needeth none o-
ther direction in that behalfe. Albeit peraduenture some small admonition be not impertinent, for we finde in our English writers many wordes and speaches amendable, & ye shall see in some   60
many inkhorne termes so ill affected brought in by men of learning as preachers and schoolemasters: and many straunge termes
of other languages by Secretaries and Marchaunts and trauailours, and many darke wordes and not vsuall nor well sounding,
though they be dayly spoken in Court. Wherefore great heed   65
must be taken by our maker in this point that his choise be good.
And peraduenture the writer hereof be in that behalfe no lesse
faultie then any other, vsing many straunge and vnaccusto-
med wordes and borrowed from other languages: and in that   70
respect him selfe no meete Magistrate to reforme the same
errours in any other person, but since he is not vnwilling to
acknowledge his owne fault, and can the better tell how to
amend it, he may seeme a more excusable correctour of other
mens: he intendeth therefore for an indifferent way and vni-   75
uersall benefite to taxe him selfe first and before any others.

    These be words vsed by th'author in this present treatise, *scientī-
ficke*, but with some reason for it auswereth the word *mechanicall*,
which no other word could haue done so properly, for when hee
spake of all artificers which rest either in science or in handy craft,   80
it followed necessarilie that *scientifique* should be coupled with
mechanicall: or els neither of both to haue bene allowed, but in
their places: a man of science liberall, and a handicrafts man, which

R iij

had not bene so cleanly a speech as the other *Maior-domo*: in truth
this word is borrowed of the *Spaniard* and *Italian*, and therefore 85
new and not vsuall, but to them that are acquainted with the affaires of Court: and so for his iolly magnificence (as this case is)
may be accepted among Courtiers,for whom this is specially written. A man might haue said in steade of *Maior-domo*, the French
word (*maistre a'hostell*) but ilfauouredly , or the right English 90
word (*Lord Steward*.) But me thinks for my owne opinion this
word *Maior-domo* though he be borrowed,is more acceptable thã
any of the rest,other men may iudge otherwise. *Politien*,this word
also is receiued from the Frenchmen , but at this day vsuall in
Court and with all good Secretaries:and cannot finde an English 95
word to match him,for to haue said a man politique,had not bene
so wel: bicause in trueth that had bene no more than to haue said a
ciuil person. *Politien* is rather a surueyour of ciuilitie than ciuil,&
a publique minister or Counseller in the state . Ye haue also this
worde *Conduict*, a French word,but well allowed of vs , and long 100
since vsuall , it soundes somewhat more than this word (leading)
for it is applied onely to the leading of a Captaine,and not as a little boy should leade a blinde man , therefore more proper to the
case when he saide, *conduict* of whole armies : ye finde also this
word *Idiome* , taken from the Greekes, yet seruing aptly, when a 105
man wanteth to expresse so much vnles it be in two words,which
surplussage to auoide, we are allowed to draw in other words single, and asmuch significatiue: this word *significatiue* is borrowed
of the Latine and French, but to vs brought in first by some No-
ble-mans Secretarie,as I thinke, yet doth so well serue the turne,as 110
it could not now be spared : and many more like vsurped Latine
and French words : as, *Methode,methodicall,placation,function, as-*
subtiling,refining,compendious,prolixe,figuratiue,inueigle . A terme
borrowed of our common Lawyers. *impression*, also a new terme,
but well expressing the matter,and more than our English word. 115
These words, *Numerous,numerositee,metricall, harmonicall* , but
they cannot be refused,specially in this place for description of the
arte. Also ye finde these words, *penetrate* , *penetrable* , *indignitie*,
which I cannot see how we may spare them,whatsoeuer fault wee
finde with Ink-horne termes : for our speach wanteth wordes to 120
               such

OF ORNAMENT. LIB. III. 113

such sence so well to be vsed : yet in steade of *indignitie*, yee haue
vnworthinesse : and for *penetrate*, we may say *peerce*, and that a
French terme also, or *broche*, or enter into with violence, but not
so well sounding as *penetrate*. Item, *sauage* for wilde : *obscure*, for
darke. Item these words, *declination, delineation, dimention*, are scho- 125
lasticall termes in deede, and yet very proper. But peraduenture
(& I could bring a reason for it) many other like words borrowed
out of the Latin and French, were not so well to be allowed by vs,
as these words, *audacious*, for bold: *facunditie*, for eloquence: *egreg-*
ious, for great or notable: *implete*, for replenished : *attemptat*, for at- 130
tempt : *compatible*, for agreeable in nature, and many more. But
herein the noble Poet *Horace* hath said inough to satisfie vs all in
these few verses.

> *Multa renascentur quæ iam cecidere cadentq́,*
> *Quæ nunc sunt in honore vocabula si volet vsus* 135
> *Quem penes arbitrium est & vis & norma loquendi.*

Which I haue thus englished, but nothing with so good grace, nor
so briefly as the Poet wrote.

> *Many a word ysalne shallest arise*
> *And such as now bene held in hiest prise*
> *Will fall as fast, when vse and custome will* 140
> *Onely vmpiers of speach, for force and skill.*

12 R. CAREW: "THE EXCELLENCY OF THE ENGLISH TONGUE" (? 1595)

Locutio is defined *Animj sensus per vocem expressio.*
On which grounde I builde these Consequences, that the
first and principall point sought in euery Languadge is
that wee maye expresse yᵉ meaning of our mindes aptlye
ech to other. Next, that we may doe it readilye without
great adoo. Then fullye, so as others maye thoroughlie 5
conceiue vs. And last of all handsomely that those to
whome we speake maye take pleasure in hearing vs, soe as
what soeuer tongue will gaine the race of perfection, must
runn on those fower wheeles, *Significancye, Easynes,*
Copiousnes, & Sweetnes, of which the two foremost importe 10
a necessitye, the two latter a delight. Now if I can
proue that our Englishe Langwadge, for all or the most is
macheable, if not preferable, before any other in vogue

at this daye, I hope the assent of any impartiall reeder   *15*
will passe on my side...

Now for the significancye of wordes, as euery *in-*
diuiduum is but one, soe in our natiue Saxon language,
wee finde many of them suitablye expressed by woordes of
one syllable, those consisting of more, are borowed from
other nations, the examples are infinite, and therfore I   *20*
will omitt them, as sufficiently notorious...

Growe from hence to the Compositione of wordes, and
therein our Languadge hath a peculier grace, a like significancy, and more shorte then the Greekes, for example,
in *Moldwarp*, wee expresse the nature of that beast, in   *25*
handkercher, the thing and his vse, in *vpright*, that vertue by a *Metaphore*, in *Wisedome* and *Doomsdaye*, soo many
sentences as wordes, and so of the rest, For I geeue only
a tast y^t may direct others to a fuller obseruation, of
what my soddaine memorye cannott represent vnto mee...   *30*

Yea soe significant are our wordes, that amongst them
sundry single ones serue to expresse diuers thinges, as
by *Bill*, are meant a weapen, a scroll, and a birdes beake,
by *Graue*, sober, a tombe, and to carue; and by *light*,   *35*
marcke, *match*, *file*, *sore*, *& praye*, the semblable...

And soe much for the significancye of our Language in
meaning, now for his easynes in learning. the same shoot-
eth oute into towe braunches. The one of others learning
our languadge, the second of our learning that of others.
For the first the most parte of our wordes (as I haue   *40*
touched) are Monasillables, and soe the fewer in tale,
and the sooner reduced to memorye neither are we loden
with those declensions, flexions, and variations, which
are incydent to many other tongues, but a few articles
gouern all our verbes and Nownes, and so wee neede a   *45*
very shorte grammer.

For easye learning of other Languages by ours, lett
these serue as prooffes, there are many Italyan wordes
which the Frenchmen cannot pronounce, as *accio*, for which
he sayes *ashio*, many of the French which the Italian cann   *50*
hardly come awaye withall, as *bayller*, *chagrin*, *postillon*,
many in ours which neither of them cann vtter, as *Hedge*,
Water, soe that a straunger though neuer soe long conuer-
sant amongst vs, carryeth euermore a watch woorde vppon
his tongue to descrye him by, but turne ann Inglishmann   *55*
at any tyme of his age into what countrey soeuer, allowe-

ing him dew respite, and you shall see him perfitt soe
well that the Imitation of his vtteraunce, will in nothing differ from the patterne of that natiue Languadge.
The wante of which towardnes cost the Ephramites their 60
skynnes, neither doth this crosse my former assertione
of others easye learninge our Language, for I meane of
the sence & wordes & not touching the pronounciation.

But I must nowe enter into ye lardge feild of our
tongues copiousnes and perhapps longe wander vp and 65
downe without finding easye way off issew, and yeat
leaue many partes thereof vnsurvayed.

My first prooff of our plentye I borowe from the
choice, which is geuen vs by the vse of diuers Languages.
The grounde of our owne apperteyneth to the old Saxon, 70
little differing from ye present low Dutch, because
they more then any of their neighbours, haue hitherto
preserued that speach from any greate forrayne mixture.
Heer amongst, the Brittons haue left diuers of their
wordes entersowed, as it weere therby making a conti- 75
nuall clayme to their Auncient possession, wee maye also
trace the footestepps of the Danish bytter (though not
longe duringe) soueraignty in these partes and the Romaine allso imparted vnto vs of his Latyne riches with noe
sparing hand. Our neighbours the French, haue been like- 80
wise contented, wee should take vp by retayle aswell
their tearmes, as their fashions, or rather wee retaine
yeat but some remnant of y^t which once heere bare all
the swaye, and daylye renewe the store. Soe haue our
Italyan trauilers brought vs acquainted with their 85
sweet relished phrases, which (soe their condicions
crept not in withall) weere the better tollerable. Yea
euen wee seeke to make our good of our late Spanish
enymye, and feare as little the hurte of his tongue as
the dinte of his sworde. Seeing then wee borowe (and 90
that not shamfully) from the Dutch, the Breton, ye Romaine, the Dane, the French, Italyan, & Spanyard, how
cann our stocke be other then exceeding plentifull.
It may be obiected, that such patchinge maketh Little-
tons hotchpot of our tongue, and in effect bringes the 95
same rather to a Babellish confusione then any one en-
tyre Language. It may againe be aunswered y^t this thefte
of woordes is not lesse warranted by the priuilidge of
a prescription, auncient and Vniuersall, then was that

of goodes amongst the *Lacedemonians* by an enacted Lawe,   100
for soe the Greekes robbed the Hebrues, the Latynes the
Greekes (which filching *Cicero* with a large discourse
in his booke *de Oratore* defendeth) and (in a manner)
all other Christiane Nations the Latyne...
For our owne partes, we imploye the borrowed ware   105
soe far to our aduantadg that we raise a profitt of new
woordes, from the same stock, which yeat in their owne
countrey are not merchantable, for example, wee deduce
diuers wordes from the Latine which in the Latyne self
cannot be yealded, as the verbes To *Aire, beard, cross,*   110
(feare), flame, (hoast, lust, minde, red, Rust) and
their deriuations *ayring, ayred, bearder, bearding,*
bearded, &c., as alsoe *closer, closely, closnes, glosing-*
ely, hourely, maiesticall, maiestically. (maiesticalnes)
In like sort wee graffe vppon Frentch wordes those bud-   115
des, to which that soyle affordeth noe growth, as
cheiffly, faulty, slauish, precisenes. Diuers wordes
alsoe wee deriue out of the Latyne at second hand by the
French, and make good English, though both Latyne and
French, haue their handes closed in that behalfe, as   120
verbes *Praye, Pointe, Paze, Prest, Rent,* &c., and alsoe
in the aduerbs *carpingly, currantly, actiuely, colourably,*
&c.
   Againe, in other languages there fall out defectes
while they want meanes to deliuer that which another   125
tongue expresseth, as (by *Ciceroes* obseruation) you can-
not interpret *ineptus* (vnapt, vnfitt, vntoward) in
Greek, neither *Procus, Capo, Vervex,* a barrow hogg, a
Capon, a wether...; noe more cann you *to stand* in *French,*
to Tye in *Cornish,* nor *Knaue* in *Latyne,* for *Nebulo* is a   130
clowdye fellow, or in *Irishe;* whereas you see our abil-
litye extendeth thereunto. Moreouer ye Copiousnes of our
languadge appeareth in the diuersitye of our dialectes,
for wee haue court, and wee haue countrye Englishe, wee
haue Northern, & Southerne, grosse and ordinary, which   135
differ ech from other, not only in the terminacions, but
alsoe in many wordes termes and phrases, and expresse the
same thinges in diuers sortes, yeat all right Englishe
alike, neither cann any tongue (as I am perswaded) de-
liuer a matter with more varietye then ours, both plainely   140
and by prouerbes and Metaphors; for example, when wee
would be rid of one, wee vse to saye *Bee going, trudge,*

pack, be faring, hence, awaye, shifte, and by circumlocu-
tion, *rather your roome then your companye, Letts see your*
backe, com againe when I bid you, when you are called,   *145*
sent for, intreated, willed, desiered, invited, spare vs
your place, another in your steede, a shipp of salte for
you, saue your credite, you are next the doore, the doore
is open for you, theres noe bodye holdes you, no bodie
teares your sleeue, &c. Likewise this worde *fortis* wee   *150*
maye *Synnonomize* after all these fashions, stoute, har-
dye, valiaunt, (stalworth), doughtye, Couragious, (sto-
mecked), aduenturous, &c.

And in a worde, to close vp these prooffes of our
copiousnes, looke into our Imitacione of all sortes of   *155*
verses affoorded, by any other Language, and you shall
finde that *Sr Phillip Sydney, Mr Stanihurst,* and diuers
moe, haue made vse how farre wee are within compasse
of a fore imagined impossibility in that behalff.

I com nowe to the last and sweetest point of the sweet-   *160*
nes of our tongue, which shall appeare the more plainelye,
yf like towe Turkeyses, or the *London Drapers* wee match
it with our neighboures. The Italyan is pleasante but
without synewes, as to stillye fleeting water, the French
delicate but ouer nice as a woman scarce daring to open   *165*
her lipps for feare of marring her countenance, the
Spanishe maiesticall, but fullsome, runninge to much on
the .O. and terrible like the deuill in a playe, the Dutch
manlike, but withall very harshe, as one ready at euery
worde to picke a quarrell. Now wee in borrowing from   *170*
them geue the strength of Consonantes to the Italyan,
the full sounde of wordes to the French, the varietye
of terminacions to the Spanish, and ye mollifieinge
of more vowells to the Dutch, and soe (like bees) gather
the honye of their good properties and leaue the dreggs   *175*
to themselues. And thus, when substantiallnes combyneth
with delightfullnes, fullnes, with fynes, seemelynes w^t
portlynes, and courrantnes with staydnes, howe canne
the languadge which consisteth of all these, sounde
other then most full of sweetnes? Againe, the longe   *180*
wordes that wee borrowe, being intermingled with the
shorte of our owne store, make vp a perfitt harmonye,
by culling from out which mixture (with Iudgment) yow
maye frame your speech according to the matter you must
worke on, maiesticall, pleasaunte, delicate, or manly,   *185*

244

more or lesse, in what sorte you please. Adde hereunto,
that what soeuer grace any other Languadge carryeth, in
Verse or Prose, in Tropes or Metaphors, in Ecchoes or
Agnominations, they maye all be liuely and exactly represented in ours. Will you haue *Platos* vayne? reede   190
Sir *Thomas Smith: The Ionick?* Sir *Tho.Moor: Ciceros?*
Aschame: Varro? Chaucer: Demosthenes? Sir *Iohn Cheeke*
(who in his treatise to the Rebells hath comprised
all the figures of Rhetorick). Will you reade Virgill?
take the *Earll of Surrey: Catullus? Shakespeare,* and   195
Marlowes fragment: *Ouid? Daniell: Lucane? Spencer: Mar-
tiall? Sir Iohn Dauis* and others. Will yow haue all in
all for prose and verse? take the miracle of our age
Sir *Philip Sydney.*

And thus, if myne owne Eyes be not blinded by affec-   200
tion, I haue made yours to see that the most renowned of
other nations haue laid vp, as in Treasure, and entrusted
the *Diuisos orbe Britannos* with the rarest Iewelles of
their lipps perfections, whether yow respect the vnderstanding for significancye, or the memorye for Easyenes,   205
or the conceipt for plentifullnes, or the Eare for
pleasauntnes: wherin if inough be deliuered, to add
more then Inough weare superfluous; if to little, I
leaue it to bee supplied by better stored capacityes;
if ought amisse, I submitte the same to the disciplyne   210
of euery able and Impartiall censurer.

13 SIR F. BACON: THE ADVANCEMENT OF LEARNING (1605)

There be therfore chiefly three vanities in Studies,
whereby learning hath been most traduced: For those
things we do esteeme vaine, which are either false or
friuolous, those which either haue no truth, or no vse:
& those persons we esteem vain, which are either   5
credulous or curious, & curiositie is either in mater
or words; so that in reason, as wel as in experience,
there fal out to be these 3. distempers (as I may tearm
them) of learning; The first fantastical learning: The
second contentious learning, & the last delicate learn-   10
ing, vaine imaginations, vaine Altercations, & vain
affectations...
   ... the ancient Authors, both in Diuinitie and in

Humanitie, which had long time slept in Libraries, began
generally to be read and reuolued. This by consequence,   *15*
did draw on a necessitie of a more exquisite trauaile in
the languages originall, wherin those Authors did write:
For the better vnderstanding of those Authors, and the
better aduantage of pressing and applying their words:
And thereof grew againe, a delight in their manner of   *20*
Stile and Phrase, and an admiration of that kinde of
writing; which was much furthered & precipitated by the
enmity & opposition, that the propounders of those
(primitiue, but seeming new opinions) had against the
Schoole-men: who were generally of the contrarie part: *25*
and whose Writings were altogether in a differing Stile
and fourme, taking libertie to coyne, and frame new
tearms of Art, to expresse their own sence, and to auoide
circuite of speech, without regard to the purenesse,
pleasantnesse, and (as I may call it) lawfulnesse of   *30*
the Phrase or word: And againe, because the great labour
that then was with the people (of whome the Pharisees
were wont to say: *Execrabilis ista turba quæ non nouit
legem*) for the winning and perswading of them, there
grewe of necessitie in cheefe price, and request, elo-   *35*
quence and varietie of discourse, as the fittest and
forciblest accesse into the capacitie of the vulgar sort:
so that these foure causes concurring, the admiration of
ancient Authors the hate of the Schoole-men, the exact
studie of Languages: and the efficacie of Preaching did   *40*
bring in an affectionate studie of eloquence, and copie
of speech, which then began to flourish. This grew spee-
dily to an excesse: for men began to hunt more after
wordes, than matter, and more after the choisenesse of
the Phrase, and the round and cleane composition of the   *45*
sentence, and the sweet falling of the clauses, and the
varying and illustration of their workes with tropes and
figures: then after the weight of matter, worth of subiect, soundnesse of argument, life of inuention, or depth
of iudgement. Then grew the flowing, and watrie vaine of   *50*
Osorius the Portugall Bishop, to be in price: then did
Sturmius spend such infinite, and curious paines vpon
Cicero the Orator, and *Hermogenes* the Rhetorican, besides
his owne Bookes of Periods, and imitation, and the like:
Then did *Car* of *Cambridge*, and *Ascham* with their Lectures   *55*
and Writings, almost deifie *Cicero* and *Demosthenes*, and

allure, all young men that were studious vnto that delicate and pollished kinde of learning. Then did *Erasmus*
take occasion to make the scoffing Eccho; *Decem annos con-*
consumpsi in legendo Cicerone: and the Eccho answered   60
in Greeke, *One; Asine.* Then grew the learning of the
Schoole-men to be vtterly despised as barbarous. In summe,
the whole inclination and bent of those times, was rather
towards copie, than weight.

Here therefore, the first distemper of learning, when   65
men studie words, and not matter: whereof though I haue
represented an example of late times: yet it hath beene,
and will be *Secundum maius & minus* in all time. And how
is it possible, but this should haue an operation to dis-
credite learning, euen with vulgar capacities, when they   70
see learned mens workes like the first Letter of a Patent,
or limmed Booke: which though it hath large flourishes,
yet it is but a Letter.

14 BEN JONSON: TIMBER OR DISCOVERIES (1640)

Custome is the most certaine Mistresse of Language, as
the publicke stampe makes the current money. But wee must
not be too frequent with the mint, every day coyning. Nor
fetch words from the extreme and utmost ages; since the
chiefe vertue of a style is perspicuitie, and nothing   5
so vitious in it, as to need an Interpreter. Words borrow'd of Antiquity, doe lend a kind of Majesty to style,
and are not without their delight sometimes. For they
have the Authority of yeares, and out of their intermis-
sion doe win to themselves a kind of grace-like new-   10
nesse. But the eldest of the present, and newest of the
past Language is the best. For what was the ancient Language, which some men so doate upon, but the ancient
Custome? Yet when I name Custome, I understand not the
vulgar Custome: For that were a precept no lesse dan-   15
gerous to Language, then life, if wee should speake or
live after the manners of the vulgar: But that I call
Custome of speech, which is the consent of the Learned;
as Custome of life, which is the consent of the good.
Virgill was most loving of Antiquity; yet how rarely   20
doth he insert *aquai*, and *pictai!* *Lucretius* is scabrous
and rough in these; hee seekes 'hem: As some doe *Chau-*

cerismes with us, which were better expung'd and banish'd.
Some words are to be cull'd out for ornament and colour,
as wee gather flowers to straw houses, or make Garlands;   25
but they are better when they grow to our style; as
in a Meadow, where though the meere grasse and green-
nesse delights; yet the variety of flowers doth heighten
and beautifie. Marry we must not play, or riot too much
with them, as in *Paronomasies*: Nor use too swelling,   30
or ill-sounding words; *Quae per salebras, altaque saxa
cadunt.* It is true, there is no sound but shall find
some Lovers, as the bitter'st confections are gratefull
to some palats. Our composition must bee more accurate
in the beginning and end, then in the midst; and in the   35
end more, then in the beginning; for through the midst
the streame beares us. And this is attain'd by Custome
more then care, or diligence. Wee must expresse readily,
and fully, not profusely. There is a difference betweene
a liberall, and a prodigall hand. As it is a great point   40
of Art, when our matter requires it, to enlarge, and
veere out all sayle; so to take it in, and contract it,
is of no lesse praise when the Argument doth aske it.
Either of them hath their fitnesse in the place. A good
man alwayes profits by his endeavour, by his helpe;   45
yea, when he is absent; nay when he is dead by his ex-
ample and memory. So good Authors in their style: A
succinct style is that, where you can take away nothing
without losse, and that losse to be manifest. The briefe
style is that which expresseth much in little. The con-   50
cise style, which expresseth not enough, but leaves
somewhat to bee understood. The abrupt style, which hath
many breaches, and doth not seeme to end, but fall. The
congruent, and harmonious fitting of parts in a sentence,
hath almost the fastning, and force of knitting, and   55
connexion: As stones well squar'd, which will rise strong
a great way without mortar. Periods are beautifull; when
they are not too long; for so they have their strength
too, as in a Pike or Javelin. As wee must take the care
that our words and sense bee cleare; so if the obscurity   60
happen through the Hearers, or Readers want of under-
standing, I am not to answer for them; no more then for
their not listning or marking; I must neither find them
eares, nor mind. But a man cannot put a word so in sense,
but some thing about it will illustrate it, if the Writer   65

understand himselfe. For Order helpes much to Perspicuity,
as Confusion hurts. *Rectitudo lucem adfert; obliquitas
et circumductio offuscat.* We should therefore speake what
wee can, the neerest way, so as wee keepe our gate, not
leape; for too short may as well be not let into the 70
memory, as too long not kept in. Whatsoever looseth the
grace, and clearenesse, converts into a Riddle; the obscurity is mark'd, but not the valew. That perisheth,
and is past by, like the Pearle in the Fable. Our style
should be like a skeine of silke to be carried, and 75
found by the right thred, not ravel'd, and perplex'd;
then all is a knot, a heape. There are words, that doe
as much raise a style, as others can depresse it. Super-
lation, and overmuchnesse amplifies.

15 J. DRYDEN: "DEFENCE OF THE
EPILOGUE" (1672)

To begin with *Language.* That an Alteration is lately
made in ours or since the Writers of the last Age (in
which I comprehend *Shakespear, Fletcher* and *Jonson*) is
manifest. Any man who reads those excellent Poets, and
compares their language with what is now written, will 5
see it almost in every line. But, that this is an *Improvement* of the Language, or an alteration for the better,
will not so easily be granted. For many are of a contrary
opinion, that the English tongue was then in the height
of its perfection; that, from *Jonsons* time to ours, it 10
has been in a continual declination; like that of the
Romans from the Age of *Virgil* to *Statius,* and so downward
to *Claudian*: of which, not onely *Petronius,* but *Quintilian*
himself so much complains, under the person of *Secundus,*
in his famous Dialogue *de causis corruptæ eloquentiæ.* 15
But, to shew that our Language is improv'd; and that
those people have not just value for the Age in which they
live, let us consider in what the refinement of a language
principally consists: that is, *either in rejecting such
old words or phrases which are ill sounding, or improper,* 20
*or in admitting new, which are more proper, more sounding
and more significant.*
The Reader will easily take notice, that when I speak
of rejecting improper words and phrases I mention not such
as are Antiquated by custome onely: and, as I may say, 25

without any fault of theirs: for in this case the refinement can be but accidental: that is when the words and
phrases which are rejected happen to be improper. Neither
would I be understood (when I speak of impropriety in
Language) either wholly to accuse the last Age, or to 30
excuse the present; and least of all my self. For all
writers have their imperfections and failings, but I may
safely conclude in the general, that our improprieties
are less frequent, and less gross than theirs. One Testimony of this is undeniable, that we are the first who 35
have observ'd them , and, certainly, to observe errours
is a great step to the correcting of them. But, malice and
partiality set apart, let any man who understands English,
read diligently the works of *Shakespear* and *Fletcher*; and
I dare undertake that he will find, in every page either 40
some *Solecism* of Speech, or some notorious flaw in Sence:
and yet these men are reverenc'd when we are not forgiven.
That their wit is great and many times their expressions
noble, envy it self cannot deny...

But it is not their Plots which I meant, principally 45
to tax: I was speaking of their Sence and Language, and
I dare almost challenge any man to show me a page together,
which is correct in both. As for *Ben. Johnson*, I am loath
to name him, because he is a most Judicious Writer; yet
he very often falls into these errors. And I once more 50
beg the Readers pardon, for accusing him or them. Onely
let him consider that I live in an age where my least
faults are severely censur'd: and that I have no way left
to extenuate my failings but my showing as great in those
whom we admire... I cast my eyes but by chance on *Catiline*; 55
and in the three or four first pages, found enough to
conclude that *Johnson* writ not correctly.

> Let the long hid seeds / Of treason, in thee, now
> shoot forth in deeds / Ranker than horrour.

In reading some bombast speeches of *Macbeth*, which are 60
not to be understood, he us'd to say that it was horrour,
and I am much afraid that this is so.

> Thy parricide, late on thy onely Son / After his mother,
> to make empty way / For thy last wicked Nuptials, worse
> than they / That blaze an act of thy incestuous life, / 65
> Which gain'd thee at once a daughter and a wife.

The Sence is here extreamly perplex'd: and I doubt the
word *They* is false Grammar.

> *And be free / Not Heaven itself from thy impiety.*

A *Synchaesis*, or ill placing of words, of which *Tully*   70
so much complains in Oratory.

> *The Waves, and Dens of beasts cou'd not receive*
> *The bodies that those Souls were frighted from.*

The Preposition in the end of the sentence; a common
fault with him, and which I have but lately observ'd in   75
my own writings.

> *What all the several ills that visit earth,*
> *Plague, famine, fire, could not reach unto,*
> *The Sword nor surfeits, let thy fury do.*

Here are both the former faults: for, besides that the   80
Preposition *unto*, is plac'd last in the verse, and at the
half period, and is redundant, there is the former *Synchæ-*
sis, in the words (*The Sword nor Surfeits*) which in construction ought to have been plac'd before the other.
Catiline sayes of *Cethegus*, that for his sake he would   85

> *Go on upon the Gods; kiss Lightning, wrest*
> *The Engine from the Cyclops, and give fire*
> *At face of a full clowd, and stand his ire.*

To *go on upon*, is onely to go on twice, to give fire at
face of a full cloud, was not understood in his own time: 90
(and stand his *ire*) besides the antiquated word *ire*
is the Article His, which makes false construction: and
giving fire at the face of a cloud, is a perfect image
of shooting, however it came to be known in those daies
to *Catiline*.   95

> *others there are*
> *Whom Envy to the State draws and pulls on,*
> *For Contumelies receiv'd; and such are sure ones.*

Ones in the plural Number: but that is frequent with him:
for he sayes, not long after.   100

> *Cæsar and Crassus; if they be ill men, / Are Mighty ones.*
> *Such Men they do not succour more the cause, &c.*

They redundant.

> *Though Heav'n should speak with all his wrath at once;*
> *We should stand upright and unfear'd.*   105

His is ill Syntax with Heaven: and by Unfear'd he means
Unaffraid, words of a quite contrary signification.

The Ports are open, He perpetually uses Ports for
Gates: which is an affected error in him, to introduce
Latine by the loss of *English* Idiom: as in the Translation   *110*
of *Tully's* Speeches he usually does.

Well placing of words for the sweetness of pronunciation was not known till Mr. *Waller* introduc'd it: and
therefore 'tis not to be wonder'd if *Ben. Johnson* has
many such lines as these   *115*

> But being bred up in his father's needy fortunes,
> Brought up in's sister's Prostitution, &c.

But meanness of expression one would think not to be
his error in a Tragedy, which ought to be more high and
sounding than any other kind of Poetry, and yet amongst   *120*
many others in *Catiline* I find these four lines together:

> So Asia, *thou art cruelly even*
> *With us, for all the blows thee given:*
> *When we, whose Vertues conquer'd thee,*
> *Thus, by thy Vices, ruin'd be.*   *125*

Be there is false *English*, for *are*: though the Rhyme
hides it.

But I am willing to close the Book, partly out of veneration to the Author, partly out of weariness to pursue
an argument which is so fruitful in so small a compass.   *130*
And what correctness, after this, can be expected from
Shakespear or from *Fletcher*, who wanted that Learning
and Care which *Johnson* had? I will therefore spare my
own trouble of inquiring into their faults: who had they
liv'd now, had doubtless written more correctly. I sup-   *135*
pose it will be enough for me to affirm (as I think I
safely may) that these and the like errors which I tax'd
in the most correct of the last Age, are such, into which
we doe not ordinarily fall. I think few of our present
Writers would have left behind them such a line as this,   *140*
Contain your Spirit in more stricter bounds. But that
gross way of two Comparatives was then, ordinary: and
therefore more pardonable in *Johnson*.

As for the other part of refining, which consists in
receiving new Words and Phrases, I shall not insist   *145*
much on it. 'Tis obvious that we have admitted many: some

of which we wanted, and, therefore our Language is the
richer for them: as it would be by importation of Bullion:
others are rather Ornamental than Necessary; yet by their
admission, the Language is become more courtly: and our   *150*
thoughts are better drest. These are to be found scatter'd
in the Writers of our Age: and it is not my business to
collect them. They who have lately written with most care,
have, I believe, taken the Rule of *Horace* for their guide;
that is, not to be too hasty in receiving of Words: but   *155*
rather to stay till Custome has made them familiar to us,
Quem penes, arbitrium est, & jus & norma loquendi.

For I cannot approve of their way of refining, who
corrupt our *English* Idiom by mixing it too much with
French: that is a Sophistication of Language, not an   *160*
improvement of it: a turning *English* into *French*, rather
than refining of *English* by *French*. We meet daily with
those Fopps, who value themselves on their Travelling,
and pretend they cannot express their meaning in *English*,
because they would put off to us some *French* Phrase of   *165*
the last Edition: without considering that, for ought
they know, we have a better of our own; but these are
not the men who are to refine us; their Tallent is to
prescribe Fashions, not Words: at best they are onely
serviceable to a Writer, so as *Ennius* was to *Virgil*.   *170*
He may *Aurum ex stercore colligere* for 'tis hard if,
amongst many insignificant Phrases, there happen not
something worth preserving: though they themselves, like
Indians, know not the value of their own Commodity.

There is yet another way of improving Language,   *175*
which Poets especially have practic'd in all Ages: that
is by applying receiv'd words to a new Signification...
By this graffing, as I may call it, on old words, has
our Tongue been Beautified by the three fore mention'd
Poets, *Shakespear, Fletcher* and *Johnson*: whose Excel-   *180*
lencies I can never enough admire. and in this, they
have been follow'd especially by Sir *John Suckling* and
Mr. *Waller*, who refin'd upon them.

16 J. EVELYN: LETTER TO WYCHE (1665)

S^r, This crude paper (which beggs y^r pardon) I should not
have presum'd to transmit in this manner, but to obey y^r
commands, and to save the imputation of being thought un-

willing to labour, though it be but in gathering straw.
My great infelicity is that the meeting being on Tuesdays   5
in ye afternoone, I am in a kind of despaire of ever grati-
fying myne inclinations in a conversation w^h I so infinitely honor, & that would be so much to mine advantage; because the very houre interferes wth an employment, w^h being of publiq concernement, I can in no way dispense with: 10
I mention this to deplore myne owne misfortune onely, not
as it can signifie to any losse of yours; w^h cannot be
sensible of so inconsiderable a member. I send you notwithstanding these indigested thoughts, and that attempt
upon Cicero wch you enjoin'd me.   15

   I conceive the reason both of additions to, and the
corruption of, the English language, as of most other
tongues, has proceeded from the same causes; namely, from
victories, plantations, frontieres, staples of commerce,
pedantry of schooles, affectation of travellers, trans-   20
lations, fancy and the style of Court, vernility and minc-
ing of citizens, pulpits, political remonstrances, theatres, shopps, &c.

   The parts affected wth it we find to be the accent,
analogy, direct interpretation, tropes, phrases, and the   25
like.

   1. I would therefore humbly propose that there might
first be compiled a Grammar for the præcepts, which (as
did the Roman, when Crates transferr'd the art to that
city, follow'd by Diomedes, Priscianus, and others who   30
undertooke it) might only insist on the rules, the sole
meanes to render it a learned & learnable tongue.

   2. That with this a more certaine Orthography were
introduc'd, as by leaving out superfluous letters, &c,
such as *o* in woomen, people, *u* in honour, *a* in reproach,   35
ugh in though, &c.

   3. That there might be invented some new periods and
accents, besides such as our grammarians & critics use,
to assist, inspirit, and modifie the pronunciation of
sentences, & to stand as markes before hand how the voice   40
and tone is to be govern'd, as in reciting of playes,
reading of verses, &c, for the varying the tone of the
voyce and affections, &c.

   4. To this might follow a Lexicon or collection of
all the pure English words by themselves; then those   45

w^h are derivative from others, with their prime, certaine, and natural signification; then, the symbolical:
so as no innovation might be us'd or favour'd, at least
till there should arise some necessity of providing a new
edition, & of amplifying the old upon mature advice.   *50*

5. That in order to this, some were appointed to collect all the technical words, especially those of the
more generous employments, as the author of the 'Essaies
des Merveilles de la Nature et des plus noble Artifices'
has don for the French, Francis Junius and others have   *55*
endeavor'd for the Latine; but this must be gleaned from
shops, not bookes, & has ben of late attempted by Mr.
Moxon.

6. That things difficult to be translated or express'd
and such as are, as it were, incommensurable one to an-   *60*
other (as determinations of weights and measures, coines,
honors, national habits, armes, dishes, drinkes, municipal
constitutions of courts, old and abrogated costomes, &c.)
were better interpreted than as yet we find them in dictionaries, glossaries, and noted in the lexicon.   *65*

7. That a full catalogue of exotic words, such as are
daily minted by our *Logodædali*, were exhibited, and that
it were resolved on what should be sufficient to render
them current, *ut Civitate donentur*, since, without re-
straining that same *indomitam novandi verba licentiam*,   *70*
it will in time quite disguise the language: there are
some elegant words introduc'd by phisitians chiefely and
philosophers, worthy to be retained; others, it may be,
fitter to be abrogated; since there ought to be a law
as well as a liberty in this particular. And in this   *75*
choyce there would be some reguard had to the well sounding and more harmonious words, and such as are numerous
and apt to fall gracefully into their cadences and periods, and so recommend themselves at the very first sight,
as it were; others, which (like false stones) will never   *80*
shine, in whatever light they be placed, but embase the
rest. And here I note that such as have lived long in
Universities doe greatly affect words and expressions
no where in use besides, as may be observed in Cleave-
land's Poems for Cambridg; and there are also some   *85*
Oxford words us'd by others, as I might instance in
severall.

8. Previous to this it would be enquir'd what particular dialects, idiomes, and proverbs were in every several county of England; for the words of ye present age   *90*
being properly the *vernacula*, or classic rather, special
reguard is to be had of them, and this consideration
admits of infinite improvements.

9. And happly it were not amisse that we had a collection of ye most quaint and courtly expressions, by way   *95*
of *florilegium*, or phrases distinct from the proverbs;
for we are infinitely defective as to civil addresses,
excuses, & formes upon suddaine and unpremeditated though
ordinary encounters: in which the French, Italians, &
Spanyards have a kind of natural grace & talent, which   *100*
furnishes the conversation, and renders it very agreeable: here may come in synonimes, homoinymes, &c.

10. And since there is likewise a manifest rotation
and circling of words, which goe in & out like the mode
& fashion, bookes would be consulted for the reduction   *105*
of some of the old layd-aside words and expressions had
formerly *in delicijs*; for our language is in some places
sterile and barren by reason of this depopulation, as I
may call it; and therefore such places should be new cultivated, and enrich'd either wth the former (if signi-   *110*
ficant) or some other; for example, we have hardly any
words that do so fully expresse the French *clinquant*,
*naiveté, ennuy, bizarre, concert, faconiere, chicane-
ries, consummè, emotion, defer, effort, chocq, entours,
debouche*, or the Italian *vaghezze, garbato, svelto*, &c.   *115*
Let us therefore (as ye Romans did the Greeke) make as
many of these do homage as are like to prove good citizens.

11. Something might likewise be well translated out of
the best orators & poets, Greek and Latin, and even out
of ye moderne languages, that so some judgement might   *120*
be made concerning the elegancy of ye style, and so a
laudable & unaffected imitation of the best recommended
to writers.

12. Finaly, there must be a stock of reputation gain'd
by some public writings and compositions of ye Members   *125*
of this Assembly, and so others may not thinke it dishonor to come under the test, or accept them for judges
and approbators; and if ye designe were ariv'd thus far,
I conceive a very small matter would dispatch the art

of rhetoric, which the French propos'd as one of the 130
first things they recommended to their late academitians.
          I am, S^r, Y^r most, &c.
Says-Court, 20 June, 1665

17 T. SPRAT: HISTORY OF THE ROYAL SOCIETY (1667)

II, xx "THEIR MANNER OF DISCOURSE"

Thus they have directed, judg'd, conjectur'd upon, and
improved *Experiments*. But lastly, in these, and all other
businesses that have come under their care; there is one
thing more, about which the *Society* has been most sollici-
tous; and that is, the manner of their *Discourse* which, 5
unless they had been very watchful to keep in due temper,
the whole spirit and vigour of their *Design*, had been soon
eaten out, by the luxury and redundance of *speech*. The ill
effects of this superfluity of talking have already over-
whelm'd most other *Arts* and *Professions*, insomuch, that 10
when I consider the means of *happy living*, and the causes
of their corruption, I can hardly forbear recanting what
I said before; and concluding, that *eloquence* ought to be
banish'd out of all *civil Societies*, as a thing fatal to
Peace and good Manners. To this opinion I should wholly 15
incline; if I did not find, that it is a Weapon, which may
be as easily procur'd by *bad men*, as *good* and that, if
these should onely cast it away, and those retain it; the
naked Innocence of vertue would be upon all occasions
expos'd to the *armed Malice* of the wicked. This is the 20
chief reason, that should now keep up the Ornaments of
speaking in any request since they are so much degene-
rated from their original usefulness. They were at first,
no doubt, an admirable Instrument in the hands of *Wise
Men*: when they were onely employ'd to describe *Goodness*, 25
Honesty, *Obedience*; in larger, fairer, and more moving
Images: to represent *Truth*, cloth'd with Bodies; and to
bring *Knowledg* back again to our very senses, from whence
it was at first deriv'd to our understandings. But now
they are generally chang'd to worse uses: They make the 30
Fancy disgust the best things, if they come sound, and
unadorn'd; they are in open defiance against *Reason*;
professing, not to hold much correspondence with that;

but with its Slaves, *the Passions*; they give the mind a
motion too changeable and bewitching, to consist with   35
right practice. Who can behold, without indignation, how
many mists and uncertainties, these specious *Tropes* and
Figures have brought on our Knowledg? How many rewards,
which are due to more profitable, and difficult *Arts*,
have been still snatch'd away by the easie vanity of   40
fine speaking? For now I am warm'd with this just Anger,
I cannot with-hold my self, from betraying the shallow-
ness of all these seeming Mysteries; upon which, *we
Writers*, and *Speakers*, look so bigg. And, in few words,
I dare say; that of all the Studies of men, nothing may   45
be sooner obtain'd, than this vicious abundance of
Phrase, this trick of *Metaphors*, this volubility of
Tongue, which makes so great a noise in the World. But I
spend words in vain; for the evil is now so inveterate
that it is hard to know whom to *blame*, or where to begin   50
to *reform*. We all value one another so much, upon this
beautiful deceipt; and labour so long after it, in the
years of our education: that we cannot but ever after
think kinder of it, than it deserves. And indeed, in most
other parts of Learning, I look on it to be a thing al-   55
most vtterly desperate in its cure, and I think, it may
be plac'd amongst those *general mischiefs*; such, as the
dissention of Christian Princes, the *want of practice*
in Religion, and the like; which have been so long spoken
against, that men are become insensible about them; every   60
one shifting off the fault from himself to others, and
so they are only made bare common places of complaint.
It will suffice my present purpose, to point out, what
has been done by the *Royal Society*, towards the correcting of its excesses in *Natural Philosophy*; to which it   65
is, of all others, a most profest enemy.
    They have therefore been most rigorous in putting in
execution, the only Remedy, that can be found for this
extravagance: and that has been, a constant Resolution,
to reject all the amplifications, digressions, and   70
swellings of style; to return back to the primitive
purity, and shortness, when men deliver'd so many *things*,
almost in an equal number of *words*. They have exacted
from all their members, a close, naked, natural way of
speaking; positive expressions; clear senses; a native   75
easiness: bringing all things as near the Mathematical

plainness, as they can: and preferring the language of
Artizans, Countrymen, and Merchants, before that, of
Wits, or Scholars.

And here, there is one thing, not to be pass'd by,   *80*
which will render this establish'd custom of the *Society*,
well nigh everlasting: and that is, the general constitu-
tion of the minds of the *English*. I have already often
insisted on some of the prerogatives of *England*; whereby
it may justly lay claim, to be the Head of a *Philo-*   *85*
sophical league, above all other Countries in *Europe*;
I have urg'd its scituation, its present Genius, and the
disposition of its Merchants; and many more such *argu-*
ments to incourage us, still remain to be us'd: But of
all others, this, which I am now alledging, is of the   *90*
most weighty, and important consideration. If there can
be a true character given of the *Universal Temper* of any
Nation under Heaven: then certainly this must be ascrib'd
to our Countrymen: that they have commonly an unaffected
sincerity; that they love to deliver their minds with a   *95*
sound simplicity; that they have the middle qualities,
between the reserv'd subtle southern, and the rough
unhewn Northern people: that they are not extreamly prone
to speak: that they are more concern'd, what others will
think of the strength, than of the fineness of what they   *100*
say: and that an universal modesty possesses them. These
qualities are so conspicuous, and proper to our Soil;
that we often hear them objected to us, by some of our
neighbour Satyrists, in more disgraceful expressions.
For they are wont to revile the *English*, with a want of   *105*
familiarity; with a melancholy dumpishness; with slow-
ness, silence, and with the unrefin'd sullenness of their
behaviour. But these are only the reproaches of partiality, or ignorance: for they ought rather to be commended
for an honourable integrity; for a neglect of circum-   *110*
stances, and flourishes; for regarding things of *greater*
moment, more than *less*; for a scorn to deceive as well
as to be deceiv'd: which are all the best indowments,
that can enter into a *Philosophical Mind*. So that even
the position of our climate, the air, the influence of   *115*
the heaven, the composition of the English blood; as well
as the embraces of the Ocean, seem to joyn with the labours of the *Royal Society*, to render our Country, a Land
of *Experimental knowledge*. And it is a good sign, that

Nature will reveal more of its secrets to the English, than to others; because it has already furnish'd them with a Genius so well proportion'd, for the receiving, and retaining its mysteries.

ON LITERATURE AND LITERARY THEORY

18A G. DOUGLAS: *VIRGIL'S ÆNEID* (1515)

Fyrst I protest, beaw schirris, be зour leif,   *(I.105–24)*
Beis weill avisit my wark or зhe repreif,
Consider it warly, reid oftar than anys:
Weill at a blenk sle poetry nocht tayn is,
And зit forsuyth I set my bissy pane   *5*
As that I couth to mak it braid and plane,
Kepand na sudron bot our awyn langage,
And spekis as I lernyt quhen I was page.
Nor зit sa cleyn all sudron I refuß,
Bot sum word I pronunce as nyghtbouris doys: *10*
Lyke as in Latyn beyn Grew termys sum,
So me behufyt quhilum or than be dum
Sum bastard Latyn, French or Inglys oyß
Quhar scant was Scottis – I had nane other choys.
Nocht for our tong is in the selwyn skant   *15*
Bot for that I the fowth of langage want
Quhar as the cullour of his properte
To kepe the sentens tharto constrenyt me,
Or than to mak my sayng schort sum tyme,
Mair compendyus, or to lykly my ryme.   *20*

Thoght venerabill Chauser, principal poet but peir,
Hevynly trumpat, orlege and reguler,   *(I.339–46)*
In eloquens balmy, cundyt and dyall,
Mylky fontane, cleir strand and royß ryall,
Of fresch endyte, throu Albion iland braid,   *25*
In his legend of notabill ladeis said
That he couth follow word for word Virgill,
Wisar than I may faill in lakar stile.

Besyde Latyn our langage is imperfite   *(I.359–67)*
Quhilk in sum part is the cauß and the wyte   *30*
Quhy that of Virgillis verß the ornate bewte
Intill our tung may nocht obseruyt be,
For thar be Latyn wordis mony ane
That in our leyd ganand translatioun haß nane
Less than we mynyß thar sentens and grauyte   *35*
And зit scant weill exponyt. Quha trewys nocht me,
Lat thame interprit "animal" and "homo"   +)

+) As for animal and homo in our langage is nocht a propir
term, and thai be bot bestis that exponys animal for a
beste. Ane beste is callit in Latyn bestia and pecus, and
animal betakynnys all corporall substans that haß ane   *40*
saull quhilk felis payn, ioy or ennoy. And vndyr animal
beyn contenyt all mankynd, beist, byrd, fowll, fisch,
serpent and all other sik thingis at lyfis and steris,
that haß a body, for al sik and euery ane of thame may be   *45*
properly callit animal. And thus animal is ane general
name for al sik maner thingis quhatsumeuer. Homo betakynnys baith a man and a woman, and we haue na term correspondent tharto, nor ʒit that signifyis baith twa in
a term alanerly.   *50*

18B W. TYNDALE: THE OBEDIENCE OF A CHRISTEN MAN (1526)

WILLIAM TYNDALE OTHERWISE CALLED HYCHINS UNTO THE READER

The sermons which thou readist in the Actes of yᵉ apostles
& all yᵗ the apostles preached were no doute preached in the
mother tonge. Why then might they not be written in the
mother tonge? As yf one of vs preach a good sermon why maye
it not be written? Saynt hierom also translated the bible   *5*
in to his mother tonge. Why may not we also? They will saye
it can not be translated in to oure tonge it is so rude.
It is not so rude as they are false lyers. For the greke
tonge agreeth moare with the english then with the latyne.
The maner of speakynge is both one so yᵗ in a thousande   *10*
places thou neadest not but to translate it in to yᵉ english
worde for worde when thou must seke a compasse in the latyne/
and yet shalt have moch worke to translate it welfaveredly/
so that it have the same grace and swetnesse/ sence and pure
vnderstandinge with it in the latyne/ as it hath in the   *15*
hebrue. A thousande partes better maye it be translated in
to the english then in to the latyne...

Fynally that this thretenynge and forbiddynge the laye
people to reade the scripture is not for love of youre soules
(which they care for as yᵉ foxe doeth for yᵉ gysse) is evi-   *20*
dente & clerer then the sonne/ in as moch as they permitte
& sofre you to reade Robyn hode & bevise of hampton/hercules/
hector and troylus with a thousande histories & fables of

love & wantones & of rybaudry as fylthy as herte can thinke/   25
to corrupte yᵉ myndes of youth with all/ clene contrary to
the doctrine of christ & of his apostles.

18C FROM THE FOREWORD OF THE RHEIMS BIBLE (1582)

THE PREFACE TO THE READER TREATING OF THESE THREE POINTS:
OF THE TRANSLATION OF THE HOLY SCRIPTURES INTO THE VULGAR
TONGUES, AND NAMELY INTO ENGLISH: OF THE CAUSES WHY THIS
NEW TESTAMENT IS TRANSLATED ACCORDING TO THE AUNCIENT
LATIN TEXT: & OF THE MANER OF TRANSLATING THE SAME.   5

   Which translation we doe not for all that publish, vpon
erroneous opinion of necessitie, that the holy Scriptures
should alwaies be in our mother tonge, or that they ought,
or were ordained by God, to be read indifferently of all,
or could be easily vnderstood of euery one that readeth   10
or heareth them in a knowen language: or that they were
not often through mans malice or infirmitie, pernicious
and much hurtful to many: or that we generally and absolutely deemed it more conuenient in it self, & more agreable to
Gods word and honour or edification of the faithful, to   15
haue them turned into vulgar tonges, then to be kept &
studied only in the Ecclesiastical learned languages:
Not for these nor any such like causes doe we translate
this sacred booke, but vpon special consideration of the
present time, state, and condition of our countrie, vnto   20
which, diuers thinges are either necessarie, or profitable and medicinable now, that otherwise in the peace of
the Church were neither much requisite, nor perchance
wholy tolerable . . .
   Wherein, though for due preseruation of this diuine   25
worke from abuse and prophanation, and for the better
bridling of the intolerable insolencie of proude, curious,
& contentious wittes, the gouernours of the Church guided
by Gods Spirit, as euer before, so also vpon more experience of the maladie of this time then before, haue taken   30
more exacte order both for the readers and translatours
in these later ages, then of old: yet we must not imagin
that in the primitiue Church, either euery one that vnderstoode the learned tonges wherein the Scriptures were
written, or other languages into which they were trans-   35

lated, might without reprehension, reade, reason, dispute,
turne and tosse the Scriptures: or that our forefathers
suffered euery schole-maister, scholer, or Grammarian that
had a litle Greeke or Latin, straight to take in hand the
holy Testament: or that the translated Bibles into the   *40*
vulgar tonges, were in the handes of euery husbandman,
artificer, prentice, boies, girles, mistresse, maide, man:
that they were sung, plaied, alleaged, of euery tinker,
tauerner, rimer, minstrel: that they were for table talke,
for alebenches, for boates and barges, and for euery pro-   *45*
phane person and companie. No, in those better times men
were neither so ill, nor so curious of them selues, so to
abuse the blessed booke of Christ: neither was there any
such easy meanes before printing was inuented, to disperse
the copies into the handes of euery man, as now there is.   *50*
  They were then in Libraries, Monasteries, Colleges,
Churches, in Bishops, Priests, and some other deuout principal Lay mens houses and hands: who vsed them with feare
and reuerence, and specially such partes as perteined to
good life and maners, not medling, but in pulpit and   *55*
schooles (and that moderately to) with the hard and high
mysteries and places of greater difficultie. The poore
ploughman, could then in labouring the ground, sing the
hymnes and psalmes either in knowen or vnknowen languages,
as they heard them in the holy Church, though they could   *60*
neither reade nor know the sense, meaning, and mysteries
of the same...
  But the case now is more lamentable: for the Protestants
and such as S.Paul calleth *ambulantes in astutia, walking
in deceitfulnes,* haue so abused the people and many other   *65*
in the world, not unwise, that by their false translations
they haue in steede of Gods Law and Testament, & for
Christes written will and word, giuen them their owne
wicked writing and phantasies, most shamefully in all their
versions Latin, English, and other tonges, corrupting both   *70*
the letter and sense by false translation, adding, detract-
ing, altering, transposing, pointing, and all other guile-
ful meanes: specially where it serueth for the aduantage
of their priuate opinions. for which, they are bold also,
partly to disauthorise quite, partly to make doubtful,   *75*
diuers whole bookes allowed for Canonical Scripture by
the vniuersal Church of God this thousand yeres and vpward:
to alter al the authentical and Ecclesiastical wordes vsed

sithence our Christianitie, into new prophane nouelties
of speaches agreable to their doctrine: to change the
title of workes, to put out the names of the authors, to
charge the very Euangelist with following vntrue translation, to adde whole sentences proper to their sect,
into their psalmes in metre, euen into the very Crede in
rime. al which the poore deceiued people say and sing as
though they were Gods owne word, being in deede through
such sacrilegious treacherie, made the Diuels word.

To say nothing of their intolerable liberty and licence
to change the accustomed callings of God, Angel, men, places, & things vsed by the Apostles and all antiquitie, in
Greeke, Latin, and all other languages of Christian nations, into new names, sometimes falsely, and alwaies
ridiculously and for ostentation taken of the Hebrues: to
frame and fine the phrases of holy Scriptures after the
forme of prophane writers, sticking not, for the same to
supply, adde, alter or diminish as freely as if they
translated Liuie, Virgil, or Terence. Hauing no religious
respect to keepe either the maiestie or sincere simplicity
of that venerable style of Christes spirit, as S.Augustine
speaketh, which kind the holy Ghost did choose of infinite
wisedom to haue the diuine mysteries rather vttered in,
then any other more delicate, much lesse in that meretri-
cious maner of writing that sundrie of these new translators doe vse...

In this our Translation, because we wish to be most
sincere, as becometh a Catholike translation, and haue
endeuoured so to make it: we are very precise & religious
in folowing our copie, the old vulgar approued Latin:
not onely in sense, which we hope we alwaies doe, but sometime in the very wordes also and phrases, which may seeme
to the vulgar Reader & to common English eares not yet
acquainted therewith, rudenesse or ignorance: but to the
discrete Reader that deepely weigheth and considereth the
importance of sacred wordes and speaches, and how easily
the voluntarie Translatour may misse the true sense of the
Holy Ghost, we doubt not but our consideration and doing
therein, shal seeme reasonable and necessarie: yea and
that al sortes of Catholike Readers wil in short time
thinke that familiar, which at the first may seeme strange,
& wil esteeme it more, when they shal otherwise be taught
to vnderstand it, then if it were the common knowen English.

... *Parasceue* is as solemne a word for the Sabboth eue,
as *Sabboth* is for the Iewes seuenth day, and now among
Christians much more solemner, taken for Good-friday onely.
These wordes then we thought it far better to keepe in   *125*
the text, and to tel their signification in the margent
or in a table for that purpose, then to disgrace bothe the
text & them with translating them. Such are also these
wordes, *The Pasche. The feast of Azymes. The bread of Pro-*
position. Which they translate *The Passeouer, The feast of*   *130*
swete bread, The shew bread ...

Moreouer, we presume not in hard places to mollifie the
speaches or phrases, but religiously keepe them word for
word, and point for point, for feare of missing, or re-
straining the sense of the holy Ghost to our phantasie.   *135*

18D FROM THE FOREWORD OF THE
AUTHORIZED VERSION (1611)

Truly (good Christian Reader) wee neuer thought from
the beginning, that we should neede to make a new Translation, nor yet to make of a bad one a good one,... but
to make a good one better, or out of many good ones, one
principall good one, not iustly to be excepted against;   *5*
that hath bene our indeauour, that our marke...
An other thing we thinke good to admonish thee of
(gentle Reader) that wee haue not tyed our selues to an
vniformitie of phrasing, or to an identitie of words, as
some peraduenture would wish that we had done, because   *10*
they obserue, that some learned men some where, haue
beene as exact as they could that way. Truly, that we
might not varie from the sense of that which we had translated before, if the word signified the same sense euery
where we were especially carefull, and made a conscience,   *15*
according to our duetie. But, that we should expresse
the same notion in the same particular word; as for example, if we translate the Hebrew or *Greeke* word once by
Purpose, neuer to call it *Intent*; if one where *Iourneying*,
neuer *Traueiling*; if one where *Thinke*, neuer *Suppose*;   *20*
if one where *Paine*, neuer *Ache*; if one where *Ioy*, neuer
Gladnesse, &c. Thus to minse the matter, wee thought to
sauour more of curiositie then wisedome, and that rather
it would breed scorne in the Atheist, then bring profite
to the godly Reader. For is the kingdome of God become   *25*

words or syllables? why should wee be in bondage to them
if we may be free, vse one precisely when wee may vse
another no lesse fit, as commodiously?

Adde hereunto, that nicenesse in wordes was alwayes
counted the next step to trifling, and so was to bee   *30*
curious about names too: also that we cannot follow a
better patterne for elocution then God himselfe; therefore
hee vsing diuers words, in his holy writ, and indifferently for one thing in nature: we, if wee will not be super-
stitious, may vse the same libertie in our English ver-   *35*
sions out of *Hebrew & Greeke*, for that copie or store
that he hath giuen vs. Lastly, wee haue on the one side
auoided the scrupulositie of the Puritanes, who leaue the
olde Ecclesiasticall words, and betake them to other, as
when they put *washing* for *Baptisme*, and *Congregation*   *40*
in stead of *Church*: as also on the other side we haue
shunned the obscuritie of the Papists, in their *Azimes*,
Tunike, *Rational*, *Holocausts*, *Præpuce*, *Pasche*, and a number of such like, whereof their late Translation is full,
and that of purpose to darken the sence, that since   *45*
they must needs translate the Bible, yet by the language
thereof, it may bee kept from being vnderstood. But we
desire that the Scripture may speake like it selfe, as
in the language of *Canaan*, that it may bee vnderstood
euen of the very vulgar.   *50*

18E G. PETTIE: THE CIUILE CONUERSATION OF M. STEPHEN GUAZZO (1586)

TO THE READER

There are some others yet who will set light by my
labours, because I write in English: and those are some
nice Trauailours, who retourne home with such queasie
stomacks, that nothing will downe them but French, Italian, or Spanish, and though a worke bee but meanelie writ-   *5*
ten in one of those tongues, and finelie translated into
our Language, yet they will not sticke farre to preferre
the Originall before the Translation: the cause is partlie,
for that they cannot so soone espie faultes in a forraine
Tongue as in their owne, which maketh them thinke that   *10*
to bee currant, which is but course, and partlie for that
straunge thinges doe more delight them, than that which

they are dailie vsed to: but they consider not the profit
which commeth by reading things in theyr owne Tongue,
whereby they shall be able to conceiue the matter much   *15*
sooner, and beare it awaie farre better, than if they
reade it in a straunge Tongue, whereby also they shall be
inabled to speake, to discourse, to write, to indite,
properlie, fitlie, finelie, and wiselie, but the worst is,
they thinke that impossible to be done in our Tongue: *20*
for they count it barren, they count it barbarous, they
count it vnworthie to be accounted of: and, which is worse,
as I my selfe haue heard some of them, they report abroade,
that our Countrie is barbarous, our manners rude, and our
people vnciuile: and when I haue stood with them in the   *25*
comparison betweene other Countries & ours, & pointed
with my finger to many grose abuses, vsed in the places
where we haue bene, when by reason they haue bene able to
defend them, they haue shronke in their necke, and tolde
me that it was the fashion of the Countrie: ...   *30*

   For the barbarousnesse of our tongue, I must likewise
saie that it is much the worse for them, and some such
curious fellowes as they are: who if one chance to deriue
anie word from the Latine, which is insolent to their
eares (as perchance they will take that phrase to be)   *35*
they forthwith make a iest at it, and tearme it an Ink-
horne tearme. And though for my part I vse those wordes
as little as anie, yet I know no reason why I should not
vse them, and finde it a fault my selfe that I do not vse
them: for it is in deed the readie waie to inrich our   *40*
tongue, and make it copious, and it is the waie which all
tongues haue taken to inrich themselues: For take the
Latine wordes from the Spanish tongue, and it shall bee
as barren as most part of their Countrie: and take them
from the Italian, & you take away in a manner the whole   *45*
tongue: take them from the French, & you marre the grace
of it: yea take from the Latine it selfe the wordes de-
riued from the Greeke, & it shall not be so flowing &
flourishing as it is. Wherfore I meruaile how our English
tongue hath crackt it credit, that it may not borrow of   *50*
the Latin as wel as other tongues: and if it haue broken,
it is but of late, for it is not vnknowen to all men, how
many wordes we haue fetcht from thence within these few
yeeres, which if they should be all counted inkpot tearmes,

I know not how we should speak anie thing without blacking   55
our mouths with inke: for what word can be more plain than
this word (plain) & yet what can come more neere to the
Latine? What more manifest than (manifest)? & yet in a manner Latine: What more commune than (rare), or lesse rare
than (commune) & yet both of them comming of the Latine?   60
But you will saie, long vse hath made these wordes currant:
and why may not vse doe as much for the posteritie, as we
haue receiued of the antiquitie? and yet if a thing be of
it selfe good, I see not how the newnesse of it can make
it naught: wherevpon I infer, that those wordes which   65
your selues confesse by vse to be made good, are good the
first time they are vttered, and therefore not to be iested
at, nor to be misliked. But how hardlie so euer you deale
with our tongue, how barbarous so euer you count it, how
little so euer you esteeme it, I durst my selfe vndertake   70
(if I were furnished with learning otherwise) to write in
it as copiouslie for varietye, as compendiously for breuitie, as choicely for words, as pithilie for sentences,
as pleasantlie for figures, & euerie waie as eloquentlie,   75
as anie writer should do in anie vulgar tongue whatsoeuer.

18F J. FLORIO: MONTAIGNE'S ESSAYS (1603)

TO THE CURTEOUS READER

Shall I apologize translation? Why but some holde (as for
their free-hold) that such conuersion is the subuersion
of Vniuersities. God holde with them, and withholde them
from impeach or empaire. It were an ill turne, the turn-   5
ing of Bookes should be the ouerturning of Libraries.
Yea but my olde fellow *Nolano* tolde me, and taught pub-
likely, that from translation all Science had it's of-
spring. Likely, since euen Philosophie, Grammar, Rhetorike, Logike, Arithmetike, Geometrie, Astronomy, Musike,   10
and all the Mathematikes yet holde their name of the
Greekes: and the Greekes drew their baptizing water from
the conduit-pipes of the Egiptians, and they from the
well-springs of the Hebrews or Chaldees. And can the wel-
springs be so sweete and deepe; and will the well-drawne   15
water be so sower and smell? And were their Countries so
ennobled, aduantaged, and embellished by such deriuing;

271

and doth it driue our noblest Colonies vpon the rockes
of ruine? And did they well? and prooued they well? and
must We prooue ill that doe so? Why but Learning would   20
not be made common. Yea but Learning cannot be too
common, and the commoner the better. Why but who is not
iealous, his Mistresse should be so prostitute? Yea but
this Mistresse is like ayre, fire, water, the more
breathed the clearer; the more extended the warmer; the   25
more drawne the sweeter. It were inhumanitie to coope her
vp, and worthy forfeiture close to conceale her. Why but
Schollers should haue some priuilege of preheminence.
So haue they: they onely are worthy Translators. Why but
the vulgar should not knowe all. No, they can not for   30
all this; nor euen Schollers for much more: I would,
both could and knew much more than either doth or can.
Why but all would not be knowne of all. No nor can: much
more we know not than we know: all know something, none
know all: would all know all? they must breake ere they   35
be so bigge. God only; men farre from God . . .

    And let confession make halfe amends, that euery lan-
guage hath it's *Genius* and inseparable forme; without
Pythagoras his *Metempsychosis* it can not rightly be translated. The Tuscan altiloquence, the *Venus* of the French,   40
the sharpe state of the Spanish, the strong significancy
of the Dutch cannot from heere be drawne to life. The
sense may keepe forme; the sentence is disfigured; the
fineness, fitnesse, featenesse diminished: as much as
artes nature is short of natures arte, a picture of a   45
body, a shadow of a substance. Why then belike I haue
done by *Montaigne*, as *Terence* by *Menander*, made of good
French no good English. If I haue done no worse, and it
be no worse taken, it is well. As he, if no Poet, yet am
I no theefe, since I say of whom I had it, rather to   50
imitate his and his authors negligence, then any backe-
biters obscure diligence . . .

    But some errors are mine, and mine by more then trans-
lation. Are they in Grammer, or Ortographie? as easie for
you to right, as me to be wrong; or in construction, as   55
mis-attributing him, her, or it, to things aliue, or dead,
or newter; you may soone know my meaning, and eftsoones
vse your mending: or are they in some vncouth termes: as
entraine, conscientious, endeare, tarnish, comporte,

efface, facilitate, ammusing, debauching, regret, effort,   *60*
emotion, and such like; if you like them not, take others
most commonly set by them to expound them, since they
were set to make such likely French words familiar with
our English, which well may beare them.

18G R. STAPYLTON: DIDO AND AENEAS (1634)

THE TRANSLATOR

In Englishing *Vergil*, I have given him a Language, not
so low as to bring downe his *Aeneis* to his *Eclogues*,
and levell the expressions of his Princes with his Shepheards: nor *so high*, that he should not be intelligent
to the Vnlearned, as if he still spake *Latin*. It is   *5*
true that wit distilled in one language, cannot be
transferred into another without losse of spirits: yet
I presume such graces are retained, as those of the
Noblest quality will favour this *Translation*, from an
Original, that was somtimes the unenvied Favorite of   *10*
the greatest Roman Emperour.

18H J. DRYDEN: FABLES ANCIENT AND MODERN (1700)

... there are other Judges who think I ought not to have
translated *Chaucer* into *English*, out of a quite contrary
Notion: They suppose there is a certain Veneration due
to his old Language; and that is little less than Pro-
fanation and Sacrilege to alter it. They are farther   *5*
of opinion, that somewhat of his good Sense will suffer
in this Transfusion, and much of the Beauty of his
Thoughts will infallibly be lost, which appear with more
Grace in their old Habit. Of this Opinion was that excellent Person, whom I mention'd, the late Earl of   *10*
Leicester, who valu'd *Chaucer* as much as Mr. *Cowley*
despis'd him. My Lord dissuaded me from this Attempt,
(for I was thinking of it some Years before his Death)
and his Authority prevail'd so far with me, as to defer
my Undertaking while he liv'd, in deference to him: *15*
Yet my Reason was not convinc'd with what he urg'd
against it. If the first End of a Writer is to be understood, then as his Language grows obsolete, his Thoughts

must grow obscure, *multa renascuntur quæ nunc cecidere;* *cadentque quæ nunc sunt in honore vocabula, si volet* *usus, quem penes arbitrium est & jus & norma loquendi.* When an ancient Word for its Sound and Significancy deserves to be reviv'd, I have that reasonable Venera- tion for Antiquity, to restore it. All beyond this is Superstition. Words are not like Land-marks, so sacred as never to be remov'd: Customs are chang'd, and even Statutes are silently repeal'd, when the Reason ceases for which they were enacted. As for the other Part of the Argument, that his Thoughts will lose of their original Beauty, by the innovation of Words; in the first place, not only their Beauty, but their Being is lost, where they are no longer understood, which is the present Case. I grant, that something must be lost in all Transfusion, that is, in all Translations; but the Sense will remain, which would otherwise be lost, or at least be maim'd, when it is scarce intelligible; and that but to a few. How few are there who can read *Chaucer,* so as to understand him perfectly? And if imperfectly, then with less Profit, and no Pleasure. 'Tis not for the Use of some old *Saxon* Friends, that I have taken these Pains with him: Let them neglect my Version, because they have no need of it. I made it for their sakes who understand Sense and Poetry, as well as they; when that Poetry and Sense is put into Words which they under- stand. I will go farther, and dare to add, that what Beauties I lose in some Places, I give to others which had them not originally: But in this I may be partial to my self: let the Reader judge, and I submit to his Decision.

20
25
30
35
40
45

19 BIBLICAL TRANSLATIONS

ACTS OF THE APOSTLES 5.25–33

WYCLIF-PURVEY *c.* 1390   but a man cam & teelde to hem/ for lo þo men whiche ȝe han put in to prisoun: ben in þe temple. & stonden & techen þe puple/ [26]þanne þe magistrat wente wiþ þe mynystris: & brouȝte hem wiþ out violence/ for þei dredden þe puple: lest þei schulden bee stoonyd/ [27] & whanne þei hadden brouȝt hem: þei settiden hem in þe coun-

5

sel/ and þe princes of prestis: axiden hem [28] & seiden/ in
comaundement we comaundiden ȝou: þat ȝe schulden not teche
in þis name/ & lo ȝe han fillid ierusalem wiþ ȝoure teching:
& ȝe wolen bringe on vs þe blood of þis man/ [29] & petre   *10*
answeride & þe apostlis & seiden/ it behoueþ to obeie to
god: more þan to men/ [30] god of oure fadris reiside ihu
whom ȝe slowen: hangynge in a tre/ [31] god enhaunside wiþ
his riȝthond þis prince and sauyour: þat penaunce were ȝyue
to israel & remissioun of synnes/ [32] & we ben witnessis   *15*
of þese wordis. & þe hooli goost whom god ȝaf to alle
obeischinge to him/ [33] whanne þei herden þese þinges:
þei weren turmentid. & þouȝten to sle hem.

TYNDALE 1534   Then came one and shewed them: beholde
the men that ye put in preson/ stonde in the temple/ and   *20*
teache the people. [26] Then went the ruler of the temple
with ministers/ and brought them with out violence. For
they feared the people/ lest they shuld haue bene stoned.
[27]And when they had brought them/ they set them before the
counsell. And the chefe preste axed them [28] sayinge: dyd   *25*
not we straytely commaunde you that ye shuld not teache
in this name? And beholde ye haue filled Ierusalem with
youre doctrine/ and ye intende to brynge this mans bloud
vpon vs. [29] Peter and the other Apostles answered and
sayde: We ought moare to obey God then men. [30] The God of   *30*
oure fathers raysed vp Iesus/ whom ye slewe and hanged on
tre. [31]Him hath god lifte vp with his right hand/ to be
a ruler and a sauioure/ for to geue repentaunce to Israell and forgeuenes of synnes. [32] And we are his recordes
concernynge these thinges and also the holy goost whom   *35*
God hath geuen to them that obey him. [33] When they hearde
that/ they claue asunder: and sought meanes to slee them.

RHEIMS 1582   And there came a certaine man and told
them, That the men, loe, which you did put in prison, are
in the temple standing, and teaching the people. [26] Then   *40*
went the Magistrate with the ministers, and brought them
without force, for they feared the people lest they should
be stoned. [27] And when they had brought them, they set
them in the Councel. And the high priest asked them,
[28]saying, Commaunding we commaunded you that you should   *45*
not teach in this name: and behold you haue filled Hierusalem with your doctrine, and you wil bring vpon vs the

bloud of this man. [29]But Peter answering and the Apostles, said, God must be obeied, rather then men. [30] The God
of our Fathers hath raised vp Iesus, whom you did kil,
hanging him vpon a tree. [31] This Prince and Sauiour God
hath exalted with his right hand, to giue repentance to
Israel, and remission of sinnes. [32]and we are witnesses
of these wordes, and the holy Ghost, whom God hath giuen
to al that obey him. [33] When they had heard these things,
it cut them to the hart, and they consulted to kil them.

AV 1611   Then came one, and tolde them, saying, Behold,
the men whom yee put in prison, are standing in the Temple,
and teaching the people. [26] Then went the captaine with
the officers, and brought them without violence: (For they
feared the people, lest they should haue bene stoned).
[27]And when they had brought them, they set them before
the Councill, and the high Priest asked them, [28] Saying,
Did not wee straitly commaund you, that you should not
teach in this Name? And behold, yee haue filled Hierusalem
with your doctrine, and intend to bring this mans blood
vpon us. [29]Then Peter, and the other Apostles answered,
and sayd, Wee ought to obey God rather then men. [30]The
God of our fathers raised vp Iesus, whom yee slew and
hanged on a tree. [31]Him hath God exalted with his right
hand to bee a Prince and a Sauiour, for to giue repentance
to Israel, and forgiuenesse of sinnes. [32] And we are his
witnesses of these things, and so is also the holy Ghoost,
whom God hath giuen to them that obey him. [33] When they
heard that, they were cut to the heart, and tooke counsel
to slay them.

NEB 1970   and then a man arrived with the report, 'Look!
the men you put in prison are there in the temple teaching
the people.' [26] At that the Controller went off with the
police and fetched them, but without using force for fear
of being stoned by the people. [27] So they brought them
and stood them before the Council; and the High Priest
began his examination. [28] 'We expressly ordered you', he
said, 'to desist from teaching in that name; and what has
happened? You have filled Jerusalem with your teaching,
and you are trying to make us responsible for that man's
death.' [29] Peter replied for himself and the apostles:
'We must obey God rather than men. [30] The God of our fa-

thers raised up Jesus whom you had done to death by hanging him on a gibbet. [31] He it is whom God has exalted with   90
his own right hand as leader and saviour, to grant Israel
repentance and forgiveness of sins. [32] And we are witnesses
to all this, and so is the Holy Spirit given by God to
those who are obedient to him.' [33] This touched them on
the raw, and they wanted to put them to death.   95

ACTS OF THE APOSTLES 7.17–29

WYCLIF-PURVEY *c.* 1390   & whanne þe tyme of biheeste cam
niȝ. which god hadde knoulechid to abraham: þe puple waxede
and multipliede in egipt/ [18]til anoþer kyng roos in egipt:
which knewe not ioseph/ [19]þis bigilide oure kyn and tur-
mentide oure fadris: þat þei schulden putte awey her ȝonge   5
children. for þei schulden not lyue/ [20] in þe same tyme
moyses was borun: and he was louyd of god/ & he was nor-
isschid þre moneþis: in þe hous of his fadir/ [21]& whanne
he was put out in þe flood: þe douȝter of farao took hym
vp and nurischide hym in to hir sone/ [22]& moyses was lerned   10
in al þe wisdom of egipcians: & he was myȝti in his wordis
& werkis/ [23]but whanne þe tyme of fourti ȝeer was fillid
to hym: it roos vp in to his herte. þat he schulde visite
hise briþeren þe sones of israel/ [24]and whanne he say a
man suffringe wronge: he vengide hym. and dide veniaunce   15
for hym þat suffride þe wronge. & he killide þe egipcian/
[25]for he gesside þat his briþeren schulden vndurstonde.
þat god schulde ȝyue to hem helpe bi þe hoond of hym. but
þei vndurstoden not/ [26]for in þe day suynge: he apperide
to hem chidinge: and he acordide hem in pees and seide/   20
men ȝe ben briþeren/ why noyen ȝe ech oþere? [27]but he þat
dide þe wronge to his neiȝbore: puttide hym awey and seide/
who ordeynede þee prince and domesman on vs? [28]wheþir þou
wolt sle me: as ȝistirdai þou killidist þe egipcian?
[29]and in þis word moises flei: and was maad a comeling in   25
þe loond of madian where he bigat twei sones/

RHEIMS 1582   And when the time drew neere of the promisse
which God had promised to Abraham, the people increased and
was multiplied in Ægypt, [18]vntil another king arose in
Ægypt, that knew not Ioseph. [19]This same circumuenting   *30*
our stocke, afflicted our fathers: that they should expose
their children, to the end they might not be kept aliue.
[20]The same time was Moyses borne, and he was acceptable
to God, who was nourished three moneths in his fathers
house. [21]And when he was exposed, Pharaos daughter tooke   *35*
him vp, and nourished him for her owne sonne. [22]And
Moyses was instructed in al the wisedom of the Ægyptians:
and he was mightie in his wordes and workes. [23]And when
he was fully of the age of fourtie yeres, it came to his
minde to visite his brethren the children of Israel.   *40*
[24]And when he had seen one suffer wrong, he defended him:
and striking the Ægyptian, he reuenged his quarel that
susteined the wrong. [25]And he thought that his brethren
did vnderstand that God by his hand would saue them: but
they vnderstoode it not. [26]And the day folowing he ap-   *45*
peared to them being at strife: and he reconciled them
vnto peace, saying, Men, ye are brethren, wherfore hurt
you one an other? [27]But he that did the iniurie to his
neighbour, repelled him, saying, *Who hath appointed thee
prince and iudge ouer vs?* [28]*What, wilt thou kil me, as*   *50*
thou didst yesterday kil the Ægyptian? [29]And Moyses fled
vpon this word: and he became a seiourner in the land of
Mádian, where he begat two sonnes.

AV 1611   But when the time of the promise drew nigh,
which God had sworne to Abraham, the people grew and mul-   *55*
tiplied in Egypt, [18]Till another king arose, which knew
not Ioseph. [19]The same dealt subtilly with our kinred,
and euill intreated our fathers, so that they cast out
their yong children, to the end they might not liue.
[20]In which time Moses was borne, and was exceeding faire,   *60*
and nourished vp in his fathers house three moneths:
[21]And when he was cast out, Pharaohs daughter tooke him
vp, and nourished him for her owne sonne. [22] And Moses
was learned in all the wisedome of the Egyptians, and was
mighty in words and in deeds. [23]And when he was ful forty   *65*
yeres old, it came into his heart to visite his brethren
the children of Israel. [24] And seeing one of them suffer

wrong, he defended him, and auenged him that was oppressed, and smote the Egyptian: [25]For hee supposed his brethren would haue vnderstood, how that God by his hand would de-liuer them, but they vnderstood not. [26] And the next day he shewed himselfe vnto them as they stroue, and would haue set them at one againe, saying, Sirs, ye are breth-ren, Why doe yee wrong one to another? [27] But hee that did his neighbour wrong, thrust him away, saying, Who made thee a ruler and a Iudge ouer vs? [28] Wilt thou kill me, as thou diddest the Egyptian yesterday? [29]Then fled Moses at his saying, and was a stranger in the land of Madian, where he begate two sonnes.

NEB 1970   Now as the time approached for God to fulfil the promise he had made to Abraham, our nation in Egypt grew and increased in numbers. [18] At length another king, who knew nothing of Joseph, ascended the throne of Egypt [19]He made a crafty attack on our race, and cruelly forced our ancestors to expose their children so that they should not survive. [20]At this time Moses was born. He was a fine child, and pleasing to God. For three months he was nursed in his father's house, [21]and when he was exposed, Phara-oh's daughter herself adopted him and brought him up as her own son. [22]So Moses was trained in all the wisdom of the Egyptians, a powerful speaker and a man of action. [23]He was approaching the age of forty, when it occurred to him to look into the conditions of his fellow-countrymen the Israelites. [24]He saw one of them being ill-treated, so he went to his aid, and avenged the victim by striking down the Egyptian. [25]He thought his fellow-countrymen would understand that God was offering them deliverance through him, but they did not understand. [26]The next day he came upon two of them fighting, and tried to bring them to make up their quarrel. "My men," he said, "you are brothers; why are you ill-treating one another?" [27]But the man who was at fault pushed him away. "Who set you up as a ruler and judge over us?" he said. "Are you going to kill me as you killed the Egyptian yesterday?" [29] At this Moses fled the country and settled in Midianite territory. There two sons were born to him.

The fyrste booke

Metrum primum.

Carmina qui
quondā stu-
dio florentē
peregi:
Flebilis heu
mestos co-
gor inire modos.

Ecce mihi lacere dictant scri-
benda camene:

Et ueris elegi fletibus ora
rigant.

Has saltem nullus potuit pros
5   uincere terror :

Ne nostrum comites prosen-
querentur iter.

Gloria felicis olim uiridisq;
iuuente :

Solantur mesti nunc mea fa
ta Senis.

Venit enim properata malis
inopina senectus,
10   Et dolor etatem iussit inesse
suam.

Intempestini funduntur uers
sice cani,

Et tremit effeto corpore
laxa cutis.

Mors hominum felix que se
nec dulcibus annis:

Inserit & mestis sepe uo-
cata uenit.

Heu heu quam surda miseros
15   auertit aure:

Et flentes oculos claudere
sena negat.

Dum leuibus malesida bonis

Boetius speaketh.

That in tyme of pros-
perite, & floryshing stu-
dye, made pleasaunte
and delectable dities,
or verses: alas now be-
yng heauy and sad ouerthrowen in
aduersitie, am compelled to fele and
tast heuines and greif. Beholde the
muses Poeticall, that is to saye : the
pleasure that is in poetes verses, do
appoynt me, and compel me to writ
these verses in meter, and y sorowfull verses do wet my wretched face
with very waterye teares, yssuinge
out of my eyes for sorowe. Whiche
muses no feare without dout coulde
ouercome, but that they wold folow
me in my iourney of exile or banishment. Sometyme the ioye of happy
and lusty delectable youth dyd comfort me, and nowe the course of so-
rowsull olde age causeth me to re-
ioyse. For hasty old age vnloked for
is come vpon me with al her incom-
modities and euyls, and sorow hath
commaunded and broughte me into
the same old age, that is to say: that
sorowe causeth me to be olde, before
my time come of olde age. The hoer
heares do growe vntimely vpon my
heade, and my reuiled skynne trem-
bleth my flesh, cleane consumed and
wasted with sorowe. Mannes death
is happy, that cometh not in youth,
when a man is lusty, & in pleasure
or welth: but in time of aduersitie,

B.i.   when

50

75

80

280

Dum levibus male fida bonis fortuna, faveret,
    paene caput tristis merserat hora meum;
nunc quia fallacem mutavit nubila vultum,   20
    protrahit ingratas impia vita moras.
        Quid me felicem totiens iactastis, amici?
        Qui cecidit, stabili non erat ille gradu.

CHAUCER *c.* 1390   Allas I wepyng am constreined to bygynne
vers of sorouful matere. ¶ þat whilom in florysching studie
made delitable ditees. ffor lo rendyng muses of poetes   25
enditen to me þinges to be writen. and drery vers of
wrecchednes weten my face wiþ verray teers. ¶ At þe leest
no drede ne my3t ouer come þo muses. þat þei ne weren fel-
awes & folweden my wey. þat is to seyne when I was exiled.
þei þat weren glorie of my [you3th] whilom weleful & grene   30
comforten now þe sorouful werdes of an olde man. for elde
is comen vnwarly vpon me hasted by þe harmes þat I haue.
& sorou haþe comaunded his age to be in me. ¶ Heeres hore
ben schad ouertymelyche vpon myne heued. and þe slak skyn
trembleþ vpon myn emty body. þilk deeþ of men is welful   35
þat ne comeþ not in 3eres þat ben swete sc. mirie. but
comeþ to wrecches often yclepid. ¶ Allas allas wiþ how
deef an eere deeþ cruel tourneþ awey fro wrecches & naieþ
to closen wepyng eyen. ¶ While fortune vnfeithful fauored
me wiþ ly3te goodes sc. temp[or]els. þe sorouful houre   40
þat is to seyne þe deeþ had almost dreynt myne heued.
¶ But now for fortune clowdy haþe chaunged hir disceyuable
chere to me warde. myn vnpitouse lijf draweþ along vnagre-
able dwellynges in me. ¶ o 3e my frendes what or wherto
auaunted 3e me to be weleful. for he þat haþe fallen stood   45
not in stedfast degree.

COLEVILE 1556   (p. 280) ... when it is often desyred. Alas
Alas howe dull and deffe be the eares of cruel death vnto   85
men in misery that would fayne dye: and yet refusythe
to come and shutte vp theyr carefull wepyng eyes. Whiles
that false fortune fauoryd me with her transitorye goodes,
then the howre of death had almost ouercom me. That is to
say deathe was redy to oppresse me when I was in prosper-   90
itie. Nowe for by cause that fortune beynge turned, from
prosperitie into aduersitie (as the clere day is darkyd
with cloudes) and hath chaungyd her deceyuable counten-
aunce: my wretched life is yet prolonged and doth continue
in dolour. O my frendes why haue you so often bosted me,   95

sayinge that I was happy when I had honor possessions
riches, & authoritie whych be transitory thynges. He
that hath fallen was in no stedefast degre.

ELIZABETH I 1593

Righmes that my groing studie ons perfourmed
   In teares, alas! cumpeld, woful staues begin.
My muses torne, behold what write I shuld indites,   100
   Wher tru woful uerse my face with dole bedews.
Thes at lest no terror might constrain,
   that felowes to our mone our way they shuld refrain.
The glory ons of happy griny Youthe,   105
   Now, fates of grounting Age, my comfort all.
Vnlookt for Age hied by mishaps is come,
   And Sorow bidz his time to add withal.
Vnseasond hore heares vpon my hed ar powrd,
   And loosed skin in feable body shakes.   110
Blessed dethe, that in switest yeres refraines,
   but, oft calld, comes to the woful wights.
O with how defe eare she from wretched wries,
   And wailing yees, cruel! to shut denies.
While gileful fortune with vading goodz did shine,   115
   My life wel ny the doleful houre bereued;
Whan her fals looke a cloude hath changed,
   My wretched life thankles abode protractz.
Why me so oft, my frendz! haue you happy cald?
   Who fauleth downe in stedy step yet neuer stode.   120

I.T. 1609

THE 1. VERSE WHEREIN BOETHIUS BEWAILETH HIS ESTATE

I that with youthfull heate did verses write,
Must now my woes in dolefull tunes endite,
My worke is fram'd by Muses torne and rude,
And my sad cheeks are with true teares bedew'd.
For these alone no terrour could affray,   125
From being partners of my weary way,
My happy and delightful ages glory,
Is my sole comfort, being old and sory.
Old age through griefe makes vnexpected hast,
And sorrow in my yeares her signes hath plac'd,   130
Vntimely hoary haires couer my head,
And my loose skin quakes on my flesh halfe dead,

O happy death, that spareth sweetest yeares,
And comes in sorrow often call'd with teares.   *135*
Alas how deafe is he to wretches cries;
And loth he is to close vp weeping eyes;
While trustles chance me with vain fauour crowned,
That saddest houre my life had almost drowned:
Now hath she clouded her deceitfull face,   *140*
My spiteful dayes prolong their weary race,
My friends, why did you count me fortunate?
He that is fall'n, ne're stood in setled state.

CONINGSBY 1664

I that was wont to sing full merrily,
Am forc'd sad tones to howl in misery: *145*
The tatter'd Muses bid me for to write
A mournful Song, while they with tears indite:
No terrour could affright these Sisters free,
But of my griefs Companions they would be.
The glory of my happy youth does give   *150*
Some comfort to the cares in which I live.
Unwelcome age (that never-failing thief)
Intrudes himself, and mixes with my grief.
My hairs untimely from my head do fall,
My skin is loose, and joints do tremble all.   *155*
That death is happy that the blithe Youth does spare,
But comes when call'd by one opprest with Care.
Alas! he will not close the weeping eye,
And deaf he is to souls in misery.
Whiles fickle Fortune faun'd me with her wing,   *160*
Each hower fear of death with it did bring.
But now that she has chang'd her cozening face,
Death takes delight to come a Tortoise pace.
O friends, why did you oft me happy call?
He ne're was firmly seated that could fall.   *165*

ELYS 1674

THE FIRST VERSE WHEREIN BOETIUS BEWAILETH HIS ESTATE

I, who was wont to make such chearfull Verse,
Must now (Alas!) Sad Notes rehearse.
The wronged Muses teach Me what to write:
My Tears true *Elegies* endite.   *170*
No Terror could them keep from following Me;

They fear not my Calamitie:
They of my Sprightly Youth the Glory were,
Of my Sad Age the Comfort are.
Old Age comes on Me hasten'd by my Cares,   175
An *Hoary Head* suits with my Tears.
Grief makes *White Hairs* spread o're mine Head, and Chin;
On my Dry Flesh hangs Shriv'led Skin.
A Happy Death, which takes not men away
In Joyfull Times! nor, Call'd, doth stay   180
When they are sunk in woe! Alas, she Flies,
And will not Close our Weeping Eyes!
Whilst Fortune did her flattring Goods bestow,
I hardly 'scap'd a *Fatall Blow*:
Now that her great Inconstancy she showes,   185
Life unregarded sticks more close.
Friends, why did yee so oft Me Happy call?
He stood not Firm, who could not 'scape this Fall.

PRESTON 1695
I who before did lofty Verse indite,
In mournful Numbers now my Griefs recite: 190
Behold! the weeping Muse hath bound her brow
With Cyprus-Wreathes, and only dictates now
Sad Elegy to me, whose teeming Eyes
Keep time with her's. The Muse who does despise
Danger, since I am gone, disdains to stay,   195
And goes the kind Companion of my way.
She whose gay Favours my brisk Youth did court,
Now courts mine Age, and is its chief Support;
Which does advance before I thought it nigh,
And yet my Cares do make it onwards fly.   200
Too soon these Temples hoary Hairs do show,
Too soon my Summer's crown'd with Alpine Snow:
My Joints do tremble, and my Skin does sit
Like a loose Garment, never made to fit.
Happy are they, whom when their Years do bloom,   205
Death does not seize, but when they call doth come!
That to the Wretched doth no Pity show;
It shuts no Eyes which Tears do overflow.
When my pleas'd Fates did smile, I once to Death
Had almost yielded my unwilling Breath: 210
But now when Fortune's gilded Favours cease,
It doth arrest my kindly Hour of Ease.

Why, O my Friends! did you me Happy call?
He stands not firm, who thus like me can fall.

21 TRANSLATIONS OF VIRGIL, *Aeneid* IV

LINES 129–35
Oceanum interea surgens Aurora reliquit.
it portis iubare exorto delecta iuventus,
retia rara, plagae, lato venabula ferro,
Massylique ruunt equites et odora canum vis.
reginam thalamo cunctantem ad limina primi   *5*
Poenorum expectant, ostroque insignis et auro
stat sonipes ac frena ferox spumantia mandit.

DOUGLAS 1515
Furth of the sey, with this, the dawyng spryngis.
As Phebus rayß, fast to the ȝettis thringis
The choß gallandis, and huntmen thame besyde,   *10*
With ralys and with nettys strang and wyde,
And huntyng sperys styf with hedis braid;
From Massilyne horsmen thik thiddir raid.
With rynnyng hundis, a full huge sort.
Nobillys of Cartage, hovand at the port,   *15*
The queyn awatys that lang in chawmyr dwellys;
Hyr ferß steyd stude stampyng, reddy ellys,
Rungeand the fomy goldyn byt gynglyng;
Of gold and pal wrocht hys rych harnasyng.

SURREY *c.* 1540
Then *from the seas, the dawning* gan arise,   *20*
The Sun once vp, *the chosen youth gan throng*
Out at the gates: the hayes so rarely knit,
The hunting staues with their *brod heads* of steele
And of Masile the horsemen fourth they brake
Of senting houndes a kenel hugh likewise.   *25*
And at the threshold of her chaumber dore,
The Carthage Lords did on the Quene attend.
The trampling steede with gold and purple trapt,
Chawing the fomie bit, there fercely stood.

PHAER 1558
The morning rose, and from the sea the sonne was comen about,   *30*
Whan to the gates assemblyth fast of noble youth a rout

With nettes and engins great, & hunter speares ful large of length.
The horsmen rush w^t noise, & dogges are brought a mighty strength.
The great estates of Moores before the doores await the quene.
In chamber long she staies, and redy brydlyd best besene   *35*
The palfrey standes in gold, attyryd riche, and ferre he stampes
For pryde, and on the fomy bitt with teeth he champes.

STANYHURST 1582

Thee whilst thee dawning Aurora fro the Ocean hastned,
And the May fresh yoonckers to the gates doo make there asemblye
With nets and catch toyls, and huntspears plentiful yrond: *40*
With the hounds quicksenting, with pricking galloper horsman.
Long for thee Princesse thee Moors gentilitye wayted,
As yet in her pincking not pranckt with trinckerye trinckets:
As they stood attending thee whilst her trapt genet hautye
Deckt with ritche scarlet, with gould stood furniture hanging,   *45*
Praunseth on al startling, and on byt gingled he chaumpeth.

VICARS 1632

And now from seas arose *Aurora* bright,
And *Lucifer*, dayes harbinger, in sight:
Young gallants nimbly flock about the gates,
And in their hands boare speares with iron plates,   *50*
Their nets, gins, grins, troops of *Massylian* sparks,
Kennels of senting hounds with loud-mouth'd barks,
Prime *Punick* peeres at the queens chamber wait,
Who there herself was dressing in great state:
Her steed in stately trappings proudly stamps,   *55*
And in his mouth his foamie bridle champs.

STAPYLTON ?1634

This while, *Aurora* rising leaves the maine.
Choice youth beare through the Ports wide nets (now day)
Cordes & broad iron toyles; then rush away
Massylian horse; flesht hounds. At the Court gate,   *60*
For the queene lingring in her Chamber, waite
The *Carthage* Lords, her foaming Courser (gay
In gold and purple) on the Bit doth play.

WALLER 1658

The morning come, early at light's first ray
The gallant youth rise with the chearfull day   *65*
Sharp Javelins in their hands, their Coursers by

They walke amidst the hound's impatient Cry:
Neerer the gates the Tyrian Peers attend,
And waite the Queen now ready to descend.
Her prouder Steed as fill'd with high disdain   70
Stamps the dull Earth, & Chawes the frothy Reine.

DRYDEN 1697
The rosy Morn was risen from the Main,
And Horns and Hounds awake the Princely Train:
They issue early through the City Gate,
Where the more wakeful Huntsmen ready wait,   75
With Nets, and Foils, and Darts, beside the force
Of *Spartan* Dogs, and swift *Massylian* Horse.
The *Tyrian* Peers and Officers of State,
For the slow Queen, in Anti-Chambers wait:
Her lofty Courser, in the Court below,   80
(Who his Majestick Rider seems to know,)
Proud of his Purple Trappings, paws the Ground.

LEWIS 1952
So now, as Aurora was rising out of her ocean bed
And the day-beam lofted, there sallied forth the *élite* of Carthage:
With fine-meshed nets and snares and the broad hunting lances   85
Massylian riders galloped behind a keen-nosed pack.
The queen dallies: the foremost Carthaginians await her
By the palace door, where stands her horse, caparisoned
In purple and gold, high-spirited, champing the foam-flecked bit.

LINES 206–18
'Iuppiter omnipotens, cui nunc Maurusia pictis   90
gens epulata toris Lenaeum libat honorem,
aspicis haec? an te, genitor, cum fulmina torques
nequiquam horremus, caecique in nubibus ignes
terrificant animos et inania murmura miscent?
femina, quae nostris errans in finibus urbem   95
exiguam pretio posuit, cui litus arandum
cuique loci leges dedimus, conubia nostra
reppulit ac dominum Aenean in regna recepit.
et nunc ille Paris cum semiviro comitatu,
Maeonia mentum mitra crinemque madentem   100
subnexus, rapto potitur: nos munera templis
quippe tuis ferimus famamque fovemus inanem.'

DOUGLAS 1515

'Almychty Ioue', quod he, 'quhamto, feill syß,
On brusyt beddis hie fest and sacryfyß
Of Mawrusya the pepill hantis thus,   *105*
Offeryng to the the honour of Bachus,
Consideris thou this? or quhidder, fader, gif we
For nocht the dredis, quhen thou lattis thundir fle?
Or gif thi fyreslauch, the blynd clowdis within,
To fley our myndis, in vane makis noys and dyn?   *110*
ʒone woman, lait exile and vagabund
Com to our boundis, that by pryce bocht the grund
A litil village to byg, and quhamto we
For to manuyr gave the strand of the see,
Quhamto our lawis and statutis we gart mak,   *115*
Our mariage gan lychtly and forsaik,
And in hir ryng heß tane Ene for lord.
And now that secund Parys, of ane accord
With his onworthy sort, skant half men beyn,
Abufe his hed and halffettis, weil beseyn,   *120*
Set lyke a mytir the Troiane foly hat,
Hys hair enoynt well prunʒeit vndir that,
By reif mantemys hir suld owris be –
Becauß onto thi templis dayly we
Bryngis offerand and in vane hallowis thi name.'   *125*

SURREY *c.* 1540

Almighty God whom the Moores nacion
Fed at rich tables presenteth with wine,
Seest thou these things? or feare we thee in vaine
When *thou lettest flye thy thonder* from the cloudes?
Or do those flames *with vaine noyse* vs affray?   *130*
A woman that wandring in our coastes *hath bought*
A plot for price: where she a citie set:
To whom we gaue the strond for to manure.
And lawes to rule her town: our wedlock lothed,
Hath chose Aeneas to commaund her realme.   *135*
That Paris now with his vnmanly sorte,
With *mitred hats*, with *oynted bush* and beard:
His rape enioyth: whiles to thy temples we
Our *offrings bring, and* folow rumors *vaine*,

PHAER 1558

Almighty Ioue, whome duely Moores esteme for God and king,   *140*
And feastes on broydred beddes to the & wynes of ioye do bryng,

Beholdst thou this? and mighty father thee with thonder dintes
Despise we thus? and yet from vs thy strokes of lightnings stintes?
Nor quake we not whan through ye cloudes thy sounding brekes aboue?
In vayn thy voyces ronne? will nothing vs to vertue moue?   *145*
A woman, lately come to land, that bought of vs the ground,
To whome the soyle we gaue to tille, and citie new to found,
And lawes also we lent, my wedlock (lo) she hath forsake:
And now *Eneas* lord of her and all her lond doth make.
And now this pranking *Paris* fyne with mates of beardles kynde,   *150*
To dropping hear and sauours nyce and vices all enclynde,
With grekishe wymple pynkyd, womanlyke: yet must the same
Enioy the spoyles of this, and we thy seruauntes take the shame,
For all our offring giftes to the we fynde no frute but fame.

STANYHURST 1582

Iuppiter almighty, who men Maurusian, eating   *155*
On the tabils vernisht, with cuprit's magnify dulye:
Eyest thow this filthood? shal wee, father heunlye, be carelesse
Of thy claps thundring? or when fiers glimrye be lifted
In clowds grim gloomming with bounce doo terrifye worldlings?
A coy tyb, as vagabund in this my segnorye wandring,   *160*
That the plat of Carthage from mee by coosinage hooked,
T'whom gaue I fayre tilladge, and eeke lawes needful enacted,
Hath scornd my wedlock: Æneas lord she reteyneth.
Now this smocktoy Paris with berdlesse coompany wayted,
With Greekish coronet, with falling woommanish hearelocks   *165*
Lyke fiest hound mylcksop trimd vp, thee victorye catcheth.
And wee beat the bushes, thee still with woorship adoring.
Onlye for our seruice soom praysed vanitye gleaming.

NN 1622

Almighty *Iuppiter*, whom *Moores* that loue   *170*
To feast on painted beds doe honour, now
With vaine feare father to thy thunder strokes,
Or doe clouds empty sounds and shining smokes
Fright vs! a woman wandring vp and downe
Our Coast bought leaue to build a little towne,   *175*
She to whom lawes with land to till we gaue,
That vs to husband would not daigne to haue,
Master Æneas takes to Lord and marries,
And now with halfe men the spruce-chind *Paris*,
Whose gofferd haire newfangled cap keeps down,   *180*
Inioyes his rape, while with rich gifts we crowne
Thy Temples, fond of such sires vaine renowne.

VICARS 1632

All powerfull *Jove*, whom we black *Moores* adore
To whom we our *Lenæan* liquors poure
On right embroidered beds; seest thou these things?   185
Or, when (great *Jove*) thou on us earthly kings
Dost flash forth lightnings, feare we this in jest?
Do those cloud-hid flames vainly fright mans breast?
Make but a skarre-crow sound? A woman (late)
Who stragling to these parts, did at a rate   190
Purchase and plant a poore, a petty town;
Whom, subject to the statutes of our crown,
We license gave to plant and plow our land,
Our princely wedlock (now) doth stiffe withstand,
And in her kingdome kindly entertains   195
One sir *Æneas*, who her solely gains.
This petty *Paris* and his stragling trains
Of beardlesse boyes, effeminately gay
With coifs and perfum'd haire, these steal the prey:
But we who fill the temples with oblations,   200
Seem onely fame to feed with vain frustrations.

STAPYLTON ?1634

All powerful *Joue*, to whom the *Moores* now tast
Grape-honours, on beds painted banqueting,
Seest thou this? Do we feare thee thundring
In vaine O father? are those lightnings blind,   205
And murmurs idle, that affright our mind?
The woman that (straid hither) built a poore
Town, and bought leaue, compeld to plow the shore
To which place we gaue Lawes (our match abhord)
Æneas ore her land receives as Lord: 210
And now that *Paris*, with's halfe-men, bold in
His *Phrygian* Miter, his oyld haire and chin,
Wins her by rape: while tis our part to bring
Gifts to thy Temple, vaine fame cherishing.

OGILBY 1649

Great *Jupiter*, to whom the *Moors* being plac'd   215
On wrought beds feasting now rich *Bacchus* taste.
Seest this oh father? or in vain our hearts
Quake at thy thunder, and when the lightning darts
From broken clouds with noise, is fond our fear?
Wandring our coasts a woman purchas'd here   220

A little seat, to whom we gave rich lands;
To whom our lawes; and This our match withstands,
And in her kingdome Lord *Æneas* states.
That *Paris* now, with his effeminate mates,
In his *Mæonian* hat, and perfum'd haire,   225
Injoyes the prise: we to thy Temple bear
Offerings, and have in vain thy name extold.

OGILBY 1654
Great King of Kings, whom *Mauritanian* Lords
Honour with Wine, feasting at stately Boards:
Behold'st thou this? or Father, are our Souls,   230
When thou dischargest Thunder from the Poles,
Frighted in vain? when dreadfull Lightning tears
Black Clouds with horrid Noyse, are fond our Fears?
A wandring Woman to our Confines toss'd,
Built a small City at a little cost;   235
I gave her Lands, for Love she gives me Hate,
Investing Lord *Æneas* in her State.
This *Paris* and his Coward Crew hath got
Her with his powder'd Hair, and tottering Hat:
Whil'st on thy Altars our Oblations flame,   240
And fondly we adore an idle Name.

DRYDEN 1697
Great *Jove*, propitious to the *Moorish* Race,
Who feast on painted Beds, with Off'rings grace
Thy Temples, and adore thy Pow'r Divine
With offer'd Victims, and with sparkling Wine: 245
Seest thou not this? or do we fear in vain
Thy boasted Thunder, and thy thoughtless Reign?
Do thy broad Hands the forky Lightnings lance,
Thine are the Bolts, or the blind work of Chance?
A wandring Woman builds, within our State,   250
A little Town, bought at an easie Rate;
She pays me Homage, and my Grants allow,
A narrow Space of *Lybian* Lands to plough.
Yet scorning me, by Passion blindly led,
Admits a banish'd *Trojan* to her Bed: 255
And now this other *Paris*, with his Train
Of conquer'd Cowards, must in *Affrick* reign!
Whom, what they are, their Looks and Garb confess;

Their Locks with Oil perfum'd, their *Lydian* dress:)
He takes the Spoil, enjoys the Princely Dame;   260
And I, rejected I, adore an empty Name.

LEWIS 1952

Almighty Jove, whom now for the first time the Moorish people
Pledge with wine as they banquet on ornamental couches,
Do you observe these things? Or are we foolish to shudder
When you shoot fire, O Father, foolish to be dismayed meaning?   265
By Lightning which is quite aimless and thunder which growls without
That woman who, wandering within our frontiers, paid to establish
Her insignificant township, permitted by us to plough up   [offer
A piece of the coast and be queen of it – that woman rejecting my
Of marriage, has taken Æneas as lord and master there.   270
And now that philanderer, with his effeminate following –
His chin and oil-sleeked hair set off by a Phrygian bonnet –
That fellow is in possession; while we bring gifts to your shrine,
If indeed you are there and we do not worship a vain myth.

22A T. BERTHELETTE, ED.: GOWER'S CONFESSIO AMANTIS (1532)

DEDICATION TO HENRY VIII

There is to my dome/ no man/ but that he may bi reding of
this warke get right great knowledge/ as wel for the vnder-
standyng of many and diuers autors/ whose resons/ sayenges/
and histories are translated in to this warke/ as for the
plenty of englysshe wordes and vulgars/ besyde the fur-   5
theraunce of the lyfe to vertue, whiche olde englysshe
wordes and vulgars no wyse man/ bycause of theyr antiquite/
wyll throwe asyde. For the wryters of later dayes/ the
whiche beganne to loth and hate these olde vulgars/ when
they them selfe wolde wryte in our englysshe tonge/ were   10
constrayned to brynge in/ their writynges/ newe termes (as some calle them) whiche they borowed out of lat-
yne/ frenche/ and other langages/ whiche caused/ that
they that vnderstode not those langages/ from whens these
newe vulgars are fette/ coude not perceyue theyr wryt-   15
ynges. And though our most allowed olde autors dydde
otherwhyle vse to borowe of other langages/ eyther by-

cause of theyr metre/ or elles for lacke of a feete
englysshe worde/ yet that ought not to be a president
to vs/ to heape them in/ where as nedeth not/ and where 20
as we haue all redy wordes approued and receyued/ of the
same effecte and strength. The whiche if any man wante/
let hym resorte to this worthy olde wryter Iohn Gower/
that shall as a lanterne gyue hym lyghte to wryte coun-
nyngly/ and to garnysshe his sentences in our vulgar 25
tonge.

22B T. SPEGHT, ED.: CHAUCER'S WORKS (1598)

F.B. TO HIS VERY LOUING FRIEND, T.S.

It is well knowne to wise and learned men, that all languages be either such as are contained in learning, or
such as be vsed amongst men in daily practise: and for
the learned tongues, they hauing *Iure testamentario*,
their legacies set downe by them that be dead, wordes 5
must be kept and continued in them in sort as they were
left without alteration of the Testators wils in any
thing. But for vsuall languages of common practise,
which in choise of wordes are, and euer will be subiect
vnto chaunge, neuer standing at one stay, but sometimes 10
casting away old wordes, sometimes renewing of them,
and alwaies framing of new, no man can so write in them,
as that all his wordes may remain currant many yeares.
... But yet so pure were *Chaucers* wordes in his owne
daies, as *Lidgate* that learned man calleth him *The* 15
Loadstarre of the English language: and so good they
are in our daies, as Maister *Spenser*, following the
counsaile of *Tullie in de Oratore*, for reuiuing of antient wordes, hath adorned his owne stile with that
beautie and grauitie, which *Tully* speakes of: and his 20
much frequenting of *Chaucers* antient speeches causeth
many to allow farre better of him, then otherwise they
would.

23A: E.K.: EPISTLE DEDICATORY TO THE SHEPHEARDES CALENDER (1579)

¶ To the most excellent and learned both
Orator and Poete, Mayster Gabriell Haruey, his
verie special and singular good frend E. K. commen-
deth the good lyking of this his labour,
and the patronage of the
new Poete.
(∵)

NCOVTHE VNKISTE, Sayde the olde famous Poete Chaucer: vvhom for his excellencie and vvonderfull skil in making, his scholler Lidgate, a vvorthy scholler of so excellent a maister, cal-leth the Loadestarre of our Language: and vvhom our Colin clout in his Æglogue calleth Tityrus the God of shepheards, comparing hym to the worthines of the Roman Tityrus Virgile. VVhich prouerbe, myne owne good friend Ma. Haruey, as in that good old Poete it ser-ued vvell Pandares purpose, for the bolstering of his baudy brocage, so very vvell taketh place in this our nevv Poete, vvho for that he is vncouthe (as said Chaucer) is vnkist, and vnknown to most mé, is regarded but of fevv. But I dout not, so soone as his name shall come into the knovvledg of men, and his vvorthines be sounded in the tromp of fame, but that he shall be not onely kiste, but also beloued of all, embraced of the most, and vvondred at of the best. No lesse I thinke, deserueth his vvittinesse in deuising, his pithi-nesse in vttering, his complaints of loue so louely, his discourses of pleasure so pleasantly, his pastorall rudenesse, his morall vvisenesse, his devve obseruing of Decorum euerye vvhere, in personages, in seasons, in matter, in speach, and generally in al seemely simply-citie of handeling his matter, and framing his vvords: the vvhich of many thinges which in him be straunge, I knovv vvill seeme the straungest, the vvords them selues being so auncient, the knitting of them so short and intricate, and the vvhole Periode & compasse of speache so delightsome for the roundnesse, and so graue for the straungenesse. And firste of the vvordes to speake, I graunt they be something hard, and of most men vnused, yet both English, and also vsed of most excellent Authors and most famous Poetes. In vvhom vvhenas this our Poet hath bene much traueiled and throughly redd, hovv could it be, (as that vvorthy Oratour sayde) but that vvalking in the sonne although for other cause he vvalked, yet needes he mought be sunburnt; and hauing the sound of those a un-cient Poetes still ringing in his eares, he mought needes in singing hit out some of theyr tunes. But whether he vseth them by such casualtye and custome, or of set purpose and choyse, as thinking them fittest for such rusticall rudenesse of shepheards, eyther for that theyr rough sounde vvould make his rymes more ragged and rusticall, or els because such olde and obsolete wordes are most vsed of country folke, sure I think, and think I think not amisse, that they bring great grace and, as one vvould say, auctoritie to the verse. For albe amongst many other faultes it specially be obiected of Valla against Liuie, and of o-ther against Saluste, that vvith ouer much studie they affect antiquitie, as coueting there-by credence and honor of elder yeeres, yet I am of opinion, and eke the best learned are of the lyke, that those auncient solemne wordes are a great ornament both in the one & in the other; the one labouring to set forth in hys worke an eternall image of antiquitie, and the other carefully discoursing matters of gratuitie and importaunce. For if my memo ry sayle not, Tullie in that booke, vvherein he endeuoureth to set forth the paterne of a

¶.ij.   perfect

294

Epiſtle.

perfect Oratour, ſayth that ofttimes an auncient worde maketh the ſtyle ſeeme graue, 40
and as it were reuerend : no otherwiſe then vve honour and reuerence gray heares for a
certein religious regard,which we haue of old age.yet nether euery where muſt old words
be ſtuffed in, nor the common Dialecte and maner of ſpeaking ſo corrupted therby, that
as in old buildings it ſeme diſorderly & ruinous. But all as in moſt exquiſite pictures they
vſe to blaze and portraict not onely the daintie lineaments of beautye, but alſo rounde 45
about it to ſhadow the rude thickets and craggy clifts,that by the baſeneſſe of ſuch parts,
more excellency may accrew to the principall;for oftimes we fynde our ſelues , I knowe
not hovv , ſingularly delighted with the ſhewe of ſuch naturall rudeneſſe,and take great
pleaſure in that diſorderly order.Euen ſo doe thoſe rough and harſh termes enlumine and
make more clearly to appeare the brightneſſe of braue & glorious vvords. So oftentimes 50
a diſchorde in Muſick maketh a comely concordaunce:ſo great delight tooke the worthy
Poete Alceus to behold a blemiſh in the ioynt of a wel ſhaped body.But if any vvill raſh-
ly blame ſuch his purpoſe in choyſe of old and vnvvonted vvords, him may I more iuſtly
blame and condemne,or of vvitleſſe headineſſe in iudging, or of heedeleſſe hardineſſe in
condemning.for not marking the compaſſe of hys bent, he vvil iudge of the length of his 55
caſt.for in my opinion it is one ſpecial prayſe,of many vvhych are dew to this Poete,that
he hath laboured to reſtore,as to theyr rightfull heritage ſuch good and naturall Engliſh
words,as haue ben long time out of vſe & almoſt cleare diſhented. VVhich is the onely
cauſe,that our Mother tonge,which truely of it ſelf is both ſul enough for proſe & ſtately
enough for verſe,hath long time ben couted moſt bare & barrein of both. which default 60
when as ſome endeuoured to ſalue & recure,they patched vp the holes with peces & rags
of other languages,borrowing here of the french,there of the Italian, euery where of the
Latine,not vveighing hovv il,thoſe tongues accorde vvith themſelues,but much vvorſe
vvith ours:So now they haue made our Engliſh tongue,a gallimaufray or hodgepodge of
al other ſpeches. Other ſome no ſo wel ſeene in the Engliſh tonge as perhaps in other lan 65
guages,if the happen to here an olde vvord albeit very naturall and ſignificant,crye out
ſtreight way,that we ſpeak no Engliſh,but gibbriſh,or rather ſuch,as in old time Euaders
mother ſpake.vvhoſe firſt ſhame is,that they are not aſhamed,in their own mother tonge
ſtraungers to be counted and alienes.The ſecond ſhame no leſſe then the firſt,that what
ſo they vnderſtand not,they ſtreight vvay deeme to be ſenceleſſe, and not at al to be vn- 70
derſtode.Much like to the Mole in Æſopes fable,that being blynd her ſelfe,vvould inno
wiſe be perſwaded,that any beaſt could ſee . The laſt more ſhameful then both,that of
their ovvne country and natural ſpeach, vvhich together vvith their Nources milk they
ſucked,they haue ſo baſe regard and baſtard iudgement ,that they vvill not onely themſelues not labor to garniſh & beautifie it,but alſo repine,that of other it ſhold be embel 75
liſhed.Like to the dogge in the maunger,that him ſelfe can eate no hay, and yet barketh
at the hungry bullock,that ſo faine vvould ſeede : vvhoſe curriſh kind though cannot be
kept from barking,yet I conne them thanke that they refrain from byting.

Novv for the knitting of ſentences,vvhych they call the ioynts and members therof,
and for al the compaſſe of the ſpeach, it is round vvithout roughneſſe,and learned wyth- 80
out hardines,ſuch indeede as may be perceiued of the leaſte , vnderſtoode of the moſte,
but iudged onely of the learned.For vvhat in moſt Engliſh wryters vſeth to be looſe,and
as it vvere vngyrt,in this Authour is vvell grounded,finely framed,and ſtrongly truſſed vp
together. In regard wherof, I ſcorne and ſpue out the rakehellye route of our ragged
rymers (for ſo theſelues vſe to hunt the letter) vvhich vvithout learning boſte, vvithout 85
iudgement

Epiſtle.

iudgement iangle, vvithout reaſon rage and ſome, as if ſome inſtinct of Poeticall ſpirite
had nevvſy rauiſhed them aboue the meaneneſſe of common capacitie. And being in the
middeſt of all theyr brauery, ſodenly eyther for vvant of matter, or of ryme, or hauing for
gotten theyr former conceipt, they ſeeme to be ſo pained and traueiled in theyr remembrance, as it vvere a woman in childebirth or as that ſame Pythia, vvhen the traunce came
vpon her.   90

Novv as touching the generall dryft and purpoſe of his Æglogues, I mind not to ſay
much, him ſelfe labouring to conceale it. Onely this appeareth, that his vnſtayed yougth
had long vvandred in the common Labyrinth of Loue, in vvhich time to mitigate and   95
allay the heate of his paſſion, or els to vvarne (as he ſayth) the young ſhepheards .ſ. his e-
qualls and companions of his vnfortunate folly, he compiled theſe xij. Æglogues, vvhich
for that they be proportioned to the ſtate of the xij. monethes, he termeth the S H E P-
HEARDS CALENDAR, applying an olde name to a nevv vvorke. Hereunto
haue I added a eertain Gloſſe or ſcholion for the expoſition of old vvordes & harder phra-
ſes : vvhich maner of gloſing and commenting, vvell I vvote, vvil ſeeme ſtraunge & rare 100
in our tongue : yet for ſomuch as I knew many excellent & proper deuiſes both in wordes
and matter vvould paſſe in the ſpeedy courſe of reading, either as vnknovve, or as not
marked, and that in this kind, as in other vve might be equal to the learned of other nations, I thought good to take the paines vpon me, the rather for that by meanes of ſome fa
miliar acquaintaunce I vvas made priuie to his counſell and ſecret meaning in them , as   105
alſo in ſundry other vvorks of his, vvhich albeit I knovv he nothing ſo much hateth, as to
promulgate , yet thus much haue I aduentured vpon his frendſhip, him ſelfe being for
long time ſuite eſtraunged , hoping that this vvill the rather occaſion him, to put forth
diuers other excellent vvorks of his, vvhich ſlepe in ſilence, as his Dreames, his Legendes, 110
his Court of Cupide, and ſondry others;

23B E. SPENSER: THE SHEPHEARDES CALENDER, "JULY"
(1579)

Thomalin.	Is not thilke same a goteheard prowde,	
	that sittes on yonder bancke,	
	Whose straying heard them selfe doth shrowde	
	emong the bushes rancke?	
Morrell.	What ho, thou iollye shepheards swayne,	5
	come vp the hyll to me:	
	Better is, then the lowly playne,	
	als for thy flocke, and thee.	
Thomalin.	Ah God shield, man, that I should clime,	
	and learne to looke alofte,	10
	This reede is ryfe, that oftentime	
	great clymbers fall vnsoft.	
	In humble dales is footing fast,	
	the trode is not so trickle:	

And though one fall through heedlesse hast,   15
    yet is his misse not mickle.
And now the Sonne hath reared vp
    his fyriefooted teme,
Making his way betweene the Cuppe,
    and golden Diademe: 20
The rampant Lyon hunts he fast,
    with Dogge of noysome breath,
Whose balefull barking bringes in hast
    pyne, plagues, and dreery death.
Agaynst his cruell scortching heate   25
    where hast thou couerture?
The wastefull hylls vnto his threate
    is a playne ouerture.
But if thee lust, to holden chat
    with seely shepherds swayne,   30
Come downe, and learne the little what,
    that Thomalin can sayne.

Morrell. Syker, thous but a laesie loord,
    and rekes much of thy swinck,
That with fond termes, and weetlesse words   35
    to blere myne eyes doest thinke.
In euill houre thou hentest in hond
    thus holy hylles to blame,
For sacred vnto saints they stond,
    and of them han theyr name.   40
S. Michels mount who does not know,
    that wardes the Westerne coste?
And of S. Brigets bowre I trow,
    all Kent can rightly boaste:
And they that con of Muses skill,   45
    sayne most what, that they dwell
(As goteheards wont) vpon a hill,
    beside a learned well.
And wonned not the great God *Pan*,
    vpon mount *Oliuet:*   50
Feeding the blessed flocke of *Dan*,
    which dyd himselfe beget?
Thomalin. O blessed sheepe, O shepheard great,
    that bought his flocke so deare,
And them did saue with bloudy sweat   55
    from Wolues, that would them teare.

GLOSSE

A Goteheard] By Gotes in scrypture be represented the wicked and reprobate, whose pastour also must needs be such.

Banck] is the seate of honor. Straying heard] which wander
out of the waye of truth.

Als] for also. Clymbe] spoken of Ambition. Great
clymbers] according to Seneca his verse, Decidunt
celsa grauiore lapsus. Mickle] much.

The sonne] A reason, why he refuseth to dwell on Moun-
taines, because there is no shelter against the
scortching sunne, according to the time of the yeare,
whiche is the whotest moneth of all.

The Cupp and Diademe] Be two signes in the Firmament,
through which the sonne maketh his course in the
moneth of Iuly.

Lion] Thys is Poetically spoken, as if the Sunne did hunt
a Lion with one Dogge. The meaning whereof is, that
in Iuly the sonne is in Leo. At which tyme the Dogge
starre, which is called Syrius or Canicula reigneth,
with immoderate heate causing Pestilence, drougth,
and many diseases.

Ouerture] an open place. The word is borrowed of the
French, & vsed in good writers.

To holden chatt] to talke and prate.

A loorde] was wont among the Britons to signifie a
Lorde. And therefore the Danes, that long time vsurped theyr Tyrannie here in Brytanie, were called for
more dread and dignitie, Lurdanes...

Recks much of thy swinck] counts much of thy paynes.
Weetelesse] not vnderstoode.

S. Michels mount] is a promontorie in the West part of
England.

A hill] Parnassus afforesayd. Pan] Christ. Dan] One
trybe is put for the whole nation per Synecdochen.

60

65

70

75

80

85

24 E. SPENSER: THE FAERIE QUEENE (1596)

(The letter to Raleigh, 1590) Sir knowing how doubtfully
all Allegories may be construed, and this booke of mine,
which I haue entituled the Faery Queene, being a continued
Allegory, or darke conceit, I haue thought good aswell for

auoyding of gealous opinions and misconstructions, as also
for your better light in reading therof, (being so by you
commanded,) to discouer vnto you the general intention &
meaning, which in the whole course thereof I haue fashioned,
without expressing of any particular purpose or by acci-
dents therein occasioned. The generall end therefore of all
the booke is to fashion a gentleman or noble person in vertuous and gentle discipline: Which for that I conceiued
shoulde be most plausible and pleasing, being coloured with
an historicall fiction, the which the most part of men delight to read, rather for variety of matter, then for profite of the ensample: I chose the historye of king Arthure,
as most fitte for the excellency of his person, being made
famous by many mens former workes, and also furthest from
the daunger of enuy, the suspition of present time ...

Lo I the man, whose Muse whilome did maske
As time her taught in lowly Shepheards weeds,
Am now enforst a far vnfitter taske,
For trumpets sterne to chaunge mine Oaten reeds,
And sing of Knights and Ladies gentle deeds;
Whose prayses hauing slept in silence long,
Me, all too meane, the sacred Muse areeds
To blazon broad emongst her learned throng:
Fierce warres and faithfull loues shall moralize my song.

Helpe then, ô holy Virgin chiefe of nine,
Thy weaker Nouice to performe thy will,
Lay forth out of thine euerlasting scryne
The antique rolles, which there lye hidden still,
Of Faerie knights and fairest *Tanaquill*,
Whom that most noble Briton Prince so long
Sought through the world, and suffered so much ill.
That I must rue his vndeserued wrong:
O helpe thou my weake wit, and sharpen my dull tong ...

With that a deadly shrieke she forth did throw,
That through the wood reechoed againe,
And after gaue a grone so deepe and low,
That seemd her tender heart was rent in twaine,
Or thrild with point of thorough piercing paine;
As gentle Hynd, whose sides with cruell steele
Through launched, forth her bleeding life does raine,
Whiles the sad pang approching she does feele,
Brayes out her latest breath, and vp her eyes doth seele.

Which when that warriour heard, dismounting straict
From his tall steed, he rusht into the thicke,
And soone arriued, where that sad pourtraict
Of death and labour lay, halfe dead, halfe quicke,   *50*
In whose white alabaster brest did sticke
A cruell knife, that made a griesly wound,
From which forth gusht a streme of gorebloud thick,
That all her goodly garments staind around,
And into a deepe sanguine dide the grassie ground.   *55*

Pittifull spectacle of deadly smart,
Beside a bubbling fountaine low she lay,
Which she increased with her bleeding hart,
And the cleane waues with purple gold did ray;
Als in her lap a louely babe did play   *60*
His cruell sport, in stead of sorrow dew;
For in her streaming blood he did embay
His litle hands, and tender ioynts embrew;
Pitifull spectacle, as euer eye did view.

Besides them both, vpon the soiled gras   *65*
The dead corse of an armed knight was spred,
Whose armour all with bloud besprinckled was;
His ruddie lips did smile, and rosy red
Did paint his chearefull cheekes, yet being ded,
Seemd to haue beene a goodly personage,   *70*
Now in his freshest flowre of lustie hed,
Fit to inflame faire Lady with loues rage,
But that fiers fate did crop the blossome of his age.

Whom when the good Sir *Guyon* did behold,
His hart gan wexe as strake, as marble stone,   *75*
And his fresh bloud did frieze with fearefull cold,
That all his senses seemd bereft attone,
At last his mightie ghost gan deepe to grone,
As Lyon grudging in his great disdaine,
Mournes inwardly, and makes to himselfe mone;   *80*
Till ruth and fraile affection did constraine,
His stout courage to stoupe, and shew his inward paine.

Out of her gored wound the cruell steele
He lightly snatcht, and did the floudgate stop
With his faire garment: then gan softly feele   *85*
Her feeble pulse, to proue if any drop
Of liuing bloud yet in her veynes did hop;
Which when he felt to moue, he hoped faire
To call backe life to her forsaken shop;
So well he did her deadly wounds repaire,   *90*
That at the last she gan to breath out liuing aire.

Which he perceiuing greatly gan reioice,
And goodly counsell, that for wounded hart
Is meetest med'cine, tempred with sweet voice;
Ay me, deare Lady, which the image art   95
Of ruefull pitie, and impatient smart,
What direfull chance, armd with reuenging fate,
Or cursed hand hath plaid this cruell part,
Thus fowle to hasten your vntimely date;
Speake, O deare Lady speake: help neuer comes too late.   100

Therewith her dim eie-lids she vp gan reare,
On which the drery death did sit, as sad
As lump of lead, and made darke clouds appeare;
But when as him all in bright armour clad
Before her standing she espied had,   105
As one out of a deadly dreame affright,
She weakely started, yet she nothing drad:
Streight downe againe her self in great despight,
She groueling threw to ground, as hating life and light.

25 J. LYLY: EUPHUES (?1578)

EPISTLE DEDICATORIE

Though the stile nothing delight the dayntie eare of the
curious sifter, yet will the matter recreate the minde of
the curteous Reader. The varietie of the one will abate
the harshnesse of the other. Things of greatest profite
are set foorth with least price. Where the wine is neat   5
there needeth no Iuie-bush. The right Coral needeth no
coulouring. Where the matter it selfe bringeth credit,
the man with his glose winneth small commendation. It is
therefore me thinketh a greater shew of a pregnant wit
then perfect wisedome, in a thing of sufficient excel-   10
lencie to vse superfluous eloquence. We commonly see that
a black ground doth best beseme a white counterfeit.
And Venus according to the iudgement of Mars, was then
most amiable, when shee sate close by Vulcan. If these
things be true which experience tryeth, that a naked tale   15
doth most truely set foorth the naked truth, that where
the countenance is faire, ther need no colours, that
painting is meeter for ragged wals, then fine Marble,
that veritie then shineth most bright, when she is in
least brauery. I shall satisfie mine owne minde though   20
I cannot feed their humors, which greatly seeke after

those that sift the finest meale, and beare the whitest
mouthes. It is a world to see how English-men desire to
heare finer speach then the language will allowe, to eate
finer bread then is made of wheat, to weare finer cloth   25
then is wrought of woll. But I let passe their finenesse,
which can no way excuse my folly...

I was driuen into a quandarie Gentlemen, whether I might
sende this my Pamphlet to the Printer or to the Pedler,
I thought it too bad for the presse, & too good for the   30
pack. But seing my folly in writing to bee as great as
others, I was willing my fortune should be as ill as
anyes. We commonly see the booke that at Easter lyeth
bounde on the Stacioners stall, at Christmas to be broken
in the Haberdashers shop, which sith it is the order   35
of proceding, I am content this Summer to haue my
dooinges read for a toye, that in Winter they may be
readye for trash. It is not straunge when as the greatest
wonder lasteth but nine dayes: That a new work should not
endure but three moneths. Gentlemen vse bookes as Gentle-   40
women handle their flowers, who in the morning sticke
them in their heades, and at night strawe them at theyr
heeles. Cherries be fulsome when they bee through ripe
bicause they be plentie, & bookes be stale when they
be printed, in that they be common. In my minde Printers   45
& Tailers are bound chiefly to pray for Gentlemen, the
one hath so many fantasies to print, the other such diuers fashions to make, that the pressing yron of the one
is neuer out of the fire, nor the printing presse of the
other at any time lyeth still. But a fashion is but a   50
daies wearing & a booke but an houres reading: which seeing it is so, I am of the shomakers minde, who careth not
so the sho holde the plucking on, nor I, so my labours
last the running ouer. He that commeth in print bicause
he would be known, is like the foole that commeth into   55
the market bicause he would be seene...

Thou art héere in *Naples* a young soiourner, I an olde
senior: thou a straunger, I a Citizen: thou secure doubt-

ing no mishappe, I sorrowfull dreading thy misfortune.
Héere mayst thou sée, that which I sigh to sée: dronken   *60*
sottes wallowing in euery house in euerye Chamber, yea,
in euerye channell. Héere mayst thou beholde that which
I cannot without blushing beholde, nor without blubber-
ing vtter: those whose bellies be their Gods, who offer
their goods as Sacrifice to theyr guttes: Who sléepe   *65*
with meate in their mouths, with sinne in their hearts,
and with shame in their houses. Héere, yea, héere, *Eu-*
phues, mayst thou sée, not the carued visard of a lewde
woman, but thé incarnate visage of a laciuious wantonne:
not the shaddow of loue, but the substaunce of lust.   *70*
My hearte melteth in droppes of bloud, to sée an harlot
wyth the one hande robbe so many cofers, and with the
other to rippe so many corses. Thou art héere amiddest
the pikes betweene *Scylla* and *Caribdis,* ready if thou
shunne *Syrtes,* to sinke into *Semphlagades.* Let the   *75*
Lacedemonian, the *Persian,* yea, the *Neapolitan,* cause
thée rather to detest such villany at the sight and
view of their vanitie. Is it not farre better to abhorre
sinnes by the remembraunce of others faults, then by
repentance of thine own follyes? Is not he accounted   *80*
most wise, whom other mens harmes do make most warie?
But thou wilt happely saye, that although there be many
thinges in *Naples* to bée iustly condempned, yet there
are some thinges of necessitie to be commended: and as
thy will doth leane vnto the one, so thy witte woulde   *85*
also imbrace the other. Alas *Euphues,* by how much the
more I loue the high climbing of thy capacitie, by so
much the more I feare thy fall. The fine Christall is
sooner crased then the harde Marble: the greenest Beech
burneth faster then the dryest Oke: the fayrest silke   *90*
is soonest soyled: & the sweetest Wine tourneth to
the sharpest Vineger. The Pestilence doth most ryfest
infect the cleerest complection, and the Caterpiller
cleaueth vnto the rypest fruite: the most delicate witte
is allured with small enticement vnto vice, and most   *95*
subiect to yéelde vnto vanytie. If therefore thou doe
but harken to the *Syrenes,* thou wilt be enamoured: if
thou haunte theyr houses and places, thou shalt bée
enchaunted. One droppe of poyson infecteth the whole
tunne of Wine: One leafe of *Coloquintida,* marreth and   *100*
spoyleth the whole pot of porredge: one yron Mole, de-

faceth the whole péece of Lawne. Descende into thine
owne conscience, and consider with thy selfe, the great
difference betweene staring and starke blinde, witte and
wisedome, loue and lust: bée merry, but with modestie: 105
bée sober, but not too sullen: bée valiant but not too
venterous. Let thy attire by comely, but not costly:
thy dyet wholsome, but not excessiue: vse pastime as the
woorde importeth, to passe the time in honest recreation.

26 SIR P. SIDNEY: ARCADIA (1590)

And is it possible, that this is *Pyrocles*, the onely
yong Prince in the world, formed by nature, and framed
by education, to the true exercise of vertue? or is it
indeed some *Amazon* that hath counterfeited the face of
my friend, in this sort to vexe me? For likelier sure I   5
I would haue thought it, that any outwarde face might
haue bene disguised, then that the face of so excellent
a mind could haue been thus blemished.

O sweete *Pyrocles* separate your selfe a little (if it
be possible) from your selfe, and let your owne minde   10
looke vpon your owne proceedings: so shall my wordes
be needlesse, and you best instructed.

See with your selfe, how fitt it will be for you in
this your tender youth, borne so great a Prince, and
of so rare, not onely expectation, but proofe, desired   15
of your olde Father, and wanted of your natiue countrie,
now so neere your home, to diuert your thoughts from
the way of goodnesse; to loose, nay to abuse your time.
Lastly to ouerthrow all the excellent things you haue
done, which haue filled the world with your fame; as if   20
you should haue drowne your ship in the long desired
hauen, or like an ill player, should marre the last act
of his Tragedie. Remember (for I know you know it) that
if we wil be men, the reasonable parte of our soule, is
to haue absolute commaundement; against which if any   25
sensuall weaknes arise, we are to yeelde all our sounde
forces to the ouerthrowing of so vnnaturall a rebellion,
wherein how can we wante courage, since we are to deale
against so weake an aduersary, that in it selfe is no-
thinge but weaknesse? Nay we are to resolue, that if   30
reason direct it, we must doo it, and if we must doo it,
we will doo it; for to say I cannot is childish, and I

will not, womanish. And see how extremely euery waye
you endaunger your minde; for to take this womanish
habit (without you frame your behauiour accordingly) is   *35*
wholly vaine: your behauiour can neuer come kindely from
you, but as the minde is proportioned vnto it. So that
you must resolue, if you will playe your parte to any
purpose, whatsoeuer peeuish affections are in that sexe,
soften your heart to receiue them, the very first downe-   *40*
steppe to all wickednes: for doo not deceiue your selfe,
my deere cosin, there is no man sodainely excellentlie
good, or extremely euill, but growes either as hee holdes
himselfe vp in vertue, or lets him self slide to vitious-
nes. And let vs see, what power is the aucthor of all   *45*
these troubles; forsooth loue, loue, a passion and the
basest and fruitlessest of all passions: feare breedeth
wit, Anger is the cradle of courage: ioy openeth and
enhableth the hart: sorrow, as it closeth, so it draweth
it inwarde to looke to the correcting of it selfe; and   *50*
so all generally haue power towards some good by the
direction of right Reason. But this bastarde Loue (for
in deede the name of Loue is most vnworthylie applied to
so hatefull a humour) as it is engendered betwixt lust
and idlenes; as the matter it workes vpon is nothing, but   *55*
a certaine base weakenes, which some gentle fooles call
a gentle hart; as his adioyned companions be vnquietnes,
longings, fond comforts, faint discomforts, hopes, iel-
ousies, vngrounded rages, causlesse yeeldings; so is the
hiest ende it aspires vnto, a little pleasure with much   *60*
paine before, and great repentaunce after. But that end
how endlesse it runs to infinite euils, were fit inough
for the matter we speake of, but not for your eares, in
whome indeed there is so much true disposition to vertue:
yet thus much of his worthie effects in your selfe is   *65*
to be seen, that (besides your breaking lawes of hospi-
tality with *Kalander* and of friendship with me) it vtterly subuerts the course of nature, in making reasons giue
place to sense, & man to woman. And truely I thinke heere-
vpon it first gatte the name of Loue; for indeede the   *70*
true loue hath that excellent nature in it, that it dooth
transform the very essence of the louer into the thing
loued, vniting, and as it were incorporating it with a
secret and inward working.
    And herein do these kindes of loue imitate the ex-   *75*

cellent; for as the loue of heauen makes one heauenly,
the loue of vertue, vertuous; so doth the loue of the
world make one become worldly, and this effeminate loue
of a woman, doth so womanish a man, that (if he yeeld to
it) it will not onely make him an *Amazon*; but a launder, 80
a distaff-spinner; or what so euer vile occupation their
idle heads can imagin, & their weake hands perform.

Therefore (to trouble you no longer with my tedious
but louing words) if either you remember what you are,
what you haue bene, or what you must be: if you consider 85
what it is, that moued you, or by what kinde of creature
you are moued, you shall finde the cause so small, the
effect so daungerous, your selfe so vnworthie to runne
into the one, or to be driuen by the other, that I doubt
not I shall quickly haue occasion rather to praise 90
you for hauing conquered it, then to giue you further
counsell, how to doo it.

27 SIR P. SIDNEY: AN APOLOGIE FOR POETRIE (1595)

Now, for the out-side of it, which is words, or (as I may
tearme it) *Diction*, it is euen well worse. So is that
honny-flowing Matron Eloquence, apparelled, or rather
disguised, in a Curtizan-like painted affectation: one
time with so farre fette words, that may seeme Monsters: 5
but must seeme straungers to any poore English man.
Another tyme, with coursing of a Letter, as if they were
bound to followe the method of a Dictionary: an other tyme,
with figures and flowers, extreamely winter-starued. But
I would this fault were only peculier to Versifiers, 10
and had not as large possession among Prose-printers;
and, (which is to be meruailed) among many Schollers;
and, (which is to be pittied) among some Preachers. Truly
I could wish, if at least I might be so bold, to wish in
a thing beyond the reach of my capacity, the diligent 15
imitators of *Tullie*, & *Demosthines*, (most worthy to be
imitated,) did not so much keep, *Nizolian* Paper-bookes
of their figures and phrases, as by attentiue translation
(as it were) deuoure them whole, and make them wholy
theirs: For nowe they cast Sugar and Spice, vpon euery 20
dish that is serued to the table; Like those Indians, not
content to weare eare-rings at the fit & naturall place

of the eares, but they will thrust Iewels through their
nose, and lippes because they will be sure to be fine.

  Tullie, when he was to driue out *Cateline*, as it were   25
with a Thunder-bolt of eloquence, often vsed that figure
of rep[et]ition, *Viuit, viuit? imo in Senatum venit, &c.*
Indeed, inflamed with a well-grounded rage, hee would haue
his words (as it were) double out of his mouth: and so
doe that artificially, which we see men doe in choller   30
naturally. And wee, hauing noted the grace of those words,
hale them in sometime to a familier Epistle, when it were
to too much choller to be chollerick. Now for similitudes,
in certaine printed discourses, I thinke all Herbarists,
all stories of Beasts, Foules, and Fishes, are rifled vp,   35
that they come in multitudes, to waite vpon any of our
conceits; which certainly is as absurd a surfet to the
eares, as is possible: for the force of a similitude, not
being to prooue any thing to a contrary Disputer, but
onely to explane to a willing hearer, when that is done,   40
the rest is a most tedious pratling: rather ouer-swaying
the memory from the purpose wherto they were applyed, then
any whit informing the iudgement, already eyther satisfied,
or by similitudes not to be satis-fied. For my part, I
doe not doubt, when *Antonius* and *Crassus*, the great fore-   45
fathers of *Cicero* in eloquence, the one (as *Cicero* testi-
fieth of them,) pretended not to know Arte, the other,
not to set by it: because with a playne sensiblenes, they
might win credit of popular eares: which credit, is the
neerest step to perswasion: which perswasion, is the   50
chiefe marke of Oratory: I doe not doubt (I say) but
that they vsed these tracks very sparingly, which who
doth generally vse, any man may see doth daunce to his
owne musick: and so be noted by the audience, more careful to speake curiously, then to speake truly.   55

  Vndoubtedly, (at least to my opinion vndoubtedly,) I
haue found in diuers smally learned Courtiers, a more
sounde stile, then in some professors of learning: of
which I can gesse no other cause, but that the Courtier
following that which by practise hee findeth fittest to   60
nature, therein, (though he know it not,) doth according
to Art, though not by Art: where the other, vsing Art to
shew Art, and not to hide Art, (as in these cases he
should doe) flyeth from nature, and indeede abuseth Art.

  But what? me thinks I deserue to be pounded, for   65

straying from Poetry to Oratorie: but both haue such an
affinity in this wordish consideration, that I thinke
this digression, will make my meaning receiue the fuller
vnderstanding: which is not to take vpon me to teach Poets
how they should doe, but onely finding my selfe sick   70
among the rest, to shewe some one or two spots of the
common infection, growne among the most part of Writers:
that acknowledging our selues somwhat awry, we may bend
to the right vse both of matter and manner; whereto our
language gyueth vs great occasion, beeing indeed capable   75
of any excellent exercising of it. I know, some will say
it is a mingled language. And why not so much the better,
taking the best of both the other? Another will say it
wanteth Grammer. Nay truly, it hath that prayse, that it
wanteth not Grammer: for Grammer it might haue, but it   80
needes it not; beeing so easie of it selfe, & so voyd of
those cumbersome differences of Cases, Genders, Moodes,
and Tenses, which I thinke was a peece of the Tower of
Babilons curse, that a man should be put to schoole to
learne his mother-tongue. But for the vttering sweetly,   85
and properly the conceits of the minde, which is the end
of speech, that hath it equally with any other tongue in
the world: and is particulerly happy, in compositions of
two or three words together, neere the Greek, far beyond
the Latine: which is one of the greatest beauties can be   90
in a language.

28 JAMES VI: THE ESSAYES OF A PRENTISE (1584)

THE PREFACE TO THE READER

The cause why (docile Reader) I haue not dedicat this
short treatise to any particular personis, (as commounly
workis vsis to be) is, that I esteme all thais quha hes
already some beginning of knawledge, with ane earnest desyre to atteyne to farther, alyke meit for the reading   5
of this worke, or any vther, quhilk may help thame to the
atteining to thair foirsaid desyre. Bot as to this work,
quhilk is intitulit, *The Reulis and cautelis to be obseruit*
& eschewit in Scottis Poesie, ze may maruell paraventure
quhairfore I should haue writtin in that mater, sen sa   10
mony learnit men, baith of auld and of late hes already
written thairof in dyuers and sindry languages: I answer,

That nochtwithstanding, I haue lykewayis writtin of it,
for twa caussis. The ane is, As for them that wrait of
auld, lyke as the tyme is changeit sensyne, sa is the   *15*
ordour of Poesie changeit. For then they obseruit not
Flowing, nor eschewit not *Ryming in termes*, besydes sindrie vther thingis, quhilk now we obserue, & eschew, and
dois weil in sa doing: because that now, quhen the warld
is waxit auld, we haue all their opinionis in writ,   *20*
quhilk were learned before our tyme, besydes our awin
ingynis, quhair as they then did it onelie be thair awin
ingynis, but help of any vther. Thairfore, quhat I speik
of Poesie now, I speik of it, as being come to mannis age
and perfectioun, quhair as then, it was bot in the in-   *25*
fancie and chyldheid. The vther cause is, That as for
thame that hes written in it of late, there hes neuer
ane of thame written in our language. For albeit sindrie
hes written of it in English, quhilk is lykest to our
language, zit we differ from thame in sindrie reulis of   *30*
Poesie, as ze will find be experience. I haue lykewayis
omittit dyuers figures, quhilkis are necessare to be vsit
in verse, for twa causis. The ane is, because they are
vsit in all languages, and thairfore are spokin of be
Du Bellay, and sindrie vtheris, quha hes written in this   *35*
airt. Quhairfore gif I wrait of thame also, it sould seme
that I did bot repete that, quhilk thay haue written, and
zit not sa weil, as thay haue done already. The vther cause
is, that they are figures of Rhetorique and Dialectique,
quhilkis airtis I professe nocht, and thairfore will   *40*
apply to my selfe the counsale, quhilk *Apelles* gaue to
the shoomaker, quhen he said to him, seing him find falt
with the shankis of the Image of *Venus*, efter that he had
found falt with the pantoun, *Ne sutor vltra crepidam.*

I will also wish zow (docile Reidar) that or ze cum-   *45*
mer zow with reiding thir reulis, ze may find in zour
self sic a beginning of Nature, as ze may put in practise
in zour verse many of thir foirsaidis preceptis, or euer
ze sie them as they are heir set doun. For gif Nature be
nocht the chief worker in this airt, Reulis wil be bot   *50*
a band to Nature, and will mak zow within short space
weary of the haill airt: quhair as, gif Nature be cheif,
and bent to it, reulis will be ane help and staff to Nature. I will end heir, lest my preface be langer nor my
purpose and haill mater following: wishing zow, docile   *55*

Reidar, als gude succes and great proffeit by reiding
this short treatise, as I tuke earnist and willing panis
to blok it, as ze sie, for zour cause. Fare weill.

I haue insert in the hinder end of this Treatise, maist
kyndis of versis quhilks are not cuttit or brokin, bot
alyke many feit in euerie lyne of the verse, and how they   *60*
are commounly namit, with my opinioun for what subiectis
ilk kynde of thir verse is meitest to be vsit.

29 JAMES VI: BASILIKON DORON (1595/1603)

(ON CONDUCT IN WAR) MS ... choose aulde experimentid
captaines & young abill soldatis, be extreamlie straite &
seuere in discipline alsuell for keiping of ordoure
(quhilke is als requisite as hardimênt in the uarres)
for punishing of sleuth (quhilke at a tyme maye putte the   *5*
haill airmie in hazairde) as lykeuayes for repressing of
mutinies (quhilke in uarres is uonderfullie dangerouse,
& looke to the Spangnoll, quhaise great successe in all
his uarres hes onlie cumd throuch straitnes of discipline
& ordoure, for sicc errouris maye be comitted in the   *10*
uarres as can not be gottin mendit againe: be in youre
awin person ualkeryfe, diligent, & painfull, using the
aduyce of thaime that are skilledest in the craft as ye
man do in all craftis, be hamlie uith youre soldatis as
youre compaignons for uinning thaire hairtis, extreamlie   *15*
liberall, for then is na tyme of spairing...

1603 ... Choose olde experimented Captaines, and young
able souldiers. Be extreamlie straite and seuere in mar-
tiall Discipline, as well for keeping of ordour, whiche
is as requisite as hardinesse in the warres, & punishing   *20*
of slouth, which at a time may put the whole army in
hazard; as likewise for repressing of mutinies whiche in
warres are wonderfull dangerous. And looke to the Spaniard,
whose great successe in all his warres hath onely come
through straitnesse of Discipline and ordour: for suche   *25*
errors may be committed in the warres, as cannot be gotten mended againe. Be in your owne person walkrife, diligent, & painfull; vsing the aduice of suche as are skil-
fullest in the craft, as ye must also doe in all other.
Be homelie with your souldiers as your companions, for   *30*

310

winning their harts; & extreamlie liberall, for then is
no time of sparing...

(ON LANGUAGE) MS In baith youre speiking & youre gesture
then use a naturall & plaine forme not fairdit uith arti-
fice, for as the frenshe men sayes, rien conterfaict fin,   *35*
bot escheu all affectate formis in baith, in your langage
be plaine, honest naturall, cumlie, clene, shorte & sen-
tentiouse escheuing baith the extremities alsueill in not
using a rusticall corrupt leid, nor yett booke langage
& penn & inkorne termes, & least of all mignarde &   *40*
æffeminate termis ...

(ON WRITING) MS Gif ye uolde uritte uorthelie choose subiects uorthie of you that be not full of uanitie but of
uertu, escheuing obscuritie & delyting euer to be plaine
& sensibill, & gif ye uritte in uerse, remember that it   *45*
is not the principall pairt of a poeme to ryme richt, &
flou ueill uith monie prettie uordis, but the cheif co-
mendation of a poeme is, that quhen the uerse sall be
shaikin sindrie in prose it sall be founde sa riche of
quike inuentions & poetike flouris, as it sall retaine   *50*
the lustre of a poeme althoch in prose, & I ualde also
aduyse you to uritte in youre awin langage for thaire is
nathing left to be said in græke & latin allreaddie,
& aneu of poore skollairs ualde matche you in these
langages, & besydes that it best becumis a king to puri-   *55*
fie & make famouse his awin langage quhairin he maye ga
before all his subiectis as it settis him ueill to doe
in all laufull things.

(THE UNION) MS For outuairde & indifferent things are
euer the shaddouis & allurairis to uertu or uyce, bot   *60*
beuaire of thrauing or constraining thaime thairto, letting it be brocht on uith tyme & at laiser, speciallie
be mixing throuch allyae & daylie conuersation the men
of euerie kingdome uith another, as maye uith tyme make
thaime to grou & uall all in ane, quhilke maye easilie   *65*
be done in this yle of brittaine being all bot ane yle,
& allreaddie ioined in unitie of religion, & langage.

1603 For these outward and indifferent things, will
serue greatlie for allurements to the people, to embrace
and followe vertue. But be ware of thrawing or constrayn-   *70*

311

ing them thereto; letting it be brought on with time,
and at leasure: speciallie by so mixing through alliance
& daylie conuersation, the inhabitants of euery kingdome
with other, as may with time make them to growe and weld
all in one. Whiche may easilie be done betwixt these   75
two nations, beeing both but one Ile of *Britaine*, and
alreadie joyned in vnitie of Religion, & language. So that
euen as in the times of our ancestors, the long warres
and many bloodie battels betwixt these two countries,
bred a naturall & hæreditarie hatred in euery of them,   80
against the other: the vniting & welding of them heer-
after in one, by all sort of friendship, commerce, & alliance: will by the contrary, produce and maintaine a naturall & inseparable vnitie of loue amongst them. As we haue
alreadie (praise be to God) a great experience of the   85
good beginning heereof, & of the quenching of the olde
hate in the harts of both the people; procured by the
meanes of this long & happie amitie, betweene the Queene
my dearest sister & me; whiche during the whole time of
both our raignes hath euer beene inviolablie obserued.   90

30 SIR F. BACON: ESSAIES, "OF STUDIES" (1597/1625)

1597 Studies serue for pastimes, for ornaments & for
abilities. Their chiefe vse for pastime is in priuatenes
and retiring; for ornamente is in discourse, and for abilitie is in iudgement. For expert men can execute, but
learned men are fittest to iudge or censure. ¶ To spend   5
too much time in them is slouth, to vse them too much for
ornament is affectation: to make iudgement wholly by their
rules, is the humour of a Scholler. ¶ They perfect *Nature*,
and are perfected by experience. ¶ Craftie men continue
them, simple men admire them, wise men vse them: For they   10
teach not their owne vse, but that is a wisedome without
them: and aboue them wonne by obseruation. ¶ Reade not
to contradict, nor to belieue, but to waigh and consider.
¶ Some bookes are to be tasted, others to bee swallowed,
and some few to bee chewed and disgested: That is, some   15
bookes are to be read only in partes; others to be read,
but cursorily, and some few to be read wholly and with
diligence and attention. ¶ Reading maketh a full man,
conference a readye man, and writing an exacte man. And
therefore if a man haue a great memorie, if he conferre   20

little, he had neede haue a present wit, and if he reade
little, he had heede haue much cunning, to seeme to know
that he doth not. ¶ Histories make men wise, Poets wittie: the Mathematickes subtle, naturall Phylosophie
deepe: Morall graue, Logicke and Rhetoricke able to   25
contend.

1625 *Studies* serue for Delight, for Ornament, and for
Ability. Their Chiefe Vse for Delight, is in Priuatenesse
and Retiring; For Ornament, is in Discourse; And for Ability, is in the Iudgement and Disposition of Businesse.   30
For Expert Men can Execute, and perhaps Iudge of particulars, one by one; But the generall Counsels, and the Plots,
and Marshalling of Affaires, come best from those that are
Learned. To spend too much Time in *Studies,* is Sloth; To
vse them too much for Ornament, is Affectation; To make   35
Iudgement wholly by their Rules is the Humour of a Scholler. They perfect Nature, and are perfected by Experience:
For Naturall Abilities, are like Naturall Plants, that
need Proyning by *Study:* And *Studies* themselues, doe giue
forth Directions too much at Large, except they be bounded   40
in by experience. Crafty Men Contemne *Studies*; Simple
Men Admire them; and Wise Men Vse them: For they teach
not their owne Vse; But that is a Wisdome without them,
and aboue them, won by Obseruation. Reade not to Contradict, and Confute; Nor to Beleeue and Take for granted;   45
Nor to Finde Talke and Discourse; but to weigh and Consider. Some *Bookes* are to be Tasted, Others to be Swallowed, and Some Few to be Chewed and Digested: That is,
some *Bookes* are to be read onely in Parts; Others to be
read but not Curiously; And some Few to be read wholly,   50
and with Diligence and Attention. Some *Bookes* also may be
read by Deputy, and Extracts made of them by Others: But
that would be, onely in the lesse important Arguments,
and the Meaner Sort of *Bookes*: else distilled *Bookes*, are
like Common distilled Waters, Flashy things. Reading   55
maketh a Full Man; Conference a Ready Man; And Writing
an Exact Man. And therefore, If a Man Write little, he
had need haue a Great memory; if he Conferre little, he
had need haue a Present Wit; And if he Reade litle, he
had need haue much Cunning, to seeme to know that, he   60
doth not. *Histories* make men Wise; *Poets* Witty: the
Mathematicks Subtill; *Naturall Philosophy* deepe; *Morall*

Graue; *Logick* and *Rhetorick* Able to Contend. *Abeunt studia
in Mores.* Nay there is no Stond or Impediment in the Wit,
but may be wrought out by Fit *Studies:* Like as Diseases   65
of the Body, may haue Appropriate Exercises. Bowling is
good for the Stone and Reines; Shooting for the Lungs and
Breast; Gentle Walking for the Stomacke; Riding for the
Head; And the like. So if a Mans Wit be Wandring, let
him *Study* the *Mathematicks*; For in Demonstrations, if   70
his Wit be called away neuer so little, he must begin
again: If his Wit be not Apt to distinguish or find differences, let him *Study* the *Schoolemen*; for they are
Cymini sectores. If he be not Apt to beat ouer Matters,
and to call vp one Thing, to Proue and Illustrate another,   75
let him *Study* the *Lawyers Cases*: So euery Defect of the
Minde, may haue a Speciall Receit.

W. SHAKESPEARE: WORKS (FIRST FOLIO 1623)

31A "TO THE GREAT VARIETY OF READERS"

From the most able, to him that can but spell: There you
are number'd. We had rather you were weighd. Especially,
when the fate of all Bookes depends vpon your capacities:
and not of your heads alone, but of your purses. Well! It
is now publique, & you wil stand for your priuiledges wee   5
know: to read, and censure. Do so, but buy it first. That
doth best commend a Booke, the Stationer saies. Then, how
odde soeuer your braines be, or your wisedomes, make your
licence the same, and spare not. Iudge your sixe-pen'orth,
your shillings worth, your fiue shillings worth at a time,   10
or higher, so you rise to the iust rates, and welcome.
But, what euer you do, Buy. Censure will not driue a Trade,
or make the Iacke go. And though you be a Magistrate of
wit, and sit on the Stage at *Black-Friers*, or the *Cock-pit*,
to arraigne Playes dailie, know, these Playes haue had   15
their triall alreadie, and stood out all Appeales; and
do now come forth quitted rather by a Decree of Court,
then any purchas'd Letters of commendation.

It had bene a thing, we confesse, worthie to haue bene
wished, that the Author himselfe had liu'd to haue set   20
forth, and ouerseen his owne writings; But since it hath
bin ordain'd otherwise, and he by death departed from that

right, we pray you do not envie his Friends, the office
of their care, and paine, to haue collected & publish'd
them; and so to haue publish'd them, as where (before)   25
you were abus'd with diuerse stolne, and surreptitious
copies, maimed, and deformed by the frauds and stealthes
of iniurious impostors, that expos'd them: euen those,
are now offer'd to your view cur'd, and perfect of their
limbes; and all the rest, absolute in their numbers, as   30
he conceiued them. Who, as he was a happie imitator of
Nature, was a most gentle expresser of it. His mind and
hand went together: And what he thought, he vttered with
that easinesse, that wee haue scarce receiued from him
a blot in his papers. But it is not our prouince, who   35
onely gather his works, and giue them you, to praise him.
It is yours that reade him. And there we hope, to your
diuers capacities, you will finde enough, both to draw,
and hold you: for his wit can no more lie hid, then it
could be lost. Reade him, therefore; and againe, and   40
againe: And if then you doe not like him, surely you
are in some manifest danger, not to vnderstand him.
And so we leaue you to other of his Friends, whom if
you need, can bee your guides: if you neede them not,
you can leade your selues, and others. And such Readers   45
we wish him.   *Iohn Heminge   Henrie Condell.*

31B THE TRAGEDIE OF HAMLET (I.4.1–194)

Enter Hamlet, Horatio, Marcellus.

Ham.	The Ayre bites shrewdly: is it very cold?
Hor.	It is a nipping and an eager ayre.
Ham.	What hower now?
Hor.	I thinke it lacks of twelue. 5
Mar.	No, it is strooke.
Hor.	Indeed I heard it not: then it drawes neere the season,
	Wherein the Spirit held his wont to walke.
	What does this meane my Lord?
Ham.	The King doth wake to night, and takes his rouse, 10
	Keepes wassels and the swaggering vpspring reeles,
	And as he dreines his draughts of Renish downe,
	The kettle Drum and Trumpet thus bray out
	The triumph of his Pledge.

| Hor. | Is it a custome? | 15 |

Hor. Is it a custome?   15
Ham. I marry ist;
　　　 And to my mind, though I am natiue heere,
　　　 And to the manner borne: It is a Custome
　　　 More honour'd in the breach, then the obseruance.
　　　　　　　Enter Ghost.   20
Hor. Looke my Lord, it comes.
Ham. Angels and Ministers of Grace defend vs:
　　　 Be thou a Spirit of health, or Goblin damn'd,
　　　 Bring with thee ayres from Heauen, or blasts from Hell,
　　　 Be thy euents wicked or charitable,   25
　　　 Thou com'st in such a questionable shape,
　　　 That I will speake to thee. Ile call thee *Hamlet*,
　　　 King, Father, Royall Dane: Oh, oh, answer me,
　　　 Let me not burst in Ignorance; but tell
　　　 Why thy Canoniz'd bones Hearsed in death,   30
　　　 Haue burst their cerments, why the Sepulcher
　　　 Wherein we saw thee quietly enurn'd,
　　　 Hath op'd his ponderous and Marble iawes,
　　　 To cast thee vp againe? What may this meane?
　　　 That thou dead Coarse againe in compleat steele,   35
　　　 Reuisits thus the glimpses of the Moone,
　　　 Making Night hidious? And we fooles of Nature,
　　　 So horridly to shake our disposition,
　　　 With thoughts beyond thee; reaches of our Soules,
　　　 Say, why is this? wherefore? what should we doe?   40
　　　　　　　Ghost beckons Hamlet.
Hor. It beckons you to goe away with it,
　　　 As if it some impartment did desire
　　　 To you alone.
Mar. Looke with what courteous action   45
　　　 It wafts you to a more remoued ground:
　　　 But doe not goe with it.
Hor. No, by no meanes.
Ham. It will not speake: then will I follow it.
Hor. Doe not my Lord.   50
Ham. Why, what should be the feare?
　　　 I doe not set my life at a pins fee;
　　　 And for my Soule, what can it doe to that?
　　　 Being a thing immortall as it selfe:
　　　 It waues me forth againe; Ile follow it.   55
Hor. What if it tempt you toward the Floud my Lord?
　　　 Or to the dreadfull Sonnet of the Cliffe,

	That beetles o're his base into the Sea,	
	And there assumes some other horrible forme,	
	Which might depriue your Soueraignty of Reason,	*60*
	And draw you into madnesse thinke of it?	
Ham.	It wafts me still: goe on, Ile follow thee.	
Mar.	You shall not goe my Lord.	
Ham.	Hold off your hand.	
Hor.	Be rul'd, you shall not goe.	*65*
Ham.	My fate cries out,	
	And makes each petty Artire in this body,	
	As hardy as the Nemian Lions nerue:	
	Still am I cal'd? Vnhand me Gentlemen:	
	By Heau'n, Ile make a Ghost of him that lets me:	*70*
	I say away, goe on, Ile follow thee.	

Exeunt Ghost & Hamlet

Hor.	He waxes desperate with imagination.	
Mar.	Let's follow; 'tis not fit thus to obey him.	
Hor.	Haue after, to what issue will this come?	*75*
Mar.	Something is rotten in the State of Denmarke.	
Hor.	Heauen will direct it.	
Mar.	Nay, let's follow him. *Exeunt.*	

Enter Ghost and Hamlet.

Ham.	Where wilt thou lead me? speak; Ile go no further.	*80*
Gho.	Marke me	
Ham.	I will.	
Gho.	My hower is almost come,	
	When I to sulphurous and tormenting Flames	
	Must render vp my selfe.	*85*
Ham.	Alas poore Ghost.	
Gho.	Pitty me not, but lend thy serious hearing	
	To what I shall vnfold.	
Ham.	Speake, I am bound to heare.	
Gho.	So art thou to reuenge, when thou shalt heare.	*90*
Ham.	What?	
Gho.	I am thy Fathers Spirit,	
	Doom'd for a certaine terme to walke the night;	
	And for the day confin'd to fast in Fiers,	
	Till the foule crimes done in my dayes of Nature	*95*
	Are burnt and purg'd away? But that I am forbid	
	To tell the secrets of my Prison-House;	
	I could a Tale vnfold, whose lightest word	
	Would harrow vp thy soule, freeze thy young blood,	
	Make thy two eyes like Starres, start from their Spheres,	*100*

Thy knotty and combined locks to part,
And each particular haire to stand an end,
Like Quilles vpon the fretfull Porpentine:
But this eternall blason must not be
To eares of flesh and bloud; list *Hamlet*, oh list   *105*
If thou didst euer thy deare Father loue.

Ham.   Oh Heauen!

Gho.   Reuenge his foule and most vnnaturall Murther.

Ham.   Murther?

Gho.   Murther most foule, as in the best it is;   *110*
But this most foule, strange, and vnnaturall.

Ham.   Hast, hast me to know it,
That with wings as swift
As meditation, or the thoughts of Loue,
May sweepe to my Reuenge.   *115*

Gho.   I finde thee apt,
And duller should'st thou be then the fat weede
That rots it selfe in ease, on Lethe Wharfe,
Would'st thou not stirre in this. Now *Hamlet* heare:
It's giuen out, that sleeping in mine Orchard,   *120*
A Serpent stung me: so the whole eare of Denmarke,
Is by a forged processe of my death
Rankly abus'd: But know thou Noble youth,
The Serpent that did sting thy Fathers life,
Now weares his Crowne.   *125*

Ham.   O my Propheticke soule: mine Vncle?

Gho.   I that incestuous, that adulterate Beast
With witchcraft of his wits, hath Traitorous guifts.
Oh wicked Wit, and Gifts, that haue the power
So to seduce? Won to to this shamefull Lust   *130*
The will of my most seeming vertuous Queene:
Oh *Hamlet*, what a falling off was there,
From me, whose loue was of that dignity,
That it went hand in hand, euen with the Vow
I made to her in Marriage; and to decline   *135*
Vpon a wretch, whose Naturall gifts were poore
To those of mine. But Vertue, as it neuer wil be moued,
Though Lewdnesse court it in a shape of Heauen:
So Lust, though to a radiant Angell link'd,
Will sate it selfe in a Celestiall bed, & prey on Garbage.   *140*
But soft, me thinkes I sent the Mornings Ayre;
Briefe let me be: Sleeping within mine Orchard,
My custome alwayes in the afternoone;

Vpon my secure hower thy Vncle stole
With iuyce of cursed Hebenon in a Violl,   145
And in the Porches of mine eares did poure
The leaperous Distilment; whose effect
Holds such an enmity with bloud of Man,
That swift as Quick-siluer, it courses through
The naturall Gates and Allies of the Body;   150
And with a sodaine vigour it doth posset
And curd, like Aygre droppings into Milke,
The thin and wholsome blood: so did it mine;
And a most instant Tetter bak'd about,
Most Lazar-like, with vile and loathsome crust,   155
All my smooth Body.
Thus was I, sleeping, by a Brothers hand,
Of Life, of Crowne, and Queene at once dispatcht;
Cut off euen in the Blossomes of my Sinne,
Vnhouzzled, disappointed, vnnaneld,   160
No reckoning made, but sent to my account
With all my imperfections on my head;
Oh horrible, Oh horrible, most horrible:
If thou hast nature in thee beare it not;
Let not the Royall Bed of Denmarke be   165
A Couch for Luxury and damned Incest.
But howsoeuer thou pursuest this Act,
Taint not thy mind; nor let thy Soule contriue
Against thy Mother ought; leaue her to heauen,
And to those Thornes that in her bosome lodge,   170
To pricke and sting her. Fare thee well at once;
The Glow-worme showes the Matine to be neere,
And gins to pale his vneffectuall Fire:
Adue, adue, *Hamlet*: remember me.   *Exit.*

Ham.   Oh all you host of Heauen! Oh Earth; what els?   175
And shall I couple Hell? Oh fie: hold my heart;
And you my sinnewes, grow not instant Old;
But beare me stiffely vp: Remember thee?
I, thou poore Ghost, while memory holds a seate
In this distracted Globe: Remember thee?   180
Yea, from the Table of my Memory,
Ile wipe away all triuiall fond Records,
All sawes of Bookes, all formes, all presures past,
That youth and obseruation coppied there;
And thy Commandment all alone shall liue   185
Within the Booke and Volume of my Braine,

Vnmixt with baser matter; yes, yes, by Heauen:
Oh most pernicious woman!
Oh Villaine, Villaine, smiling damned Villaine!
My Tables, my Tables; meet it is I set it downe,   190
That one may smile, and smile and be a Villaine;
At least I'm sure it may be so in Denmarke;
So Vnckle there you are: now to my word:
It is; Adue, Adue, Remember me: I haue sworn't.

31C THE TRAGEDIE OF KING LEAR (IV.6.232–52)

Stew. Wherefore, bold Pezant,
        Dar'st thou support a publish'd Traitor? Hence,
        Least that th'infection of his fortune take
        Like hold on thee. Let go his arme.
Edg. Chill not let go Zir,   5
        Without vurther 'casion.
Stew. Let go Slaue, or thou dy'st.
Edg. Good Gentleman goe your gate, and let poore volke
        passe: and 'chud ha'bin zwaggerd out of my life,
        'twould not ha'bin zo long as 'tis, by a vortnight.   10
        Nay, come not neere th'old man: keepe out che vor'ye,
        or ice try whither your Costard, or my Ballow be
        the harder; chill be plaine with you.
Stew. Out Dunghill.
Edg. Chill picke your teeth Zir: come, no matter vor   15
        your foynes.
Stew. Slaue thou hast slaine me: Villain, take my purse;
        If euer thou wilt thriue, bury my bodie,
        And giue the Letters which thou find'st about me,
        To *Edmund* Earle of Glouster: seeke him out   20
        Vpon the English party, Oh vntimely death, death.

31D THE TRAGEDIE OF JULIUS CAESAR (III.2.171–232)

Ant. If you haue teares, prepare to shed them now.
        You all do know this Mantle, I remember
        The first time euer *Cæsar* put it on,
        'Twas on a Summers Euening in his Tent,
        That day he ouercame the *Neruij*.   5
        Looke, in this place ran *Cassius* Dagger through:
        See what a rent the enuious *Caska* made:
        Through this, the wel-beloued *Brutus* stabb'd,

And as he pluck's his cursed Steele away:
Marke how the blood of *Cæsar* followed it,   *10*
As rushing out of doores, to be resolu'd
If *Brutus* to vnkindely knock'd, or no:
For *Brutus*, as you know, was *Cæsars* Angel.
Iudge, O you Gods, how deerely *Cæsar* lou'd him:
This was the most vnkindest cut of all.   *15*
For when the Noble *Cæsar* saw him stab,
Ingratitude, more strong then Traitors armes,
Quite vanquish'd him: then burst his Mighty heart,
And in his Mantle, muffling vp his face,
Euen at the Base of *Pompeyes* Statue   *20*
(Which all the while ran blood) great *Cæsar* fell.
O what a fall was there, my Countrymen?
Then I, and you, and all of vs fell downe,
Whil'st bloody Treason flourish'd ouer vs.
O now you weepe, and I perceiue you feele   *25*
The dint of pitty: These are gracious droppes.
Kinde Soules, what weepe you, when you but behold
Our *Cæsars* Vesture wounded! Looke you heere,
Heere is Himselfe, marr'd as you see with Traitors.

1.	O pitteous spectacle! *30*
2.	O Noble *Cæsar*!
3.	O wofull day!
4.	O Traitors, Villaines!
1.	O most bloody sight!
2.	We will be reueng'd: Reuenge *35*
	About, seeke, burne, fire, kill, slay.
	Let not a Traitor liue.
Ant.	Stay Country-men.
1.	Peace there, heare the Noble *Antony*.
2.	Wee'l heare him, wee'l follow him, wee'l dy with him. *40*
Ant.	Good Friends, sweet Friends, let me not stirre you vp

To such a sodaine Flood of Mutiny:
They that haue done this Deede, are honourable,
What priuate greefes they haue, alas I know not,
That made them do it: They are Wise, and Honourable, *45*
And will no doubt with Reasons answer you.
I come not (Friends) to steale away your hearts,
I am no Orator, as *Brutus* is;
But (as you know me all) a plaine blunt man
That loue my Friend, and that they know full well,   *50*
That gaue me publike leaue to speake of him:

For I haue neyther writ nor words, nor worth,
Action, nor Vtterance, nor the power of Speech,
To stirre mens Blood. I onely speake right on:
I tell you that, which you your selues do know,   55
Shew you sweet *Cæsars* wounds, poor poor dum mouths
And bid them speake for me: But were I *Brutus*,
And *Brutus Antony*, there were an *Antony*
Would ruffle vp your Spirits, and put a Tongue
In euery Wound of *Cæsar*, that should moue   60
The stones of Rome, to rise and Mutiny.

31E TROYLUS AND CRESSIDA (I.3.75–138)

Vlys.   Troy yet vpon his basis had bene downe,
And the great *Hectors* sword had lack'd a Master
But for these instances.
The specialty of Rule hath beene neglected;
And looke how many Grecian Tents do stand   5
Hollow vpon this Plaine, so many hollow Factions.
When that the Generall is not like the Hiue,
To whom the Forragers shall all repaire,
What Hony is expected? Degree being vizarded,
Th'vnworthiest shewes as fairely in the Maske,   10
The Heauens themselues, the Planets, and this Center,
Obserue degree, priority, and place,
Insisture, course, proportion, season, forme,
Office, and custome, in all line of Order:
And therefore is the glorious Planet Sol   15
In noble eminence, enthron'd and sphear'd
Amid'st the other, whose med'cinable eye
Corrects the ill Aspects of Planets euill,
And postes like the Command'ment of a King.
Sans checke, to good and bad. But when the Planets   20
In euill mixture to disorder wander,
What Plagues, and what portents, what mutiny?
What raging of the Sea? shaking of Earth?
Commotion in the Windes? Frights, changes, horrors,
Diuert, and cracke, rend and deracinate   25
The vnity, and married calme of States
Quite from their fixure? O, when Degree is shak'd,
(Which is the Ladder to all high designes)
The enterprize is sicke. How could Communities,
Degrees in Schooles, and Brother-hoods in Cities,   30

Peacefull Commerce from diuidable shores,
The primogenitiue, and due of Byrth,
Prerogatiue of Age, Crownes, Scepters, Lawrels,
(But by Degree) stand in Authentique place?
Take but Degree away, vn-tune that string,   35
And hearke what Discord followes: each thing meetes
In meere oppugnancie. The bounded Waters,
Should lift their bosomes higher then the Shores,
And make a soppe of all this solid Globe:
Strength should be Lord of imbecility,   40
And the rude Sonne should strike his Father dead:
Force should be right, or rather, right and wrong,
(Betweene whose endlesse iarre, Iustice recides)
Should loose her names, and so should Iustice too.
Then euery thing includes it selfe in Power,   45
Power into Will, Will into Appetite,
And Appetite (an vniuersall Wolfe,
So doubly seconded with Will, and Power)
Must make perforce an vniversall prey,
And last, eate vp himselfe.   50
Great *Agamemnon:*
This Chaos, when Degree is suffocate,
Followes the choaking:
And this neglection of Degree, is it
That by a pace goes backward in a purpose   55
It hath to climbe. The Generall's disdain'd
By him one step below; he, by the next,
That next, by him beneath: so euery step
Exampled by the first pace that is sicke
Of his Superiour, growes to an enuious Feauer   60
Of pale, and bloodlesse Emulation.
And 'tis this Feauer that keepes Troy on foote,
Not her owne sinewes. To end a tale of length,
Troy in our weaknesse liues, not in her strength.

31F LOVE'S LABOUR'S LOST (V.1.1–30)

Enter the Pedant, Curate and Dull.
Pedant. Satis quid sufficit.
Curat. I praise God for you sir, your reasons at dinner
    haue beene sharpe & sententious: pleasant without
    scurrillity, witty without affection, audacious   5
    without impudency, learned without opinion, and

strange without heresie: I did conuerse this *quondam*
day with a companion of the Kings, who is intituled,
nominated, or called, *Don Adriano de Armatho.*

Ped. *Noui hominum tanquam te,* His humour is lofty, his   10
discourse peremptorie: his tongue filed, his eye
ambitious, his gate maiesticall, and his generall
behauiour vaine, ridiculous, and thrasonicall. He is
too picked, too spruce, too affected, too odde, as
it were, too peregrinat, as I may call it.   15

Curat. A most singular and choise Epithat.

Draw out his Table-booke.

Peda. He draweth out the thred of his verbositie, finer
then the staple of his argument. I abhor such phana-
ticall phantasims, such insociable and poynt deuise   20
companions, such rackers of ortagriphie, as to speake
dout fine, when he should say doubt; det, when he
shold pronounce debt; d e b t, not det: he clepeth
a Calf, Caufe: halfe, haufe: neighbour *vocatur* nebour;
neigh abreuiated ne: this is abhominable, which he   25
would call abbominable: It insinuateth me of infamie:
ne inteligis domine, to make franticke, lunaticke?

Cura. *Laus deo, bene intelligo.*

Peda. *Bome boon for boon prescian,* a little scratcht,
'twil serue.   30

31G SONNETS (1609)

46

M Ine eye and heart are at a mortall warre,
  How to deuide the conqueſt of thy ſight,
Mine eye,my heart their pictures ſight would barre,
My heart,mine eye the freecdome of that right,
My heart doth plead that thou in him dooſt lye,   5
(A cloſet neuer pearſt with chriſtall eyes)
But the defendant doth that plea deny,
And ſayes in him their faire appearance lyes.
To ſide this title is impannelled
A queſt of thoughts,all tennants to the heart,   10
And by their verdict is determined
The cleere eyes moyitie,and he deare hearts part.
    As thus,mine eyes due is their outward part,
      And my hearts right,their inward loue of heart.

118

Lke as to make our appetites more keene   15
With eager compounds we our pallat vrge,
As to preuent our malladies vnſeene,
We ſicken to ſhun ſickneſſe when we purge.
Euen ſo being full of your nere cloying ſweetneſſe,
To bitter ſawces did I frame my feeding;   20
And ſicke of wel-fare found a kind of meetneſſe,
To be diſeaſ'd ere that there was true needing.
Thus pollicie in loue t'anticipate
The ills that were,not grew to faults aſſured,
And brought to medicine a healthfull ſtate   25
Which rancke of goodneſſe would by ill be cured.
   But thence I learne and find the leſſon true,
   Drugs poyſon him that ſo fell ſicke of you.

139

O Call not me to iuſtifie the wrong,
   I that thy vnkindneſſe layes vpon my heart,   30
Wound me not with thine eye but with thy toung,
Vſe power with power,and ſlay me not by Art,
Tell me thou lou'ſt eiſe-where;but in my ſight,
Deare heart forbeare to glance thine eye aſide,
What needſt thou wound with cunning when thy might   35
Is more then my ore-preſt deſence can bide?
Let me excuſe thee ah my loue well knowes,
Her prettie lookes haue beene mine enemies,
And therefore from my face ſhe turnes my foes,
That they elſe-where might dart their iniuries :   40
   Yet do not ſo,but ſince I am neere ſlaine,
   Kill me out-right with lookes,and rid my paine.

32 ANON.: THE PINDER OF WAKEFIELD (1632)

HOW GEORGE *SERUED ONE THAT GOT HIS PURSE.*

In the time of Lent your Players doe range all the Countries
from place to place: and comming to *Wakefield*, they had
great audience euery day. *George* amongst the rest would
needes bee one; but it chanced when he came from the Play,   5
and going to *Bankes* house to drinke with some associates,
looking for his Purse, it was gone, which put him in a pelting chafe. Well, hee brooked it so well as he could vntill
next day, hammering in his head, now to take the theefe, at
last an odde conceit came in his head, he got a many fish-   10
hooks and sowed them full in his pockets, the beards downe-

ward, that it was no hurt to trust downe ones hand, but to
get out impossible, without great tearing of the hand to
peeces: then hee gets many Counters and puts them in his
pocket also, and to the Play he goes amongst the greatest   *15*
crowd, still iustling & gingling his pocket to draw the
fish to the bait: *George* seemed to affect the Play very well,
and carelesse of his pockets still gingling of the Counters,
which being noted by a notable nimmer, hee was quickly in
George his pocket: which he perceiuing, wrings his body   *20*
on one side then on the other. Oh, quoth the Cutpurse,
thinking to draw out his hand, but alacke hee was fast
enough. *George* being in the crowd would not take any notice
that he had caught, but still wrested his body from place
to place vntill all the hookes had got hold; which made   *25*
the Cutpurse cry out vehemently, that all about him wondred
what he ayled, at last *George* seemed to take notice; saying,
what the Diuell aylest thou, art thou mad. Oh my hand, my
hand, good Master, quoth the Cutpurse; what the Diuell doth
thy hand in my pocket? quoth *George*, pull it out or I will   *30*
so baste you, and so he was as good as his word, for he
pummelled him soundly: the theefe cryed, *George* stroue to
goe out of doores, the Players stood still, all the Audience
bent their eyes that way, people about them wondred to see
the mans hand in *George* his pocket, and could not pull it   *35*
out, euery one said *George* was a coniuerer, some said he had
a Diuell in his pocket, some one thing, some another thing:
but *George* he got out of the house, the man of force must
needs follow, crying out still with his hand in his pocket.
People thronged after to see this new Comedy, and so for-   *40*
sooke the other Play, the Players being left alone, they
followed also. But *George* perceiuing such a multitude stood
still, and desired them to make a stand for a while, and
they should all see him release him presently: With that
the people all stood still, and *George* walkt along with   *45*
his prize, certifying him hee had lost a purse the day before, and some forty shillings and odde in it, and he knew
hee had it, or that he knew that some of his fellowes had
it: and therefore willed him without any more trouble to
deliuer it, or else hee would haue him hang'd, and should   *50*
also walke before the Iustice with your hand in my pocket:
you fared so well yesterday that made you bee so ready in
the same place to day. Come, come, quoth *George*, you must
re-deliuer, or goe. The Cutpurse seeing that there was no

remedy, and sich a multitude of people about him, also   *55*
perceiuing *George* to be much beloued, prayed him for Gods
sake to forgiue him, and not to let the people to wrong him,
and hee would giue him all that he had, and that was a purse
with fiue pounds odde mony in it: which *George* taking and
making him to sweare also to forsake his trade; tooke a   *60*
knife and cut out his pocket, for there was no other way
to release him: and then tooke his girdle and did so bebaste
him; crying, runne, runne, you Rogue, the fellow being at
liberty, ranne so fast, that none could ouertake him, and
so escaped. The people all did wonder what the matter should   *65*
bee, but knew not any thing. All flocked about *George*, but
hee hasted to *Bankes* his house, where hee told all the passages to his friends: some were mad that he let the Cutpurse
goe, because they had lost their purses. Nay, it is no matter, quoth *George*, you laught at mee because I had lost   *70*
mine. Come, giues a little drinke, quoth *George*, where he
spent an Angell of his money for ioy amongst his friends,
which reioyced them much, euery one praised *George* for his
wit, especially for this of the fishookes, to catch those
that sought to catch, euery one commended him for it, both   *75*
old and yong: and to this day it is remembred there to his
praise.

33 J. MILTON: REASON OF CHURCH GOVERNMENT (1641)

... in the priuate academies of Italy... I began... to assent... to an inward prompting which now grew daily upon me,
that by labour and intent study (which I take to be my
portion in this life) joyn'd with the strong propensity of
nature, I might perhaps leave something so written to   *5*
aftertimes, as they should not willingly let it die. These
thoughts at once possest me, and these other. That if I
were certain to write as men buy Leases, for three lives
and downward, there ought no regard be sooner had than to
Gods glory by the honour and instruction of my country.   *10*
For which cause, and not only for that I knew it would be
hard to arrive at the second rank among the Latines, I
apply'd my selfe to that resolution which *Ariosto* follow'd
against the perswasions of *Bembo*, to fix all the industry
and art I could unite to the adorning of my native tongue;   *15*
not to make verbal curiosities the end, that were a toyl-
som vanity, but to be an interpreter & relater of the best

and sagest things among mine own Citizens throughout this
Iland in the mother dialect. That what the greatest and
choycest wits of *Athens, Rome*, or modern *Italy*, and those 20
Hebrews of old did for their country, I in my proportion
with this over and above being a Christian, might doe for
mine: not caring to be once nam'd abroad, though perhaps
I could attaine to that, but content with these British
Ilands as my world, whose fortune hath hitherto bin, that 25
if the Athenians, as some say, made their small deeds
great and renowned by their eloquent writers, *England* hath
had her noble atchievments made small by the unskilfull
handling of monks and mechanicks.

34 J. MILTON: PARADISE LOST (1667)

Of Mans First Disobedience, and the Fruit *(I.1)*
Of that Forbidden Tree, whose mortal tast
Brought Death into the World, and all our woe,
With loss of *Eden*, till one greater Man,
Restore us, and regain the blissful Seat, 5
Sing Heav'nly Muse, that on the secret top
Of *Oreb*, or of *Sinai*, didst inspire
That Shepherd, who first taught the chosen Seed,
In the Beginning how the Heav'ns and Earth
Rose out of *Chaos*: Or if *Sion* Hill 10
Delight thee more, and *Siloa's* Brook that flow'd
Fast by the Oracle of God; I thence
Invoke thy aid to my adventrous Song,
That with no middle flight intends to soar
Above th'*Aonian* Mount, while it pursues 15
Things unattempted yet in Prose or Rhime.
And chiefly Thou O Spirit, that dost prefer
Before all Temples th'upright heart and pure,
Instruct me, for Thou know'st; Thou from the first
Wast present, and with mighty wings outspread 20
Dove-like satst brooding on the vast Abyss
And mad'st it pregnant: What in me is dark
Illumine, what is low raise and support:
That to the highth of this great Argument
I may assert th'Eternal Providence 25
And justifie the wayes of God to men ...

Thus Satan talking to his neerest Mate *(I.192)*
With Head up-lift above the wave, and Eyes

That sparkling blaz'd, his other Parts besides
Prone on the Flood, extended long and large   30
Lay floating many a rood, in bulk as huge
As whom the Fables name of monstrous size,
Titanian, or *Earth-born*, that warr'd on *Jove*,
Briarios or *Typhon*, whom the Den
By ancient *Tarsus* held, or that Sea-beast   35
Leviathan, which God of all his works
Created hugest that swim th'Ocean stream:
Him haply slumbring on the *Norway* foam
The Pilot of some small night-founder'd Skiff,
Deeming some Island, oft, as Sea-men tell,   40
With fixed Anchor in his skaly rind
Moors by his side under the Lee, while Night
Invests the Sea, and wished Morn delayes:
So stretcht out huge in length the Arch-fiend lay
Chain'd on the burning Lake, nor ever thence   45
Had ris'n or heav'd his head, but that the will
And high permission of all-ruling Heaven
Left him at large to his own dark designs,
That with reiterated crimes he might
Heap on himself damnation, while he sought   50
Evil to others, and enrag'd might see
How all his malice serv'd but to bring forth
Infinite goodness, grace and mercy shewn
On Man by him seduc't, but on himself
Treble confusion, wrath and vengeance pour'd.   55
Forthwith upright he rears from off the Pool
His mighty stature; on each hand the flames
Drivn backward slope their pointing spires, and rowld
In billows, leave i'th'midst a horrid Vale.
Then with expanded wings he stears his flight   60
Aloft, incumbent on the dusky Air
That felt unusual weight, till on dry Land
He lights, if it were Land that ever burn'd
With solid, as the Lake with liquid fire;
And such appear'd in hue, as when the force   65
Of subterranean wind transports a Hill
Torn from *Pelorus*, or the shatter'd side
Of thundring *Ætna*, whose combustible
And fewel'd entrals thence conceiving Fire,
Sublim'd with Mineral fury, aid the Winds,   70
And leave a singed bottom all involv'd

With stench and smoak: Such resting found the sole
Of unblest feet ...

Which when *Beelzebub* perceiv'd, then whom,   *(II.299)*
Satan except, none higher sat, with grave   75
Aspect he rose, and in his rising seem'd
A Pillar of State; deep on his Front engraven
Deliberation sat and publick care;
And Princely counsel in his face yet shon,
Majestick though in ruin: sage he stood   *80*
With *Atlantean* shoulders fit to bear
The weight of mightiest Monarchies; his look
Drew audience and attention still as Night
Or Summers Noon-tide air, while thus he spake...

ON THE HISTORY OF THE
PERIOD AND ITS CULTURE

35 J. FROISSART AND J. BOURCHIER: THE CHRONYCLES
(1523)

*THE PREFACE OF JOHAN BOURCHIER KNYGHT LORDE
BERNERS/ TRANSLATOUR OF THIS PRESENT CRONYCLE*

What condygne graces and thankes ought men to gyue to the
writers of historyes? Who with their great labours/ haue
done so moche profyte to the humayne lyfe. They shewe/   5
open/ manifest and declare to the reder/ by example of
olde antyquite: what we shulde enquere/ desyre/ and folowe:
And also/ what we shulde eschewe/ auoyde/ and vtterly flye.
For whan we (beynge vnexpert of chaunces) se/ beholde/ and
rede the auncyent actes/ gestes/ and dedes: Howe/ and   10
with what labours/ daungers/ and paryls they were gested
and done: They right greatly admonest/ ensigne/ and teche
vs: howe we maye lede forthe our lyues. And farther/ he
that hath the perfyte knowledge of others ioye/ welthe/
and highe prosperite: and also trouble/ sorowe and great   15
aduersyte: hath thexpert doctryne of all parylles. And
albeit/ that mortall folke are marueylously separated/
bothe by lande & water/ and right wonderously sytuate:
yet are they and their actes (done paraduenture by the
space of a thousande yere) compact togyder/ by thisto-   20
graphier: as it were the dedes of one selfe cyte/ and in
one mannes lyfe. Wherfore I say that historie may well be
called a diuyne prouydence: For as the celestyall bodyes
aboue/ complecte all and at euery tyme the vniuersall
worlde/ the creatures therin conteyned/ and all their   25
dedes: semblably so dothe history. Is it nat a right
noble thynge for vs/ by the fautes and errours of other/
to amende and erect our lyfe in to better? we shuld nat
seke and acquyre that other dyd/ but what thyng was most
best/ most laudable/ and worthely done: we shulde putte   30
before our eyes to folowe. Be nat the sage counsayles of
two or thre olde fathers in a cyte/ towne/ or countre:
whom long age hath made wyse/ dyscrete/ and prudent:
farre more praysed/ lauded/ and derely loued: than of
the yonge menne? Howe moche more than ought hystories   35
to be commended/ praysed/ and loued? In whom is encluded
so many sage counsayls/ great reasons/ & hygh wisedoms:
of so innumerable persons/ of sondry nacyons and of euery

age: and that in so long space/ as four or fyue hundred
yere. The most profytable thyng in this worlde/ for the
instytucion of the humayne lyfe/ is hystorie. Ones the
contynuall redyng therof/ maketh yonge men equall in
prudence to olde men: and to olde fathers stryken in age/
it mynystreth experyence of thynges. More it yeldeth
priuate persons worth of dignyte/ rule/ and gouernaunce.
It compelleth themperours/ hygh rulers and gouernours/
to do noble dedes: to thende they may optayne immortall
glory. It exciteth/ moueth/ and stereth the strong hardy
warriours/ for the great laude that they haue after they
ben deed/ promptly to go in hande with great and harde
parels/ in defence of their countre. And it prohibyteth
reprouable persons to do mischeuous dedes/ for feare of
infamy and shame...

36 J. BELLENDEN: BOECE'S CRONIKLIS OF SCOTLAND
(1531)

Schort tyme eftir Makbeth returnit to his innative cruelte,
and become furious, as þe nature of all tyrannis is quhilkis conquessis realmez be wrangwis menis, traisting all
pepill to doo siclike cruelteis to him as he did afoir to
vtheris. Forthir, remembring þe weirdis gevin to him, as
is rehersit, þat Banquhois posterite suld reioise þe crovne
be lang progressioun, he callit Banquho and his son Fleance
to ane supper, quhilkis suspeckitt na thing leß þan his
treson. Makbeth, quhen þe bankett wes done, thocht he
wald nocht slay þame oppinlie, for rumour of pepill, bot
laid ane band of armyt men to slay thame at þair return-
yng hayme. Thir men quhilkis war laid in waitt to þis
effect slew Banquho, nochtþeles Fleance eschapitt be cov-
irt of þe nycht, and sauffitt, as apperit, be singular
favoure of God to ane bettir fortoun.

   Fleance, eschaping in þis wise, and seyng new waching
laid for his slauchter ilk daye, fled in Walis, quhair he
wes plesandlie ressauit be þe Prince þairof, and maid sa
familiar that he lay with þe Princes dochter, and maid
hir with childe. The Prince of Walis, fynding his dochter foulʒeitt, slew Fleance, and held his dochter, becaus scho consentit to his pleseir, in maist schamfull
seruitude. At last scho wes deliuer of ane son, namyt
Walter, quhilk grew finalie, quhill he was of xx ʒeris,

Texts

36A W. HARRISON: "THE HISTORIE OF SCOTLAND" (1587)

(B1–15) *Shortlie after,* he began to shew what he was, in stead of equitie practising *crueltie.* For the pricke of conscience (*as it chanceth euer in tyrants, and such as atteine to anie estate by vnrighteous means*) caused him euer to feare, least he should be serued of the same cup, as he had ministred to his predecessor. *The woords also of the three weird sisters, would not out of his mind,* which as they promised him the kingdome, so likewise did they promise it at the same time vnto *the posteritie of Banquho. He willed therefore the same Banquho with his sonne named Fleance, to come to a supper* that he had prepared for them, which was in déed, as he had deuised, present death at the hands of certeine murderers, whom he hired to execute that déed, appointing them to meete with the same Banquho and his sonne without the palace, *as they returned to their lodgings, and there to slea them,* so that he would not haue his house slandered, but that in time to come he might cleare himselfe, if anie thing were laid to his charge vpon anie suspicion that might arise.

It chanced yet *by the benefit of the darke night,* that though the father were slaine, the sonnet yet *by the helpe of almightie God reseruing him to better fortune, escaped* that danger: and afterwards hauing some inkeling (by the admonition of some friends which he had in the court) how his life was sought no lesse than his fathers, who was slain not by chance medlie (as by the handling of the matter Makbeth would haue had it to appeare) but euen vpon a prepensed deuise: wherevpon to auoid further perill he *fled into Wales...*

(B16–34) Fleance therefore (as before said) fled into Wales, where shortlie after by his courteous and amiable behauiour, he grew into such fauor and estimation with the prince of that countrie, that he might vnneath haue wished anie greater; at length also *he came into such familiar acquaintance with the said princes daughter,* that she of courtesie in the end *suffered him to get hir with child;* which being once vnderstood, hir father the prince conceiued such hatefull displeasure towards Fleance, that he finallie *slue him, & held his daughter in most vile estate of seruitude, for that she had consented* to be on this wise *defloured* by a stranger. *At the last yet, she was*

335

richt lusty, of gretar curage and spreitt þan ony man
þat wes nurist in landwert, as he wes. And þocht he was
haldin with þe Prince of Walis, his gudeserr, in law
estaitt, 3ite he had ane hye mynde, and abill to na thing
mair þan to attempt grete chargis. It happynnit at last
þat he fell at contencioun with his compan3eoun, quhilk
obieckit to him that he was nocht gottin of lauchfull bed
and for þat cauß he wes sa impacient þat he slew his com-
pan3eon, and syne fled in Scotlannd to seyk support of
his freyndis ...

Na thing succedit happelie to Makbeth eftir þe slauchter of Banquho, for ilk man eftir his slauchter began to
haif fere of þair lyfe, and durst nocht compere quhair
he wes, throw quhilk followit ilk daye mor displeseir.
For quhen þis tiran persauit all men havand him in dreid,
he began to dreid all men in þe samyn maner, and be that
way grew maist odius to his subdittis, slaying his nobillis be vane causis for breking of his new lawis, or
ellis eschaieting þair gudis. And quhen he had gottin
grete proffitte be slauchter & proscripcioun of his nobillis, he began to put his handis mair pertlie in þair
blude, becaus þe proffitt þairof apperitt ilk day moir
sweit. For euery man quhom he mystraistit war slayn be
this waye, and þair gudis spendit on ane strang gard to
keip him fra iniuris of þame quhilkis had him in hattrent.
Forthar, þat he mycht invaid þe pepill with mair tyranny,
he biggitt ane strang castell in þe hicht of Donsynnane,
ane hill in Gowry, x mylis fra Perth ...

On þe samyn maner Makbeth, evir in fere of inymys
for his tresonabill murdir, come haistlie with ane grete
power about Makduffis houß, and þai quhilkis war within
þe houß, traisting na evill, randrit þe samyn sone eftir
his cuming. Howbeit, he left na thing of his cruelte, bot
slew baith Makduffis wyfe and his barnis with all vtheris
personis quhom he fand in þat castell, incontinent con-
fiscatt Makduffis gudis, and put him to þe horne.

Makduff, banyst in þis maner, fled in Ingland to
Macolme Canmoir, to se gif he mycht fynd ony waye at his
hand to revenge þe slauchter maid sa cruelly on his wyiff
and bayrnis, and declarit finalie to Malcolme þe grete
oppressioun done to him be Makbeth, and schew als how
þe said tiran wes richt odius to all his pepill for þe
slauchter of his nobillis & commonis and vþeris sindry

deliuered of a sonne named Walter, who within few yeares   *T36A*
prooued a man *of greater courage and valiancie, than anie*
other had commonlie béene found, although he had no better
bringing vp than (by *his grandfathers* appointment) *among*   *45*
the baser sort of people. Howbeit he shewed euer euen from
his infancie, *that there reigned in him a certaine stout-*
nesse of stomach, readie to attempt high enterprises.

   It chanced that falling out with one of his companions,
after manie tawnting words which passed betwixt them,   *50*
the other to his reproch obiected that he was a bastard,
and begotten in vnlawfull bed; wherewith being sore kind-
led, in his raging furie he ran vpon him and *slue him* out
of hand. *Then* was he glad to *flée* out of Wales, and comming
into Scotland to séeke some friendship there, he happen-   *55*
ed into the companie of such Englishmen,...

   (B35–52)   *after the* contriued *slaughter of Banquho,*
nothing prospered with the foresaid Makbeth: for in maner
euerie man began to doubt his owne life, and durst vnneth
appeare in the kings presence; and euen as there were   *60*
manie that *stood in feare of him,* so likewise stood he in
feare of manie, in such sort that he began *to make those*
awaie by one surmized cauillation or other, whome he thought
most able to worke him anie displeasure.

   At length *he found such swéetnesse* by putting his no-   *65*
bles thus to death, that his earnest thirst after bloud
in this behalfe might in no wise be satisfied: for ye must
consider he wan double profit (as hée thought) hereby: for
first they were rid out of the way whome he feared, and
then againe *his coffers were inriched by their goods which*   *70*
were forfeited to his vse, whereby his might better main-
teine *a gard of armed men* about him *to defend his person*
from iniurie of them whom he had in anie suspicion. Further,
to the end he might the more cruellie oppresse his subiects
with all tyrantlike wrongs, he builded a strong castell   *75*
on the top of an hie hill called Dunsinane, situate in
Gowrie, ten miles from Perth...

   (B53–69)   Immediatelie then, being aduertised whereabout
Makduffe went, he *came hastily with a great power* into Fife,
and foorthwith besieged the castell where Makduffe dwelled,   *80*
trusting to haue found him therein. *They that kept the*
house, without anie resistance opened the gates, and suf-
fered him to enter, mistrusting none euill. But neuerthe-

cruelteis nocht wourthy to be rehersitt. And quhen he saw
Malcolme siche for compassioun of his sorrowis, he sayid:
'How lang sall þou suffer þe murdir of þi fader and vther
freyndis to be vnpuneist? Quhen sall þou be saciatt with
þe afflicccioun of þi realme, quhilk, beand opprest, mycht
nocht defend þe? ...

Sone aftir Makduff send lettrez to þe nobillis of Scotland, schawin þe conspiracioun maid aganis þe tiran
Makbeth, praying þame, sen Macolme was iust heritour to
þe croun, to assist to him, þat he may recovir þe samyn.
In þe mene tyme Macolme purchest þe Erle of Northumberland
to cum with x^m men to help him to recovir his realme.
Thir tythingis cumin in Scotland drew þe nobillis in
twa sindry faccionis, of þe quhilk þe tane assistit to
Makbeth and this wther to Macolme, throu quhilk rayß
oftymes frequent skarmising betuix þir partis, for þe
nobillis quhilkis war of Malcolmez opinioun wald nocht
ioparde þame to chance of batale quhill his cumin out
of Yngland to þair support. Makbeth, seyng at last his
inemyß incres ilk daye with mayr pyssance and his freyndis
grow leß, fled in Fife, and abaid with þe freyndis quhilkis war of his opinioun at Donsynnane, with purpoß to
fecht with his inemyß erar þan to fle out of þe realme
schamefullie but ony straik. His freyndis gaiff counsale
othir to tak peace with Macolme, or ellis to fle haistelie
with his tresour and gold in þe Ilis, quhair he mycht fee
sindry gret capitanis and cum agane with new army aganis
Macolme. Nochtþeles, he had sik confidence in his fretis
þat he belewit fermlie neuer to be wincust quhill þe
Wode of Binan war brocht to Donsynnan, nor ȝit to be
slane with ony man borne of ane woman.

Macolme, folloving haistlie on Makbeth, come þe nycht
afoir his wictorie to þe Wod of Birnane; and quhen his
army had refreschit þame ane schort tyme, he commandit
ilk man to tak ane branche of þe wod, and cum þe nixt
morow arrayt in þat samyn maner in þair inemys sicht.
Makbeth, seyng him cum in þis gyse, wnderstude þe prophecy was completit þat þe wiche schew to him, nochtþeles arrayt his men. Skarslie had his inymyß cassin fra
þame þe branschis and cumand forthwert in batal, quhen
Makbeth tuke þe flycht, on quhome follovit Makduff
with gret haitrent, sayng: 'Tratour, now þi insaciabill
crewelte sall haue ane end!' Þan sayd Makbeth: 'Þou fol-

lesse Makbeth most cruellie *caused the wife and children*   T36A
of Makduffe, with all other whom he found in that castell,
to be slaine. Also he confiscated the goods of Makduffe,
proclamed him traitor, and confined him out of all the
parts of his realme; but Makduffe was alreadie escaped out
of danger, and *gotten into England vnto Malcome Cammore,*
to trie what purchase hée might make by means of his sup-   90
port, *to reuenge the slaughter so cruellie executed on his*
wife, his children, and other friends. At his comming vnto
Malcolme, *he declared* into what *great miserie* the estate
of Scotland was brought, by the detestable cruelties exercised by the tyrant Makbeth, hauing committed *manie*   95
horrible slaughters and murders, both as well of the nobles
as commons, for the which *he was hated right mortallie of*
all his liege people desiring nothing more than to be deliuered of that intollerable and most heauie yoke of thral-
dome, which they susteined at such a caitifs hands.   100
   Malcolme hearing Makduffes woords, which he vttered
in verie lamentable sort, *for méere compassion* and verie
ruth that pearsed his sorowfull hart, bewailing the miserable state of his countrie, *he fetched a deepe sigh...*

   (B74–98) *Soone after,* Makduffe repairing to the borders   105
of Scotland, *addressed his letters* with secret dispatch
vnto the nobles of the realme, declaring how Malcolme was
confederat with him, to come hastilie into Scotland to
claime the crowne, and therefore *he required them, sith*
he was right inheritor thereto, to assist him with their   110
powers *to recouer the same* out of the hands of the wrongful usurper. In the meane time, Malcolme purchased such
fauor at king Edwards hands, that old Siward earle of
Northumberland was appointed with ten thousand men to
go with him into Scotland, to support him in this enter-   115
prise, for recouerie of his right. *After these newes were*
spread abroad in Scotland, the nobles drew into seuerall
factions, the one taking part with Makbeth, and the other
with Malcolme. Héerevpon insued oftentimes sundrie bicker-
ings, & diuerse light skirmishes: for those that were   120
of Malcolmes side, would not ieopard to ioine with their
enimies in a pight field, *till his comming out of England*
to their support. But after that Makbeth perceiued his
enimies power to increase, by such aid as came to them
foorth of England with his aduersarie Malcolme, he *recoiled*   125

lowis me in wayne, for nane þat is borne of ane wife may
slay me.' Þan said Makduff: 'I am þe samyn man, for I was
schorne out of my moderis wayme'; incontinent schure of
his heid, and brocht þe samyn on ane staik to Macolme.
This was þe end of Makbeth in þe xvij ȝeir of his regne,
quhilk in the begynnyng of his empire did mony proffi-
tabill thingis for þe commoune wele, and sone aftir be
illusioun off dewillis wes degeneratt fra his honest
begynnyng in maist terribill crewelte, and slane fra þe
Incarnacioun j^m lxj, quhilk was in þe xvj ȝeir of þe
proscripcioun of Malcolme.

backe into Fife, there purposing to *abide* in campe forti-
fied, at the castell of Dunsinane, and to fight with his
enimies, if they ment to pursue him; howbeit *some of his*
friends aduised him, that it should be best for him,
either to make some agréement with Malcolme, or else to
flée with all spéed into the Iles, and to take his trea-
sure with him, to the end *he might wage sundrie great*
princes of the realme to take his part, & reteine strangers,
in whome he might better trust than in his owne subiects,
which stale dailie from him: *But he had such confidence*
in his prophesies, that he beléeued he should neuer be
vanquished, till Birnane wood were brought to Dunsinane;
nor yet to be slaine with anie man, that should be or
was borne of anie woman.

(B99–121) *Malcolme following hastilie after Makbeth,*
came the night before the battle *vnto Birnane wood, and*
when his armie had rested a while there to refresh them,
he commanded euerie man to get a bough of some trée or
other of that wood in his hand, as big as he might beare,
and to march foorth therewith in such wise, that *on the*
next morrow they might come closelie and without sight
in this manner within view of his enimies. On the morrow
when *Makbeth beheld them comming in this sort*, he first
maruelled what the matter ment, but in the end *remembred*
himselfe that the prophesie which he had heard long before
that time, of the comming of Birnane wood to Dunsinane
castell, was likelie to *be now fulfilled. Neuerthelesse,*
he brought his men in order of battell, and exhorted them
to doo valiantlie, howbeit *his enimies had scarselie cast*
from them their boughs, when Makbeth perceiuing their

T36

115

120

T36A

130

135

140

145

150

155

numbers, *betooke him* streict *to flight, whom Makduffe*
pursued with great hatred euen till he came vnto Lunfan-
naine, where Makbeth perceiuing that Makduffe was hard at
his back, leapt beside his horsse, *saieng: 'Thou traitor,*
... *now shall thine insatiable crueltie haue an end, for*   160
I am euen he that thy wizzards haue told thée of, who was
neuer borne of my mother, but *ripped out of her wombe;'*
therewithall he stept vnto him, and slue him in the place.
Then *cutting his head from his shoulders, he set it vpon*
a pole, and brought it vnto Malcolme. This was the end   165
of Makbeth, after he had reigned 17 yeeres ouer the Scot-
ishmen. *In the beginning of his reigne he accomplished*
manie woorthie acts, verie profitable to the common-wealth
(as he haue heard) *but afterward by illusion of the diuell,*
he defamed the same with most terrible crueltie. He was   170
slaine in the yéere of the incarnation, 1057, and in the
16 yeere of king Edwards reigne ouer the Englishmen.

37A HENRY VIII: PROCLAMATION (1530)

Mense Junii, Anno regni metuendissimi domini nostri regis
Henrici octaui. xxii.
   A proclamation made and diuysed by the kyngis highnes,
with the aduise of his honorable counsaile, for dampning
of erronious bokes and heresies, and prohibitinge the   5
hauinge of holy scripture, translated into the vulgar
tonges of englisshe, frenche, or duche, in suche maner,
as within this proclamation is expressed.
   The kinge out most dradde soueraigne lorde, studienge
and prouidynge dayly for the weale, benefite, and honour   10
of this most noble realme, well and euidently perceiueth,
that partly through the malicious suggestion of our gostly enemy, partly by the yuell and peruerse inclination
and sedicious disposition of sundry persons, diuers heresies and erronious opinions haue ben late sowen and   15
spredde amonge his subiectes of this said realme, by
blasphemous and pestiferous englisshe bokes, printed in
other regions, and sent in to this realme, to the entent
as well to peruerte and withdrawe the people from the
catholike and true fayth of Christe, as also to stirre   20
and incense them to sedition, and disobedience agaynst
their princes, soueraignes, and heedes, as also to cause
them to contempne and neglect all good lawes, customes,

and vertuous maners, to the final subuersion and desolation of this noble realme, if they myght haue preuayled
(whiche god forbyd) in theyr most cursed persuasions and   25
malicious purposes. Where vpon the kynges hignes, by his
incomparable wysedome, forseinge and most prudently
considerynge, hath inuited and called to hym the primates
of this his gracis realme, and also a sufficient nombre   30
of discrete vertuous and well lerned personages in diui-
nite, as well of either of the vniuersites, Oxforde and
Cambrige, as also hath chosen and taken out of other
parties of his realme: gyuinge vnto them libertie, to
speke and declare playnly their aduises, iudgementes,   35
and determinations, concernynge as well the approbation
or reiectynge of suche bokes as be in any parte suspected,
as also the admission and diuulgation of the olde and
newe testament translated in to englisshe. Wher vpon
his highnes, in his owne royall person, callynge to hym   40
the said primates and diuines, hath seriously and depely,
with great leisure and longe deliberation, consulted, de-
bated, inserched, and discussed the premisses: and finally, by all their free assentes, consentes, and agrementes,
concluded, resolued, and determined, that these bokes   45
ensuynge, That is to say, the boke entitled the wicked
Mammona, the boke named the Obedience of a Christen man,
the Supplication of beggars, and the boke called the
Reuelation of Antichrist, the Summary of scripture, and
diuers other bokes made in the englysshe tonge, and im-   50
printed beyonde the see, do conteyne in them pestiferous
errours and blasphemies: and for that cause, shall from
hensforth be reputed and taken of all men, for bokes of
heresie, and worthy to be dampned, and put in perpetuall
obliuion. The kynges said highnes therfore straitly charg-   55
eth and commaundeth, all and euery his subiectes, of what
astate or condition so euer he or they be, as they wyll
auoyde his high indignacion and most greuous displeasure,
that they from hensforth, do not bye, receyue, or haue,
any of the bokes before named ..., that he or they, with-   60
in fyftene dayes next after the publisshynge of this
present proclamation, do actually delyuer or sende the
same bokes and euery of them, to the bisshop of the dio-
cese, wherin he or they dwelleth, or to his commissary,
or els before good testimonie, to theyr curate or par-   65
isshe preest, to be presented by the same curate or par-

isshe preest, to the sayd bisshop or his commissary.
And so doynge, his highnes frely pardoneth and acquiteth
them, and euery of them, of all penalties, forfaitures,
and paynes, wherin they haue incurred or fallen, by
reason of any statute, acte, ordinaunce, or proclamation
before this tyme made, concernynge any offence or trans-
gression by them commytted or done, by or for the kepynge
or holdynge of the sayde bokes.

70

37B EDWARD VI: PROCLAMATION (1547)

The xxiiij daie of Maie. A Proclamation, concernyng tale
tellers.

For so muche as the kynges highnes, the lord protector,
and the residue of the Kynges Maiesties counsaill is en-
formed, that there hath been nowe of late, diuerse leude
and light tales told, whispered, and secretly spred
abrode, by vncertain aucthors, in Markettes, Faires, and
Alehouses, in diuerse and sondry places of this realme,
of innouacions and chaunges in religion and ceremonies
of the Churche feined to be doen and appoyncted by the
Kynges highnes, the Lorde Protector, and other of his
highnes priuey Counsaill, whiche, by his grace or theim,
was neuer begon nor attempted, and also of other thynges
and factes, soundyng to the dishonor and slaunder of the
kynges moste royall maiestie, the Lorde Protectors grace,
and other the kynges moste honorable Counsaill, and no
lesse to the disquietnesse and disturbaunce of the kynges
highnes louing subiectes, contrary to diuerse wholsome
lawes and ordinaunces, vpon graue and weightie considerations, heretofore made and ordeined by the kynges highnes moste noble progenitours, to reforme, punishe and
chastice, al maner of leude and vagaraunt persones,
tellyng and reportyng false newes and tales to the dis-
quietyng and disturbyng of the Kynges highnes, his
nobles and subiectes, of this Realme. The Kynges moste
royall Maiestie, by the moste circumspect and laudable
aduise, of his moste derely beloued vncle, Edward Duke
of Somerset, Lorde Protector of the Kynges maiesties
realmes, dominions and subiectes, & gouernour of his
moste royall persone, and other of his highnes priuey
counsaill, consideryng and graciously ponderyng, the

5

10

15

20

25

30

great hurt, damage, losse and disquietnes, emonges his
graces subiectes, which might ensue of suche false and
slaunderous tales and newes, and that nothyng is more
necessary, then to prouide and se, that good and wholsome   *35*
lawes be put in vre and full execucion, to the intent no
maner of person, maie, or shall haue iustly any occasion
to surmise, inuent, or disperse, any kynde of false tales
or newes, to the discorde or disturbaunce of the subiectes of this realme: streightly chargeth and commaund-   *40*
eth, al maner of officers, ministers and iustices, that
the saied former lawes and statutes, be earnestly put
in execucion, that is to saie, that no maner or persone
from hencefurthe, be so hardie to finde, saie, or tell
any false newes, messages, or other suche false thynges,   *45*
whereof discord, or any slander, might arise within this
realme, betwene the kyng, his people, or the nobles,
and that he that so doeth, shalbe kept in prisone. vntill he haue brought in him, which was the aucthor of
the tale...   *50*

38 ELIZABETH I: PROCLAMATION (1559)

❧ By the Queene.

Orasmuche as the tyme wherein common Interludes in the Englishe tongue are wont vsually to be played, is now past vntyll AllHallontyde, and that also some that haue ben of late vsed, are not conuenient in any good ordzed Christian Common weale to be suffred. The Quenes Maiestie doth straightly forbyd al maner Interludes to be playde eyther openly oz priuately, except the same be notified befoze hande, and licenced within any Citie oz towne corpozate, by the Maioz oz other chiefe officers of the same, and within any shyze, by suche as shalbe Lieuetenaunts foz the Queenes Maiestie in the same shyze, oz by two of the Iustices of peax inhabytting within that part of the shire where any shalbe played.

AND foz instruction to euery of the sayde officers, her maiestie doth likewise charge euery of them as they will aunswere: that they permyt none to be played wherin either matters of religion oz of the gouernaunce of the estate of the commõ weale shalbe handled oz treated, beyng no meete matters to be wzytten oz treated vpon, but by menne of aucthozitie, learning and wisedome, noz to be handled befoze any audience, but of graue and discreete persons: All which partes of this proclamation, her maiestie chargeth to be inuiolably kepte. And if any shal attempte to the contrary: her Maiestie giueth all maner of officers that haue authozitie to see common peax kepte in commandement, to arrest and enpzison the parties so offending foz the space of fourteene dayes oz moze, as cause shall nede: And surder also vntill good assuraunce may be founde and gyuen, that they shalbe of good behauiour, and no moze to offende in the like.

AND further her Maiestie gyueth speciall charge to her nobilitie and gentilmen, as they professe to obey and regarde her maiestie, to take good ozder in thys behalfe wyth their seruauntes being players, that this her Maiesties commaundement may be dulye kepte and obeyed.

Yeuen at our Palayce of Westminster the xvi. daye of Maye, the first yeare of oure Raygne.

Imprinted at London in Powles Churchyarde, by *Richard Iugge* and *Iohn Cawood* Printers to the Quenes Maiestie.

Cum priuilegio Regiæ Maiestatis.

39 H. LATIMER: THE SERMON ON THE PLOUGHERS (1549)

Amende therfore and ye that be prelates loke well to your
office, for right prelatynge is busye labourynge and not
lordyng. Therfore preache and teach and let your ploughe
be doynge, ye lordes I saye that liue lyke loyterers, loke
well to your office, the ploughe is your office and charge. 5
If you lyue idle and loyter, you do not your duetie, you
folowe not youre vocation, let your plough therfore be
going and not cease, that the ground maye brynge foorth
fruite. But nowe me thynketh I heare one saye vnto me,
wotte you what you say? Is it a worcke? Is it a labour? 10
how then hath it happened yat we haue had so manye hundred yeares so many vnpreachinge prelates, lording loyterers and idle ministers? Ye would haue me here to make
answere and to showe the cause thereof. Nay thys land is
not for me to ploughe, it is to stonye, to thorni, to 15
harde for me to plough. They haue so many thynges yat
make for them, so many things to laye for them selues
that it is not for my weake teame to plough them. They
haue to lay for them selues customes Cerimonyes, and
authoritie, plaeyng in parliamente and many thynges more. 20
And I feare me thys lande is not yet rype to be ploughed.
For as the saying is, it lacketh wethering this greare
lacketh wetheringe at leaste way it is not for me to
ploughe. For what shall I loke for amonge thornes but
prickyng and scrachinge? what among stones but stumblyng? 25
What (I had almost sayed) among serpenttes but stingyng?
But this muche I dare say, that sence lording and loytry-
ing hath come vp, preaching hath come downe contrarie to
the Apostells times. For they preached and lorded not.
And nowe they lorde and preache not. 30
   For they that be lordes wyll yll go to plough. It is
no mete office for them. It is not semyng for their state.
Thus came vp lordyng loyterers. Thus crept in vnprech-
inge prelates, and so haue they longe continued.
   For howe many vnlearned prelates haue we now at this 35
day? And no meruel. For if ye plough men yat now be, were
made lordes they wolde leaue of theyr labour and fall to
lordyng outright, and let the plough stand. And then bothe
ploughes not walkyng nothyng shoulde be in the common
weale but honger. For euer sence the Prelates were made 40

Loordes and nobles, the ploughe standeth, there is no
worke done, the people sterue.

Thei hauke, thei hunt, thei card, they dyce, they pas-
tyme in theyr prelacies with galaunte gentlemen, with
theyr daunsinge minyons, and with theyr freshe companions, so that ploughinge is set a syde. And by the lord-
inge and loytryng, preachynge and ploughinge is cleane
gone. And thus if the ploughemen of the countrey, were as
negligente in theyr office, as prelates be, we shoulde
not longe lyue for lacke of sustinaunce. And as it is
necessarie for to haue thys ploughinge for the sustenta-
cion of the bodye: so muste we haue also the other for
the satisfaction of the soule, or elles we canne not lyue
longe gostly. For as the bodie wasteth & consumeth
awaye for lacke of bodily meate: so doeth the soule
pyne away for default of gostly meate.

40 H. MACHYN: DIARY (1557)

The vij day of Junj was a proclamassyon in london by y^e
quen grace, of ye latt duke of Northumberland was sup-
portyd & furdered by Henry ye Frenche kyng and ys
menysters, & by ye heddes of dudley, asheton, and by
ye consperacy of Wyatt & ys trayturs band & ye sayd
kynges mynysters dyd secretly practysse and gyff &
they favorabull w^t trumpeters blohyng, & a x harroldes
of armes, & w^t my lord mayre & ye althermen; & by y^e
lat stafford & w^t odur rebelles whom he had interteynyd
in ys rayme, & dyver odur mo ye wyche be ther yett
on taken...

The viij of Junj cam a goodly prossessyon vnto
powlles & dyd oblassyon at ye he auter sant clementes
parryche w^t out tempyll bare, with iiij^{xx} baners &
stremars & ye whettes of ye cete playing and a iij^{xx}
copes and prest & clarkes, and dyuer of the ennes
of ye cowrt whent next ye prestes: & then cam y^e
parryche w^t whytt rodes in ther handes and so bake
agayne w^t the whettes playng, & prestes & clarkes
syngyng home warde.

The x day of June ye kyng & ye quen toke ther jor-
ney toward hamtun cowrte for to hunt & to kyll a grett
hartt w^t serten of ye consell & so ye howsswold tared

at ye whytt hall tyll ye saterday ffolowhyng they came
a gayne to whytthall.

The xvj day of Junij my yong duke of Norffoke rod
abrod & at stamfford hyll my lord havyng a dage hangyng
on ys sadyll bow & by mysse ffortune dyd shutt yt & yt
on of ys men y^t ryd a for & so by mysse fforten ys
horsse dyd fflyng, & so he hangyd by on of ys sterope
& so thatt ye horsse knokyd ys brayns owtt w^t fflyngyng
owtt w^t ys leges...

The xviij day of Junj was ij cared to be bornyd beyonde sant gorgeus almust at Nuwhyngtun ffor herese &
odur matters.

The xix day of June was bered in ye parryche of sant
benett sheyroge old masters Hall, the mother of master
Edward Hall, of Gray in, ye wyche he sett fforthe the
cronnacle the wyche hes callyd master Hall cronnacull
& she dyd giue sserten good gownes boyth for men and
vomen a xx & ij ffeyre whytt branchys and x stayffes
torches & master Garrett & my lade behyng secturs &
my lade War... & master mosscar and ys wyff and dyuer
odur had blake gownes.

41 R. LANEHAM: A LETTER (1575)

Me thought it my part sumwhat to empart vnto yoo, hoow
it iz héer with me, & hoow I lead my life, which in
déed iz this.

A mornings I rize ordinarily at seauen a clok: Then
reddy, I go intoo the Chappell: soon after eyght, I get
me commonly intoo my Lords Chamber, or intoo my Lords
prezidents. Thear at the cupboord after I haue eaten y^e
manchet, serued ouer night for liuery (for I dare be az
bolld, I promis yoo, az any of my freends the seruaunts
thear: and indéed coold I haue fresh if I woold tary,
but I am of woont iolly & dry a mornings) I drink me vp
a good bol of Ale: when in a swéet pot it iz defecated
by al nights standing, the drink iz ye better, take that
of me: & a morsell in a morning with a sound draught iz
very holsome and good for the eysight. Then I am az
fresh all ye forenoon after, az had I eaten a hole pées
of béef. Noow syr, if the Councell sit, I am at hand,
wait at an inch I warrant yoo If any make babling, peas
(say I) wot ye whear ye ar? if I take a lystenar, or a

25

30

35

40

5

10

15

348

priar in at the chinks or at ye lokhole, I am by & by   20
in the bones of him, but now they kéep good order, they
know me well inough: If a be a fréend or such one az I
lyke: I make him sit dooun by me on a foorm, or a rheast,
let the rest walk a Gods name.

   And héer doth my langagez now and than stond me in   25
good sted, my French, my Spanish, my Dutch, & my Latten:
sumtime amoong Ambassadours men, if their Master be within with the Councel, sumtime with the Ambassadour himself,
if hee bid call hiz lacky, or ask whats a clok, and I
warrant ye I aunswer him roundly that they maruell to see   30
such a fello thear: then laugh I & say nothing. Dinner &
supper I haue twenty placez to go to, & hartly prayd to:
And sumtime get I too Master Pinner by my faith a worshipfull Gentlman, and az carefull for his charge az any hir
highnez hath: thear find I alway good store of very good   35
viaunds we eat and bee merry thank God & the Quéene. Himself in féeding very temperat & moderat az ye shall sée
ony: and yet by your leaue of a dish, az a colld pigeon
or so, that hath cum to him at meat more than he lookt
for, I haue seen him éen so by and by surfit, az he hath   40
pluct of hiz napkin, wyept his knife, & eat not a morsell
more: lyke ynoough to stik in hiz stomake a too dayz after..

   But alwayez among the Gentlwemen by my good will (O,
yee kno that cum alweyez of a gentle spirite) & when I
sée cumpany according than can I be az lyuely to, sum-   45
tyme I foote it with daunsing: noow with my Gittern, and
els with my Cittern, then at the Virginalz: ye kno nothing
cums amisse with mee: then carroll I vp a song withall:
that by and by they com flocking about me lyke béez too
hunny: and euer they cry, anoother good Langham anoother.   50
Shall I tell yoo? when I sée Misterz – (A, sée a madde
knaue, I had almost tollde all) that gyue shee onz but an
ey or an ear: why then, man, am I best, my grace, my courage, my cunning iz doobled: ...

   Héerwith ment I fully to bid ye farewell, had not   55
this doubt cum to my minde, that heer remainz a doout in
yoo, which I ought (me thought) in any wyze to cléer.
Which, iz, ye maruel perchauns to sée me so bookish. Let
me tell yoo in, few woords: I went to scool forsooth both
at Pollez, & allso at saint Antoniez: in the fifth   60
foorm, past Esop fabls iwys, red Terens. *Vos istæc intro
auferte*, & began with my Virgill *Tytire tu patulæ*. I coold

conster & pars with the best of them syns, that (az partly
ye kno) haue I traded the feat of marchaundize in sundry
Cuntreyz, & so gat me Langagez: which do so littl hinder   *65*
my Latten, az (I thank God) haue mooch encreast it. I haue
leizure sumtime, when I tend not vpon the coounsell: whear-
by, now Look I on one booke, noow on an other. Stories I
delight in, the more auncient & rare, the more likesum
vntoo me: If I tolld ye, I lyked William of Malmesbery   *70*
so well, bicauz of hiz diligenz & antiquitée...

42 ELIZABETH I AND JAMES VI: CORRESPONDENCE (1586–8)

(Elizabeth to James, c. 1 Feb., 1586–7)
Be not caried away, my deare brother, with the lewd per-
swations of suche, as insteade of infowrming you of my
to nideful and helpeles cause of defending the brethe
that God hath given me, to be better spent than spilt by
the bloudy invention of traitors handz, may perhaps make   *5*
you belive, that ether the offense was not so great, or
if that cannot serue them, for the over-manifest triall
wiche in publik and by the greatest and most in this land
hathe bine manifestly proved, yet the wyl make that her
life may be saved and myne safe, wiche wold God wer true,   *10*
for whan you make vewe of my long danger indured thes
fowre – wel ny fiue – moneths time to make a tast of, the
greatest witz amongs my owne, and than of French, and
last of you, wyl graunt with me, that if nide wer not mor
than my malice she shuld not have her merite.   *15*
   And now for a good conclusion of my long-taried-for
answer. Your commissionars telz me, that I may trust her
in the hande of some indifferent prince, and have all her
cousins and allies promis she wil no more seake my ruine.
Deare brother and cousin, way in true and equal balance   *20*
wither the lak not muche good ground when suche stuf
serves for ther bilding. Suppose you I am so mad to
truste my life in anothers hand and send hit out of my
owne? If the young master of Gray, for curring faueur
with you, might fortune say hit, yet old master Mylvin   *25*
hath yeres ynough to teache him more wisdome than tel a
prince of any jugement suche a contrarious frivolous
maimed reason. Let your councelors, for your honour, dis-
charge ther duty so muche to you as to declaire the absur-

ditie of such an offer; and, for my part, I do assure   *30*
myselfe to muche of your wisdome, as, thogh like a most
naturall good son you charged them to seake all meanes
the could deuis with wit or jugement to save her life,
yet I can not, nor do not, allege my fault to you of thes
persuations, for I take hit that you wil remember,   *35*
that advis or desiars aught ever agree with the surtye
of the party sent to and honor of the sendar, wiche whan
bothe you way, I doute not but your wisdome wil excuse my
nide, and waite my necessitie, and not accuse me ether of
malice or hate.   *40*
    And now to conclude. Make account, I pray you, of my
firme frindeship loue and care, of which you may make sure
accownt, as one that never mindz to faile from my worde,
nor swarve from our league, but wyl increase, by all good
meanes, any action that may make true shewe of my stable   *45*
amitie; from wiche, my deare brother, let no sinistar
whisperars, nor busy troblars of princis states, persuade
to leave your surest, and stike to vnstable staies. Suppose them to be but the ecchos to suche whos stipendaries
the be, and wyl do more for ther gaine than your good.   *50*
And so, God hold you ever in his blessed kiping, and make
you see your tru frinds. Excuse my not writing sonar, for
paine in one of my yees was only the cause.
    Your most assured lovinge sistar and cousin ELIZABETH R.

(James to Elizabeth, March 1586–7)
Madame and dearest sister, Quhairas by your lettir and   *55*
bearare, Robert Carey youre seruand and ambassadoure, ye
purge youre self of yone unhappy fact. As, on the one
pairt, consideddring your rank and sex, consanguinitie and
longe professed good will to the defunct, together with
youre many and solemne attestationis of youre innocentie,   *60*
I darr not wronge you so farre as not to iudge honorablie
of youre unspotted pairt thairin, so, on the other syde,
I uishe that youre honorable behauioure in all tymes heir-
after may fully persuaide the quhole uorlde of the same.
And, as for my pairt, I looke that ye will geue me at   *65*
this tyme suche a full satisfaction, in all respectis,
as sall be a meane to strenthin and unite this yle, establish and maintaine the treu religion, and obleig me to
be, as of befoire I war, youre most louing. .

This bearare hath sumquhat to informe you of in my name,   *70*
quhom I neid not desyre you to credit, for ye knou I loue
him.

(Elizabeth to James, August 1588)
Now may appeare, my deare brother, how malice conioined
with might strives to make a shameful end to a vilanous
beginning, for, by Godz singular fauor, having ther flete   *75*
wel-beaten in our narow seas, and pressing, with all violence, to atcheue some watering place, to continue ther
pretended invation, the windz have carried them to your
costes, wher I dout not the shal receaue smal succor and
les welcome; vnles thos lordz that, so traitors like,   *80*
wold belie ther owne prince, and promis another king re-
liefe in your name, be suffred to live at libertye, to
dishonor you, peril you, and aduance some other (wiche
God forbid you suffer them live to do). Therfor I send
you this gentilman, a rare younge man and a wise, to   *85*
declare vnto yov my ful opinion in this greate cause,
as one that neuer wyl abuse you to serve my owne turne;
nor wyl you do aught that myselfe wold not perfourme if
I wer in your place. You may assure yourselfe that, for
my part, I dout no whit but that all this tirannical   *90*
prowd and brainsick attempt wil be the beginning, thogh
not the end, of the ruine of that king, that, most unking-
ly, euen in midz of treating peace, begins this wrongful
war. He hathe procured my greatest glory that ment my
sorest wrack, and hathe so dimmed the light of his svn-   *95*
shine, that who hathe a wyl to obtaine shame let them kipe
his forses companye. But for al this, for yourselfe sake,
let not the frendz of Spain be suffred to yeld them forse;
for thogh I feare not in the end the sequele, yet if, by
leaving them unhelped, you may increase the Englisch   *100*
hartz unto you, you shal not do the worst dede for your
behalfe; for if aught shuld be done, your excuse wyl play
the *boiteux*; if you make not sure worke with the likely
men to do hit. Looke wel unto hit, I besiche you.
    The necessity of this matter makes my skribling the   *105*
more spidye, hoping that you wyl mesure my good affection
with the right balance of my actions, wiche to you shalbe
euer suche as I haue professed, not douting of the reci-
proque of your behalfe, according as my last messengier
unto you hathe at large signefied, for the wiche I ren-   *110*

dar you a million of grateful thankes togither, for the
last general prohibition to your subiectz not to fostar
nor ayde our general foe, of wiche I dout not the obseruation if the ringeleaders be safe in your handz; as
knoweth God, who euer haue you in his blessed kiping,   *115*
with many happy yeres of raigne.

    Your most assured louing sistar and cousin ELIZABETH R.
To my verey good brother the king of Scottz.

(James to Elizabeth, Sept. 1588)
Madame and dearest sister, The suddaine pairting of this
honorable gentleman, youre ambassadoure, upon thaise   *120*
unfortunatt and displeasant neuis of his onkle, hes mouit
me with the more haist to trace theis feu lynes unto you;
first, to thanke you, as uell for the sending so rare a
gentleman unto me, to quhose brother I was so farre be-
holden; as also, for the tayce sending me such summes   *125*
of money, quhiche, according to the league, I sall thank-
fullie repaye with forces of men, quhensoeuer youre
estait sall so requyre, according as my last letter hath
maid you certified; not doubting but, as ye haue honorable begunn, so ye uill follou foorth youre course to-   *130*
uardis me, quhiche thairby I shall so procure the con-
currence of all my goode subjectis with me in this course
as sall make my friendshippe the more steadable unto you.
The next is to pray you most hairtly, that in any thing
concerning this gentleman fallin out by the death of   *135*
his onkle, ye will haue a fauorable consideration of him
for my sayke, that he may not haue occasion to repent him
of his absence at suche a tyme. All other things I remitt
to his credite, praying you to thinke of me as of
one quho constantlie shall contineu his professed   *140*
course, and remaine,
    Youre most louing and affectionat brother and cousin,
                  JAMES R.
Postcrip. I thocht goode, in kaice of sinistre reportis,
madame, hereby to assure you that the Spanishe flete   *145*
neuer entered uithin any roade or heauen within my dominion, nor neuer came uithin a kenning neere to any of my
costis.

43 A. DAY: THE ENGLISH SECRETORIE (1586)

CAP. II: WHAT IS CHIEFLY TO BE RESPECTED IN FRAMING OF AN EPISTLE

For somuch as by the necessarye vse of letters before layd
downe, a commendable maner of writing & orderly framing
of the same, hath in some sort been already remembred:
it shal not be amisse in continuing the intended order
hereof, that in this chapter we do now more fully indeuour   5
to aunswere the purpose, therein supposed. For the better
manifestation of which, & to the intent the ignorant and
studious herein, may by degrees be led to the attaining
of that which vnto the matter therof may be approued most
conuenient: I haue first thought good to draw vnto your   10
consideration, certaine speciall points in this action
of all other principally to be regarded. It shall then
beseme that for such performance the better to enable him
whose forwardnes requireth the same, these three notes
in writing of all maner of Epistles be chiefly admitted.   15
First aptnes of wordes & sentences respecting that they
be neat and choisly piked, orderly laid downe & cunningly
handled, next breuity of speach according in matter &
dilation to be framed vpon whatsoeuer occurrent: lastly
comelines in deliuerance, concerning the person and cause,   20
whervpon is intended the direction to be framed. These
three, as they are seldome in our common vse of writinge,
amonge the ignorant at any time pursued, so vnto him that
desireth by skilfull obseruation and practize, to become
therin more wary and circumspect, are greatlye auaileable   25
to be vsed. And that we may the more conueniently distin-
guishe each part of these properties in sort as they are
to bee followed, we will first in the course of this
Chapiter examine and laye out the seuerall distinctions,
wherein this kinde of aptnes is principally to be con-   30
sidered.

As nothing therefore in the common vse and conuersation
of men deserueth more praise, then that which is well ordered, and according to the time place and presence vsually appointed and discreetly furnished: so in this matter   35
of writing Epistles, nothing is more disordered, fonde,
or vaine, then for anye one, of a thinge well done, to
take forth a president, and thinke to make vnto him selfe
thereof, a common platforme for euery other accident, who

without consideration of the grauity or lightnes of   *40*
the cause he taketh in hand (much like vnto a foolish
Shoemaker, that making his shoes after one fashion, quan-
titye and proportion: supposeth the same forthwith of
abilitie fitte to serue euery mans foot) includeth in
like sort a common methode vnto euery matter. Such imi-   *45*
tators who rather by rote then reason make hauocke of wit
with purchase of small discretion, by such vnnecessary
capitulations, beeing often times farre different from
their owne intended purposes, are better prepared to deliuer vnto viewe, the ridiculous Pike of *Horace* with an   *50*
Asses heade monstrouslye shaped, whereat the Readers may
laugh, and euery one may sport, then certainely to manifest their argument with such correspondent speaches as
thervnto may be deemed incident.

　To auoyd this so great and hard an imperfection, it   *55*
shall speciallye behoue him that endeuoureth well to write,
aduisedly with him selfe first to consider, the foremost
motion inducing argument to the cause whereof he is intended to debate, and beeing well studied and read in the
purest and best kind of writers, (wherof great plenty do   *60*
now remaine in our English tongue) seeke to frame his
inuention accordaunt to the example herein for that purpose (or to the like effect) before him deliuered, not in
the selfe same speaches, but in the selfe same order (the
intendment whereof was not otherwise layd downe, but   *65*
onelye to such an ende, and for the like obseruation)
which order beeing distinguished in the seuerall partes
of euery Epistle, shall conduct the follower, to what
ende, and vpon what occasion, each matter therein was in
that sort particularly framed.   *70*

　Next let him deliberate with him selfe, how much or
how greatlye importeth the matter he taketh in hande, to
whom he writeth the same, and what in the handling therof
it shall principally concerne, that according to the validitie or forceles conceit of the same, the matter of his   *75*
Epistle by aptnes of wordes may be measured and composed:
Hereon lyeth the chiefest waight & burthen of each mans
discretion, wherevnto oportunitye also seemeth a thing
so necessary to be adioyned, as laboring the one perfectly,
and attending the other circumspectly, I see no reason,   *80*
but he that can frame him selfe to the varietie of these,
may with greater facilitie reache vnto the reste, the bet-

ter to enhable him selfe hereafter if aduauncement draw
him to it to become a Secretorie.

And in asmuch as Letters are onely messengers of each   *85*
mans intendments, it shalbe as apt vnto euery one, as anye
aptnes of wordes in anye of them to bee deliuered, to take
notice of time and place, needfull to giue opportunity to
whatsoeuer in suche occasions by him continuallye to bee
handled, the necessarye consideration whereof, because   *90*
the same also somewhat hereunto importeth, I will in place
conuenient, where more at large the same may be required,
endeuour to enlarge it, pursuing in the meane tyme as in
this Chapter intended, the purposes therein to bee considered.   *95*

Now the matter and importance of your letter thus
deliberately aduised, the best forme and manner of deliu-
ery shal then next to the same be considered. Wherin it
appeareth that kinde of writing to haue bene deemed alwayes most excellent that in sentences is most exquisite,   *100*
in words of the best choyce, and the same most effectual,
which to the argument, place, time, and person, is
most meet and appertinent, which entreating of hye matters is weighty, in meaner causes neate and pliable, in
the lowest plesaunt and more familiar, in iesting that   *105*
procureth cause of delight, in praising commendable, in
stirring vehement and bold, in aduising gentle and frend-
ly, in perswasion sententious, and vsing grauitie, in nar-
ration playne and resolute, in requiring shamefast, in
commending officious, in prosperous causes glad, in   *110*
troubles serious and more sad. And finally, that attem-
parating vnto euery circumstance their sundry motions,
in such fashion and order as vnto the matter therof is
most consonant, can most fitly and redely deliuer the
same vpon whatsoeuer occasion to be ordered.   *115*

And herein is especially to be considered, that of what
validitie or inualiditie soeuer, the matter to be dis-
coursed or written of may appeare, and to whomesoeuer of
hye meane or low accompt the same shall passe or be directed, that the aptnes of speach be therein so deemed,   *120*
as ye choysest and best maner of speaking may to euery
of these occasions be admitted. For a weightie cause,
and common direction, may not all in one kinde of termes
be deliuered, neyther is it fit that in a letter framed
to one of good calling, a man should therein deale with   *125*

him in speeches: as when he directeth his seruaunt to
seeche a peece of saltfish, or dresse a messe of potage,
but such shalbe the stile as is the account of the partie
to whome it must goe, and the weight of the cause that is
to be handled, that is loftie when it is required, neate,
pliable, or more meane, if so it ought to be respected,   *130*
onely prouiding that whatsoeuer or to whome soeuer we
write, we alwayes giue our selues as neere as may be, to
the moste likely and best kinde of deliueraunce, auoyding
all nicenesse and farre fet fines to be vsed therein,
the matter hereof being but such, as if a man would by   *135*
orderly speache, eyther weightily, grauely, pleasantly,
or familiarly, discourse or commune of his affaires re-
spectiuely, touching the person & cause, and in no poynt
otherwise. This onely difference in letters as in all
other speaches, that eche man studie for his indeuour   *140*
to write commendably, as in speeche he gaineth moste
praise that speaketh most excellently.

AN EPISTLE MONITORIE TO A FATHER,
TOUCHING THE LEWD AND ILL DEMEANOR OF HIS SONNE

Exordium.   Though it seeme an approued follye to caste   *145*
pearles before swine, or to offer a golden saddle to an
Asses backe; yet (not that I thinke either the Sowe worthy
of the pearles, or the Asse fit for the saddle), I haue
written vnto you, the one reason to manifest vnto you,
the vile and bad parts of your sonne whereof you   *150*
will take no notice, and of which this letter heerein
closed shall beare sufficient testimony, the other for
charities sake, to admonish you which are his father,
to his benefit & timely looking to, to winde him from
that, which by small sufferance may breed your woes   *155*
and his irrecuperable destruction.

Propositio.   I haue vnderstoode that hauing beene found
heretofore in the like pilfering with two M. that he
serued, and the secreat information thereof being brought
to your eares, you misliked his courtesie that tolde you,   *160*
iustefied the matter to be false that was deliuered you,
and not so much as examining the action at all (which a
good father would haue done by all maner of industry) you
allowed your sonne for honest, and affirmed that it was
vnpossible he shoulde enter into any such theiuerie.   *165*

Distributio.   If I see the childe of such a father come
to an euill ende I will not maruaile at all, seeing that
besides the ordinary inclinations alreadye graffed in
his yong yeares, his parentes are content by winking at
it, to giue him furtheraunce, and in maner to affirme   *170*
that it shall so be, insomuch as thereby seemeth, the
sonne hath sworne he will neuer liue honestlye, and the
father hath promised that he will set him forward to
Tiburne for his vilany. Is it reason that men (of zeal
and conscience) should go about to pitty their misfor-   *175*
tunes, who haue protested neuer by compassion to preuent
in them selues, the iust and appropriate reward of their
own euils?

Dicæologia.   What shal I say to the vnhappy father of
such a sonne, or rather vnhappy childe of such a father,   *180*
whether shal I forwarne him or thee, the one purposing,
the other animating, to what vnto ech of you in the end
must become a particular desolation? Truly these things
wil not continue, they cannot long hold.

Finitio.   Wel (not in respect that either of you haue   *185*
deserued so much at my hands) but for pitties sake, I am
content to beare with your infirmities, and (so you wil
not vrge me to your owne harmes) by your courteous,
though not so much as honest vsage (for honesty willeth
I should haue mine owne againe, or reasonable recompence)   *190*
wil part with my losses: but yet therwithall warne you
(to which ende I haue written this letter) that you
preuent your mischeiues betimes, you do consider the
successe of your owne harmes,

Adagium.   *so long the pot goeth to the riuer, that at*   *195*
last it commeth broken home, euerye man will not deale
with you as I doe.

Confirmatio.   It can not chuse but you must needes know,
nay rather be a partaker of your sons euils, how euer
you dissemble with the world, & face out the matter be-   *200*
fore people. *God when he striketh, smiteth home*, you
will els repent it, for it will none otherwise be.

Mitigatio.   Because I haue yet some hope, that by
driuing into your conceipt the enormity hereof, and dis-
couering the packe which you said was lockt vp from your   *205*

seeing, I haue hoped that at the least wise for the feare
of God & to saue him from the gallowes you wil endeuor
to chastise him. I haue lent this bearer, who can inform
you of the truth, time & place of that which you go about
to shrowd vp so couertly, and if afterwards you will   210
not bridle him, I protest his shameles forhead must be
corrected by iustice, and the lawes must further passe
vpon him. Surely, not for enuy of the person, but for
the shameles brow he beareth, as one that had don none
offence. to prouoke me by euil vsage to blaze his faults,   215
that otherwise by good councel would haue couered them.
I think it a deed meritorious to haue him punished.

Epilogus. If you haue a desire as a father to cherish
him, haue regard as a friend betimes to correct him,
otherwise you shal soner see him come to shame then any   220
waies climb vnto credit. But for ought I can heare both
father and mother are so addicted to the bolstring of his
doings as that it semeth they haue already vowed their
infamy to the worlde, and his lyfe to the gallowes. Good
councel may do much, & thogh in tast I seeme a bitter   225
enemy, the proof in trial shal be better then a fawning
friend.

44 A. BOORDE: THE BREUIARY OF HELTHE (1547)

THE BREUIARY OF HELTHE, FOR ALL MANER OF SYCKENESSES AND
DISEASES THE WHICHE MAY BE IN MAN, OR WOMAN DOTH FOLOWE.
EXPRESSYNGE THE OBSCURE TERMES OF GREKE, ARABY, LATYN,
AND BARBARY, INTO ENGLYSH CONCERNING PHISICKE AND CHIER-
URGYE COMPYLED BY ANDREW BOORD OF PHYSICKE DOCTOUR AN   5
ENGLYSH MAN

A PROLOGUE TO PHISICIONS

Egregiouse doctours and maysters of the Eximiouse and
Archane Science of Phisicke of your Vrbanyte Exasperate
nat yourselfe againste me for makynge of this lytle vol-   10
ume of phisicke. Consideryng that my pretence is for an
vtilite and a comon welth. And this nat onely but also
I do it (for no detriment) but for a preferment of your
laudable science that euery man shuld esteme, repute,
and regarde, the excellent faculty. And also you to be   15
extolled and hyghly to be preferred that hath and dothe
study practyse, and labour, this sayde archane science,
to ye whiche none marciouse persons can nor shal attynge

to the knowlege: yet this natwithstanding fooles and
incipient persons, ye and many ye whiche doth thynke
them selfe wyse (the whiche in this faculte be fooles
in dede) wyll enterpryce to smatter & to medle to ministre medecynes, and can nat tell how when, and what
tyme the medecine shuld be ministred, but who is bolder
then blynd Bayerd, for a Lady, a gentylwoman, a blind
prest, a fye on such a one now a daies wyl practyse other
by a blynde boke, eyther els that they haue ben in
the company of some doctoure of phisicke, or els hauynge
an Auctour of phisicke, or Auctours and wyll ministre
after them, and can nat tel what the auctour ment in
his ministration. The philosopher sayth, when the philosopher dothe make an ende, the phisicion dothe begyn,
where shall he or she begyn that can but wryte and rede
and dothe vnderstande lytle lerninge or none.

O lord what a great detriment is this to ye noble science of phisicke that ignoraunt persons wyll enterpryce
to medle with the ministration of phisicke y^t Galen
prince of phisicions in his Terapentyk doth reprehend
and disproue sayeng. Yf phisicions had nothing to do with
Astronomy, Geomatry, Logycke, and other sciences, Coblers,
Curryars, of ledder, Carpenters and Smythes and such maner
of people wolde leue theyr craftes, and be phisicions,
as it appereth nowe a dayes that theyr by many Coblers,
be fye on such ons ...

Auenzoar sayth euery phisicion ought to knowe fyrst
lernynge and then practyce, that is to saye fyrste to haue
gramer to vnderstand what he doth rede in latyn. Than to
haue Logycke to discusse or dyffine by argumentation the
trouth from the falshod, and so econuerse. And then to
haue a Rethorycke or an eloquent tonge the whiche shulde
be placable to the herers of his worde. And also to haue
Geomatry, to ponder & way the dregges or porcions the
whiche ought to be ministred. Arythmetrycke is necessary
to be had concerninge numeration but aboue al thynges
next to gramer a phisicion muste haue surely his Astronomy to knowe howe whan & what tyme euery medecine ought
to be ministred. And than fynally to knowe naturall philosophy, the which consysteth in the knowlege of natural
thynges. And al these thinges had, than is a man apt to
study phisicke by speculacion. And speculacion obtayned
than boldly a man maye practyse phisicke. And who so euer

he or she be that wyl practyse phisicke in ministryng
medecines and nat hauyng these aforesayde sciences, shal
kyll many more than he shall saue, for and any suche
blynd phisicion helpe or heale one person, the person 65
so heled, is heled more by chaunce than by any cunnynge,
euen lyke as the blynde man doth cast his staffe, per-
auenture he hyt ye thynge that he doth cast at, perauen-
ture nat hit it . . .

A PROHEME TO CHIERURGIONS 70

Chierurgy is a laudable science, and worthy to be estemed
& regarded for ye great vtilitie of it, for it is a science vrgent, nedefull, and necessary, for the preseruation
of mans lyfe, wherefore maysters of Chierurgy ought to be
expert in theyr facultie, hauynge good wyttes & memory, 75
euermore to be diligent & tendable about theyr cures, and
to be of a good iudgement in the knowynge of the disease,
and to minister such salues and medecines as is accordynge to the infyrmyte, syckenes, or sore. Also they must
haue a good eye and a stedfast hande. . . Also Chierurgions 80
ought to be wyse, gentyll, sober, and nat dronken, circumspect, and lerned, and to promyse no more than they
be able to performe with goddes helpe, and nat to be
boystiouse aboute his pacientes but louyngly to comfort
them. Also euery Chierurgion ought to know the complexion 85
of his pacient, and to consyder the age, the weaknes, and
strength, and diligently to consyder yf the sickenes, sore,
or impedyment, be perticuler by him selfe: or els that it
haue any other infyrmyte concurraunt with it: or els that
the sicnes in the exteriall partes haue any fedyng from 90
the interyall partes, and that they be circumspect in
insycyons and Scaryfycations and Flebothomy, and sure in
Anothomy, and in no wyse to let blode in any particuler
place theyr where ye signe hath any dominion. Forthermore
Chierurgions must be circumspect in serchynge grene 95
woundes that be festered and fystylyd, and that they clen-
se and skoure the woundes from all corruption, and that
they heale nat ye woundes to quycly makyng the wound hole
aboue and false vnderneth. And in any wyse let them be
sure in serchyng of the depnes of woundes and fystles, 100
and accordynge to the deepnes to make the tentes. Moreouer Chierurgions must knowe the oposicion and the con-

iunction of the mone, and in what signe ye mone is in
euery day, and to knowe what sygnes be attractyue, what
signes by recentyue, what signes be expulcyue, and what   *105*
signes be dygestiue. Also they muste knowe the operation
of all maner of breades, of drynkes, and of meates. And
to haue euer in a redynes theyr instrumentes and theyr
salues and theyr oyntmentes, and in periculus causes one
Chierurgion ought to consult with an other, and to haue   *110*
the counsell of a doctour of phisicke, for there is no
man can be to sure to helpe a man as god knoweth who kepe
vs all Amen.

A PREAMBLE TO SYCKE MEN AND TO THOSE THAT BE WOUNDED

I do aduertyse euery sycke man, and al other men the   *115*
whiche hathe any infyrmite sicknes or impediment, aboue
all thynges to pacify him selfe, or to arme him selfe
with pacience, and to fixe his harte and mynd in christes
death & passion and to call to his remembraunce, what
paines, what aduersyte, and what penury, and pouertye   *120*
Christ dyd suffer for vs. And he that can thus pacyfy
him selfe, and feele his owne payne in christes passion,
shal mitigate his paynes and anguyshe be it neuer so
great. And therfore let euery sycke person stycke as fast
to Christ in his paynes and sickenes as Christ dyd stycke   *125*
fast to the crosse for our synnes and redempcion. And
than yf the pacient wyll haue any councell in phisicke.
Fyrste let him call to him his spyrytuall phisicion
which is his goostly father, and let him make his con-
science clene and that he be in perfyte loue and charite   *130*
and yf he haue done any wronge let him make restitucion
yf he can, and yf he be in det let him loke to it and
make a formal wyl or testament settinge euery thynge in
a dew order for the welth of his soule, wyse men be sure
of theyr testamentes makynge many yeres before they dye   *135*
& dothe renewe it ons a yere as they increase or decrease
in goodes or substance. All these aforesayd thynges
goostly and godly prouided for the soule. Than let the
pacient prouyde for his body, and take counsell of some
expert phisicion, howe and in what wyse the body may be   *140*
recouered of his infyrmite, and than to commyt his body
to the industry of his phisicion and at all tymes redy
to folowe the wyll mynd and counsell of his phisicion ...

Texts

¶ *THE 53. CAPYTLE DOTH SHEWE OF A CANKER*

Cancer is the latyn word. In englyshe it is named a canker   *145*
the whiche is a sore the whiche doth corode & cat the
flesshe corruptynge ye Arters the vaynes & the sinewes
corodyng or eatynge the bone and doth putryfy & corrupt
it. And then it is seldome made whole.
¶ *The cause of this infyrmyte.* ¶ This infyrmyte doth come   *150*
of a melancholy humour, or of a coleryke humour adusted,
or it may spryng of an hurt or a harme taken and nat loked
vnto betyme doth fystle and festure.
¶ *A remedy.* ¶ Yf the bone be blacke there is no remedye
but to cut the bone flesshe and al, specially if it be   *155*
in the armes or legges, yf the bone be nat putrified
fyrste skoure the cankerous place .iii. or .iiii. daies
with white wine. After that take burnt leed and myxe it
with the oyle of Roses and anoynt ye place dyuers tymes,
and vse pilles named pillule iude. And after that take   *160*
of white popy an vnce, of opium and henbane of either
of them a drame, of gumme arabicke halfe an vnce, of the
oyle of Roses .iiii. vnces incorporate this togyther and
anoynte the canker oft, or els vse the oyle of iuneper.
Or els take of terre sigillate, or boyle armoniake of   *165*
eche an vnce, of Ceruce, of muscilage of either halfe an
vnce, compounde al this togyther with the iuce of letuce
and the water or iuce of houseleke, and vse yeralogodion
and the confection of hamech.

¶ *THE 79. CAPTYLE DOTH SHEWE OF AN HUMOUE NAMED COLER*   *170*

Colera is ye latyn worde. In greke it is named *Cholæ*.
In englysh it is named Coler, the whiche is one of the
.iiii. humours. And it is hote and drye, lyenge or beyng
in the stomake and is mouable. There be .v. kyndes of coler.
The fyrst is natural coler which is reedyshe clere and   *175*
pure. The seconde is glasey, the which is ingendred of
wateryshe fleume, and of reed clere coler. The thyrde is
whityshe viscus and clammy lyke the white of a rawe egge,
the which is ingendred of congellacion of fleume and and
of clere reed coler. The .iiii. is grene the originall   *180*
of the which cometh of malyce of the stomake. The .v. is
a darke grene coler, and doth burne in the stomake, and
is ingendred of to much adusted humours.

¶ *A remedy to purge coler.* ¶ Coler adusted doth purge, the
pilles of Lapidis lazule, and so doth yeralogodion ruffi   *185*
and the confection of Hamech. And to purge citrine coler
is good the confection of Manna, and the pilles the which
be good against coleryke feuers, & pillule psilii. And to
purge grosse and viscus coler vse sirupus acetosus.
And it is good for reed coler and for al superfluous   *190*
coler, vse the pilles named pillule scomatice, pilles of
turbyth, or pilles of coloquintida & so doth sirupus
acetosus laxatiuus and so doth the confection made of
fumiterre, this must be done of a potycary the which hath
yᵉ practyce of al suche matters, for I nor no man els   *195*
can nat in theyr maternall tonge expresse the whole
termes of phisicke.

¶ *THE 122. CAPYTLE DOTH SHEWE OF THE PESTYLENCE*

Epidemia is the greke worde. In latin it is named *Pesti-*
lencia or *Febris pestilencialis.* In englyshe it is   *200*
named the pestilence.
¶ *The cause of this infyrmyte.* ¶ This infyrmyte dothe come,
either by the punyshment of god, either els of a corrupt
and contagious ayre, and one man infected with this sicknes may infect many men, this sicknes may come also with   *205*
the stenche of euyl dyrty stretes, of channelles nat kept
clene, of standynge puddels, and stynkynge waters, of
seges & stynkinge draughtes of shedynge of mannes blode,
and of deed bodies nat depely buried, of a great company
beynge in a lytle or smal rome, of comon pyssynge places,   *210*
and of many such lyke contagious ayers as be rehersed
in the dyetarye of helthe.
¶ *A remedy.* ¶ The chiefe remedy that I do know is for
euery man to submyt him selfe to god and than to amende
our lyuinge, and to fle farre from infectious places   *215*
and nat to go into the company of them which be infected,
or do resort to infectious persons and to beware of the
clothes, or any other thynge that doth pertayne to such
infectiue persons. Than vse a good dyet in eatynge and
drynkyng and vse perfumes in your chambers and houses,   *220*
go nat abrode in the open ayre, late in the nyght, nor
rise nat early in the mornynge, let the sonne haue dominion ouer the ground to waste and consume al contagious
mystes and ayers or you aryse, and than arise and serue

god which doth giue helth to all men, and folowe my 225
counsell in this matter as I haue shewed in the dyetary
of helth.

45 J. SKEYNE: ANE BREVE DESCRIPTIOVN OF THE PEST
(1586)

*QVHAIRIN THE CAVSIS, SIGNIS AND SUM SPECIALL PRESERUATION
AND CURE THAIROF AR CONTENIT.*

SET FURTH BE MAISTER GILBERT SKEYNE, DOCTOURE IN MEDICINE

TO THE READAR

Sen it hes plesit the inscrutabill Consall, and Iustice of 5
God (Beneuolent readar) that this present plaig and maist
detestabil diseise of Pest, be laitlie enterit in this
Realme, it becummis euerie one in his awin vocatione to be
not only most studious by perfectioun of lyfe to mitigat
apperandlie the iuste wrathe of God touart vs, in this 10
miserable tyme: Bot also to be maist curagius in suffering
of trauail, for the aduancement of the commoun weilth.
I beand mouit in y part seand the pure of Christ inlaik,
without assistance of support in bodie, al men detestand
aspectioun, speche, or communicatioun with thame, thoucht 15
expedient to put schortlie in wryte (as it hes plesit God
to supporte my sober knawlege) quhat becummis euerie ane
baith for preseruatioun and cure of sic diseise quhairin
(gude readar) thou sall nather abyde greit eruditioun nor
eloquence, bot onlie tho sentence and iugement of the 20
maist ancient writaris in medicine expressit in vulgar
langage without poleit or affectionat termis. And howbeit
it become me rather (quha hes bestouit all my Zouthe in
the Sculis) to had vrytin the samin in Latine, Zit vnderstanding sic interpryses had bene nothing profitable to 25
the commoun and wulgar people, thocht expedient and neidfull to express the sam in sic langage as the vnlernit
may be als weil satisfyit as Masteris of Clargie. Quhilk
beand acceptable and allowit be the Magistratis of this
Noble Burgh conforme to my gude mynde, sall God willing 30
as occasioun and tyme sufferis treit this samin argument
at more lenthe, quhilk presentlie for vtilitie of ye pure,
& schortnes of tyme, is mouit to set furthe almaist rude
and imperfite, nor doutand gentill Readar, bot thou will 35
appryse the samyn with siclyk mynd as the pure Womanis

oblatioun was apprysit be the Gude Lord, quha mot pre-
serue the in the helthe of Saule and bodie for euer &
euer.　　So be it.

¶ *ANE COMPENDIOUS DESCRIPTIOUN OF THE PEST　CAP. 1*

Ane pest is the corruptioun or infectioun of ye Air, or　　40
ane venemous qualytie & maist hurtfull Wapor thairof,
quhilk hes strenthe and wikitnes abone al natural putri-
factioun & beand contractit first maist quietlie infectis
the Spiritall partis of mannis bodie, thairefter the humoris, puttand sairest at the naturall Humiditie of the hart,　45
quhilkis tholand corruptioun ane feuir mast wikit quietlie
and theiflie strikis the patient: quhais bodie exteriour-
lie apperis weil at eis, bot interiourlie is maist heuelie
vexit. Quhilk schortly may be descryuit. Ane feuerable
infectioun, maist cruelle and sindre wayis strikand doun　50
mony in haist. Heirfor it is maist vehement & hait diseis
that may put at mannis bodie, & maist dangerous, because
it is difficil to knaw all thingis, quhilkis makis ane
man propense to becum Pestilential. Alwais quhilk hes the
cause frome the Heiuins or corruptioun of Air, is properlie　55
be maist learnit, callit ane pest: and quilk is generit
within vs or of vther causis is callit ane Malignant feuer.

¶ *THE CAUSIS OF PEST　CAP. 2*

It war difficill & tediouse to descryue all the causis of
ane Pestilence. Heirfoir at this present I sall comemorat
the principalis onlie be the quhilkis the rest may be　　60
vnderstand. Certane it is, the first and principal cause
may be callit, and is ane scurge and punischment of the
maist iust God, without quhais dispositioun in all thingis,
vtheris secund causis wirkis no thing. So the Heauine
quhilk is the admirable instrument of God blawis that　65
contagioun vpone the face of the Earth, as quhan the
maist nocent Sterres to man kynd conuenis, quhilkis be
Astrologis ar callit infortunat. Or quhan Cometis with
other wikit impressionis ar generit and preseruit in the　70
Air, quhilk, of it self, beand maist simple substance,
and so incorruptible & necessar for mannis lyfe: nottheles
resauis and admittis, baith frome the Heauinis, and inferiour Elementis mony infectionis and corruptioun quhilkis

ar the seid & cheif causis of sindre diseisis quhilkis   75
ar callit Epidimiall, & thir causis in maist part ar vniuersall. Inferiour causis ar quhilkis occupeis ane Realme,
ane people ane Citie, or ane house thairof. Cause thairof
is standand vatter, sic as Stank, Pule, or Loche moste
corrupte, and filthie: Erd, dung, stinkand Closettis,   80
deid Cariounis vnbureit in speciale of man kynd quhilkis
be similitude of nature in maist nocent to man, as euerie
brutall is maist infectand and Pestilentiall to thair awin
kynd. Forther continuall schouris of Veit with greit sow-
thin wynde or the samin blawand from pestiferous placis.   85
The cause of pest in ane priuat Citie is stinkand corruptioun & filth, quhilkis occupeis the commune streittis
and gaittis, greit reik of colis without vinde to dispache
the sam, corruptioun of Herbis, sic as Caill & growand
Treis. Moist heuie sauer of Lynt, Hemp, & Ledder steipit   90
in Vater. Ane priuat house infectis ather of stinkand
closettis, or corrupte Carioun thairin, or neir by, or
gif the inhabitantis hes inuiseit vther infectis Rowmis,
or drinking corrupte Vatter, eating of Fruttis, or vder
meittis quhilkis ar corrupte, as we see dalie the pure   95
mair subiecte to sic calamitie, nor the potent, quha ar
constrynit be pouertie to eit ewill and corrupte meittis,
and diseisis contractit heirof ar callit Pandemiall.
In euerie ane the cause is abundance of corruptible hu-
moris collectit and generit of metis and drinke, quhilkis   100
of ony lycht cause becummis corrupt, in mannis bodie als
wikit as deidlie poysone. Finallie & principallie infectit
Air quhilk all men drauis of be inspiratioun of necessitie
for continuatioun of lyfe. By the quhilk first the
Spirituall partis, secundlie the humoris & naturall   105
partis ar sair put at, in sum hastelie, in otheris
laitlie or neuer, as ane be ane other is accustumit to
diuersitie of meitis as the bodie is preparit & propense
to corruptioun and finalie as dwelling and passioun of
the forsaidis causis seruis.

46 P. STUBBS: THE ANATOMIE OF ABUSES (1583)

Spudaeus. Is ye playing at football, reding of mery
bookes & such like delectations, a violation or prophanation of the Sabaoth day?
Philoponus. Any exercise which w^{t}draweth vs from godlines,

either vpon ye sabaoth, or any other day els, is wicked 5
& to be forbiden. Now who is so grosly blinde, y^t seeth not
y^t these aforesaid exercises not only w^{t}draw vs from godlines & vertue, but also haile & allure vs to wickednes and
sin: for as concerning football playing: I protest vnto you, it may rather be called a freendly kinde of 10
fight, then a play or recreation. A bloody and murthering
practise, then a felowly sporte or pastime.

For dooth not euery one lye in waight for his Aduersarie, seeking to ouerthrowe him & to picke him on his nose,
though it be vppon hard stones, in ditch or dale, in 15
valley or hil, or what place soeuer it be, hee careth not
so he haue him down. And he that can serue ye most of this
fashion, he is counted the only felow, and who but he?
so that by this meanes, somtimes their necks are broken,
sometimes their backs, sometime their legs, sometime 20
their armes, sometime one part thurst out of ioynt, sometime another, sometime the noses gush out with blood, sometime their eyes start out: and sometimes hurt in one place,
sometimes in another. But whosoeuer scapeth away the best
goeth not scotfrée, but is either sore wounded, craised 25
and bruseed, so as he dyeth of it, or els scapeth very
hardly: and no meruaile, for they haue the sleights to
meet one betwixt two, to dashe him against the hart with
their elbowes, to hit him vnder the short ribbes with
their griped fists, and with their knees to catch him 30
vpon the hip, and to pick him on his neck, with a hundered
such murdering deuices: and hereof, groweth enuie, malice,
rancour, cholor, hatred, displeasure, enmitie and what not
els? and sometimes fighting, brawling, contention, quarrel
picking, murther, homicide and great effusion of blood, 35
as experience dayly teacheth.

Is this murthering play now an exercise for the Sabaoth
day? is this a christian dealing for one brother to mayme
and hurt another, and that vpon prepensed malice, or set
purpose? this to do to another, as we would wish another 40
to doo to vs, *God make vs more careful ouer the bodyes of*
of our Bretheren.

As for the reading of wicked Bookes, they are vtterly
vnlawfull, not onely to bee read, but once to be named,
& that not (onely) vpon the Sabaoth day, but also vppon 45
any other day: as which tende to the dishonour of God,
deprauation of good manners and corruption of christian

soules. For as corrupt meates doo annoy the stomack, and
infect the body, so the reading of wicked and vngodly
Bookes (which are to the minde, as meat is to the body)   50
infect the soule, & corrupt ye minde, hailing it to dis-
truction: if the great mercy of God be not present.

And yet notwithstanding, whosoeuer wil set pen to paper
now a dayes, how vnhonest soeuer, or vnseemly of christian
eares his argument be, is permitted to goe forward, and   55
his woork plausibly admitted and fréendly licensed, and
gladly imprinted without any prohibition or contradiction
at all: wherby it is growen to this issue, that bookes &
pamphlets of scurrilitie and baudrie, are better esteemed
and more vendible then the godlyest and sagest bookes   60
that be: for if it be a godly treatise, reproouing vice,
and teaching vertue, away with it ...

47 J. ASTLEY: THE ART OF RIDING (1584)

*THE ART OF RIDING DEFINED, WITH NOTES OF COURAGE IN A
HORSSE, THE USING AND ABUSING OF AN HORSSE, AND WHAT
IS IUSTLIE CALLED THE HARDNESSE OF A HORSSES MOUTH, &C.*

Nothing is reckoned more proper to mans nature, than the
desire to know a truth, nor any thing counted more foule,   5
or grosse, than to erre & be deceiued. Seeing then that
the thing purposed is for the knowledge of the true vse
of the hand in this Art of Riding and Horsemanship, which
belongeth to the warre and feates of armes; and that in
reason, the substance of a part of any thing cannot well   10
be vnderstood without the knowledge of the verie nature
of the thing it selfe whereof it is part (as the vse of
the hand is but part of the Art of Riding) I haue thought
good therfore First, to seeke out what the verie substance
of the Art it selfe is, that thereby wee may the better   15
vnderstand this part whereof we purpose to treate. And
thus not meaning to hold you long, I will saie foorthwith
mine opinion thereof, the rather to saue the band, whereby I stand indebted vnto you all, than that I thinke my
selfe able to satisfie your skilfull expectations, and   20
so vnder the correction of diuerse Noble and many other
Gentlemen besides your selfe, with a great number of
others that at this daie are growne to some excellencie
in this kind of Horssemanship, I saie (for my part) that
the said kinde of Riding is an Art to make an horsse,   25

for the seruice aforesaid, obedient to his Rider. In
this short kind of speech (as I take it) the verie whole
substance of the said Art is fullie conteined, and therefore the words thereof are diligentlie to be weighed,
but especiallie these here following: as ART, an HORSE,   *30*
a RIDER, and OBEDIENCE: which I meane for the better
explaning of my conceipt, to passe ouer with a short discourse.

The art is the cause efficient. ART therefore is an
obseruation of certaine experiences tried & gathered   *35*
togither, to be put in order, and taught to some good end.
Three things are chieflie to be required in Art, that is:
easines, readines, and perfectnes. Art also is said to
imitate nature.

The materiall cause. An HORSE is the matter and sub-   *40*
iect wherevpon this Art worketh, and is a creature sensible, and therefore so farre as he is mooued to doo anie
thing, he is thervnto mooued by sense and feeling. Further,
this is common to all sensible creatures, to shunne all
such things as annoy them, and to like all such things   *45*
as doo delight them.

The cause formall is the manner of teaching. The
instrument wherby this Art is wrought, is the RIDER, a
creature reasonable, and therefore ought to be able to
render a reason of euerie thing that he teacheth, in mak-   *50*
ing the horsse obedient to his will, the which if he cannot doo, hee is to be suspected as one vnskilfull of the
Art, and knoweth not what hee dooth.

The cause finall is obedience. OBEDIENCE, is a
readie willingness to doo the will of him that dooth   *55*
command. But now by the waie, though euerie Rider be a
creature reasonable, yet euerie reasonable creature is
not a Rider, but he which only is skilfull in that Art.

Finally, the patterne that Art should imitate, that
excellent Philosopher and valiant captaine XENOPHON in   *60*
his booke *De re equestri* doth verie gallantlie set forth
in these words: Note when you see a Horsse (saith he)
make haste to meet with other horsses, that be in his
view, or mares rather, and then shall you see how nature
mooueth him to shew himselfe in his best forme and lus-   *65*
tines of courage, yea, both terrible and beautiful to
behold: for then he will set vp his crest, bow in his
head, pricke vp his eares, gather vp his legs high and
nimble, swell in his nostrils, and start out his taile,

&c. This is now the patterne that the curious painter   70
with all his skill dooth diligentlie indeuor to imitate,
but how much more should the skilfull Rider doo the same?

Of these horsses thus to be made, as XENOPHON also
writeth, there be twoo kinds: the one, for the seruice
aforesaid, the other for pompe and triumph the which   75
we call stirring horsses, the vse of which are verie
profitable for this seruice, bicause they teach a man to
sit surelie, comelie, and stronglie in his seate, which
is no small helpe to him that must fight and serue on
horssebacke: but of this last I meane not now to speake.   80

48 J. HORTROP: THE TRAUAILES OF AN ENGLISH MAN
(1591)

*CONTAINING HIS SUNDRIE CALAMITIES INDURED BY THE SPACE
OF TWENTIE AND ODD YERES IN HIS ABSENCE FROM HIS NATIUE
COUNTRIE: WHEREIN IS TRULY DECYPHERED THE SUNDRIE
SHAPES OF WILDE BEASTS, BIRDS, FISHES, FOULES, ROOTES,
PLANTS, &C*   5

> *With the description of a man that appeared in the Sea:*
> *and also of a huge Giant brought from China to the*
> *King of Spaine*

NO LESSE PLEASANT THAN APPROUED

TO THE MOST HIGH AND MIGHTIE PRINCESSE, ELIZABETH BY   10
THE GRACE OF GOD QUEENE OF ENGLAND, FRANCE, AND IRELAND,
DEFENDRES OF THE FAITH, &C.

Your Highnes most humble subiect I.H. heartely praieth
for the continuance of your Maiesties most prosperous
raigne.   15
About xxiii. yeeres past (most gracious and renowmed Soue-
raigne) being prest forth for one of the Gunners in your
Maiesties ships for the West Indian voiage, (of which Sir
Iohn Haukins was general) such was our successe before
his returne into England, we were distrest through want   20
of victuals, nor could we obtaine anie for money: by
meanes whereof many of vs (though vnto our Generals
greate griefe) were constrained to be set on shoare in
the West Indies, amongst the wilde Indians. Since which
time (most dread Soueraigne) I haue passed sundrie per-   25
illes there in the wildernesses, and escaped many dangers,
wherein my life stood often in hazard, yet by the proui-
dence of the Almightie I was preserued. And being now
returned into my natiue Countrie of England, I doe in all

humblenesse prostrate myselfe (together with the discourse   30
of my trauels) at your Highnes feete, humbly beseeching
your Maiestie to accept the same at your subiects hands,
as our Sauiour Iesus Christ accepted the poore widowes
mite. And thus I humbly take my leaue, praying for the
prosperous raigne of your most excellent Maiestie.   35

THE LATE AND WONDERFULL TRAVAILE OF AN ENGLISHMAN,
WITH HIS SLAUERIE AND MISERIE SUSTAINED FOR 23.
YEERES SPACE TOGETHER

Not vntruly nor without cause, said *Iob* the faithful ser-
uant of God (whome the sacred Scriptures tell vs, to haue   40
dwelt in the lande of Hus) that man beeing borne of a
woman, liuing a short time, is replenished with many miseries, which some knowe by reading of histories, many by
the viewe of others calamities, and I by experience in my
selfe, as this present Treatise insuing shall shew.   45
    It is not vnknowne vnto many that I *I.H.* pouder-maker
was borne at *Bourne*, a Towne in Lincolnshire, from my age
of twelue yeeres brought vp in Redriffe neere London, with
M.Frauncis Lee, who was the Queenes Maiesties powder-maker,
whome I serued, vntill I was prest to goe on the voiage   50
to the West Indies, with the Right worshipfull Sir Iohn
Haukins, who appointed mee to be one of the Gunners in
her Maiesties shippe called the Iesus of Libbicke, who
set saile from Plimmouth in the moneth of October 1567,
hauing with him an other shippe of her Maiesties, called   55
the Minion, and foure shippes of his owne namely, the
Angell, the Swallow, the Iudith, and the William and Iohn.
He directed his Vizeadmirall, that if foule weather did
separate them, to meete at the Iland of Tennerif. After
which by the space of seuen daies and seuen nights, we   60
had such storms at Sea, that we lost our long boates and
a pinnisse, with some men comming to the Tennerif: there
our Generall heard that his vizeadmirall with the Swallow,
and the William and Iohn, were at the Iland called the
Gomero, where finding his vizeadmirall hee ancored, tooke   65
in fresh water and set saile for Cape Blanke, where in
the way we tooke a Portugall Caruill, laden with fish
called Mullets: from thence to Cape de Verde. In our course
thither we met a Frenchman of Rochell called Captaine
Bland, who had taken a Portugall Caruill, whome our vize-   70
admirall chased and tooke. Sir Frauncis Drake was made

Master and Captaine of the Caruill, and so wee kept our
way till wee came to Cape de Verde, and there we ancored,
tooke our boates, and set soldiers on shore. Our Generall
was the first that leapt on land, & with him Captain   75
Dudley there we tooke certain Negros, but not without
damage to our selues for our General, Captaine Dudley,
and eight other of our company were hurt with poysoned
arrowes, about nine daies after the eight that were wound-
ed died. Our Generall was taught by a Negro, to draw   80
the poyson out of his wound with a cloue of garlicke,
whereby he was cured. From thence we went to Surroleon,
where be monstrous fishes called Sharkes, which wil deuoure men, I amongst others was sent in the Angell with
two pinnaces into the riuer called the Calouses, that were   85
there trading with the Negros, we tooke one of them with
the Negroes, & brought them away. In this riuer in the
nighttime we had one of our pinnaces bulged by a sea-horse,
so that our men swimming about the riuer, were all taken
into the other pinnaces, except two that tooke holde one   90
of another, and were carried awaie by the sea horse, who
hath the iust proportion of a horse, sauing that his legs
be short, his teeth verie great and a span in length, he
vseth on the night to go on land into the woodes, seek-
ing at vnawares to deuouer the Negros in their cabbins,   95
whom they by their vigilancie preuent, and kill them in
this manner. The Negros keepe watch, and diligently attend
their comming, and when they are gone into the woods, they
forthwith laie a great tree ouerthwart the waie, so that
at their returne, for that their legs be so short, they   100
cannot go ouer it: then the Negroes set vppon them with
their bowes, arrowes and darts, and so destroy them.

   From thence we entered the riuer called the Causterus,
where there were other Caruelles trading with the Negros,
and them we tooke. In this Iland betwixt the riuer and   105
the maine, Trees grow with their rootes vpwards, and
Oisters vpon them. There grow Palmita trees, which be as
high as a ships maine mast, & on their tops grow nuts,
wine and oyle, which they call Palmita oyle. The Plantine
trees also grow in that countrie, the tree is as big as   110
a mans thigh, and as high as a firre pole, the leaues
thereof be long & broade, and on the top grow the fruit
which is called Plantaines, they are crooked and a cubite
long, and as big as a mans wrist, they grow on clusters:

when they be ripe they be verie good and daintie to eate, 115
Sugar is not more delicate in tast than they be. In this
land bee Elyphants, which the Negros kill in this manner:
they seke out their hants where they rest in the night,
which is against a tree, that they saw three partes in
sunder, so that when the Elephant leaneth and stretch 120
himselfe against it, the tree falleth, & he with it,
then he roareth, wherby the Negros know he is fallen,
then they come vpon him and kill him.

From thence with the Angell, the Iudith and the pinnaces, wee sailed to Surreleon, where our Generall at 125
that time was, who with the Captaines and souldiers went
vp into the riuer called the Faggarine, to take a towne
of the Negroes, where he found three kings of that Countrie with fiftie thousand Negroes beseeging the same
towne, which they could not take in many yeeres before 130
that they had warred with it. Our Generall made a breach,
entered, and valiantlie tooke the towne, wherein were
founde fiue Portugals, which yeelded themselues to
his mercie, and hee saued their liues, we tooke and carried thence for trafficke of the West Indies fiue hundred 135
Negroes. The three kings droue seuen thousand Negros into
the sea at low water, at the point of the land, where
they were all drowned in the oze, for that they could not
take their canowes to saue themselues. Wee retourned
backe againe in our pinnaces to the shippes, and there 140
tooke in fresh water, and made readie sayle towarde Reo-
grande. At our comming thether we entred with the Angel,
the Iudith, and the two pinnasses, we found there seuen
Portugall Caruils, which made great fight with vs. In the
end by Gods helpe wee won the victory, and droue them 145
to the shore, from whence with the Negroes they fled, we
fetcht the caruils from the shore into the riuer. The next
morning sir Frances Drake with his Caruell, the Swallow,
the William and Iohn came into the riuer, with Captaine
Dudley and his soldiers, who landed being but a hundred 150
souldiers, and fought with seauen thousande Negroes,
burned the towne, and returned to our Generall with the
losse of one man.

49 J. MURRELL: A NEW BOOKE OF COOKERIE (1615)

TO BAKE A NEATES TONGUE TO BE EATEN HOT

Boyle it tender, and pill off the skinne, take the flesh
out at the but-end: mince it small with Oxe suit, and
marrow. Season it with Pepper, Salt, Nutmeg, parboyld
Currens, and a minced Date cut in pieces. Take the yolkes   5
of two new layd Egges, and a spoonefull of sweet Creame,
worke all together with a siluer spoone, in a Dish, with
a little powder of a dryed Orange pill: sprinckle a little
Vergis ouer it, and cast on some Sugar. Then thrust it in
againe as hard as you can cram it. Bake it on a Dish in   10
the ouen: baste it with sweet Butter, that it may not
bake drye on the outside: when it is to be eaten sawce it
with Vinegar and Butter, Nutmeg, Sugar, and the iuyce of
an Orenge.

TO BAKE A SWAN   15

Scald it, and take out the bones: then parboyle it, and
season it well with Pepper, Salt, and Ginger. Then Lard it,
and put it in a deepe Coffin of Rye paste with store of
Butter. Let it soake well, when you take it out of the
Ouen put in more Butter moulten at the venthole.   20

A RYCE PUDDING

Steep it in faire water all night: then boyle it in new
Milke, and draine out the Milke through a Cullinder:
mince beefe Suit handsomely, but not too small, and put
it into the Rice, and parboyld Currins, yolkes of new layd   25
Egges, Nutmeg, Sinamon, Sugar, and Barberryes: mingle all
together: wash your scoured guttes, and stuffe them with
the aforesaid pulp: parboyle them, and let them coole.

50 G. FOX: THE JOURNAL (*c.* 1674)

(1651) And afterwards I passed away through ye Country & att
night came to an Inn: & there was a rude Company of people &
I askt ye woman if shee had any Meate to bringe mee some: &
shee was somethinge strange because I saide thee & thou to
her: soe I askt her if shee had any milke but shee denyed it. .   5

(1651) .. & before I was brought in before him ye garde
saide It was well if ye Justice was not drunke before wee
came to him for hee used to bee drunke very early: & when I
was brought before him because I did not putt off my hatt &
saide thou to him he askt ye man whether I was not Mased or   *10*
fonde: & hee saide noe: Itt was my principle: & soe I warned
him to repent & come to ye light y^t Christ had enlightned
him withall...

And when I was at Oram before in ye steeplehouse there
came a professor & gave mee a push in ye brest in ye steeple-   *15*
house & bid mee gett out of ye Church: alack poore man saide
I dost thou call ye steeplehouse ye Church: ye Church is y^e
people whome God has purchased with his bloode: & not ye house.

(1653) But att ye first convincement when freinds coulde
not putt off there hatts to people nor say you to a particu-   *20*
lar but thee & thou: & coulde not bowe nor use ye worldes
salutations nor fashions nor customes: & many freindes beinge
tradesmen of severall sortes: they lost there custome at y^e
first: for ye people woulde not trade with y^m nor trust y^m &
for a time people y^t were tradesmen coulde hardely gett money   *25*
enough to by breade butt afterwards when people came to see
freinds honesty & truthfulnesse & yea & nea att a worde in
there dealinge & there lifes & conversations did preach &
reach to ye wittnesse of God in all people & they knew & saw
y^t they would not cuzen & cheate y^m for conscience sake to-   *30*
wards God. And y^t at last they might sende any childe & bee
as well used as y^{m}selves att any of there shopps.

(1656) And in y^t time many freindly people out of severall
parts of ye county came to visitt us & was convinct: & a
great rage there was amongst professors & preists: for saide   *35*
they they thee & thou all people without respect: & will not
doffe there hatts to one nor bowe ye knee to any man: and
this troubled y^m fearefully: butt at ye assisses they expected wee shoulde have beene all hanged: & then saide they letts
us see whether they dare thou & thee & keepe on there hatts   *40*
before ye Judge: but all this was litle to us: for wee saw
howe God woulde staine ye worlds honor & glory: ffor wee was
commanded not to seeke y^t honor nor give it butt know y^e
honor y^t came from God onely & seekt for y^t.

(1657) ... & when they were gonne there came uppe another   *45*
rude company of professors & some of ye heads of ye tounde
& they caled for ffaggotts & drinke though wee forbad y^m:
whoe were as rude a carriaged people as ever I mett with-

all but ye Lords power chained y^m t^t they had not power to
doe us any mischeife: but when they went there ways they left   *50*
all there faggotts & beere y^t they had caled for Into y^e
roome for us to pay in y^e morninge & wee shewed y^e Inkeeper
what an unworthy thinge it was: yett hee tolde us wee must
pay it: & pay it wee did.

ADDITIONAL TEXTS

51 D. LYNDSAY: THE FIRST BUKE OF THE MONARCHIE
(1574)

ANE EXCLAMATION TO THE REDAR, TWICHING THE
WRYTTING OF VULGAR, AND MATERNALL LANGUAGE.

Gentill Redar, haue at me none dispyte,
Thinkand that I presumpteously pretend,
In vulgar toung so hie mater to wryte: 5
Bot quhair I mys, I pray the till amend,
Till vnlernit, I wald the cause wer kend,
Of our most miserabill trauell and torment,
And how in eirth, no place bene permanent, ...

Howbeit that diuers deuot cunning Clerkis,   10
In Latyne toung hes written sindrie buikis.
Our vnleirnit knawis lytle of thir werkis:
More than thay do, the rauing of the ruikis:
Quhairfoir to Colȝearis, Carteris, & to cuikis
To Iok and Thome, my Ryme sal be directit,   15
With cunning men, howbeit it wil be lactit.

Thocht euerie commoun may not be ane clerk
Nor hes no Leid, except thair toung maternall:
Quhy suld of God, yᵉ maruellous heuinlie werk,
Be hid from thame, I think it nocht fraternall: 20
The Father of heuin, quhilk wes, & is eternall
To Moises gaue the Law, on Mont Sinay,
Nocht into Greik nor Latyne, I heir say.

He wrait the Law, in Tablis hard of stone,   25
In thair awin vulgare language of Hebrew,
That all the Barnis of Israell euery one
Micht knaw the Law, & so the same ensew.
Had he done wryt, in Latyne or in Grew,
It had to thame bene bot ane sauirles Iest.   30
Ze may weill wit, God wrocht all for yᵉ best...

Of languagis, the first Diuersitie,
Wes maid be Goddis maledictioun,
Quhen Babilon wes beildit in Caldie:
Those beildaris gat none vther afflictioun,   35
Afore the tyme of that punitioun:
Was bot ane toung, quhilk Adam spak him self
Quhare now of toungis, thare bene thre score and twelf.

Nochtwithstanding, I think it greit plesour,
Quhair cunning men hes languagis anew,
That in thair ȝouth, be diligent laubour,
Hes leirnit Latyne, Greik, and auld Hebrew,
That I am nocht of that sort, sore I rew:
Quhairfoir I wald all buikis necessare,
For our Faith, wer in till our toung vulgare... 40

Sanct Ierome in his proper toung Romane, 45
The Law of God he trewly did translait,
Out of Hebrew, and Greik in Latyne plane:
Quhilk hes bene hid from vs lang tyme, God wait
Vnto this tyme, bot efter myne consait:
Had sanct Ierome bene borne in till Argyle, 50
Into Irische toung his bukis had done compyle...

Lat Doctouris wryte thair curious questionis
And argumentis, sawin full of Sophistrie:
Thair Logick, and thair hich Opinionis,
Thair dirk Iugementis of Astronomie, 55
Thair Medecine, and thair Philosophie:
Lat Poetis schaw thair glorious Ingyne,
As euer thay pleis, in Greik, or in Latyne,

Bot lat vs haue the buikis necessare,
To commoun weill and our Saluatioun, 60
Iustlie translatit in our toung vulgare:
And als I make the Supplicatioun:
O gentill Redar, haue none Indignatioun:
Thinkand I mell me with so hie matair,
Now to my purpose fordwart will I fair.

52 R. STANYHURST, THE HISTORIE OF IRELANDE (1577)

But of all other places, Weiseforde with the territorye
bayed, and perclosed within the riuer called the Pill, was
so quite estranged from Irishry, as if a trauailer of the
Irish (which was rare in those dayes) had picht his foote
within the pile and spoken Irishe, the Weisefordians would 5
commaunde hym forthwith to turne the other ende of his
tongue, and speake Englishe, or else bring his trouchman
with him. But in our dayes they haue so aquainted themselues with the Irishe, as they haue made a mingle mangle,
or gallamaulfrey of both the languages, and haue in such 10

medley or checkerwyse so crabbedly iumbled them both togyther, as commonly the inhabitants of the meaner sort
speake neyther good English nor good Irishe.

There was of late dayes one of the Péeres of England
sent to Weiseford as Commissioner, to decide the contro- 15
uersies of that countrey, and hearing in affable wise the
rude complaintes of the countrey clownes, he conceyued
here and there, sometyme a worde other whyles a sentence.
The noble man beyng very glad that vpon his first commyng
to Ireland, he vnderstood so many wordes, told one of hys 20
familiar friends, that he stoode in very great hope, to
become shortly a well spoken man in the Irishe, supposing
that the blunte people had pratled Irishe, all the while
they iangled Englishe. Howbeit to this day, the dregs of
the olde auncient Chaucer English, are kept as well there 25
as in Fingall. As they terme a spider, an attercop, a
wispe, a wad, a lumpe of bread, a pocket or a pucket, a
Sillibuck a copprouse, a faggot, a blease, or a blaze,
for the short burning of it, as I iudge, a Phisition, a
leache, a gappe, a sharde, a base court or quadrangle, 30
a bawen, or rather, as I suppose, a barton, ye household
or folkes, meany, Sharppe, kéene, estraunge, vncouth,
easie, éeth or éefe, a dunghill, a mizen, as for the
worde bater, that in English purporteth a lane, bearing
to an high way, I take it for a méere Irishe worde, that 35
crepte vnawares into the English, thorough the daily
entercourse of the English and Irish inhabitants.

And where as commonly in all countreys, the women speake
most neately and pertely, whiche *Tully* in hys thirde booke
de Oratore, speakyng in the person of *Crassus*, séemed to 40
haue obserued, yet notwithstandyng in Ireland it falleth
out contrary. For the women haue in their English tongue
an harrish and broade kynd of pronunciation, with vtteryng
their wordes so péeuishly & faintly, as though they were
halfe sicke, and ready to call for a possette. And most
commonly in words, of two sillables, they giue the last the 45
accent. As they say, Markeate, Baskeate, Gossoupe, Pussoate,
Robart, Niclase, etc. which doubtlesse doth disbeautifie
their Englishe aboue measure. And if they could be weaned
from that corrupt custom, there is none that could dislyke
of their English. 50

53 ANON., THE STATUTES OF IONA (1616)

Forsamekle as, the Kingis Majestie haveing a speciall care
and regaird that the trew religioun be advanceit and establisheit in all the pairtis of this kingdome, and that all
his Majesties subjectis, especiallie the youth, be exercised
and trayned up in civilitie, godlines, knawledge, and   5
learning, that the vulgar Inglishe toung be universallie
plantit, and the Irishe language, whilk is one of the cheif
and principall causis of the continewance of barbaritie and
incivilitie amongis the inhabitantis of the Ilis and Hey-
landis, may be abolisheit and removit; and quhairas thair   10
is no meane more powerfull to further this his Majesties
princelie regaird and purpois than the establishing of
scooles in the particular parrocheis of this kingdome whair
the youthe may be taught at the least to write and reid,
and be catechiesed and instructed in the groundis of reli-   15
gioun; thairfore the Kingis Majestie, with advise of the
Lordis of his Secreit Counsall, hes thocht it necessar and
expedient that in everie parroche of this kingdome, whair
convenient meanes may be had for interteyning a scoole
that a scoole salbe establisheit, and a fitt persone ap-   20
pointit to teache the same, upoun the expensis of the parrochinnaris according to the quantitie and qualitie of the
parroche, at the sight and be the advise of the bischop
of the diocie in his visitatioun; commanding heirby all
the bishoppis within this kingdome that thay and everie   25
ane of thame within thair severall dioceis deale and tra-
vell with the parrochinnaris of the particular parrocheis
within thair saidis dioceis to condescend and aggree upoun
some certane, solide, and sure course how and by quhat
meanes the said scoole may be intertenyned. And, gif ony   30
difficultie sall arryse amongis thame concerning this
mater, that the said bishop reporte the same to the saidis
Lordis, to the effect thay may tak suche ordour heiranent
as thay sall think expedient. And that letteris be direct
to mak publicatioun heirof, quhairthrow nane pretend   35
ignorance of the same.

Forsamekle as the Kingis Majestie, with advise of the
Lordis of his Secreit Counsall, hes found it verie neces-
sair and expedient for the better establisheing of the
trew religioun that childrene be catechesed and educate in   40
the knowledge of the groundis thairof frome thair tender

yeiris; and seeing mony parentis ar so careles and negligent in that point as thair childrene, being ather alto-
gidder ignorant or cairleslie instructed, ar quhen thay
come to aige easilie pervertit and drawne to Poperie, –   *45*
thairfore his Majestie, with advise foirsaid, hes commandit and ordanit, and by thir presentis straitlie commandis,
chairges, and ordanes, all and sindrie parentis to use the
ordinar meanes of instructing thair young childreen, to
present thame to thair ordinar pastour at all usuall tymes   *50*
of catechiesing and examinatioun, and to bring thame to the
bishop of the diocie at everie visitatioun within the parroche to be tryed and confirmed be him, under the panes
particularlie underwrittin, to be incurrit *toties quoties*
be everie persone that sall failyee to present thair chil-   *55*
drene to the bischop at his visitatioun as said is: that
is to say, be everie nobilman fourty pundis, be every barone
fourty merkis, and be everie inferiour persone twenty merkis or lesse according to the meanes of the said persone:
and that letteris be direct to mak publicatioun heirof,   *60*
quhairthrow nane pretend ignorance of the same.

54 W. BRADFORD, HISTORY OF PLIMOUTH PLANTATION
(1630)

OF THEIR VOYAGE, AND HOW THEY PASSED THE SEA,
AND OF THEIR SAFE ARRIVAL AT CAPE COD

But to omite other things, (that I may be breefe,) after
longe beating at sea they fell with that land which is called Cape Cod; the which being made and certainly knowne to   *5*
be it, they were not a litle joyfull. After some deliberation
had amongst them selves and with the m^r of the ship, they
tacked aboute and resolved to stande for the southward (the
wind and weather being faire) to finde some place aboute
Hudsons river for their habitation. But after they had sail-   *10*
ed that course aboute halfe the day, they fell amongst deangerous shoulds and roring breakers, and they were so farr
intangled ther with as they conceived them selves in great
danger; and the wind shrinking upon them withall, they resolved to bear up againe for the Cape, and thought them   *15*
selves hapy to gett out of those dangers before night over-
tooke them, as by Gods providence they did. And the next day
they gott into the Cape-harbor wher they ridd in saftie ...
   Being thus arived in a good harbor and brought safe to

land, they fell upon their knees and blessed the God of   20
heaven, who had brought them over the vast and furious ocean,
and delivered them from all the periles and miseries therof,
againe to set their feete on the firme and stable earth,
their proper elemente. And no marvell if they were thus
joyefull, seeing wise Seneca was so affected with sailing   25
a few miles on the coast of his owne Italy; as he affirmed,
that he had rather remaine twentie years on his way by land,
then pass by sea to any place in a short time; so tedious
and dreadfull was the same unto him.

But hear I cannot but stay and make a pause, and stand   30
half amased at this poore peoples presente condition; and so
I thinke will the reader too, when he well considers the same.
Being thus passed the vast ocean, and a sea of troubles before
in their preparation (as may be remembred by that which wente
before), they had now no freinds to wellcome them, nor inns   35
to entertaine or refresh their weatherbeaten bodys, no houses
or much less townes to repaire too, to seeke for succoure. It
is recorded in scripture as a mercie to the apostle and his
shipwraked company, that the barbarians shewed them no smale
kindnes in refreshing them, but these savage barbarians,   40
when they mette with them (as after will appeare) were readier
to fill their sids full of arrows then otherwise. And for the
season it was winter, and they that know the winters of that
cuntrie know them to be sharp and violent, and subjecte to
cruell and feirce stormes, deangerous to travill to known   45
places, much more to serch an unknown coast. Besids, what
could they see but a hidious and desolate wildernes, full of
wild beasts and willd men? and what multituds ther might be
of them they knew not. Nether could they, as it were, goe up
to the tope of Pisgah, to vew from this willdernes a more   50
goodly cuntrie to feed their hops; for which way soever they
turnd their eys (save upward to the heavens) they could have
litle solace or content in respecte of any outward objects.
For summer being done, all things stand upon them with a
weatherbeaten face; and the whole countrie, full of woods   55
and thickets, represented a wild and savage heiw. If they
looked behind them, ther was the mighty ocean which they had
passed, and was now as a maine barr and goulfe to seperate
them from all the civill parts of the world. If it be said they
had a ship to sucour them, it is trew; but what heard they   60
daly from the m^r and company? but that with speede they should
looke out a place with their shallop, wher they would be at

some near distance; for the season was shuch as he would not
stirr from thence till a safe harbor was discovered by them
wher they would be, and he might goe without danger; and   65
that victells consumed apace, but he must and would keepe
sufficient for them selves and their returne. Yea, it was mut-
tered by some, that if they gott not a place in time, they
would turne them and their goods ashore and leave them ...

What could now sustaine them but the spirite of God and   70
his grace? May not and ought not the children of these fathers
rightly say: Our faithers were Englishmen which came over this
great ocean, and were ready to perish in this willdernes, but
they cried unto the Lord, and he heard their voyce, and looked
on their adversitie, etc. Let them therfore praise the Lord,   75
because he is good, and his mercies endure for ever. Yea, let
them which have been redeemed of the Lord, shew how he hath
delivered them from the hand of the oppressour. When they wan-
dered in the deserte willdernes out of the way, and found no
citie to dwell in, both hungrie, and thirstie, their sowle   80
was overwhelmed in them. Let them confess before the Lord his
loving kindnes, and his wonderfull works before the sons of
men.

55 ANON., DUNDONALD SCHOOL REGULATIONS (c. 1640)

Orders to be subscribed be him who shall have charge of
instructing the youth heirefter at the Kirk of Dundonald
quhairunto he shall ty himself under paine of deposition
from his office incaice of failzie after dew tryall and
admonitions.   5

1. The maister shall attend at all tymes quhen the
children ar in schoole and not suffer himself to be with-
drawen by drinking, playing or any other avocatioun.

2. If ony (other) inevitable necessitie draw him away a
whole day or the great part of it he shall not faill to   10
have some other in his absence to teach the shollers and
keip them in ordour.

3. If it shall happen that the maister have necessarie
bussiness to withhold him longer nor the space of one day
he shall acquaint the Sessioun therwith, or at leist the   15
minister if the haist of the matter cannot admit delay till
the Sessioun meit, that he may obtean libertie therto.

4. Let the childrein in the moneths of October, November,
December, Januar, Februar, meit in the morning at the sunne

ryssing and be dismissed at the sunne setting at nicht, 20
except some younger ones or those quho ar farder distant
from the shoole, of quhom some consideratioun must be had.
All the rest of the yeir let the hour of gathering in the
morning be seaven of clock and the hour of skailing six,
and such as learns Latein wold always prevent the rest a 25
prettie space.

5. Let the shollers goe to breckfast at 9 hours and con-
vein againe at 10; to dinner lykwayes at 12 hours and returne
at one efternoone, so neir as may be; for quhilk purpose
thair must be a sand glasse to measour the hours. 30

6. Let the maister pray gravelie and religiouslie everie
morning before the shoole at thair first meiting and so at
evin before he dismisse them.

7. Let a task be prescribed everie evining to ilk sholler
in the Lords Prayer, Belief, Commands, Graces or Catechisme, 35
according thair age and progresse, quhilk let them say
everie morning before they enter to thair ordinar lessoun...

12. For the childreins better profiting let these quho
ar farder advanced in reiding Scottish, quhither print or
writ, each of them have the charge of a yong sholler, quho 40
shall sit besyde them, quhom they shall mak perfyte
of his lessoun against the tyme come he shall be called to
say, on the negligent parteis quhilk of the two soever it
shall be fund to have bein; and let the elder shollers them
selfs speir at the maister quhat words they ar ignorant of 45
in thair own lessoun, it being alwayes provyded that the
elder sholler his furdering of the yonger hinder not himself in his learning.

13. Let a speciall care be had of the childreins writing
quho ar meit for it. Let the hour named betwixt xj and 12 50
be alloted to that exercise every day and forder to those
whoise speciall ayme that is. Let the maister mak or mend
thair pens, rule thair paper, cast thair coppes, tak in-
spection particularlie of everie ons writing, point out the
faults and learn them by ocular demonstratioun in his own 55
practeise before them how to mend...

16. And finallie as without disciplein no companie can
be keipit in ordour so leist of all unbrydled youth, therfor
it shall be necessarie that thair shall be in the shoole a
commoun censor quho shall remark all faults and delate them 60
to the maister ... and according to the qualitie of the
faults the maister shall inflict punishment, streking some on

the leg with a birk wand, belt or paire of taws, others on the
hips as thair fault deservs, bot none at ony tyme or in ony
caice on the heid or cheiks. And heirin especiallie is the 65
maister to kyth his prudence in taking up the severall inclinations of his shollers and applying himself thairunto by
lenitie, allurements, commendations, fair words, some littill
rewards, drawing from vice and provocking to vertue such as
may be wone thairby, and others by moderat severitie if 70
that be fund most convenient for thair stubbornes; and let
the wyse maister rather by a grave, austere and authoritative
countenance and cariage represse insolenceis and gaine everie
one to thair dewtie than by stroks, yit not neglecting the
rod quhair it is neidfull. 75

56 H. MANWAYRING, THE SEA-MANS DICTIONARY (1644)

*THE STATE OF A CHRISTIAN, LIVELY SET FORTH BY AN ALLEGORIE
OF A SHIPPE UNDER SAYLE:
TAKEN OUT OF THE* VICTORY OF PATIENCE

My Body is the Hull; *the* Keele *my Backe; my Neck the* Stem;
the Sides *are my Ribbes; the* Beames *my Bones; my flesh the* 5
plankes; *Gristles and ligaments are the* Pintells *and* knee-
timbers; *Arteries, veines and sinewes the severall* seames
of the Ship; my blood is the ballast; *my heart the* principall hold; *my stomack the* Cooke-roome; *my Liver the*
Cesterne; *my Bowels the* sinke; *my Lungs the* Bellowes; *my* 10
teeth the Chopping-knives; *except you divide them, and then
they are the* 32. *points of the Sea-card both agreeing in
number; Concoction is the* Caldron; *and hunger the* Salt *or*
sawce; *my belly is the* lower Decke; *my kidnies* Close Cabbins
or receptacles; my thighes are long Galleries *for the grace* 15
of the Ship; my armes and hands the Can-hookes, *my Midriffe
is a large Partition or* bulk-head; *within the circumference
of my head is placed the* Steeridge-roome *and* chiefe Cabbins,
with the Round house *where the* Master *lyeth, and these for
the more safety and decency are inclosed with a double* 20
fence, the one Dura mater *something hard and thicke, the
other* Pia mater *very thin and soft, which serveth in stead
of hangings; The eares are two doores or* Scuttles *fitly
placed for entertainment; the two Eyes are* Casements *to let
in light; under them is my Mouth the* Stowidge *or* Stewards 25
roome; *my Lipps are* Hatches *for receit of goods; my two*

Nostrils serve as Gratings *to let in ayre; at the one end
stands my chin which is the* Beakehead...

A Bend. Is the outwardmost tymber on the ships-side,
and is also called a Wale: these are the chiefe strength of   30
the Ships-side, to which the Futtocks and knees of the
Beames are Boleed...

A Berth. Is a convenient distance and roome to Moore a
ship in: Also when they would goe cleere of a Point, or a
Rock, they say, take a good *berth*, that is, goe a pretty   35
distance off to sea-Boord of it.

Berthing. They call the raising or bringing-up of Ship-
sides, the *Berthing* of her: as they say, A Clincher, hath
her sides *Berthed*-up, before any beame be put into her.

A Bight. By a *Bight*, is meant any part of a Roape, as it   40
is taken compassing, as when we cannot, or meane not to take
the end in hand, because of a Cabell, or other small Roape
being Quoiled up; we say, give me the *Bight*; that is,
one of the fakes, which lyes rowled up one over the other.

Bildge, or *Buldge.* The *Bildge* of the Ship, is the bredth   45
of the flooce, whereon the ship doth rest, when she is a-
ground. A ship is *Bilged*, that is, when she strikes on a
Rock, or an Anchor, or the like, and breakes off her Timbers or planckes there, and so springs a Leake.

57 T. HOBBES, LEVIATHAN, "OF SPEECH" (1651)

The Invention of *Printing*, though ingenious, compared with
the invention of *Letters*, is no great matter. But who was
the first that found the use of Letters, is not known. He
that first brought them into *Greece*, men say was *Cadmus*, the
sonne of *Agenor*, King of Phænicia. A profitable Invention   5
for continuing the memory of time past, and the conjunction
of mankind, dispersed into so many, and distant regions of
the Earth; and with all difficult, as proceeding from a
watchfull observation of the divers motions of the Tongue,
Palat, Lips, and other organs of Speech; whereby to make   10
as many differences of characters, to remember them. But
the most noble and profitable invention of all other, was
that of SPEECH, consisting of *Names* or *Appellations*, and
their Connexion; whereby men register their Thoughts; recall
them when they are past; and also declare them one to an-   15
other for mutuall utility and conversation; without which,
there had been amongst men, neither Common-wealth, nor

Society, nor Contract, nor Peace, no more than amongst Lyons,
Bears, and Wolves. The first author of Speech was *God* himself, that instructed *Adam* how to name such creatures as   *20*
he presented to his sight; For the Scripture goeth no further in this matter. But this was sufficient to direct him
to adde more names, as the experience and use of the creatures should give him occasion; and to joyn them in such
manner by degrees, as to make himself understood; and so   *25*
by succession of time, so much language might be gotten,
as he had found use for; though not so copious, as an Orator
or Philosopher has need of. For I do not find any thing in
the Scripture, out of which, directly or by consequence can
be gathered, that *Adam* was taught the names of all Figures,   *30*
Numbers, Measures, Colours, Sounds, Fancies, Relations;
much less the names of Words and Speech, as *Generall, Speciall, Affirmative, Negative, Interrogative, Optative, Infin-
itive*, all which are usefull; and least of all, of *Entity, Intentionality,*   *35*
Quiddity, and other insignificant words of the School.
   But all this language gotten, and augmented by *Adam* and
his posterity, was again lost at the tower of *Babel*, when by
the hand of God, every man was stricken for his rebellion,
with an oblivion of his former language. And being hereby   *40*
forced to disperse themselves into severall parts of the
world, it must needs be, that the diversity of Tongues that
now is, proceeded by degrees from them, in such manner, as
need (the mother of all inventions) taught them; and in
tract of time grew every where more copious.   *45*
   The generall use of Speech, is to transferre our Mentall
Discourse, into Verbal; or the Trayne of our Thoughts, into
a Trayne of Words; and that for two commodities; whereof one
is, the Registring of the Consequences of our Thoughts;
which being apt to slip out of our memory, and put us to a   *50*
new labour, may again be recalled, by such words as they
were marked by. So that the first use of names, is to serve
for *Markes*, or *Notes* of remembrance. Another is, when many
use the same words, to signifie (by their connexion and
order), one to another, what they conceive, or think of   *55*
each matter; and also what they desire, feare, or have any
other passion for. And for this use they are called *Signes*.
Speciall uses of Speech are these; First, to Register, what
by cogitation, wee find to be the cause of any thing, present or past; and what we find things present or past may   *60*
produce, or effect: which in summe, is acquiring of Arts.

Secondly, to shew to others that knowledge which we have
attained; which is, to Counsell, and Teach one another.
Thirdly, to make known to others our wills, and purposes,
that we may have the mutuall help of one another. Fourthly,   *65*
to please and delight our selves, and others, by playing
with our words, for pleasure or ornament, innocently.

    To these Uses, there are also foure correspondent Abuses.
First, when men register their thoughts wrong, by the inconstancy of the signification of their words; by which   *70*
they register for their conceptions, that which they never
conceived; and so deceive themselves. Secondly, when they
use words metaphorically; that is, in other sense than that
they are ordained for; and thereby deceive others. Thirdly,
when by words they declare that to be their will, which is   *75*
not. Fourthly, when they use them to grieve one another:
for seeing nature hath armed living creatures, some with
teeth, some with horns, and some with hands, to grieve an
enemy, it is but an abuse of Speech, to grieve him with
the tongue, unless it be one whom wee are obliged to   *80*
govern; and then it is not to grieve, but to correct and
amend.

    The manner how Speech serveth to the remembrance of the
consequence of causes and effects, consisteth in the im-
posing of *Names*, and the *Connexion* of them.   *85*

58 R. BLOME, BRITANNIA (1673)

ISLES OF GREAT BRITAIN

England is blest with a sweet and temperate Air; the *Summers*
(by reason of the continual and gentle winds) so abating the
heats, and the thickness of the *air*, with frequent showers
in the Winter so aswaging the *cold*; that neither the one,   *5*
nor the other, are found obnoxious to its *Inhabitants*: the
Summer not scorching, nor the *Winter* benumning them.

    The whole *Country* is extreamly fertile, and grateful to
the *Husbandman*, abounding in all things necessary for the
use of man, both for *food*, and *rayment*. For what *Commodi-*   *10*
ties it hath not of its own natural product, those defects
(if properly so tearmed) are supplyed from other Countries,
in exchange of ours. The Particulars whereof doth, and may
at large appear in a Volume lately published by me ...

    The *Earth*, for the most part, produceth great plenty of   *15*

grains, as *Wheat*, *Rye*, *Barly*, *Oats*, *Pease*, *Beans*, and
Tares. And its rich *Meadows* and *Pastures* feed innumerable
quantities of *Cattle*, as *Oxen* and *Sheep*, insomuch that
the *English* are observed to eat more *flesh* then any *Nation*
in the *World*. Here are bred excellent *Horses*, both for   20
comliness of *shape*, and *service*, either for *Sadle*, *Coach*,
Cart, or *Plow*. In the *bowels* of the *earth* are store of
excellent *Mines* of *Lead*, *Tynn*, *Iron*, *Copper*, and some of
Silver; and from these *Mines*, especially from the *Lead*
and *Tynn*, great profit is drawn by the vast quantities   25
both wrought and unwrought, not only used at home, but
sent into other Countries. Here are also aboundance of *Mines*
of *Coals*, which with the *Wood* which groweth, plentifully
serveth the *Inhabitants* for *Fewel*. So that if one part is
destitute of *Wood*, that defect is supplyed by *Coals*...   30
    It is every where replenished with fresh and delightful
streams, many of which are *Navigable*; in which said *Rivers*,
as also in the *Seas* that environ the whole *Countrey*, are
found sufficient plenty of excellent *Fish*, as *Salmons*,
Carps, *Trouts*, *Pikes*, *Tench*, *Eels*, *Flounders*, *Smelts*,   35
Perches, *Lampres*, *Mullets*, &c. these are *fresh-water Fish*.
Then in the *Seas*, *Soles*, *Lobstars*, *Oysters*, *fresh Codd*,
Mackarells, *Crabs*, *Prawns*, *Whitings*, *Plaice*; and lastly
Herrings and *Pilchards*, which bring a considerable profit
to this Kingdom, they finding great vent in *Spain*, *Italy*,   40
and elsewhere...

AMERICAN PLANTATIONS

NEW-ENGLAND, seated North of *Mary-land*, conteineth according to the report of Captain *Smith*, 70 *miles* of *Sea-coast*,
in which track are found divers good *Havens*, some of which   45
are capable to harbour about 500 sail of Ships from the
fury of the Sea or Winds, by reason of the interposition
of the great number of *Isles* that lye about the Coast. And
although the Country is seated in the midst of the *Temper-*
ate Zone, yet is the *Clime*, as to *heat* and *cold*, more un-   50
certain then those *European Kingdoms* which lye *parallel*
with it; and as to *Virginia* this may be compared as *Scotland*
is to *England*.
    The *air* is here found very agreeable to the *English*,
which induces them to possess divers potent Colonies...   55

393

The Country is well watered with *Rivers*, the chief amongst
which are *Agamentico, Conectecut, Kinebequy, Merrimeck, Mishuin,
Mistick, Neraganset, Pascataway, Pemnaquid, Tachobacco*, &c.
And in these, as also in the Sea, are taken excellent *fish*,
as *Codd, Thornback, Sturgeon, Porpuses, Hadock, Salmons,
Herrings, Mackrill, Oysters, Lobsters, Crab-fish, Tortoise,*   60
*Cockles, Muscles, Clams, Smelts, Eels, Lamprons, Basses,
Alewives, Hollibuts, Sharks, Seals, Grampus, Whales*, with
sundry other sorts.

Here are great variety of Fowls, as *Phesants, Partridges,
Heath-Hocks, Turks, Pullain, Geese, Ducks, Herns, Cranes,*   65
*Cormorants, Swans, Widgins, Sheldrakes, Snipes, Doppers,
Black-birds*, the *Hum-bird, Loon*, with abundance of others too
tedious to name... Their *Wild-beasts* of chief note, are
*Lyons, Bears, Foxes, Rackoons, Mooses, Musquashs, Otters,
Bevers, Deer, Hares, Coneys*, &c., and for Tame, *Cows,*   70
Sheep, Goats, Swine, and *Horses*... Here are sundry sorts of
Trees, as the *Oak, Cyprus, Pine, Cedar, Firr, Ash, Asp,
Elm, Alder, Maple, Birch, Sasafras, Sumach*, &c. and for
Fruit-trees, the *Apple, Pear, Plumb, Walnut, Chesnut*, ...

The *English* now here inhabiting, are very numerous and   75
powerful; They are governed by *Laws* of their own making;
have their several *Courts* of *Judicature*, and assemble together at their set times and places, as well for the making
of new *Laws*, abolishment of old, hearing and determining of
Causes, as for the electing of a *Governour, Deputy-Gover-*   80
nour, Assistants, Burgesses, and other *Magistrates*; every
Town having two *Burgesses*, and each County annually electing
such like *Officers*, for the looking after the affairs in the
said *Colony*. And in matters that concern *Religion* and *Church
Government*, they are very strict, and make a great shew,   85
being much of the stamp of the rigid *Presbyterians*.

Here are several *Towns* of good account, the chief amongst
which are *Boston* the Metropolis, seated very commodious for
traffick on the *Sea-shoar*; at present a very large and spacious *Town*, or rather *City*, composed of several well-ordered   90
Streets, and graced with fair and beautiful *Houses*, which are
well inhabited by *Merchants* and *Trades-men*, who drive a considerable *trade* for such *commodities* as the Country affordeth, to *Jamaica, Barbados*, and other the *Caribbe Isles*, as
also to *England* and *Ireland*. It is a place of good strength,   95
having two or three hills adjoyning, on which are raised
Fortifications, with great *Guns* mounted thereon ...

NEW-YORK, adjoyning to *New-England* Southwards, so called
from his *Royal Highness James* D. of *York*, the Proprietor
thereof, by grant from his Majesty, and is that part of
New-England which the *Dutch* called the *New-Netherlands*...
It is also possessed by divers sorts of *people*, not much
unlike the *Indians* in *Virginia, Mary-land*, and the other
parts, & are well proportionate, stout, swarthy, black hair'd,
which they wear exceeding long, they are expert at their
bow and *arrows*, which is their chief weapon of *war*, they
are of a ready wit, and apt to receive instructions; ...

100

105

59 E. COLES, ENGLISH DICTIONARY (1676)

TO THE READER

The several Climates of the World, have influenced the Inhabitants with Natures very different from one another. And their
several speeches bear some proportion of Analogy with their
Natures. The *Spanish* and the *Spaniard* both are Grave, the
Italian and th' *Italians* Amourous, the *Dutch* as boisterous
as the *Germans*, and the *French* as light as they themselves
are. But the moderate Clime of *England* has indifferently
temper'd us as to both: and what excess there is in either,
must be attributed to the accession of something Foreign.
Our changes are all professedly owing to the Conquests,
especially of *Sax* and *Normandy*.

5

10

The first was far the greater, and by virtue of That the
body of our Language is still Teutonick: But the Last is
that which more nearly concerneth us; because, though its
first irruption was not a violent Inundation, yet it forced
us to such a Communication with *France*, that our Genius is
wrought into some resemblance of theirs: and (to imitate
them) we bring home fashions, terms and phrases from every
Nation and Language under Heaven. Thus we should fill one
another with Confusion and Barbarity, were it not for some
such faithful Interpreter as is here presented to the
Prince of Isles...

15

20

In that which I have done, I do not warrant absolute perfection. The pains that are taken in it, will appear at first
sight. The addition that is made to the number of words in
former Authors of this kind, is almost incredible (considering the bulk) being raised from seven in th' Expositor to
almost thirty thousand here; which is some thousands more

25

than are in Mr. *Blunts Glossographia* or Mr. *Philips World
of Words*. The order I observe is altogether Alphabetical; 30
for that best answers the design of Informing others. If
any would have the proper Names, Terms of Law, Navigation
(or any other Art) by themselves, they may go through the
whole and (with delight and profit) reduce them all to
their particular Heads... 35

Poetical expressions may be allowed to Poetical Relations
and Fictions; yet here and there I give a hint, to let you
know, that I take them not for real verities. The history
of the Bible I suppose to be so well known, as that I only
give the plain English of the *Hebrew, Chaldee, Syriack* and 40
Greek Names.

Here is a large addition of many words and phrases that
belong to our English Dialects in the several Counties,
and where the particular Shire is not exprest, the distinction (according to the use) is more general into North and 45
South-Country words.

'Tis no disparagement to understand the Canting Terms.
It may chance to save your throat from being cut, or (at
least) your Pocket from being pickt. I have not only retain'd, but very much augmented the number of Old Words. 50
For though Mr. *Blount* (as he saies expressly) shunn'd them,
because they grew obsolete; yet doubtless their use is very
great: not only for the unfolding those Authors that did
use them, but also for giving a great deal of light to other
words that are still in use. Those that I call Old Words are 55
generally such as occurr in *Chaucer, Gower, Pierce Ploughman*
and *Julian Barns*.

And whosoever has a mind, instead of them (or other vulgar
terms) to use expressions that are more polite; he sees what
words are markt for Latin, Greek or French, and may himself 60
make such Collections as will be far more advantageous, than
if they had been gathered to his hand.

Finally, that I might be the more comprehensive (for here
is very much in very little room) I have signified the derivation of the words from their several Originals, and the 65
Names of the Counties in which they are used, by one or two
of their initial letters; the meaning of which is exprest
in the following Table.

60 J. BUNYAN, THE PILGRIM'S PROGRESS (1678)

Then said *Evangelist*, If this be thy condition, why standest
thou still? He answered, Because I know not whither to go.
Then he gave him a *Parchment-Roll*, and there was written
within, *Fly from the wrath to come*.

The Man therefore Read it, and looking upon *Evangelist*   5
very carefully; said, Whither must I fly? Then said *Evangelist*, pointing with his finger over a very wide Field,
Do you see yonder *Wicket-gate*? The Man said, No. Then said
the other, Do you see yonder shining light? He said, I think
I do. Then said *Evangelist*, Keep that light in your eye,   10
and go up directly thereto, so shalt thou see the Gate;
at which when thou knockest, it shall be told thee what thou
shalt do.

So I saw in my Dream, that the Man begun to run; Now he
had not run far from his own door, but his Wife and Child-   15
ren perceiving it, began to cry after him to return: but
the Man put his fingers in his Ears, and ran on crying,
Life, Life, Eternal Life: so he looked not behind him, but
fled towards the middle of the Plain ...

Now I saw in my Dream, that just as they had ended this   20
talk, they drew near to a very *Miry Slough*, that was in the
midst of the Plain, and they being heedless, did both fall
suddenly into the bogg. The name of the Slow was *Dispond*.
Here therefore they wallowed for a time, being grieviously
bedaubed with the dirt; And *Christian*, because of the bur-   25
den that was on his back, began to sink in the Mire.

Pli. Then said Pliable, *Ah, Neighbour* Christian, *where
are you now?*

Ch. Truly, said *Christian*, I do not know.

Pli. At that, *Pliable* began to be offended; and angerly   30
said to his Fellow, *Is this the happiness you have told me
all this while of? if we have such ill speed at our first
setting out, what may we expect, 'twixt this, and our Journey's end? May I get out again with my life, you shall possess the brave Country alone for me.* And with that he gave   35
a desperate struggle or two, and got out of the Mire,
on that side of the Slough which was next to his own
House: So away he went, and *Christian* saw him no more.

Wherefore *Christian* was left to tumble in the Slough
of *Dispondency* alone, but still he endeavoured to struggle   40
to that side of the Slough, that was still further from his

own House, and next to the Wicket-gate; the which he did, but could not get out, because of the burden that was upon his back. But I beheld in my Dream, that a Man came to him, whose name was *Help*, and asked him, *What he did there?*...   45

Now *Christian* looked for nothing but death, and began to cry out lamentably, even cursing the time in which he met with Mr. *Worldly-Wiseman*, still calling himself a thousand fools for hearkening to his counsel: he also was greatly ashamed to think that this Gentlemans arguments, flowing   50 only from the flesh, should have that prevalency with him, to forsake the right way. This done, he applied himself again to *Evangelist* in words and sense as follows.

Chr. Sir, what think you? is there hopes? May I now go back, and go up to the *Wicket-gate*, shall I not be abandon-   55 ed for this, and sent back from thence ashamed. I am sorry I have hearkened to this man's counsel, but may my sin be forgiven.

Evang. Then said *Evangelist* to him, Thy sin is very great, for by it thou hast committed two evils; thou hast forsa-   60 ken the way that is good, to tread in forbidden paths: yet will the man of the Gate receive thee, for he has good will for men; only, said he, take heed that thou turn not aside again, lest thou perish from the way when his wrath is kindled but a little. Then did *Christian* address himself   65 to go back, and *Evangelist* after he had kept him, gave him one smile, and bid him God speed: so he went on with hast, neither spake he to any man by the way; nor if any man asked him, would he vouchsafe them an answer. He went like one that was all the while treading on forbidden ground, and   70 could by no means think himself safe, till again he was got into the way which he left to follow Mr. *Worldly-Wiseman's* counsel: so in process of time, *Christian* got up to the Gate. Now over the Gate there was Written, *Knock and it shall be opened unto you.*   75

61 G. MERITON, A YORKSHIRE DIALOGUE (1683)

A YORKESHIRE DIALOGUE IN ITS PURE NATURAL DIALECT, AS IT (IS) NOW COMMONLY SPOKEN IN THE NORTH PARTS OF YORKESHIRE, BEING A MISCELLANEOUS DISCOURSE, OR HOTCHPOTCH OF SEVERAL COUNTRY AFFAIRES, BEGUN BY A DAUGHTER AND HER MOTHER, AND CONTINUED BY THE FATHER, SON, UNCLE, NEESE, AND LAND-LORD;   5

    D. Mother our Croky's Cawven sine't grew dark,
        And Ise flaid to come nar, she macks sike wark.

M. Seaun, seaun Barn, bring my Skeel and late my tee
   Mack hast, and hye Thee ore to'th Laer to me:
   Weese git a Battin and a Burden Reap,   10
   Though it be mirke, weese late it out by grape;
   Than wee'l toth Field and give the Cow some Hay,
   And see her Clean, before we come away;
   For flaid she git some water before she Cleen,
   And marr her Milk, Ise greet out beath my Neen: 15
D. Whaugh Mother how she Rowts, Ise varra Arfe
   Shee'l put, and rive my good Prunella Scarfe,
M. Ise dinge thy harnes out, thou base mucky Sewe,
   Thou macks sike Anters, Thou'l mistetch my Cow;
   What need thou be seay flaid. She will nut mell,   20
   Nor Hipe, if there war neane here but thy sell;
D. Wally, wally, here's a deft Tinye Cawfe,
   It's better than a Keausteril behawfe,
M. It's newly gitten Feaut, tack haud on't *Tibb*,
   Wee'l suckl't weel, and put it into'th Cribb.   25
   And Bed it Strangly, with good clean Streay,
   And see it lye'th sell down before we geay,
   Now let us hame, and late for Bowles and Sile,
   Thy Father'l meause whore we are all this while.
F. Ise nut farr, ist Cow Cawv'd that's a gooddin,   30
   Now *Tibb* weese git some Beestling puddin,
   Let's Spang our gates for it is varra Snithe,
   And Ise flaid wife, it will be frost belive,
   Leake yonder ist Lad comming, to late for you,
   Hee'd be in Bed, to Morn, we gang to plewe,   35
M. Wya, wya, did'th pot play when you com.
   Wheay keauks the Supper now when Ise fra hame
   What *Hob* ist Beefe aneugh, ist Groats put in
   Till all war deaun, I knawe thou wad not lin.
S. Ey Mother the Groats are in, Ive tane of'th pot,   40
   And'th Cael I seaure are cawd eneugh to Sup; ...

62 ANON., BOG-WITTICISMS (*c.* 1687)

Bryan having been sent in an Errant to a Gentlemans house in
the Country, fell deeply in Love with a *Welch* Maid, who be-
longed to the Kitching there, sometime after he met a Footman
belonging to the same Gentleman; *Bryan* desired him *to tauke*
a pot of *drenk vid him, for a quarter of an hour, vile he*   5
did mauke request to shom Skrivishner to vrite a Letter for

him to *Vrsula*; which being done, *be me shoul Y did pray him to shend it upon* Ursula *by de Waaterman indede*.

Shweet Mrs. Ursula,   The Letter.

Be de ham of me Moddarsh Smock, aund be aul de Usquebah   *10*
daat vash drunk at mine Fadersh Vedding; de Deevil take me
indede, but Y be sho much in Lofe vid dee, daat Y cannot go
to Bed aul the long Night for sleeping upon dee; aund Y cannot be upon vaaking but the Deevil take me, Y do fall upon
dreaming consharning thy shweet shelfe indede, daan do Y tink,   *15*
vaat is the matre? vaat is de maatre vid mine awn shelfe; Aund
Y do feend it is aal for much Love consharning dee, in fait:
Be me shalwashion Y vill tall dee vaat Y vill do indede, and Y vill
put kish upon dy faush indeede, and Y vill be for mauking
Child upon dy Body indeede, aund Y will mauke a great del   *20*
more consharning dee dan dyne own Moddar in fait. Noow de
Deevil tauke de fashion, daat van two yong Cople of Man and
Voman be for coming togedder vid on anodder, daat dare
musht be mauking upon the great Sherimony of de Presht, aund
aul de People to mauke Witnesh upon it: Be me Shoul Y vill   *25*
not mauke staying sho long; but Y vill be dyne Husband
vidout aal daat now, aund be Shaint *Pautrick*, Y vill love
dee like auny ting indede. Y vill shend to *Tredagh* for mine
Moddarsh tree Goats, four Sheep, one Filly Mare, and the
tauny Coow, and vee will be for mauking a Daury in *Lincolns-*   *30*
Inn-Fields be Chreest, aund vee will mauke Butter and Chese,
aund Eggs, and shell our shelves into Plauce and Conferrmant
every day indede. And we vill shing Curds and Crame be
Chreest, and Buttar and Eggs, Bony-Clabber, and Tiff, untel
de Coow shall have Cauf, de Maure shall have Colt, de Goats   *35*
shall have Kidd, aund *Ursulah* shall hauve Child indede;
Aund dan vee vill shet up Housh-kepin and be for livein aul
togadder, be Chreest, as it is de fashion in mine awn Country, in fait. Noow de Deevil tauke me, dear Joy, dou shaut
be for sending Aunswer to vaat Y hauve sent dee by de   *40*
Skriviwnar, aund if dee vilt mete me to morrow morning at
four of de Clock in de aufter noons, aut de Hole in de Vaal,
vee vill go to Bed aund be Mawrry'd presantly indede, vidd-
out de Charge of de Vedding, aund de Priests fese be Chreest,
aund vee vill put de grate Chete upon our Parantsh, aund   *45*
be me Shoul vee vill be Mawrried, dear Joy; aund none body
shaul be vysher for it indede; Aund being at such dishtansh
daat Y cannot come to put Kish upon dy shweet faush, Y vill

put a hoondrad Kishes upon dish Pauper, and shend me Shar-
vish, aund me Affuction to dee indede, and my shalwashion 　　　*50*
Y vill alwash be
　　　　　　Dine owne Dear Joy, BRYAN.
Y have geeven de Vaaterman Shixpensh to breng it to dee,
to shave de charge of de Penny-Posht in fait.

63 J. LOCKE, AN ESSAY CONCERNING HUMANE UNDERSTANDING (1690)

§1　God having designed Man for a sociable Creature, made
him not only with an inclination, and under a necessity to
have fellowship with those of his own kind; but furnished
him also with Language, which was to be the great Instrument, and common Tye of Society. *Man* therefore had by Nature　*5*
his Organs so fashioned, as to be *fit to frame articulate
Sounds*, which we call Words. But this was not enough to
produce Language; for Parrots, and several other Birds, will
be taught to make articulate Sounds distinct enough, which
yet, by no means, are capable of Language.　　　　　　　*10*

§2　Besides articulate Sounds therefore, it was farther
necessary, that he should be *able to use these Sounds, as
signs of internal Conceptions*; and to make them stand as
marks for the *Ideas* within his own Mind, whereby they might
be made known to others, and the Thoughts of Mens Minds　*15*
be conveyed from one to another.

§3　But neither was this sufficient to make Words so useful as they ought to be. It is not enough for the perfection
of Language, that Sounds can be made signs of *Ideas*, unless those *signs* can be so made use of, as *to comprehend*　　*20*
several particular Things: For the multiplication of Words
would have preplexed their Use, had every particular thing
need of a distinct name to be signified by.

§4　*Words* then are made to be signs of our *Ideas*, and *are
general or particular, as the Ideas they stand for are general*　*25*
or particular. But besides these Names which stand for *Ideas*,
there be others which Men have found and make use of, not to
signifie any *Idea*, but the want or absence of some *Ideas*,
simple or complex, or all *Ideas* together; such are the Latin
words, *Nihil*, and in English, *Ignorance* and *Barrenness*. All　*30*
which negative or privative Words, cannot be said properly
to belong to, or signifie no *Ideas*: for then they would be per-

fectly insignificant Sounds; but they relate to positive
Ideas, and signifie their absence.

§5   It may also lead us a little towards the Originall of   35
all our Notions and Knowledge, if we remark, how great a
dependence our *Words* have on common sensible *Ideas*; and how
those which are made use of, to stand for Actions and Notions
quite removed from sense, *have their Original*, and are transferred *from obvious sensible Ideas*; *v.g.* to *Imagine, Apprehend,*   40
Comprehend, Adhere, Conceive, Instill, Disgust, Disturbance,
Tranquillity, &c. are all Words taken from the Operations
of sensible Things, and applied to certain Modes of Thinking.
Spirit, in its primary signification, is Breath; *Angel*, a
Messenger: And I doubt not, but if we could trace them to   45
their Originals, we should find, in all Languages, the names,
which stand for Things that fall not under our Senses, to
have had their first rise from sensible *Ideas*.

64 SALEM WITCHCRAFT PAPERS (1692)

(Joseph Morgan v. Dorcas Hoar)   The depotion of Joseph morgin
aged abought 46 years of their aboughts Testifyeth and saith
that gooday hoer being at my hous did pretend sum thing of
forting telling and thair said that I shuld dy before my wife
and that my oldest dauter shuld not Live to be a woman and   5
further saith that oldest dauter shuld not live to be a
woman. and further sayth that my self being caled to sit on
the Jurey to sarch the body of goodman hore he dying very
sudingly: that then on desiering to have his body stript
thee; said Goody hoar did fly out in a great pation and said   10
what do you think that I have kild my husband you retches
you and

(John Tuck v. Dorcas Hoar)   The depersision of John tuck aged
about 18 years this deponant doth testif and say that I the
s'd. deponant being at the hous of Dorkas hore about 3 year   15
agone with John neal which was then thomas whitredges servant then the s'd. neal brought a hin of the said whors which
he the s'd. neal had kiled doing damage in his s'd. masters
Corn. & I the s'd deponant being thare when the s'd. neal
presented the hen to hear: the s'd hore did then break out   20
in grreat pashan and told the s'd. John neal that it should
be the worst weaks work that Ever he did farder saith not
Jurat in Curia

(Isaac Cummings, Sr. v. Elizabeth How) Jun 27. 1692   25
The disposition of Isaac commins iyner aged about sixty yers
or thare abouts who testyfyeth and saith that about aight yers
agon James how jun'r of ipswech. came to my hous to borow a
hors I not being at home my son isaac told him as my son
told me whan i cam home i hade no hors to ride on but my son   30
isaac did tell the said how that his father hade no hors to
ride on but he hade a mare the which he thought his father
would not be wiling to lend this being upon a thursday the
next day being Fryday I took the mare and my self and my wif
did ride on this maer abute half a mile to an naighbours hous   35
and home again and when we came home I turned the maer out
the maer being as well to my thinking as ever she was next
morning it being saterday about sun rising this said maer stood
neer my doore and the said maer as i did aperehand did show
as if she head bin much abused by riding and here flesh as I   40
thoug much wasted and her mouth (much) read semenly to my
aperehantion much abused and hurt with the bridel bits I seing the maer in such a sad condition I toke up the said maer
and put her into my barn and she wold eate no maner of things
as for provender or any thing w'c i gave her then i sent for   45
my brother thomas andros which was living in boxford the
said anderos came to my hous. I not being at home when I came
home a litil afore night my brother anderos told me he head
giving the said mear somthing for the bots but as he could
pursev it did do her no good but said he I can not tell but   50
she may have the baly ach and said he i wil try one thing
more my brother anderos said he wold take a pipe of tobaco
and lite it and put itt in to the fundement of the maer I
told him that I thought it was not lawfull he said it was lawfull for man or beast then I toke a clen pipe and filled it   55
with tobaco and did lite it and went with the pipe lite to
the barn then the said anderos used the pipe as he said before
he wold and the pip of tobaco did blaze and burn blew then I
said to my brother anderos you shall try no more it is not
lawful he said I will try again once mor which he did and then   60
thar arose a blaze from the pipe of tobaco which seemed to
me to cover the butocks of the said mear the blaz went up
ward towards the roof of the barn and in the roof of the barn
thar was a grate crackling as if the barn wOld have falen or
bin burnt which semed so to us which ware with in and some   65
that ware with out and we hade no other fier in the barn
(b)ut only a candil and a pipe of tobaco and then I said I

thought my barn or my mear most goe the next day being Lords
day I spoke to my brother anderos at noone to come to see the
said mear and said anderos came and what h(e) did I say not
the same Lords day at night my naighbour John hunkins came   *70*
to my hous and he and I went in to my barn to see this mear
said hunkins said and if I ware as you i wolud cute of a
pece of this mear and burn it I said no not to day but if she
lived til tomorow morning he might cut of a pece off of her
and burn (if) he would presently as we hade spoken these   *75*
words we stept out of the barn and emedeiatly this said mear
fell downe dade and never stured as we coold purseve after
she fell down but lay (stone) dead

    Isac Commings sen'r declared: to the Jury of inquest: that
the above written evidence: is the truth: upon oath June 30th   *80*
1692.

65 E. WALLER, "OF ENGLISH VERSE" (1693)

Poets may boast, as safely vain,
Their works shall with the world remain;
Both, bound together, live or die,
The verses and the prophecy.

But who can hope his lines should long   *5*
Last in a daily changing tongue?
While they are new, envy prevails;
And as that dies, our language fails.

When architects have done their part,
The matter may betray their art;   *10*
Time, if we use ill-chosen stone,
Soon brings a well-built palace down.

Poets that lasting marble seek,
Must carve in Latin, or in Greek;
We write in sand, our language grows,
And, like the tide, our work o'erflows.   *15*

Chaucer his sense can only boast;
The glory of his numbers lost!
Years have defaced his matchless strain;
And yet he did not sing in vain.   *20*

66 SIR W. SCOTT, KENILWORTH (1821)

He exclaimed to the smith in turn, 'Wayland, touch him not,
or you will come by the worse! – the gentleman is a true
gentleman, and a bold.'

'So thou hast betrayed me. Flibbertigibbet?' said the
smith; 'it shall be the worse for thee!'   5

'Be who thou wilt,' said Tressilian, 'thou art in no danger from me, so thou tell me the meaning of this practice,
and why thou drivest thy trade in this mysterious fashion.'

The smith, however, turning to Tressilian, exclaimed, in
a threatening tone, 'Who questions the Keeper of the Crys-   10
tal Castle of Light, the Lord of the Green Lion, the Rider
of the Red Dragon? – Hence! – avoid thee, ere I summon Tal-
pack with his fiery lance, to quell, crush, and consume!'
These words he uttered with violent gesticulation, mouthing
and flourishing his hammer.   15

'Peace, thou vile cozener, with thy gipsy cant!' replied
Tressilian, scornfully, 'and follow me to the next magistrate, or I will cut thee over the pate.'

'Peace, I pray thee, good Wayland!' said the boy; 'credit
me, the swaggering vein will not pass here; you must cut   20
boon whids.' . . .

'Why, so thou didst, thou peevish fool,' answered the
youth; 'thou didst lie on that bench even now, didst thou
not? But art thou not a hasty coxcomb, to pick up a wry word
so wrathfully? Nevertheless, loving and honouring my lord   25
as truly as thou, or any one, I do say, that should Heaven
take him from us, all England's manhood dies not with him.'

'Ay,' replied Blount, 'a good portion will survive with
thee, doubtless.'

Sources of shorter texts (t1–t57)

References are to *STC* (*Short Title Catalogue*) and Wing; abbreviations of text or facsimile series: EE = English Experience; EETS = Early English Text Society; EL = English Linguistics; ScM = Scolar Press, Menston; *ScR* = *Scholar's Reprints*; STS = Scottish Text Society (for details see Bibliography); B.L. = British Library

t1 Jonathan Swift, *A Proposal for Correcting, Improving and Ascertaining the English Tongue*... (London, 1712); from Bolton 1966:117

t2 John Hart (see T6), 1569: fol. 21r

t3 Robert Reyce, *The Breviary*: MS Ipswich; from Harlow 1970:171

t4 Richard Verstegan (R. Rowlands), *A restitution of decayed intelligence* (Antwerp, 1605, 3rd ed. 1634); from Moore 1910:126

t5 John Ray, *A collection of English words* (London, 1674), sig. A5r–A6r: Wing R388, B.L., 435.a.26

t6 Samuel Daniel, *The poeticall essayes* (London, 1599), sig. F2v: *STC* 6221

t7 Murdoch Nisbet, *The New Testament in Scots ... c.1520*, ed. T. G. Law, STS, 3 vols. (1901–5)

t8 Anon.; from Barber 1976:27–8

t9 William Harrison (see T36A), 1808: V, preface

t10 William Shakespeare, *As You Like It*, V,1.47ff.; from Hinman 1968:222

t11 George Puttenham (see T11), 1589:123

t12 *Batman vppon Bartholome* (London, 1582), sig. π: facs. Anglistica & Americana 161 (Hildesheim, 1976). *On the Properties of Things*: John Trevisa's translation of Bartholomæus Anglicus, *De proprietatibus rerum*, ed. M. C. Seymour *et al.* (Oxford, 1975), I, 41

t13   Henry Peacham, *The Garden of Eloquence* (London, 1577), sig. Gii^v: *STC* 19497; facs. Gainesville, 1954, EL 267

t14   Ralph Lever, *The arte of reason, rightly termed, witcraft*... (London, 1573), sig. **i^v: *STC* 15541; facs. EL 323, "The Forespeache"

t15   Ulpian Fulwell, *The Flower of Fame* (London, 1575), sig. Bii^v: *STC* 11475; cf. Jones 1953:99–100

t16   Thomas Becon, *The worckes* (London, 1564, 1560, 1563): *STC* 1710, fols. 475v, 478r; cf. Jones 1953:60

t17 &   Joseph Glanvill, *The Vanity of Dogmatizing* (London, 1661, 2nd
t18   ed. 1664, 3rd ed. 1676): Wing G834; from Jones, in Fish 1971:64

t19   John Wilkins, *Ecclesiastes* (London, 1646): Wing W2188; from Jones, in Fish 1971:196–7

t20   Ben Jonson (see T14); from King 1941:xv

t21   Joseph Addison, *The Spectator*, No. 285 (26.1.1712), ed. D.F. Bond (Oxford, 1965), III, 11

t22   Sir Thomas Elyot, *The boke named the Gouernour* (London, 1531), fol. 19v: *STC* 7635; facs. EL 246

t23   John Palsgrave, *The Comedy of Acolastus*... *(1540)*, ed. P.L. Carver, EETS 202 (1937); from Rusch 1972:23

t24   Roger Ascham, *Toxophilus* (London, 1545), sig. Aiij^r: *STC* 837; facs. EE 79

t25   Joseph Addison, *The Spectator*, No. 417 (28.6.1712), ed. Bond, III, 566 (see t21)

t26   Martin Billingsley, *The Pens Excellencie*... (London, 1618): *STC* 3062

t27   Elizabeth I (see T20D), 5 Metr. 1–9; from EETS 113, p. 32

t28   James VI (see T28), MS Bodley 165 (1583/4), stanza from the poem *Phœnix*; from Croft 1973, no. 24; the text was printed, in slightly anglicized form, in *Essays* (T28), 1584: sig. Hij^r

t29   John Milton (see T33f.), Trinity MS 1634; from Croft 1973, no. 47; passage from *Comus* 890ff.

t30   Sir John Cheke, *The Gospel according to St. Matthew*..., ed. J. Goodwin (London, 1843)

t31   John Hart (see t2, T6), *A Methode*... (London, 1570): *STC* 12889; B.L., C.54.b.15, sig. Di^{rv}; facs. from R. Kaiser, ed., *Medieval English*, 3rd ed. (Berlin, 1958), plate III

t32   John Bullokar (see T7), title page and p. 43 (p. 43 also in
t33   Dobson 1968:100)

t34   Alexander Gil, *Logonomia Anglica* (London, 1619, 2nd ed. 1621): *STC* 11873–4, 1619:110, 1621:114; from Dobson

1968:134–5. Text quoted: Spenser, *Faerie Queene*, I, 4, 10

t35   Richard Mulcaster (see T8); 1582:155

t36   John Hart (see t2, T6), 1569: fols. 18v–19r

t37   Ben Jonson (see T14), *The Alchemist*, II, 1, 89–104, ed. C. H. Herford and P. Simpson (Oxford, 1937), V, 317; passage also in Graband 1965:136

t38   James Howell, *Familiar Letters*, book II, no. 56 (9.8.1630); from Tucker 1961:28

t39   Sir Thomas More, *The Apologye of Syr Thomas More, knyght*, ed. A. I. Taft, EETS 180 (1930); from S. Brook, *The Language of the Book of Common Prayer* (London, 1965), p. 86

t40 &   John Wilkins, *An Essay Towards a Real Character, and a*
t41   *Philosophical Language* (London, 1668): Wing W2196; facs. EL 119, pp. 8 and 278–9

t42   P. Ashton, *A short treatise vpon the Turkes chronicles* (London, 1556), sig. *vi^v: *STC* 11899; from Bennett 1952: I, 175

t43   Robert Cawdrey, *A Table Alphabeticall . . .* (London, 1604), title page: facs. Gainesville 1966; EE 226

t44   Henry Cockeram, *The English Dictionarie* (London, 1623, 2nd ed. 1626), sig. A3v: STC 5462; facs. Anglistica & Americana 54 (Hildesheim, 1970)

t45   Edward Phillips, *The New World of English Words* (London, 5th ed. 1696), preface: Wing P2073; from Osselton 1958:18

t46   J.K. (John Kersey?), *A New English Dictionary* (London, 1702), title page and preface

t47   Randle Cotgrave, *A Dictionarie of the French and English Tongues* (London, 1611): *STC* 5830; facs. Columbia, 1950; EL 82

t48   Sir Thomas Elyot, *Of the knowledg which maketh a wise man* (London, 1533), sig. A3^{rv}: *STC* 7668; passage also in Moore 1910:82

t49   Sir Thomas Elyot (see t22), 1531:94r; quotation also in Jones 1953:80

t50   Sir Thomas Hoby (see T5); quotation also in Jones 1953:47

t51   Anon., *A Hundred Mery Talys* (London, 1526), from H. Oesterley, ed., *Shakespeare's Jest Book* (1866, Gainesville, rev. ed. 1970), p. 17; quotation also in Jones 1953:6

t52   Angel Day (see T43); from Jones 1953:106

t53   Henry Peacham (see t13), 1577: sig. Gii^v

t54   John Hart (see t31); from Jones 1953:107

t55 &   Nathaniel Fairfax, *A Treatise of the Bulk and Selvedge of the*
t56   *World* (London, 1674), sig. A5^v–A6^r: Wing F131

t57   John Wilkins (see t40–1), 1668:216

Bibliographical notes on texts T1–T66

Summarized from the *Dictionary of National Biography*, Dobson (1968) and editions of the individual texts. The information starts with biographical data and a characterization of the passage chosen; there follows (S) = source/edition used; and (L) = relevant literature, especially as an aid to linguistic analysis. (These specialized titles are not repeated in the general bibliography.)

1   William Caxton (?1422–91), England's first printer; translator particularly of French texts and editor of ME texts, here of Trevisa's translation (*c.* 1387) of the Latin original of Ranulph Higden (†1364). Passages added by Trevisa relating to contemporary conditions are here italicized.

(S)   Higden, Ranulphus, *Description of Britayne, & also Irlonde taken oute of Policronicon* (1480): *STC* 13440a; facs. EE 386 (1971). The excerpt is from ch. xv (no pagination).

(L)   N. F. Blake, *Caxton and His World* (London, 1969), pp. 171ff.

2   William Caxton, translation of a French prose-rendering of Virgil's *Aeneid*.

(S)   *Eneydos* (Westminster, 1490): *STC* 24796; B.L., IC 55135. The prologue was edited by W. J. B. Crotch, EETS 176 (1928), pp. 107–10; Bolton 1966:1–4; Fisher and Bornstein 1974:179–88, with facs.; excerpt from sig. Ai^r–ii^r.

(L)   Fisher and Bornstein 1974:179–81

3   William Lily (?1468–1522), grammarian, Headmaster of St Paul's School, London (1512–22). John Colet (?1467–1519), dean of St Paul's and founder of St Paul's School, for which he wrote his *Latin Grammar* in 1509. The text is from the first edition of his school grammar, which was authorized by the king and of which some 350 editions were published.

(S)   William Lily and John Colet, *A shorte Introduction of Grammar, generally to be vsed in the Kynges Maiesties dominions, for the bryngynge vp of all those that entende to atteyne the knowlege of the Latine tongue* (1549): *STC* 15611; facs. EL 262 (1970). The excerpt is from sig. Aii^r–iii^r.

4   Sir Thomas Wilson, secretary of state and scholar (?1525–81). *Rule of Reason* 1551. His *Arte of Rhetorique* is the most typical sixteenth-century handbook of Ciceronian rhetoric.

(S)   *The Arte of Rhetorique, for the vse of all suche as are studious of Eloquence, sette forth in English* (London: R. Grafton, 1553): *STC* 25799; facs. EE 206 (1969). *ScR* (1962). The excerpts are from book III, fols. 86^r–88^r.

(L)   Baugh 1978:262–4; Barber 1976:82–7; Howell 1956:98–110; Jones 1953:100–2

5   Sir John Cheke (1514–57), professor of Greek at Cambridge (1540–51), tutor to Edward, Prince of Wales, 1544, introduced the modern pronunciation of Greek. He was in favour of a spelling reform of English and against excessive borrowing of Latin words. His partial translation of the New Testament (*c.* 1550) includes the Lord's Prayer (t30). The letter here printed was probably written in 1557; it forms part of the preface to Hoby's translation and is often quoted in modernized form.

(S)   *The Courtier of Count Baldessar Castilio ... done into Englyshe by Thomas Hoby* (London, 1561): *STC* 4778; B.L., 1030.c.13. The excerpt is from sig. Aiii^r.

(L)   Baugh 1978:261; Dobson 1968:38–46; Jones 1953:102–3, 121–2

6   John Hart, Chester Herald (†1574), probably the most important phonetician and spelling reformer of the sixteenth century; his marginal headings are here italicized and incorporated.

(S)   *An Orthographie, conteyning the due order and reason, howe to write or paint thimage of mannes voice, most like to the life or nature* (London, 1569): *STC* 12890; facs. EL 209 (1969); ed. by B. Danielsson (Stockholm, 1955–63). The excerpt is from fols. 3^r–5^v.

(L)   Danielsson 1955; Dobson 1968:62–8; Jones 1953:137–8, 147–50

7   William Bullokar (*c.* 1530–1609), "the most persistent of spelling reformers" (Dobson 1968:93).

(S)   *Booke at large, for the Amendement of* Orthographie *for English speech: wherein, a most perfect supplie is made, for the wantes and double* sounde of letters in the olde Orthographie... (London: H. Denham, 1580): *STC* 4086; facs. EE 24 (1968); facs. ed. by J. R. Turner (Leeds, 1970). The excerpt is from fols. 1ᵛ–2ᵛ.

(L)   Dobson 1968:93–117; Jones 1953:154–6

8   Richard Mulcaster (?1530–1611), born in Cumberland, but educated in the south, was one of the outstanding pedagogues of the sixteenth century. When he was Headmaster of Merchant Taylors' School (1561–86), his pupils probably included Edmund Spenser; Headmaster of St Paul's School (1596–1608). His book on English spelling is the first part of a projected grammar which was never completed.

(S)   *The First Part of the Elementarie which entreateth chefelie of the right writing of our English tung* (London: T. Vautroullier, 1582): *STC* 18250; facs. EL 219 (1970); ed. by E. T. Campagnac 1925. The excerpts are from pp. 158, 159, 253–9.

(L)   Dobson 1968:117–28; Jones 1953:157–67, 192–4, 205–7

9   Thomas Harman, country gentleman from Kent.

(S)   *A Caueat or Warening for Common Cursetors, vulgarely called Vagabones*... (London, 1567, 1573): *STC* 12787–8. The textual history of the early editions is uncertain. There is no critical edition; E. Viles and F. J. Furnivall's EETS edition (es 9, 1868) is not satisfactory; the text is therefore from Holzknecht 1954:243–4.

10   William Harrison (1535–93), topographer and historian. Apart from the introductory description of Britain, he also contributed Book V to Holinshed's *Chronicle*, a rendering of Boetius' *Scottish Chronicle* (T36 and T36A) (also see T52).

(S)   Raphael Holinshed, *The firste volume of the Chronicles of Englande, Scotlande, and Irelande* (London, for J. Harrison, 1577, 2nd ed. 1587; ed. London, 1807–8; repr. New York, 1965), pp. 24–6 (1807) (cf. Bolton 1966:13–21). The second edition has significant alterations and additions by John Hooker (?1526–1601) which illustrate the linguistic-stylistic progress made by English and Scots and a considerably altered attitude towards the vernaculars (cf. especially lines 4–21, 43–7, 53–72, 95–101).

11   George Puttenham (†1590); the ascription is uncertain (Richard Puttenham?, Lord Lumley?).

(S)   *The arte of English poesie* (London: R. Field, 1589): *STC* 20519; facs. EE 342 (1971); EL 110 (1968). The facsimile is from pp. 119–23; (cf. t11).

Texts

(L)   Barber 1976:26–7, 37–8; Howell 1956:327–9; Jones
1953:129–39; *The Arte...*, ed. G. D. Willcock and A. Walker
(Cambridge, 1936), pp. lxxxiv–xciv

12   Richard Carew (1555–1620), country gentleman from
Cornwall, M.P., antiquary, translated Tasso and wrote a
Description of Cornwall. The essay from which the excerpt is
taken was prompted by Henri Estienne's (1528–98) *De la
précellence du langage françois* (Paris, 1579). Carew's text became
widely known by being included in Camden (1614).

(S)   *The Excellency of the English Tongue* (written in 1595–6?, 1605?)
in MS B.L., Cotton Jul.F.xi, from which it was printed in
William Camden, *Remaines concerning Britaine: But especially
England, and the Inhabitants thereof* (London, 1614): *STC* 4522;
ed. from the MS in Smith 1904:II,285–95. The excerpts are
from fols. 265^r–7^v (Camden 1614:36–44).

(L)   D. N. C. Wood, "Elizabethan English and Richard Carew", in
Neophilologus 61 (1977), 304–15

13   Sir Francis Bacon, Baron Verulam, Viscount St Albans
(1561–1626), Lord Chancellor, Attorney-General, Privy
Councillor, etc., philosopher and essayist, wrote in English and
Latin. He translated and expanded his *Advancement* as *De
augmentis scientiarum* (1623) – which was in turn 'Englished' by
Wats (Oxford, 1640).

(S)   *The Twoo Bookes of Francis Bacon. Of the proficience and
aduancement of learning, diuine and humane* (London: H.
Tomes, 1605): *STC* 1164, B.L., C.38e.26; facs. EE 218 (1970).
The excerpts are from fols. 17^v–19^r.

(L)   Brekle 1975:281–7; Howell 1956:365–75; M. W. Croll, "Attic
Prose: Lipsius, Montaigne, Bacon" (1923), reprinted in Fish
1971:3–25; B. Vickers, *Bacon and Renaissance Prose* (Cambridge,
1968); K. R. Wallace, *Francis Bacon on Communication and
Rhetoric* (Chapel Hill, 1943)

14   Ben Jonson (1572–1637), poet and dramatist. *Timber* contains
jottings and reflections, most of which were translated from, or
suggested by, reading Latin authors. (The excerpt paraphrases
Quintilian, *Institutio oratoria*, 1.6.)

(S)   *Timber: or, Discoveries; Made vpon Men and Matter: as they have
flow'd out of his daily Readings; or had their refluxe to his peculiar
Notion of the Times (The Workes of Benjamin Jonson)* (London,
1641; written in ?1637): B.L., C.39.k.9; facs. ScM 1975. (The
passage is also in Bolton 1966:37–45.) The excerpt is from
pp.118–20.

15   John Dryden (1631–1700), poet laureate (1670–89), dramatist,
      adapter of Shakespeare and translator of Chaucer (T18H),
      Virgil (T21L), Boccaccio, etc.

(S)   *Defence of the Epilogue, or, An Essay on the Dramatique Poetry of
      the last Age*, printed as an appendix to *The Conquest of Granada
      by the Spaniards*... (London: for H. Herringman, 1672): Wing
      D2256; Bodleian Library, Malone L.36. (The passage is also in
      Bolton 1966:55–69.)

(L)   J. M. Bately, "Dryden's revisions in the *Essay of Dramatic
      Poesy*...", *Review of English Studies* 15 (1964), 268–82

16   John Evelyn (1620–1706), instigator and from 1672 secretary
      of the Royal Society; his *Diary* was first published in 1818–19.
      Sir Peter Wyche (1628–99?), diplomat and translator.

(S)   "Letter to Sir Peter Wyche, 1665", printed in Spingarn
      1908–9:II,312–15.

(L)   See no. 17

17   Thomas Sprat (1635–1713), Bishop of Rochester and Dean of
      Westminster, in 1663 became one of the first members of the
      Royal Society; praised for the style of his sermons.

(S)   *The History of the Royal-Society of London, For the Improving of
      Natural Knowledge* (London, 166): Wing S5032; B.L., 740.c.17;
      ed. Spingarn 1908–9:116–19. The excerpt is from book II, ch.
      xx, pp. 111–13.

(L)   Barber 1976:132–3; Howell 1956:388–90; R. F. Jones,
      "Science and English prose style in the third quarter of the
      seventeenth century", *Publications of the Modern Language
      Association* 45 (1930), 977–1009.

18A   Gavin Douglas (?1474–1522), poet, translator, Archbishop of
      St Andrew's (1514), Bishop of Dunkeld (1516–20). His
      translation of the *Aeneid* (which was not published until 1553)
      circulated in manuscript form, thus influencing Surrey's
      (T21C).

(S)   *Virgil's Aeneid Translated into Scottish Verse*, ed. from MS
      Trinity College Cambridge 0.3.12 (copied by Douglas'
      secretary M. Geddes, *c.* 1515) by C. F. C. Coldwell, STS III,
      25, 27, 28, 30 (1962–). The excerpts are from III, 25:6, 12–13.

(L)   Coldwell 1964:111–15

18B   William Tyndale (†1536), reformer and biblical translator,
      lived in Germany from 1524; he started printing the New
      Testament in Cologne in 1525 and finished it in Worms in
      1526. He was imprisoned and killed in Vilvorde in 1535.

(S)   *The Obedience of a Christen Man and how Christen Rulers ought to*

Texts

Governe/where in also (yf thou marke diligently) thou shalt fynde eyes to perceave the crafty conveyaunce of all iugglers (Marlborow, in the lande of Hesse [Antwerp?]: H. Luft, 1528): *STC* 24446; B.L., C.53.b.1; facs. ScM (1970). The excerpts are from fols. 15ʳᵛ.

(L) N. Davis, *William Tyndale's English of Controversy* (London, 1971)

18C *The New Testament of Iesvs Christ, translated faithfvlly into English, out of the authentical Latin, according to the best corrected copies of the same, diligently conferred with the Greeke and other editions in diuers languages: With Arguments of bookes and chapters, Annotations, and other necessarie helpes, for the better vnderstanding of the text, and specially for the discouerie of the Corrvptions of diuers late translations, and for cleering the Controuersies in religion, of these daies. In the English College of Rhemes* (Reims: I. Fogny, 1582): *STC* 2884; facs: ScM (1975)

18D *The Holy Bible, Conteyning the Old Testament, and the New: Newly Translated out of the Originall tongues: & with the former Translations diligently compared and reuised, by his Maiesties speciall Commandement. Appointed to be read in Churches* (London: R. Barker, 1611, the "Authorized Version"): *STC* 2216; ed. by W.A. Wright (Cambridge, 1909).

18E George Pettie (1548–89), writer of romances. The translation of 1579 (first printed in 1586) is from the French rendering of the Italian original.

(S) *The Ciuile Conuersation of M. Stephen Guazzo ... translated ... by G. pettie* (London, 1586): *STC* 12423; Cambridge, University Library, Syn.7.58.18. The excerpt comes from sig. Aviᵛ–.

(L) Barber 1976:86–7; Jones 1953:177–8, 205

18F John Florio (?1553–1625), compiler of the best contemporary Italian–English dictionary (1598), translator of Montaigne, and possibly caricatured by Shakespeare as Holofernes, cf. T31F.

(S) *The Essayes or Morall, Politike and Millitarie Discourses of Lo: Michaell de Montaigne ... First written by him in French And now done into English...* (London: for E. Blount, 1603): *STC* 18041, B.L., C.59.i.18. The excerpts come from sig. A5ʳᵛ.

18G Stapylton (see 21H)

18H John Dryden (cf. 15), *Fables Ancient and Modern* (London, 1700): Wing D2278. Passage also in W.P. Ker, ed., *Essays of John Dryden* (New York, 1961), II, 266–7.

19A   *Later Version* of the Wyclif Bible, *c.* 1395, in MS B.L., Royal 1 C viii., ed. by J. Forshall and F. Madden, *The Holy Bible, containing the Old and New Testaments with the Apocryphal Books, in the earliest versions made from the Latin Vulgate by John Wycliffe about A.D. 1380 and revised by John Purvey about A.D. 1388* (Oxford, 1879); excerpts from MS Royal, fols. 355^{rb-vb}.

19B   *The newe Testament/dylygently corrected and compared with the Greke by Willyam Tyndale...* (Antwerp: de Keyser, 1534): *STC* 2826, Herbert 13; ed. by N. H. Wallis (Cambridge, 1909)

19C and 19D   See 18C and 18D

19E   *The New English Bible with the Apocrypha* (London, 1970; N.T.: 1961, 2nd ed., 1970)
       19A–19D are found (somewhat unreliably transcribed) together with other Renaissance versions in *The English Hexapla exhibiting the Six Important English Translations of the New Testament* (London, 1841?).

(L)   F. F. Bruce, *The English Bible: A History of Translations* (London, 1961); J. M. Grainger, *Studies in the Syntax of the King James Version*, Studies in Philology 2 (1907); A. C. Partridge, *English Biblical Translation* (London, 1973); H. W. Robinson, ed., *The Bible in Its Ancient and English Versions* (London, 1940).

20A   Boethius, Anicius M.S. (*c.* 480–525), philosopher and politician, wrote on philosophy, music, theology, mathematics and logic. He was an important mediator between classical antiquity and the medieval world. His best known work is *De consolatione philosophiae* (written in prison).

(S)   Boethius, *Consolationis philosophiae libri quinque*, ed. by K. Büchner (Heidelberg, 1947).

20B   Geoffrey Chaucer (1340–1400).

(S)   MS B.L., Add.10340; ed. R. Morris, EETS ES 5 (1868); cf. Caxton's printing (?1478): *STC* 3199; facs. EE 644 (1974). The excerpt comes from MS fol. 3va.

(L)   R. W. F. Elliott, *Chaucer's Language* (London, 1974), pp. 153–70

20C   George Colville (or Coldewel), translator. Biographical data (as with the other translators below) are scant or lacking altogether.

(S)   *Boetivs de Consolatione philosophiae* (London: J. Cawoode, 1556):

STC 3201; B.L., 231.f.13. The excerpt comes from sig. Bi^{rv}; the facsimile page is from Isaac 1936.

20D Elizabeth I (1533–1603), queen of England from 1558, daughter of Henry VIII and Anne Boleyn, was educated in the humanities by her tutor Ascham.

(S) *Queen Elizabeth's Englishings of Boethius, Plutarch and Horace*, ed. by C. Pemberton, EETS 113 (1899). The excerpt comes from S.1f (cf. t27).

(L) F. Fehlauer, *Die englischen Übersetzungen von Boethius De consolatione philosophiae* (Berlin, 1909); G. B. Riddehough, 'Queen Elizabeth's Translation of Boethius' *De consolatione philosophiae*', in *Journal of English and Germanic Philology* 45 (1946), 88–94

20E I.T.: the translator's identity is unknown.
(S) *Fiue bookes of philosophicall comfort. Newly translated* (London: for M. Loanes, 1609): STC 3202; B.L., 1385.c.16. The excerpt comes from sig. Bi^{rv}.

20F Sir Harry Coningsby, *The Consolation of Philosophy* (London: J. Flesher, 1664): Wing B3428, B.L., 11623.a.3

20G Edmund Elys (*fl.* 1707), parson at East Allington 1659–89, published Quaker treatises and religious poetry.
(S) *Summum Bonum, or an Explication of the Divine Goodness in the Words of the Most Renowned Boetivs. Translated by a Lover of Truth, and Virtue* (Oxford, 1674): Wing B3434, B.L., 8461.a.18

20H Richard Graham, Viscount Preston (1648–95), politician and ambassador, was repeatedly imprisoned in the Tower, where he drafted his translation of the *Consolation*, which remained the standard rendering until well into the twentieth century.
(S) *A.M.S. Boetius on the consolation of philosophy* (London, 1695): Wing B3433; B.L., 8461.bb.22
Other passages from several translations are found in Rigg 1968:114–35 (King Alfred, Chaucer, Walton, Queen Elizabeth, Green).

21A Publius Vergilius Maro (70–19 BC), Roman poet. His works are among the most translated texts of the European Renaissance and the classical movement. The *Aeneid*, and – owing to the contents – especially Book IV, was very popular. Apart from the versions here printed, cf. Caxton's translation of a French prose version (T2) and – in Spenserian stanzas – Sir Richard Fanshawe, *The fourth book of the Aeneid on the loves of Dido and Aeneas done into English* (London, 1652; ed. by A. L. Irvine, Oxford, 1924); Sir John Harington, *Virgil's Aeneis* (1659; Books I–VI); Sir Robert Howard, *The fourth book of Virgill: of the loves of Dido and Aeneas* (in *Poems*, 1660); and Nahum Tate's Libretto for Purcell's opera *Dido and Aeneas* (*c.*1690).

(S)   *P. Vergilii Opera*, ed. by F. A. Hirtzel (Oxford, 1900)

21B   Douglas, III, 25:162, 166 (see 18A)

21C   Henry Howard, Earl of Surrey (?1517–47), courtier and poet, influenced by Petrarch; with Wyatt, introduced the sonnet into English literature. His translation of the *Aeneid* survives in two printed versions and in manuscript form, which appear to represent different stages of the translation. The influence of Douglas is particularly conspicuous in the earliest version; borrowings from T20B are here in italics (following Ridley).

(S)   *Certain bokes of Virgiles Æneis* (London: R. Tottell, 1557): *STC* 24798; ed. by F. H. Ridley (Berkeley, 1963)

(L)   Ridley 1963; O. Fest, *Über Surreys Aeneisübersetzung* (Berlin, 1903)

21D   Thomas Phaer (?1510–60), lawyer, physician and translator; wrote legal handbooks and medical treatises. His partial translation of the *Aeneid* (1555–60) was completed by Thomas Twyne in 1584.

(S)   *The seuen first bookes of the Eneidos conuerted in Englishe meter* (London: for R. Jugge, 1558): *STC* 24799

(L)   E. J. W. Brenner, *Thomas Phaer, mit besonderer Berücksichtigung seiner Aeneisübersetzung...* (Heidelberg, 1913)

21E   Richard Stanyhurst (1547–1618) translated parts of the *Aeneid* and contributed the "Description of Ireland" and "History of Ireland" to Holinshed's *Chronicle* (T52). As a Roman Catholic, he lived in exile from *c.*1580.

(S)   *The First Foure Bookes of Virgil his Aeneis Translated intoo English heroical verse* (Leiden, 1582): *STC* 24806; B.L., C.56.d.3; ed. by D. van der Haar (Amsterdam, 1933); see van der Haar 6–50.

21F   John Vicars (?1580–1652), Presbyterian and poetaster, mentioned in Butler's *Hudibras* (I.640).

(S)   *The XII Aeneids of Virgil* (London: N. Alsop, 1632): *STC* 24809

21G   The translation is anonymous, the translator's identity very doubtful (Sir D. Digges?).

(S)   *Didos death* (London: for W. Burre, 1622): *STC* 24811

Texts

21H   Sir Robert Stapylton (?–1669), dramatist and translator.
(S)   *Dido and Aeneas. The fourth booke of Virgils Aeneis* (London: W.
       Cooke, 1634?): *STC* 24812

21J   John Ogilby (1600–76), translator, geographer, dancing-master
       and publisher, made fun of by Dryden and Pope.
(S)   *The Works of Publius Virgilius Maro. Translated by*... (London:
       J. Crook, 1649): Wing V608; B.L., 833.d.26 (2nd edn.,
       completely revised (London, 1654): Wing V610; B.L.,
       1872.a.33)

21K   Edmund Waller (1606–87), poet, praised by contemporaries
       for the harmony of his verse (T15/113, 183) completed the
       translation by Sidney Godolphin (1610–43) of the fourth book
       of the *Aeneid*; cf. T65.
(S)   *The Passion of Dido for Æneas. As it is Incomparably exprest in the*
       Fourth Book of Virgil (London, 1658; text identical with 2nd
       edn., 1679): Wing V633; B.L., C.58.a.28; excerpt from sig.
       B7^r.

21L   John Dryden (T15), *The Works of Virgil: Containing his*
       Pastorals, Georgics, and Æneis. Translated into English Verse
       (London, 1697): Wing V61; B.L., 74.k.10; excerpts from p.
       301, lines 182–92.

21M   C. Day Lewis (1904–72), poet and literary critic.
(S)   *The Aeneid of Virgil* (London, 1952)
       Compare the parallel translations printed in Rigg 1968:147–73
       (II, 199–233; IV, 1–30, 173–94, 642–62 in ABCLM).

22A   Thomas Berthelet(te) (†1555), printer to the crown (1530–55),
       pupil of Pynson; John Gower (?1325–1408), one of the major
       poets in the age of Chaucer.
(S)   *Jo. Gower de Confessione Amantis* (London: T. Berthelette,
       1532): *STC* 12143; B.L., 641.k.3. The excerpt is from sig.
       aa.ii^v.

22B   Thomas Speght (*fl.* 1598), Headmaster of Ely Cathedral
       School (?) 1572, editor of Chaucer's *Works*.
(S)   *The workes of our antient, and lerned English poet, G. Chaucer*
       newly printed (London: G. Bishop, 1598): *STC* 5077; facs.
       Geoffrey Chaucer. The Works 1532, ed. by D. S. Brewer, ScM
       (1969)

23A–B E.K., presumably Spenser's friend Edward Kirke (1553–1613),
       who possibly also had a hand in the glossary. Edmund Spenser,

poet. His father was from Lancashire, a fact reflected in the language of the *Shepheardes Calender*. Sidney (T26 and T27) and Spenser were members of the influential literary club "Areopagus". Spenser's poetry, especially his *Faerie Queene* (T24), greatly influenced English poetic diction, especially in its archaizing tendencies.

(S)   *The Shepheardes Calender Conteyning twelue Aeglogues proportionable to the twelue monethes* (London: H. Singleton, 1579), *STC* 2308; facs. (with an introduction by H. O. Sommer, London, 1890), ScM (1968). The facsimile and excerpt are from sign. π ii^{rv}, fols. 26^r–27^r, 29^v–30^r.

24   Edmund Spenser, *The Faerie Queene* (London, 1590, 1596): *STC* 23080, 23082; facs. (1596) ScM (1976). The excerpts are from sig. A2, pp. 197–200; "Letter to Raleigh", pp. 592–3.

(L)   T23B. Barber 1976:96–9; McElderry 1932; B. Groom, *The Diction of Poetry from Spenser to Bridges* (Toronto, 1955); A. W. Sugden, *The Grammar of Spenser's Faerie Queene* (Philadelphia, 1936)

25   John Lyly (?1554–1606), dramatist and prose writer, main representative of Euphuism, a fashionable form of literary prose in the late sixteenth century.

(S)   *Euphues. The Anatomy of Wyt. Very pleasant for all Gentlemen to reade, and most necessary to remember*... (London, 1578): *STC* 17051; facs. ScM (1968). The excerpts are from sign. Aiii^r–iiij^r, fols. 4^v–5^r.

(L)   R. W. Zandvoort, "What is Euphuism?", in *Festschrift Mossé* (Paris, 1959), pp. 508–17.

26   Sir Philip Sidney (1554–86), courtier and poet. The *Arcadia* was written for his sister; the first manuscript version is dated 1581–2, expanded and revised version 1584–6, posthumously printed in 1590.

(S)   *The Covntesse of Pembrokes Arcadia, written by Sir Philippe Sidnei* (London, 1590): *STC* 22538a; B.L., 10440; excerpt from pp. 51–3.

(L)   A. P. Duhamel, Sidney's *Arcadia* and Elizabethan Rhetoric, *Studies in Philology* 45 (1948), 134–50; A. Fraunce, *Arcadian Rhetorike* (London, 1588).

27   Sir Philip Sidney, *Apologie for Poetrie* (written 1581–3?). The passage here printed is part of a much-quoted digression, in which the author discusses defects of contemporary poetry and the potentials of the English language in this field.

Texts

(S)   *An Apologie for Poetrie. Written by the right noble, vertuous and learned, Sir Phillip Sidney, Knight* (London: H. Olney, 1595): *STC* 22534; facs. EE 413 (1971). The excerpt is from sig. K4^r–L1^v.

28   James VI (1566–1625), King of Scotland, and from 1603, as James I and VI, of both England and Scotland (cf. T29, T42, t28).

(S)   *The Essayes of a Prentise. 'A Treatise of the airt of Scottis Poesie'* (Edinburgh, 1584): *STC* 14373; facs. EE 209 (1969). The excerpt is from sign. K2^r–3^r.

29   James VI, ΒΑΣΙΛΙΚΟΝ ΔΩΡΟΝ, MS B.L., Royal 18 B xv, autograph of *c.*1595, with corrections in the author's hand; *B.D., or his Maiesties Instructions to his Dearest Sonne, Henry the Prince* (Edinburgh, 1603): *STC* 14349, Bodleian Library, Don. f.23. Edited by J. Craigie, together with the edition of 1599, *STC* 14348; STS III, 16, 18 (1944–50). The excerpts are from fols. 16^{rv}, 29^{rv}, 30^{rv}, 32^{rv}, 1603: pp. 58–9, 149–50.

(L)   Craigie, "Introduction"

30   Sir Francis Bacon (T13), *Essayes* (London, 1597), fols. 1^r–2^r: *STC* 1137; facs. EE 17 (1968). *The Essayes or Covnsels, civill and Morall, of Francis Lo. Verulam, Viscount St Alban. Newly written* (London, 1625): *STC* 1148; B.L., C.57.e.32; facs. ScM (1971); excerpt from pp. 292–5.

31A–F William Shakespeare (1564–1616). John Heming (†1630) and Henry Condell (?–1627) were leading actors of the time and closely allied with Shakespeare, whose collected plays they edited in 1623 ('First Folio' = F1). Of the plays here represented, *Hamlet* (1603) was first printed as a 'Bad Quarto'; *Lear* (1608) as a 'Doubtful Quarto'; *LLL* (1598), *Hamlet Q2* (1604–5) and *Troilus* (1609) as 'Good Quartos', but *Julius Caesar* is first recorded in F1. (The early versions are conveniently collected in facsimile in M. J. B. Allen and K. Muir, eds., *Shakespeare's Plays in Quarto*. Berkeley: California University Press, 1981.)

(S)   *Mr William Shakespeares Comedies, Histories, & Tragedies. Published according to the True Originall Copies* (London: I. Iaggard and E. Blount, 1623): *STC* 22273; facs. *The Norton Facsimile…*, prep. by C. Hinman (New York, 1968)

(L)   *Hamlet* 603–796 = pp. 256b–8a (1968:764–6); *Lear* 2683–2703 = p. 304b (p. 812); *Julius Caesar* 1706–67 = p. 122a

(p. 730); *Troilus* 534–97 = sig. π 1ᵛ (p. 592); *LLL*
1739–68 = pp. 135b–6a (pp. 153–4); *(Preface)* = sig. A3ʳ (p. 7)

31G   *Shake-speares Sonnets* (London: G. Eld for T.T., 1609); facs.
1938. The facsimiles are taken from sig. D2ᵛ, H1ᵛ, I1ᵛ⁻.

(L)   Abbott (1870), Blake (1983), Brook (1976), Franz (1939),
Gordon (1928), Hussey (1982), Kökeritz (1953), Partridge
(1977), Quirk (1971), Salmon and Bourke (1985), Schäfer
(1973), Scheler (1982) and Shakespeare dictionaries and
concordances.

32   Anon. (George à Greene), *The Pinder of Wakefield: Being the
merry History of* George a Greene *the lusty Pinder of the North.
Briefly shewing his manhood and his braue merriments amongst his
boone Companions. A Pill fit to purge melancholy in this drooping
age. Reade and then judge ... Full of pretty Histories, Songs,
Catches, Iests, and Ridles* (London: for E. Blackamoore, 1632):
STC 12212; ed. by E. A. Horsman (Liverpool, 1956). The
excerpt is from 1956:41–3.

33   John Milton (1608–74), poet and prolific prose writer; sided
with Cromwell in the Civil War. (For his early poems cf. t29;
Paradise Lost T34.)

(S)   *The Reason of Church-governement Urg'd against Prelaty*
(London, 1641): Wing M2175, B.L., E137 (9); facs. ScM in
Prose Works, I (1968). The excerpt is from pp. 37–9.

34   *Paradise Lost* (London, 1667): Wing M2136; facs. ScM (1968).
The excerpts are from sig. A1ʳ, A4ʳᵛ, E2ᵛ.

(L)   R. D. Emma, *Milton's Grammar* (The Hague, 1964); K. G.
Hamilton, "The Structure of Milton's Prose", in Emma and
J. T. Shawcross, eds., *Language and Style in Milton* (New York,
1976), pp. 304–32; J. Richardson, "Virgil and Milton Once
Again", in *Comparative Literature* 14 (1962), 321–31

35   Jean Froissart (1337–c. 1410), French historiographer. John
Bourchier, Baron Berners (1467–1533), politician and
translator.

(S)   *The First Volume of Sir Johan Froyssart of the Chronycles of
Englande/ Fraunce/ Spayne ...* (London: R. Pinson, 1523): *STC*
11396; facs. EE 257 (1970). The excerpt is from sig. Ai–Aiii.

(L)   G. Schleich, *Archiv* 160 (1931), 34–50; 163 (1933), 203–17;
164 (1933), 24–35

36   Hector Boetius (Boece) (?1465–1536), historian and co-
founder of the University of Aberdeen; *Scotorum Historiae*

(Paris, 1527). John Bellenden (Ballentyne) (*fl.* 1533–87), poet, was commissioned by James V to translate Boece and Livy. The *Chronicle* was paraphrased (t9) by Harrison (who also wrote the "Introduction" to the book (T10)) to form part of Holinshed's *Chronicle* (1577, 2nd ed. 1587); this paraphrase in turn came to be used as the main source for Shakespeare's plays. T36A is here printed in synoptical fashion with his source T36; Harrison's more substantial expansions have been omitted.

(S)   *The Chronicles of Scotland. Compiled by Hector Boece. Translated into Scots by John Bellenden, 1531*, ed. by R. W. Chambers *et al.*, MS Pierpont Morgan; STS III, 10, 15 (1938–41); excerpt from 15:154–62.

(L)   R. W. Chambers and W. W. Seton, "Bellenden's Translation of the History of Hector Boece", in *Scottish Historical Review* 17 (1919–20), 5–15

36A   See T36; printed from Holinshed, 2nd ed. 1587: V, 271–7 (cf. T10).

37A   Henry VIII (1491–1547), King of England from 1509. *A proclamation*... (London: T. Berthelette, 1530): *STC* 7775; B.L., C.52.k.8; ed. by A. W. Pollard, *Records of the English Bible* (London, 1911).

37B   Edward VI (1537–53), King of England from 1547; son of Henry VIII and Jane Seymour, educated by John Cheke and Roger Ascham.

(S)   *All suche Proclamations*... (London: R. Grafton, 1550): *STC* 7758; B.L., C.12.b.17. The excerpt is from fols. 2^v–4^r.

38   Elizabeth I (T20D), *Proclamation* (London, 1559): *STC* 7896; facs. EE 369 (1971) "Forbidding Unlicensed Plays"

39   Hugh Latimer (?1485–1555), Bishop of Worcester (1535–9), burnt as a heretic with Ridley in Oxford.

(S)   *A notable Sermon of ye reuerende father Maister Hughe Latimer* ... *("The Sermon of the Ploughers")* (London, 1548) B.L., 11845; ed. by E. Arber (London, 1869). The excerpt is from sig. Biii^r–Bv^r (Arber, pp. 24–5).

(L)   P. Janton, *L'éloquence et le rhétorique dans les sermons de Latimer* (Paris, 1968)

40   Henry Machyn (?1498–?1563), London undertaker and diarist (1550–63).

(S)   *Diary*, MS B.L., Cotton Vit.F.v.; ed. by J. G. Nichols, Camden

Soc., 42 (1848), fols. 72^v–73^v = Nichols pp. 138–9. The text is from the manuscript with the additions from Nichols, because parts of the manuscript are no longer legible.

(L) A. Wijk, *The Orthography and Pronunciation of Henry Machyn, the London Diarist* (Uppsala, 1937); W. Matthews, *Cockney Past and Present* (London, 1938), pp. 12–16, 106–17, 162–99; R.M. Wilson, "The Orthography and Provenance of Henry Machyn", in *Festschrift Hugh Smith* (London, 1963), pp. 202–16

41 Robert Laneham, London merchant, who attended the festivities at Kenilworth in 1575, reporting on the event in semi-phonetic spelling.

(S) *A Letter: whearin, part of the entertainment vntoo the Queenz Maiesty, at Killingworth Castl, in Warwik Shéer in this Soomerz Progress 1575, iz signified: from a freend officer attendant in the Coourt, vntoo his fréend a Citizen, and Marchaunt of London* (London, 1575): *STC* 15191; facs. EL 60 (1968). The excerpt is from p. 82.

42 Elizabeth I (T20D) and James VI (T28–9). The letters are part of an extensive correspondence. Elizabeth here justifies the death of James' mother Mary Stuart; James accepts the reasons given. Elizabeth warns him not to support what remains of the Armada.

(S) *Letters of Queen Elizabeth and King James VI of Scotland*..., ed. by J. Bruce, Camden Soc., 46 (1849). The excerpts are from no. 26 (pp. 43–5); no. 27 (pp. 45–6); no. 31 (pp. 52–4)

43 Angel Day (*fl.*1586), writer, translator of Longus.

(S) *The English Secretorie, or, Methods of Writing Epistles and Letters* (London, 1586): *STC* 6401; B.L., C.116.bb.33; facs. EL 29 (1968). The excerpts are from pp. 3–7, 229–31.

(L) J. Robertson, *The Art of Letter Writing: an Essay on the Handbooks Published in the Sixteenth and Seventeenth Centuries* (Liverpool, 1942)

44 Andrew Boorde (?1490–1549), doctor, traveller, writer of medical and other popular scientific works.

(S) *The Breuiary of Helthe*... (London, 1547): not in *STC*; facs. EE 362 (1971). The excerpts are from fols. 2^r–5^r, 28^{rv}, 38^{rv}, 54^{rv}.

45 Gilbert Skeyne (Skene) (?1522–99), writer of the first medical book in Scots.

(S) *Ane breve descriptiovn of the pest* (Edinburgh: R. Lekprevik,

1586): *STC* 22626.5; facs. EE 415 (1971). The excerpt is from sig. A2^r–A4^r.

46   Philip Stubbs (*fl.*1583–91), puritan. His book contains the most caustic criticism of contemporary amusements; Nashe retorted in his *Anatomie of Absurdities.*

(S)   *The Anatomie of Abuses* (London: R. Jones, 1583): *STC* 23376; facs. EE 489 (1972)

47   John Astley (?–1595), Master of the Jewel House 1558–95, M.P., prompted his friend Thomas Blundeville to write *The arte of ryding* (?1560), which complements the present book.

(S)   *The art of riding, set foorth in a breefe treatise* (London: H. Denham, 1584): *STC* 884; B.L., 58.b.8(1); facs. EE 10 (1968). The excerpt is taken from pp. 1–4.

48   Job Hortrop was a member of Sir John Hawkins' unsuccessful expedition; his naive and often quite unreliable report was used by Hakluyt.

(S)   *The trauailes of an English man...* (London: for W. Wright, 1591): *STC* 13828; facs. EE 469 (1972). The excerpt is taken from pp. 3–9.

49   John Murrell (*fl.* 1630); the excerpt comes from his second cookery book.

(S)   *A New Booke of Cookerie* (London: for J. Browne, 1615): *STC* 18299; facs. EE 479 (1972); excerpt from pp. 20–1, 27, 39.

50   George Fox (1624–91), son of a Leicestershire weaver, founder of the "Society of Friends" (1668), a movement directed against the Presbyterian establishment. Missionary trips to Ireland, America, Holland. The Quaker W. Penn founded the American colony named after him in 1682.

(S)   *The Journal of George Fox*, ed. from the MSS by T. E. Harvey (Cambridge, 1911). The excerpts are from pp. 20/1–6, 31/11–19, 32/29–34, 138/20–34.

(L)   T. E. Harvey, *Quaker Language* (London, 1928); J. I. Cope, "Seventeenth-Century Quaker Style", *Publications of the Modern Language Association* 71 (1956), 725–54; again in Fish 1971:200–35; Finkenstaedt 1963:174–213

51   Lyndsay, David (*c.* 1490–1555), born near Cupar (Fife), poet, dramatist and courtier (knighted 1529). Though notable for various courtly poems, his fame mainly rests on the first great Scottish play, *Ane Pleasant Satyre on the Thrie Estaitis* (1540).

His "Defense of the Vernacular" represents a type of praise of the mother tongue widespread in Renaissance Europe.

(S)   *The First Buke of the Monarchie, in The warkis of the famous and worthie knight, Schir Dauid Lyndesay. Newly corectit and augmentid*, Edinburgh, Thomas Bassandyne, 1554: *STC* 15660; repr. EE 352 (1971).

52   Richard Stanyhurst (1547–1618), translated parts of Virgil's *Aeneid* (cf. T21E) and contributed the "Description of Ireland" and "History of Ireland" to Holinshed's *Chronicle* (also see the entry for T10).

53   *Statutes of Iona* (1609, ratified 1616), regulations aiming at the complete removal of Gaelic (because it had from the Reformation onwards been equated with "barbarity and the dregs of papistry"); "the old bards of the heroic tradition were to be banished and the sons of the chiefs were to be educated in the Lowlands" (Murison in Aitken and McArthur 1979:10). As the text makes clear, no proper distinction was made between English and Scots, not even in the written form.

(S)   David Masson, ed., *Register of the Privy Council of Scotland*, vol. x. Edinburgh: Register House, 1891: 671–2

(L)   C. W. J. Withers, "The language geography of Scottish Gaelic", in *Scottish Literary Journal*, supplement no. 9 (1979), 41–54

54   William Bradford (1590–1657), emigrated to Holland (Amsterdam, Leiden, 1607–20), one of the leading men of the Pilgrim Fathers of the *Mayflower* 1620, second governor of Plymouth, New England, 1621; author of the *History* which remained in MS until 1856.

(S)   *Bradford's History "of Plimoth Plantation" from the Original Manuscript*. Boston: Wright & Potter 1893. The excerpts are from ch. ix (1620), pp. 93–7; the text is slightly modernized in the following features: occurrences of *u/v, i/j; the, that, and* for *y^e, y^t, &* in the MS. All other idiosyncrasies of the spelling are retained.

55   Dundonald School regulations (*c.* 1640), describing, in a mixture of English with Scots interferences, the administration of, and teaching at, the newly built Ayrshire School "for them quho learns Scots" (T12a:67).

(S)   For similar texts cf. "School regulations printed", in *The Urban Experience. A Sourcebook. English, Scottish and Welsh Towns*

1450–1700, R. C. Richardson and T. B. James, eds., Manchester: University Press, 1983

56 Henry Manwayring, seventeenth-century naval officer and author of the *Dictionary*.

(S) *The Sea-Mans Dictionary: or, an Exposition and Demonstration of all the Parts and Things belonging to a Shippe;...*, London: by G.M. for John Bellamy, 1644: Wing M551; repr. facs. EL 328 (1972)

57 Thomas Hobbes (1588–1679), philosopher, educated at Malmesbury and Oxford, tutor and secretary to William Cavendish and his son; mathematical tutor to Charles II. Widely travelled and in contact with most important European scholars of his age. Wrote in Latin and English; important treatises: "De Cive" (1642/1651), "Human Nature" (1650), "Leviathan" (1651), "De Homine" (1658), "De Corpore Politico"/"Elements of Law" (1680).

(S) *Leviathan, or The Matter, Forme, & Power of A Common-wealth Ecclesiasticall and Civill.* London: Andrew Crooke, 1651: Wing H2246–47. The excerpt is from part I, ch. 4 (pp. 12–13); the complete chapter is printed in Bolton 1966:46–54.

58 Richard Blome (†1705), publisher and compiler. He had published a *Geographical Description of ... the World* (1670) and a work on Jamaica (1672) before compiling *Britannia*.

(S) *Britannia, or, A Geographical Description of the Kingdoms of England, Scotland, and Ireland, with the Iles and Territories thereto belonging...*, London: T. Roycroft, 1673: Wing B3207. The excerpts are from pp. 10–11 and 326–8.

59 Elisha Coles, the younger (?1640–80), teacher of Latin and English in London (1663), usher of Merchant Taylors' School (1677) and master of Galway School (?–1680); author of a treatise on short hand (1674) and lexicographer. Although his dictionary is largely derivative, it is remarkable for its inclusion of special lexis for which he drew on recent publications: the canting terms are from Richard Head's *The Canting Academy* (1673), the dialect words from John Ray (1674).

(S) *An English Dictionary: Explaining The difficult Terms that are used in Divinity, Husbandry, Physick, Phylosophy, ... By E. Coles*, School-Master and Teacher of the Tongue to Forreigners. London: S. Crouch, 1676, "To the Reader": Wing C5070; repr. L. Menston: Scolar, 1971.

(L) Dewitt T. Starnes and G. E. Noyes, *The English Dictionary from*

Cawdrey to Johnson, 1604–1755. Chapel Hill: University of North Carolina Press, 1946:58–63

60 John Bunyan (1628–88), tinsmith, soldier (in the parliamentary forces?), became deacon and preacher, wrote pamphlets against the Quakers 1656–7, repeatedly imprisoned on the laws against unlicensed preaching; prolific writer of devotional literature (*Collected Works*, 1736).

(S) *The Pilgrim's Progress as originally published by John Bunyan.* Being a Fac-simile reproduction of the First Edition. (London: Ponder, 1678, Wing B5557.) London: Elliot Stock, 1875. The excerpts are from pp. 5–6, 12–14, 30–31; the references to the sources of biblical quotations have been omitted in my transcript.

61 George Meriton (1634–1711), the most likely author of the piece which goes under "G.M. Gent." in the second and third editions; lawyer at Northallerton, who went to Dublin, 1684, and writer of legal, historical and moral treatises.

(S) The text is from the 2nd ed. (York: John White 1683: Wing M1814; (1st ed. 1673)); ed. by A.C. Cawley, *George Meriton's A Yorkshire Dialogue (1683)*, Yorkshire Dialect Society Reprint II. Kendal, 1959:14–15

(L) Cawley, "Introduction", pp. 1–13; Francis Brokesby, "Some Observations concerning the Dialect and various Pronunciation of words in the East-Riding of Yorkshire", added to the 3rd ed. of 1697; C. Dean, *The Dialect of G.M. ... Studies in the Stressed Vowels*, Yorkshire Dialect Society Reprint III. Kendal, 1962

62 *Bog-Witticisms*. The first edition of the anonymous pamphlet is undated. Its title page reads: "Bogg-Witticisms:/or, *Dear Joy's* Common-Places. Being a Compleat Collection of the most Profound *Punns*, Learned *Bulls*, Elaborate *Quibbles*, and Wise *Sayings* of some of the Natives of *Teague-Land*...": Wing B3437A; reproduced in Bliss 1979:52.

(S) Alan Bliss, ed., *Spoken English in Ireland, 1600–1740. Twenty-seven Representative Texts Assembled and Analysed*. Dublin: Dolmen, 1979:124–5 (Text XV = 1687:45–50)

(L) Bliss 1979:173–326

63 John Locke (1632–1704), philosopher, student at Westminster and Oxford, lecturer at Oxford, expelled in 1684, lived in Holland; after his return became commissioner of appeals. Important treatises: "Of Civil Government" 1689; "On

Toleration" 1689; "On Education" 1693 and cf. below; the "unquestioned founder of the analytic philosophy of mind" (J. S. Mill).

(S) *An Essay Concerning Humane Understanding*, London: Eliz. Holt for Thomas Basset, 1690 (Wing L2738), book III, ch. 1. The excerpt here printed is from Bolton 1966:83–5 (who prints a larger section, 83–90).

64 *Salem Witchcraft Papers*, the testimonies given in court during the notorious witch trials in 1692, in which more than 150 persons, mainly of Essex County, were charged of witchcraft and 19 of them hanged. Most of the depositions came from less educated speakers and were taken down by uneducated scribes; they thus provide evidence of varieties close to spoken New England English among second- and third-generation Americans.

(S) *The Salem Witchcraft Papers, Verbatim Transcripts of the Legal Documents of the Salem Witchcraft Outbreak of 1692 (in 3 vols.)*, ed. by Paul Boyer and Stephen Nissenbaum. New York: Da Capo Press, 1977; pp. 400, 403, 444–5.

65 Edmund Waller (1606–87), of a wealthy country family and a complex political career during the Civil War, Commonwealth and Restoration periods; poet, who was credited with "sweetness" by Pope and who was much imitated in his own days (cf. T21K).

(S) "Of English Verse", 1693, here printed from Frank Kermode, *et al.*, eds., *The Oxford Anthology of English Literature*, I, Oxford: University Press, 1973:1135

66 Sir Walter Scott (1771–1832), novelist and poet. Trained as a lawyer, he started collecting Scottish ballads and then concentrated on his novels mainly on Scottish history. In tune with contemporary interest in the Middle Ages and the Renaissance he also wrote historical novels of the more distant past for which he invented period languages in which selected lexical and morphological features were intended to signal the speech of the times described. (The unrealistic nature of the language is even more obvious in his 'medieval' *Ivanhoe* than it is in the pseudo-EModE of *Kenilworth*.)

(S) *Kenilworth. Waverley Novels*, Border Edition, ed. by Andrew Lang. London: Macmillan, 1901. The excerpts here included are from pp. 167–8 and 232.

(L) Graham Tulloch, *The Language of Sir Walter Scott*. London: Deutsch, 1980

Bibliography

Abbott, E.A. (1870). *A Shakespearean Grammar*. 3rd edn. London: Macmillan; reprinted New York: Dover 1966

Agutter, A. (1988). "Middle Scots as a literary language", in Jack (1988:13–26)

Aitken, A.J. (1977). "How to pronounce older Scots", in *Bards and Makars*, ed. by A.J. Aitken. Glasgow: University of Glasgow Press. 1–21

Aitken, A.J., and Tom McArthur, eds. (1979). *Languages of Scotland*. Edinburgh: Chambers

Alston, R.C. (1974). *A Bibliography of the English Language from the Invention of Printing to the Year 1800*. Vols. 1–10, part 1. Leeds: Arnold; corrected reprint Ilkley: Menston

Altenberg, B. (1982). *The Genitive v. the of-Construction. A Study of Syntactic Variation in 17th Century English*. Lund: Gleerup

Anderson, J.M. (1973). *Structural Aspects of Language Change*. London: Longman

Anderson, P.M. (1987). *A Structural Atlas of the English Dialects*. London: Croom Helm

Atkins, J.W.H. (1947). *English Literary Criticism: The Renascence*. London: Methuen

Bähr, D. (1974). *Standard English und seine geographischen Varianten*. Munich: Fink

Bailey, R.W. (1978). *Early Modern English. Additions and Ante-datings to the Record of English Vocabulary*. Hildesheim and New York: Olms

(1985). "The conquests of English", in *The English Language Today*, ed. by S. Greenbaum, Oxford: Pergamon. 9–19

Bailey, R.W., J.W. Downer, Jay L. Robinson, with Patricia V. Lehman (1975). *Michigan Early Modern English Materials*. Ann Arbor: Xerox University Microfilms

Bald, M.A. (1926). "The anglicisation of Scottish printing", *Scottish Historical Review* 23:107–15

Bibliography

(1928). "Contemporary references to the Scottish speech in Scotland", *Scottish Historical Review* 25:163–79

Baldinger, K. (1980). *Semantic Theory*. Oxford: Blackwell (Spanish original 1970)

Baldwin, T. W. (1944). *William Shakespeare's Small Latin & Lesse Greeke*. 2 vols. Urbana, Ill.: University of Illinois Press

Barber, C. (1976). *Early Modern English*. London: Deutsch

Bately, J. M. (1964). "Dryden's revisions in the *Essay of Dramatic Poesy*: The preposition at the end of the sentence and the expression of the relative", *Review of English Studies* 15:268–82

Bauer, L. (1983). *English Word-Formation*. Cambridge: Cambridge University Press

Baugh, A. C., ed. (1967). *A Literary History of England*. 2nd edn. New York: Routledge and Kegan Paul

Baugh, A. C. and T. Cable (1978). *A History of the English Language*. 3rd ed. London: Routledge and Kegan Paul

Beek, M. van (1969). *An Enquiry into Puritan Vocabulary*. Groningen: Wolters-Noordhoff

Behrens, W. (1937). *Lateinische Satzformen im Englischen. Latinismen in der Syntax der englischen Übersetzungen des Humanismus.* Emsdetten, Westf.: Lechte

Bennett, H. S. (1952; 1965; 1970). *English Books and Readers: 1475–1557; 1558–1603; 1603–40.* Cambridge: Cambridge University Press

Benson, L. D., ed. (1987). *The Riverside Chaucer*. New York: Houghton Mifflin; Oxford: Oxford University Press, 1988

Biese, Y. M. (1941). *Origin and Development of Conversions in English*. Helsinki: Suomalaisen Kirjallisuuden Seuran Kirjapainon

Blake, N. F. (1969). *Caxton and His World*. London: Deutsch
(1981). *Non-standard Language in English Literature*. London: Deutsch
(1983). *Shakespeare's Language*. London: Macmillan

Bliss, A. J. (1979). *Spoken English in Ireland, 1600–1740*. Dublin: Dolmen

Bolton, W. F., ed. (1966). *The English Language, vol. 1*. Cambridge: Cambridge University Press

Bradley, H. (1916). "Shakespeare's English", in *Shakespeare's England*. Oxford: Oxford University Press. Vol. 2

Braidwood, J. (1964). "Ulster and Elizabethan English", in *Ulster Dialects: An Introductory Symposium*, ed. by G. B. Adams. Holywood, Co. Down: Ulster Folk Museum. 5–109

Breejen, B. den (1937). *The Genitive and Its of-Equivalent in the Latter Half of the Sixteenth Century*. Amsterdam: Diss

Bibliography

Brekle, H. (1975). "The seventeenth century", *Current Trends in Linguistics* 13:277–382

Brook, G. L. (1976). *The Language of Shakespeare*. London: Deutsch

Brose, B. (1939). *Die englischen Passivkonstruktionen vom Typus "I am Told a Story" und "I Am Sent For"*. Würzburg-Aumühle: Triltsch

Bruce, F. F. (1962). *The English Bible: A History of Translations*. London: Lutterworth

Brunner, K. (1960–2). *Die englische Sprache in ihrer geschichtlichen Entwicklung*. 2 vols. 2nd edn. Tübingen: Niemeyer

Buchmann, E. (1940). *Der Einfluss des Schriftbildes auf die Aussprache im Neuenglischen*. SKGRV 35. Breslau: Priebatsch

Bühler, K. (1978). *Sprachtheorie. Die Darstellungsfunktion der Sprache* (1965). 2nd edn. Stuttgart: Gustav Fischer: reprinted Frankfurt: Ullstein

Bynon, T. (1977). *Historical Linguistics*. Cambridge: Cambridge University Press

Byrne, M. St Clare (1964). "The foundations of Elizabethan language", *Shakespeare Survey* 17:223–39

Carroll, W. (1976). *The Great Feast of Language in 'Love's Labour's Lost'*. Princeton: Harvard University Press

CED (1970). *A Chronological English Dictionary*, ed. by T. Finkenstaedt, E. Leisi and D. Wolff. Heidelberg: Winter

Cercignani, F. (1981). *Shakespeare's Works and Elizabethan Pronunciation*. Oxford: Oxford University Press

Chambers, R. W. and W. W. Seton (1919–20). "Bellenden's translation of the history of Hector Boece", *Scottish Historical Review* 17:5–15

Charlton, K. (1965). *Education in Renaissance England*. London: Routledge & Kegan Paul

Chomsky, N. (1966). *Cartesian Linguistics*. New York, London: Harper & Row

Cohen, M. (1977). *Sensible Words. Linguistic Practice in England 1640–1785*. Baltimore: Johns Hopkins University Press

Cope, J. I. (1956). "Seventeenth-century Quaker style", *Publications of the Modern Language Association* 71:725–54; reprinted in Fish (1971:200–35)

Copley, J. (1961). *Shift of Meaning*. London: Oxford University Press

Coseriu, E. (1974). *Synchronie, Diachronie und Geschichte*. Munich: Fink

Craigie, W. A. (1946). *The Critique of Pure English from Caxton to Smollett* (Society for Pure English Tract 65). Oxford: Oxford University Press

Crane, W. G. (1937). *Wit and Rhetoric in the Renaissance*. New York: Columbia University Press

Croft, P.J. (1973). *Autograph Poetry in the English Language.* 2 vols. London: Cassell

Croll, M.W. (1923). "Attic prose: Lipsius, Montaigne, Bacon", in *Schelling Anniversary Papers.* 117–50; reprinted in Fish (1971:3–25)
(1929). "The baroque style in prose"; reprinted in Watson (1970:84–110)

Crystal, D. and D. Davy (1973). *Investigating English Style.* London: Longman

Curtis, S.J. (1967). *History of Education in Great Britain.* 7th edn. Foxton: University Tutorial Press

Davies, H.S. (1952). "Sir John Cheke and the translation of the Bible", *Essays & Studies* 5:1–12

Davis, N. (1971). *William Tyndale's English of Controversy.* London: University of London

Dawson, G.E. and L. Kennedy Skipton (1981). *Elizabethan Handwriting 1500–1650.* New York: Norton

De Beaugrande, R. and W. Dressler (1981). *Introduction to Text Linguistics.* London: Longman

Dekeyser, X. (1988). "Socio-historical aspects of relativization in late 16th century English: ca. 1550–1600", *Studia Anglia Posnaniensia* 21:25–39

DEMEP (1976). *English Pronunciation 1500–1800. Report based on the DEMEP Symposium,* ed. by B. Danielsson. Stockholm: Almqvist & Wiksell

Devitt, A.J. (1989). *Standardizing Written English: Diffusion in the Case of Scotland 1520–1659.* Cambridge: Cambridge University Press

Dobson, E.J. (1955). "Early Modern Standard English", *Transactions of the Philological Society.* 25–54
(1968). *English Pronunciation 1500–1700.* 2nd edn. Oxford: Clarendon

DOST (1931–83). *A Dictionary of the Older Scottish Tongue from the Twelfth Century to the End of the Seventeenth Century* [A–P completed], ed. by W. Craigie and A.J. Aitken. Aberdeen: Aberdeen University Press

Duhamel, A.P. (1948). "Sidney's 'Arcadia' and Elizabethan rhetoric", *Studies in Philology* 45:134–50

EDD (1898–1905). *The English Dialect Dictionary,* ed. by J. Wright. 6 vols. London: H. Frowde

Ekwall, E. (1975). *A History of Modern English Sounds and Morphology,* trans. and ed. by A. Ward. Oxford: Blackwell (German original, 4th edn. Berlin: de Gruyter, 1965)

Ellegård, A. (1953). *The Auxiliary Do: The Establishment and Regulation of Its Use.* Gothenburg Studies 2. Stockholm: Almqvist & Wiksell

Bibliography

Elliott, R. W. F. (1974). *Chaucer's Language*. London: Deutsch

Emma, R. D. (1964). *Milton's Grammar*. The Hague: Mouton
and J. T. Shawcross, eds. (1976). *Language and Style in Milton*. New
York: Ungar

The English Experience. Its Record in Early Printed Books Published
in England between 1475 and 1640 (1966–78). Amsterdam:
Walter J. Johnson

English Linguistics 1500–1800 (1967–72). 365 vols. Menston: Scolar
Press

Finkenstaedt, T. (1963). *You and Thou. Studien zur Anrede im
Englischen*. Berlin: E. Schmidt
et al. (1973). *Ordered Profusion. Studies in Dictionaries and the English
Lexicon*. Heidelberg: Winter

Fish, S. E., ed. (1971). *Seventeenth Century Prose. Modern Essays in
Criticism*. New York: Oxford University Press

Fisher, J. H. (1977). "Chancery and the emergence of Standard
Written English in the fifteenth century", *Speculum* 52:870–99
and D. Bornstein (1974). *In Forme of Speche is Chaunge. Readings in
the History of the English Language*. Englewood Cliffs, N.J.:
Prentice-Hall

Flasdieck, H. M. (1928). *Der Gedanke einer englischen Sprachakademie in
Vergangenheit und Gegenwart*. Jena: Frommann

Franz, W. (1939). *Die Sprache Shakespeares in Vers und Prosa*. Halle and
Saale: Niemeyer; reprinted Tübingen: Niemeyer, 1987 (4th edn.
of the *Shakespearegrammatik*)

Fraunce, A. (1588). *The Arcadian Rhetorike*. London; reprinted in EL
176, Menston: Scolar Press, 1969

Fridén, G. (1948). *Studies on the Tenses of the English Verb from Chaucer
to Shakespeare*. Uppsala: Almqvist & Wiksell

Fries, C. C. (1940). "On the development of the structural use of
word-order in modern English", *Language* 16:199–208

Görlach, M. (1982). *Einführung in die englische Sprachgeschichte*. 2nd
edn. Heidelberg: Quelle & Meyer
(1985a). "Renaissance English (1525–1640)", in *The English
Language Today*, ed. by S. Greenbaum. Oxford: Pergamon.
30–40
(1985b). "Scots and Low German: The social history of two
minority languages", in *Focus on: Scotland*, ed. by M. Görlach.
Amsterdam: Benjamins. 19–36
(1987). "Lexical loss and lexical survival: The case of English and
Scots", *Scottish Language* 6:1–24
(1988). "The study of Early Modern English variation – the
Cinderella of English historical linguistics?", in *Historical*

Bibliography

Dialectology. Regional and Social, ed. by J. Fisiak. Berlin: Mouton de Gruyter. 211–28

(forthcoming). "Regional and social variation in Early Modern English", in *The Cambridge History of the English Language*, vol. III ed. by R. Lass. Cambridge: Cambridge University Press

Gordon, G.S. (1928). *Shakespeare's English* (Society for Pure English Tract 29). Oxford: Oxford University Press

Graband, G. (1965). *Die Entwicklung der frühneuenglischen Nominalflexion*. Tübingen: Niemeyer

Grant, W. and D. Murison, eds. (1931–76). *The Scottish National Dictionary*. Edinburgh: Scottish National Dictionary Association. 10 vols. Introduction to vol. 1

Gray, D. (1988). "A note on sixteenth-century purism", in *Words. For Robert Burchfield's Sixty-Fifth Birthday*, ed. by E.G. Stanley and T.F. Hoad. Cambridge: Cambridge University Press. 103–19

Groom, B. (1939). *The Formation and Use of Compound Epithets in English from 1579* (Society for Pure English Tract 49). Oxford: Oxford University Press. 295–322

(1955). *The Diction of Poetry from Spenser to Bridges*. Toronto: Toronto University Press

Halliday, M.A.K. and R. Hasan (1976). *Cohesion in English*. London: Longman

Hamilton, K.G. (1976). "The structure of Milton's prose", in Emma and Shawcross (1976:304–32)

Harlow, C.G. (1970). "An unnoticed observation on the expansion of sixteenth-century Standard English", *Review of English Studies* 21:168–73

Harris, J. (1985). *Phonological Variation and Change. Studies in Hiberno-English*. Cambridge: Cambridge University Press

(1986). "Expanding the superstrate: Habitual aspect markers in Atlantic Englishes", *English World-Wide* 7:171–99

Harvey, T.E. (1928). *Quaker Language*. London

Holmberg, B. (1964). *On the Concept of Standard English and the History of Modern English Pronunciation*. Lund: Gleerup

Holzknecht, K.J., ed. (1954). *Sixteenth-Century Prose*. New York: Harper

Horn, W. and M. Lehnert (1954). *Laut und Leben. Englische Lautgeschichte der neueren Zeit (1400–1950)*. 2 vols. Berlin: Deutscher Verlag der Wissenschaften

Howatt, A.P.R. (1984). *A History of English Language Teaching*. Oxford: Oxford University Press

Howell, W.S. (1956). *Logic and Rhetoric in England 1500–1700*. Princeton: Princeton University Press

Hussey, S. S. (1982). *The Literary Language of Shakespeare*. London: Longman

Isaac, F. (1936). *English Printers' Types of the Sixteenth Century*. London: Oxford University Press

Jack, R. D. S., ed. (1988). *The History of Scottish Literature*. I: *Origins to 1660*. Aberdeen: Aberdeen University Press

Jacobsson, B. (1951). *Inversion in English with Special Reference to the Early English Period*. Uppsala: Almqvist & Wiksell

Jespersen, O. (1946). *Growth and Structure of the English Language*. 9th edn. Oxford: Blackwell

(1909–49). *A Modern English Grammar on Historical Principles*. Heidelberg: Winter; Copenhagen: Munksgaard

Jiriczek, O. L. (1923). *Specimens of Tudor Translations from the Classics*. Heidelberg: Winter

Johnson, F. R. (1944). "Latin versus English: The sixteenth century debate over scientific vocabulary", *Studies in Philology* 41:109–35

Johnson, S. (1755). *A Dictionary of the English Languages*. London: for J. & P. Knapton, etc.; reprinted London: Times Books, 1983 ("Preface" reprinted in Bolton 1966: 127–56)

Jones, R. F. (1930). "Science and English prose style in the third quarter of the seventeenth century", *Publications of the Modern Language Association* 45:977–1009

(1932). "Science and language in England of the mid-seventeenth century", *Journal of English and Germanic Philology* 31:315–31; reprinted in Fish (1971:94–111)

(1953). *The Triumph of the English Language*. Stanford: Stanford University Press

Joseph, M. (1947). *Shakespeare's Use of the Arts of Language*. New York: Columbia University Press. Shorter version: *Rhetoric in Shakespeare's Time*. New York: Harcourt, Brace & World, 1972

Kermode, F. *et al.* (1973). *The Oxford Anthology of English Literature*. London: Oxford University Press. Vol. 1

King, A. H. (1941). *The Language of the Satirized Characters in Poetaster. A Socio-Stylistic Analysis 1597–1602* (Lund Studies 10). Lund: Gleerup

Kökeritz, H. (1935). "English pronunciation as described in shorthand systems of the 17th and 18th centuries", *Studia Neophilologica* 7:73–146

(1953). *Shakespeare's Pronunciation*. New Haven: Yale University Press

(1961). "Elizabethan prosody and historical phonology", *Annales Uppsalienses* 5:79–102

Knorrek, M. (1938). *Der Einfluß des Rationalismus auf die englische*

Sprache. Beiträge zur Entwicklungsgeschichte der englischen Syntax im 17. und 18. Jahrhundert. SKGRV 30. Breslau: Priebatsch

Knowlson, J. (1975). *Universal Language Schemes in England and France 1600–1800.* Toronto: Toronto University Press

Kohonen, V. (1978). "On the development of an awareness of English syntax in early (1550–1660) descriptions of word order by English grammarians, logicians and rhetoricians", *Neuphilologische Mitteilungen* 79:44–58

Kopytko, R. (1988). "The impersonal use of verbs in William Shakespeare's plays", *Studia Anglia Posnaniensia* 21:41–51

Kytö, M. and M. Rissanen (1983). "The syntactic study of early American English. The variationist at the mercy of his corpus?", *Neuphilologische Mitteilungen* 84:470–90

Labov, W. (1973). "The social setting of linguistic change", *Current Trends in Linguistics* 11:195–251

  (1975). "The use of the present to explain the past", in *Proceedings of the Eleventh International Congress of Linguists.* Bologna. 825–51

Lambley, K. (1920). *The Teaching and Cultivation of the French Language During Tudor and Stuart Times.* Manchester: Manchester University Press

Lass, R. (1976). *English Phonology and Phonological Theory. Synchronic and Diachronic Aspects.* Cambridge: Cambridge University Press

  (1987). *The Shape of English. Structure and History.* London: Dent

  (forthcoming). "Phonology and morphology", in *Cambridge History of the English Language, III (1476–1776).* Cambridge: Cambridge University Press

Lausberg, H. (1967). *Elemente der literarischen Rhetorik.* 3rd edn. Munich: Fink

Lehmann, W. P. (1973). *Historical Linguistics: An Introduction.* 2nd edn. New York: Holt, Rinehart & Winston

Leith, D. (1983). *A Social History of English.* London: Routledge & Kegan Paul

Leonard, S. A. (1929). *The Doctrine of Correctness in English Usage 1700–1800* (University of Wisconsin Studies, 25). Madison, Wis.: University of Wisconsin

Lewis, C. S. (1954). *English Literature in the Sixteenth Century Excluding Drama.* Oxford: Clarendon

  (1974). *Studies in Words.* 2nd edn. Cambridge: Cambridge University Press

Lightfoot, D. W. (1979). *Principles of Diachronic Syntax.* Cambridge: Cambridge University Press

Lowth, R. (1762). *A Short Introduction to English Grammar.* London; reprinted Menston: Scolar Press, 1967

Bibliography

Luick, K. (1914–21). *Historische Grammatik der englischen Sprache, I.* Leipzig: Tauchnitz

Lyons, J. (1968). *Introduction to Theoretical Linguistics.* Cambridge: Cambridge University Press

Marchand, H. (1969). *The Categories and Types of Present-day English Word-formation.* 2nd edn. Munich: Beck

Matthews, W. (1938). *Cockney Past and Present.* London: Routledge & Kegan Paul

McConchie, R.W. (1988). " 'It hurteth memorie and hindreth learning': attitudes to the use of the vernacular in sixteenth century English medical writings", *Studia Anglia Posnaniensia* 21:53–67

McElderry, B.R. (1932). "Archaism and innovation in Spenser's poetic diction", *Publications of the Modern Language Association* 47:144–70

McLaughlin, J. (1970). *Aspects of the History of English.* New York: Holt, Rinehart & Winston

Menner, R.J. (1945). "Multiple meaning and change of meaning in English", *Language* 21:59–76

Michael, I. (1970). *English Grammatical Categories and the Tradition to 1800.* Cambridge: Cambridge University Press

 (1987). *The Teaching of English: From the Sixteenth Century to 1870.* Cambridge: Cambridge University Press

Moore, J.L. (1910). *Tudor–Stuart Views on the Growth, Status, and Destiny of the English Language* (SEP 41). Halle Saale: Niemeyer

Nehls, D. (1974). *Synchron-diachrone Untersuchungen zur Expanded Form im Englischen.* Munich: Hueber

Nelson, W. (1952). "The teaching of English in Tudor grammar schools", *Studies in Philology* 49:119–43

Neuhaus, H.J. (1971). "Towards a diachronic analysis of vocabulary", *Cahiers de Lexicologie* 19:113–26

Nevalainen, T. (1983). "A corpus of colloquial Early Modern English for a lexical-syntactic study: Evidence for consistency and variation", in *Papers from the Second Scandinavian Symposium on Syntactic Variation* (Acta Univ. Stockh. 57). Stockholm. 109–22

Nugent, E.M. (1956). *The Thought and Culture of the English Renaissance. An Anthology of Tudor Prose 1481–1555.* Cambridge: Cambridge University Press

ODEE (1966). *The Oxford Dictionary of English Etymology,* ed. by C.T. Onions. Oxford: Oxford University Press

OED (1933). *The Oxford English Dictionary,* ed. by J.A.H. Murray and William Craigie. Oxford. *Supplements I–IV.* ed. by W. Burchfield (1972–86). 2nd edn. Oxford: Oxford University Press, 1989

Bibliography

Ó Muirithe, D. (1978). *The English Language in Ireland*. Dublin: Mercier

Ong, W.J. (1944). "Historical backgrounds of Elizabethan and Jacobean punctuation theory", *Publications of the Modern Language Association* 59:349–60

Onions, C.T. (1919). *A Shakespeare Glossary*. Oxford: Clarendon. 2nd edn rev. by R. Eagleson

Osselton, N.W. (1958). *Branded Words in English Dictionaries before Johnson*. Groningen: Wolters

1985). "Spelling-book rules and the capitalization of nouns in the seventeenth and eighteenth centuries", in *Historical and Editorial Studies in Medieval and Early Modern English*, ed. by Mary-Jo Arn and Hanneke Wirtjes. Groningen: Wolters-Noordhoff. 49–62

Padley, G.A. (1976, 1985). *Grammatical Theory in Western Europe, 1500–1700: The Latin Tradition* (1976) and *Trends in Vernacular Grammar I* (1985). Cambridge: Cambridge University Press

Partridge, A.C. (1953). *The Accidence of Ben Jonson's Plays, Masques, and Entertainments*. Cambridge: Bowes & Bowes

(1964). *Orthography in Shakespeare and Elizabethan Drama*. London: Arnold

(1969). *Tudor to Augustan English*. London: Deutsch

(1973). *English Biblical Translation*. London: Deutsch

(1976). *A Substantive Grammar of Shakespeare's Nondramatic Texts*. Charlotteville

Percival, W.K. (1975). "The grammatical traditions and the rise of the vernaculars", *Current Trends in Linguistics* 13:231–75

Petti, A.G. (1977). *English Literary Hands from Chaucer to Dryden*. London: Arnold

Pollard, A.W. and G.R. Redgrave (1926). *A Short-Title Catalogue of Books Printed in England, Scotland & Ireland and of English Books Printed Abroad 1475–1640*. London: Bibliographical Society. 2nd edn rev. by W.A. Jackson, vol. 1 (1984), vol. 2 (1976). London: Oxford University Press for the Bibliographic Society

Price, H.T. (1910). *A History of Ablaut in the Strong Verbs from Caxton to the End of the Elizabethan Period*. Bonn: Hanstein

Prins, A.A. (1974). *A History of English Phonemes: From Indo-European to Present-day English*. 2nd edn. Leiden: Leiden University Press

Quirk, R. (1971). "Shakespeare and the English Language", in *A New Companion to Shakespeare Studies*, ed. by K. Muir and S. Schoenbaum. Cambridge: Cambridge University Press. 67–82; reprinted in Salmon and Burness (1987:3–21)

(1985). *A Comprehensive Grammar of the English Language*. London: Longman

Bibliography

Quirk, R., S. Greenbaum, G. Leech and J. Svartvik (1972). *A Grammar of Contemporary English*. London: Longman

Reuter, O. (1936). *Verb Doublets of Latin Origin in English*. Helsingfors: Akademische Buchhandlung; Leipzig: Harrassowitz

(1938). "On continuative relative clauses in English", *Societas Scientiarum Fennica, Commentationes Humanarum Litterarum* 9,3:1–61

Richardson, J. (1962). "Virgil and Milton once again", *Comparative Literature* 14:321–31

Riddehough, G. G. (1946). "Queen Elizabeth's translation of Boethius' De consolatione philosophiae", *Journal of English and Germanic Philology* 45:88–94

Rigg, A. G. (1968). *The English Language. A Historical Reader*. New York: Appleton Century Crofts

Robertson, J. (1942). *The Art of Letter Writing: An Essay on the Handbooks Published in the Sixteenth and Seventeenth Centuries*. Liverpool: Liverpool University Press; London: Hodder & Stoughton

Robinson, H. W., ed. (1940). *The Bible in Its Ancient and English Versions*. London

Roget's Thesaurus of English Words and Phrases, ed. by R. A. Dutch. London: Longman. Rev. ed. by D. C. Browning. London: Longman, 1983

Romaine, S. (1982). *Socio-Historical Linguistics, Its Status and Methodology*. Cambridge: Cambridge University Press

Ross, C. H. (1893). "The absolute participle in Middle and Modern English", *Publications of the Modern Language Association* 8:245–302

Rudskoger, A. (1952). *Fair, Foul, Nice, Proper ... A Contribution to the Study of Polysemy* (Gothenburg Studies 1). Gothenburg: Almqvist & Wiksell

Rusch, J. (1972). *Die Vorstellung vom Goldenen Zeitalter der englischen Sprache im 16., 17. und 18. Jahrhundert* (SAA 69). Bern: Francke

Rydén, M. (1966). *Relative Constructions in Early Sixteenth-Century English*. Uppsala: Almqvist & Wiksell

Rydén, M. and S. Brorström (1987). *The BE/HAVE Variation with Intransitives in English* (Stockholm Studies 70). Stockholm: Almqvist & Wiksell

Salmon, V. (1965). "Sentence structures in colloquial Shakespearean English", *Transactions of the Philological Society*. 105–40; reprinted in Salmon and Burness (1987:265–300)

(1967). "Elizabethan colloquial English in the Falstaff plays", *Leeds Studies in English*, n.s. 1, 27–70; reprinted in Salmon and Burness (1987:37–70)

Bibliography

(1969). "Review of Chomsky's *Cartesian Linguistics* (1966)", *Journal of Linguistics* 5:165–87

(1970). "Some functions of Shakespearean word-formation", *Shakespeare Survey* 23:13–26; reprinted in Salmon and Burness (1987:193–206)

(1972). *The Works of Francis Lodwick: A Study of his Writings in the Intellectual Context of the Seventeenth Century.* London: Longman

(1988). "English punctuation theory", *Anglia* 106:285–314

Salmon, V. and E. Burness, eds. (1987). *Reader in the Language of Shakespearean Drama.* Amsterdam: Benjamins

Samuels, M. L. (1972). *Linguistic Evolution.* Cambridge: Cambridge University Press

Schäfer, J. (1973). *Shakespeares Stil.* Frankfurt: Athenäum

(1980). *Documentation in the O.E.D. Shakespeare and Nashe as Test Cases.* Oxford: Clarendon

Scheler, M. (1977). *Der englische Wortschatz.* Berlin: E. Schmidt

(1982). *Shakespeares Englisch. Eine sprachwissenschaftliche Einführung.* Berlin: E. Schmidt

Schlauch, M. (1959). *The English Language in Modern Times (since 1400).* Warsaw: Polish Scientific Publishers

(1987). "The social background of Shakespeare's malapropisms", in *Poland's Homage to Shakespeare* (1965), 203–31; reprinted in Salmon and Burness (1987:71–99)

Schmidt, A. and G. Sarrazin (1962). *Shakespeare-Lexicon.* 2 vols. Berlin: de Gruyter

Scholar's Reprints. Gainesville, later Delmar, N.Y. With critical introductions

Scragg, D. G. (1974). *A History of English Spelling.* Manchester: Manchester University Press

Serjeantson, M. S. (1935). *A History of Foreign Words in English.* London: Routledge & Kegan Paul

Shaaber, M. A. (1957). *Seventeenth-Century English Prose.* New York: Harper

Slaughter, M. M. (1982). *Universal Languages and Scientific Taxonomy in the Seventeenth Century.* Cambridge: Cambridge University Press

Smith, C. A. (1902). "The chief differences between the first and second folios of Shakespeare", *English Studies* 30:1–20

Smith, G. G., ed. (1902). *Specimens of Middle Scots.* Edinburgh, London: Blackwood

(1904). *Elizabethan Critical Essays.* 2 vols. London: Oxford University Press

Sonnino, L. A. (1968). *A Handbook to Sixteenth-Century Rhetoric.* London: Routledge & Kegan Paul

Sórensen, K. (1957). "Latin influence in English syntax", *Travaux du cercle linguistique de Copenhague* 11:131–55

Spevack, M. (1972). *Shakespeare Concordance*. Hildesheim: Olms
(1977). "SHAD (A Shakespeare Dictionary): Toward a taxonomic classification of the Shakespeare Corpus", in *Computing in the Humanities*, ed. by S. Lusignan. Waterloo, Ont. 107–14

Spevack, M. *et al.* (1974). "SHAD: A Shakespeare dictionary", in *Computers in the Humanities*, ed. by J. L. Mitchell. Edinburgh. 111–23

Spingarn, J. E. (1908–9). *Critical Essays of the Seventeenth Century*. 3 vols. Oxford: Clarendon Press

Starnes, Dewitt T. and G. E. Noyes (1946). *The English Dictionary from Cawdrey to Johnson 1604–1755*. Chapel Hill: University of North Carolina Press

Stein, D. (1986). "Stylistic aspects of syntactic change", *Folia Linguistica Historia* 6:153–78

Strang, B. M. H. (1970). *A History of English*. London: Methuen

Sugden, H. W. (1936). *The Grammar of Spenser's Faerie Queene*. Philadelphia: Linguistic Society of America

Taylor, E. W. (1976). "Shakespeare's use of *eth* and *es* endings of verbs in the First Folio", *CLA Journal* 19,4:437–57; reprinted in Salmon and Burness (1987:349–70)

Templeton, J. M. (1973). "Scots. An outline history", in *Lowland Scots*, ed. by A. J. Aitken. Edinburgh: Association for Scottish Literary Studies. 4–19

Tieken-Boon van Ostade, I. (1987). *The Auxiliary DO in Eighteenth-century English. A Sociohistorical-Linguistic Approach*. Dordrecht: Foris

Tilley, M. P. (1950). *A Dictionary of the Proverbs in England in the Sixteenth and Seventeenth Centuries*. Ann Arbor: University of Michigan Press

Traugott, E. C. (1972). *The History of English Syntax*. New York: Holt, Rinehart & Winston

Treip, M. (1970). *Milton's Punctuation and Changing English Usage 1582–1676*. London: Methuen

Trnka, B. (1930). *On the Syntax of the English Verb from Caxton to Dryden*. Prague; reprinted Nendeln: Kraus, 1987

Tucker, S., ed. (1961). *English Examined*. Cambridge: Cambridge University Press

Ullmann, S. (1963). *The Principles of Semantics*. 3rd edn. Oxford: Blackwell

Vachek, J. (1962). "On the interplay of external and internal factors in the development of language", *Lingua* 11:433–48

Bibliography

Vickers, B. (1968). *Bacon and Renaissance Prose*. Cambridge: Cambridge University Press
 (1970). *Classical Rhetoric in English Poetry*. London: Macmillan
Visser, F. T. (1949). *Some Causes of Verbal Obsolescence*. Nijmegen: Dekker & van de Vegt
 (1963–73). *An Historical Syntax of the English Language*. 3 vols. Leiden: Brill
Vorlat, E. (1975). *The Development of English Grammatical Theory 1586–1737*, with special reference to the theory of parts of speech. Leuven: Leuven University Press
Vos, A. (1976). "Humanistic standards of diction in the inkhorn controversy", *Studies in Philology* 73:376–96
Wakelin, M. F. (1982). "Evidence for spoken regional English in the sixteenth century", *Revista Canaria de Estudios Ingleses* 5:1–25
Waldron, R. A. (1978). *Sense and Sense Development* (1967). 2nd edn. London: Deutsch
Wallace, K. R. (1943). *Francis Bacon on Communication and Rhetoric*. Chapel Hill: University of North Carolina Press
Watson, F. (1908). *The English Grammar Schools to 1660*. Cambridge: Cambridge University Press (2nd edn published by Frank Cass (1968))
Watson, G. (1974). *The New Cambridge Bibliography of English Literature, I, 600–1660*. Cambridge: Cambridge University Press
Watson, G., ed. (1970). *Literary English Since Shakespeare*. London: Oxford University Press
Weinreich, U. (1959). *Languages in Contact*. The Hague: Mouton
Weinreich, U., W. Labov and M. Herzog (1972). "Empirical foundations for a theory of language change", in *Directions for Historical Linguistics*, ed. by W. P. Lehmann and Y. Malkiel. Austin: University of Texas Press. 95–195
Wermser, R. (1976). *Statistische Studien zur Entwicklung des englischen Wortschatzes* (SAA 91). Bern: Francke
West, M. (1953). *A General Service List of English Words*. 2nd edn. London: Longman
Wijk, A. (1937). *The Orthography and Pronunciation of Henry Machyn, the London Diarist*. Uppsala: Appelberg
Willcock, G. D. (1954). "Shakespeare and Elizabethan English", *Shakespeare Studies* 7:12–24
Willcock, G. D. and A. Walker, eds. (1936). *The Arte of English Poesie*. Cambridge: Cambridge University Press
Williams, F. B., Jr. (1978). "Lost books of Tudor England", *The Library*, V, 33:1–14
Williamson, M. (1929). *Colloquial Language of the Commonwealth and*

Restoration (The English Association Pamphlet 73). Oxford: Oxford University Press

Wilson, R.M. (1963). "The orthography and provenance of Henry Machyn", in *Festschrift Hugh Smith*. London: Methuen. 202–16

Wing, D. (1945–51). *Short-Title Catalogue of Books Printed in England ... 1641–1700*. 3 vols. New York (2nd edn of vol 1, 1972)

Wood, D.N.C. (1977). "Elizabethan English and Richard Carew", *Neophilologus* 61:304–15

Wright, L.B. (1935). *Middle-Class Culture in Elizabethan England*. Chapel Hill: University of North Carolina Press

Wyld, H.C. (1923). *Studies in English Rhymes from Surrey to Pope*. London: Murray

(1936). *A History of Modern Colloquial English*. 3rd edn. Oxford: Blackwell

Zachrisson, R.E. (1914). "Northern or London English as standard pronunciation", *Anglia* 38:405–32

Zandvoort, R.W. (1959). "What is Euphuism?", in *Festschrift Mossé*. Paris. 508–17

Index of persons

This selective index includes all occurrences of names of British persons of historical importance, but not all foreigners. A few titles of works are also listed; for geographical names see the index of topics. The information given in the Index is listed as follows: name; text number if author of text; mention of name in discursive text, and in EModE text; mention in sources of shorter texts or bibliographical notes on texts in Text Section (pages containing more important information are underlined).

Index of persons

Index of persons

Harvey, William 39, 206
Heming, John T31A; 420
Henslowe, Philipp 3
Henry VIII T37A; 422
Hobbes, Thomas T57; 168; 426
Hoby, Sir Thomas t50; 159; T5/1;
　408, 410
Holinshed, Raphael (T36A); 21; 411,
　417, 422, 425
Homer 36
Hooker, John (T10); 22; 411
Horace 25, 156; T11/133–5,
　T15/157, T18H/19–21, T43/50
Hortrop, Job T48; 169, 183; 424
Hoskins, John 29
Howell, James t38; 98; 408

I.T. (translator) T20E; 416

James VI/I t28, T28, T29, T42; 14,
　20, 41, 43, 44; 420
Jerome (Hieronymus) T18B/5,
　T51/50
Johnson, Samuel 41, 55, 56, 166
Jonson, Ben t20, t37, T14; 11, 14, 26,
　34, 63, 74, 80, 81, 82, 84, 99, 107,
　144, 162, 178; T15/3, 10, 48,
　55–126, 133, 180; 408, 412

Kersey?John t46; 152; 408
Kirke, Edward? (E.K.) T23A, T23B/
　57–89; 144, 150; 418
Knox, John 19

Labov, William 5, 8, 62
Laneham, Robert T41; 423
Latimer, Hugh T39; 12; 422
Lever, Ralph t14; 31, 156, 164, 174;
　407
Lewis, C. Day T21M; 173; 418
Lily, William T3; 6; 409
Lisle, William 40
Livius, Titus T18C/96, T23/38
Locke, John T63; 37, 39, 303, 182;
　427
Lydgate, John 6, 18; T10/36, T11/41,
　T22B/15, T23A/9

Lyly, John T25; 28, 29, 31, 88, 89,
　107; 419
Lyndsay, Sir David T51; 18; 424–5

Machyn, Henry T40; 422–3
Malherbe, François de 38
Manwayring, Henry T56; 183; 426
Marlowe, Christopher 88, T12/193
Marston, John 162
Martinet, André 2
Meriton, George T61; 14, 146; 427
Milton, John t29, T33, T34; 28, 35,
　38, 39, 40, 41, 43, 44, 55, 100–1,
　105, 113, 130, 173; 407, 421
Montaigne, Michel de (T18F); 414
More, Sir Thomas t39; 39, 107,
　121–2; 408
Moses T51/22
Mulcaster, Richard t35, T8; 38, 40,
　41, 54, 55, 57, 98, 150; 408, 411
Murrell, John T49; 424

Nashe, Thomas 107; 162, 177, 178,
　180
New English Bible 129
Newton, Isaac 39
Nisbet, Murdoch t7; 19; 406
North, Sir Thomas 168

Ogilby, John T21J; 78; 418
Ovid, P.O. Naso T12/193

Palsgrave, John t23; 37, 153, 167,
　208; 407
Parker, Matthew 145
Peacham, Henry t13, t53; 31, 162,
　183, 191; 407–8
Pecock, Reginald 10
Pepys, Samuel 50, 155
Petrarch, Francesco 32
Pettie, George T18E; 414
Phaer, Thomas T21D; 417
Phillips, Edward t45; 36, 41, 152;
　T59/29; 408
Piers Plowman (by Langland) T11/41,
　T59/56
Pléiade 38, 173

446

Index of topics

This selective index of topics includes terms mentioned in the Introduction and those found in the original texts (T1–T66); synonyms or related topics are often listed under cover terms.

Index of topics

Index of topics

Index of topics

Index of topics

morpheme 79ff., 190
morphology 79–94, 157, 170–81
'naive' spellings 62, 73
national language 22; T11/10–13,
    T18A/7, T28/28–30, T29/56, 67
native language (mother tongue)
    T4/7, 10, T11/19, T18B/3ff.,
    T18C/3, T23A/59, T29/52, T33/
    15–19 (cf. vernacular)
negation 101, 102, 118–20; T63/31–4
neologism 36, 137–8, 158, 170;
    T14/11–12, T15/155–6,
    T16/66–75
New York T58/98–101
norm 22, 29, 171; T15/52–5, 135–43,
    T16/28
Normans T10/1
noun phrase 102–4
nurse 37

obsolescence 139–43, 175; T16/108,
    T18H/25–30 (cf. archaism)
Old English T10/1, T11/22
    (Anglesaxon)
onomasiology 183, 185–6
opacity 171
ornament (ornature) T8/27, 39,
    T10/41, T17/21ff., T22B/19,
    T23A/75–6, T25/11, 24,
    T27/20ff., T30/3, 7
oversea language 155, 168; T4/14

paradigmatic relations 183, 186ff.
parataxis 95, 121–3
participle 90–3, 99, 101, 109, 123,
    126–8, 157
parts of speech 97–100
passive 116–17
pastoral 16; T23B
pejoration 202, 208
periods of English 9–11
perspicuity T14/59–76, T29/36–38,
    44–5
phonaestheme 143, 170; t57
phonetics T7/7, T11/1–8
phonemes 64–75
phonemic loss 69

phonemic merger 68–9
phonemic split 66, 70
phonetic spelling 56
phonological change 66–70
phonology 61–78
phrasal verbs 106–7
pidgin 18
Pilgrim Fathers 169; T54
plain(ness) 31–3; t42, t43/4, t53/5,
    T4, T8/141–3, T17/70–7,
    T18A/6, T29/34–41, T44/19–28,
    T45/21–8
plural 79–80
poetic diction 34, 35–6, 104, 143–5,
    173; T4/21–4, T11/17ff.,
    T23B/71, T27, T29/47–51,
    T59/36–8
polysemy 109–10, 143, 181, 189,
    191–3, 203, 206; T12/31–6
polysyllabic words T10/47,
    T12/19–21
'possessive dative' 81–2, 102
preaching (language of) 12, 31–3,
    132; t19, T8/141–3, T10/9–11,
    T13/40ff., T16/22, T18B/1–3,
    T27/13, T39
preposition 108–10; T15/74, 81
Presbyterians T58/86
prescriptivism 27, 138
prestige 40, 62
preterite 90–3, 99
printing 3–4, 25, 37, 42–7, 55;
    T7/53–7, 69, T18C/49, T57/1
productivity 170–2, 175
progressive (pronunciation) 68–70
pronouns 84–7, 102–3; T15/92–103
pronunciation 15, 24; t22, T6/30–44,
    T52/43, T57/8–10, T63/5–10
proverbs (paroemia) 190–1; T4/22
pun 61
punctuation 58–9; T16/37–43
purism 26, 144, 163–6, 168;
    T5/13–28, T11/26, T12/73,
    T13/29, T15/158–69, T29/55ff.
Puritans 39

Quakers 85, 147; T50

Index of topics

Index of topics

Index of words

The following index lists a few words from the introduction and the texts; it provides the best examples of words whose spelling, form or meaning illustrate typical features of EModE.

Index of words